Green Day FAQ

Green Day FAQ

All That's Left to Know About the World's Most Popular Punk Band

Hank Bordowitz

An Imprint of Hal Leonard LLC

Published in 2018 by Backbeat Books
An Imprint of Hal Leonard LLC
7777 West Bluemound Road
Milwaukee, WI 53213

Trade Book Division Editorial Offices
33 Plymouth St., Montclair, NJ 07042

The FAQ series was conceived by Robert Rodriguez and developed with Stuart Shea.

All images are from the author's collection, unless otherwise noted.

Printed in the United States of America

Book design by Snow Creative

Library of Congress Cataloging-in-Publication Data
Names: Bordowitz, Hank, author.
Title: Green Day FAQ : all that's left to know about the world's most popular punk band / Hank Bordowitz.
Description: Montclair, NJ : Backbeat Books, 2018. | Series: FAQ Series | Includes bibliographical references and index.
Identifiers: LCCN 2017036090 | ISBN 9781495051678 (pbk.)
Subjects: LCSH: Green Day (Musical group)--Miscellanea.
Classification: LCC ML421.G74 B67 2018 | DDC 782.42166092/2 [B] --dc23
LC record available at https://lccn.loc.gov/2017036090

www.backbeatbooks.com

To my family 2000 light-years away

Contents

Foreword

It was the summer of 1994 when I first saw the potential impact of Green Day. As the Artist Liaison for the Lollapalooza tour, I had one of the strangest jobs in the business. My job ranged from teaching basketball to the Buddhist monks who traveled with the Beastie Boys to dealing with any artist's problems or issues.

For the first half of the tour the opening act was a band called the Boredoms, from Japan. As per usual the opening act had some talent but wasn't well known and had a nice response from the small crowd that had entered the venue. As the midpoint of the tour approached, and as a fan of punk rock, I personally was excited about a young band called Green Day from the Bay Area joining the tour.

Their first record, *Dookie*, was released in February 1994, and by the time they joined us it was starting to take off. If my memory is correct, they were to join us in New York, and I was truly happy to have them on the tour. The first two shows went well since we were playing open fields and people had a lot of room to move around.

After those two shows we were moving back into our amphitheatre setup, where there were 7,000 reserved seats before you got to the open lawn. By now the buzz had taken full effect and the venue was filling up fast as Green Day took the stage for their 1:40 p.m. opening set. This is when things started to go sideways. The band walked out to a large number of open seats, which I am pretty sure they had never seen, and immediately told the crowd to come on down front, before breaking into their opening song.

We then immediately saw the power Billie Joe had over the crowd, and a sea of people poured past the ushers and rushed the stage. Looking back, I can now understand that the band probably should have been prepped for this type of setup since up until this point they had only played general admission shows. However, chaos broke out, seats were broken, and kids were hurt.

It was one of those moments where time stood still and a thirty-minute set seemed to go on forever. We did the best we could but it was a scary time, and when it was over we were happy no one was seriously injured. However, I was pissed and went after the band for the disregard of the public's safety.

There were heated words among us, and at the end of the day I was told by the promoter to come to the dressing room. The room was destroyed and the promoter was now yelling at me, and I spent the next hour with a few of the crew cleaning it up the best I could.

I was hoping to put the incident behind me, but the dressing room antics continued for a couple of days, and I felt something had to be done. So at the next show I took all of the band's food into the parking lot and put a sign on it that said they would have no dressing room and piggies live in the lot. This started a whole other issue, but it brought everything to a head and led to a productive meeting with the band where I was able to explain the power of the microphone and how the liability had fallen on them for telling the audience to rush the stage. I told them that they wouldn't need to do that anymore since the fans were going to do it naturally, and then responsibility fell on the venue.

Through that summer we built a good working relationship, and I was asked to help get their first arena tour together. Originally I was asked to stay on the road with them, but I had other responsibilities. We went in opposite directions, only to be reunited on the 2000 Vans Warped Tour. I am not sure it was their first choice for a tour since in an earlier article I read that there were two things in life they wouldn't do: watch *Titanic* and play the Warped Tour. On the first day of the tour I taped a copy of the movie to the window of their bus and said, "Now you can say you have done both." This tour was before the release of *Warning*, and the set list was almost exclusively made up of songs from their early roots.

However, the memories I do have of that summer usually ended up in a blur but started out with Fat Mike, Dickie Barret, Billie Joe, or Tré, along with assorted other characters, all deciding on riding on a bus overnight together. Sometimes that would be my bus, and a night that stood out ended with us in a lineup at the US border wondering if we were going to be let back into the country. After about an hour we were cut loose and made it to load-in in Detroit. Everyone except me got to sleep it off, and I went straight to work.

Though I haven't been part of Green Day's universe for many years, they continue to influence so many artists who have come up through the ranks and will come up in the future. They have survived and prospered by never forgetting their roots but also by not dwelling on them. They are not afraid of what others say, but they blaze their own trail, continuing to surprise their fans and critics alike.

They have run a thread through the fabric of my life and touched it twice in the forty-eight hours preceding the request to write this. I was on a long flight from Asia the day before I got the request and was scanning the available movies when I saw a description for a movie called *Ordinary World*, about an aging punk rocker. I thought, "Perfect, this should be an easy one," not knowing that Billie Joe was the lead in the movie.

I sat watching that movie, thinking about how Green Day continue to tell amazing stories—from their early days channeling youthful angst to this movie about our inevitable need to face the reality of aging and responsibility. Is it possible to be "punk rock and slip into middle age gracefully?" It is a challenge so many of us have faced, and once again we can turn to them to see that we are not alone.

The other way Green Day recently touched my life was when I saw that they would be playing the Rose Bowl in Pasadena, California, this coming summer. This is the largest venue you can play in the Los Angeles area. I had a flashback to those early days and wondered if they ever thought it would lead to this.

With the world turned upside down, we need bands like Green Day—bands who are not afraid to speak against authority and will continue to challenge the status quo—more than ever!

Respectfully,
Kevin Lyman
February 15, 2017

Acknowledgments

The author wishes to acknowledge and thank the following people:

Bernadette Malavarca and John Cerullo at Hal Leonard, one a new acquaintance and one of very long standing.

Lindsay Wagner (the bionic woman of Hal Leonard Books), who produced the tome you now hold in your hands, and Micah White for a very thorough, sometimes maddening copy edit.

My accountant, Mark Zuckerman, so ill as I write this.

Jeffery and Justin Jacobson, my legal guardians.

The Music and English Composition Departments at Bergen Community College.

My mother, one of the most caring and generous people I know, and my father, one of the wisest and most decent.

Caren, Michael, Larry, and Will: "2000 Light Years Away."

Beth, Rich, Lisa, David, and Henry.

My buddy Larry Solomon for his support of this project and for tearing me away from it sometimes.

Rick, Jane, and Scott of whatever the band is calling itself today.

Pierre Lamoureux, mon bon ami toujours, the man with the golden contact manager!

Kevin Lyman, for the stunningly good foreword. I hope this is the beginning of a beautiful friendship.

The members of BHSS, who were always behind me.

Frank White, an auld acquaintance renewed.

My son Larry (again) for running an errand to Berkeley for me at zero hour.

Jim Testa and Sandra Castillo for answering the call on Facebook.

The people at Getty Images for having pictures of almost anything.

All of the people who made their most excellent Green Day art available via Creative Commons, especially Sven-Sebastian Sajak, Cristycroad, Chuchitogd 13, Naomi Lir, Fryede, and Deidre Woolard.

Dan Sheehan for insight into his unusual encounter during the band's early days.

The cast and crew at the Sidney Silverman Library in Paramus, New Jersey, and the New York Library for the Performing Arts at Lincoln Center.

The Google Alerts System for providing an avalanche of information on a daily basis.

Vivek Tiwary—The book is out, and I'm holding you to your promise. ;)

Mitch Hayes at Rusty for going to bat for me, and Geoff Backshall for his permission. Sorry it didn't make it in.

To three generations of Green Day fans.

And, of course, to Green Day for making three generations of excellent and challenging music for those fans.

> "Where's the truth in the written word if no one reads it?"
>
> —*Billie Joe Armstrong, "Troubled Times"*

Introduction

When you're talking dynamism in rock and roll, few bands stand out like Green Day. Dynamics cover a lot of ground, and so do Billie Joe Armstrong, Mike Dirnt, Tré Cool, and the fourth entity that (like all great bands) they become when they play music together. In the words of one of their own songs, they are walking contradictions, a three-man collection of oxymorons. Take their niche genre, pop punk, a phrase that the band's singer and guitarist, Billie Joe Armstrong, hoped to eliminate from the language several times. For over a decade he has failed to do away with the notion, brilliantly.

As self-identified punks, they got started in one of the world's punk hotbeds, the Bay Area in the late eighties. They had the punk ethic, but they also had something else. Where their music was informed by the Clash, the Ramones, and all the bands that played at 924 Gilman Street—which spanned the punk spectrum from local heroes like Operation Ivy to punk heroes like Jello Biafra—it was also influenced by groups like the Beatles, the Kinks, and the Who. Their music had thrash and edge, but it also had *melody*. From the beginning, Green Day songs came packaged in tightly written, tightly composed two-to-three minute audio bombs that expressed their own angst and invited anyone to share in it.

They sang about boredom and slacking, but they were among the most driven bands imaginable. By the time they were eighteen, they had toured the United States twice, had played throughout Europe, and had done it all on their own earnings. At a time when there was limited interest in punk from a mainstream audience, they grew their audience every time they played.

This led to another major juxtaposition. Punk (especially Bay Area punk) required cred, something that few of the arbiters of cred, like the punk zines, seemed willing to give Green Day. Yet their following grew to the point where they could no longer play small clubs, backyards, and Elks halls because too many people wanted to see them. To play more "mainstream" professional venues, they had to deal with club and concert hall owners that thrived on taking advantage of naïve nineteen-year-olds. Aware enough to realize this, the group made the decision to take themselves to the next level. This involved eschewing the DIY ethic of punk and actually aligning with the business of music. They already had two albums and several EPs that sold very well. They were not on their own label but on a fairly substantial independent enterprise, Lookout! Records. In order to maintain their integrity, however, they had to "sell out."

They got management, they signed to a major label, and suddenly they lost many of their old "friends." The folks at 924 Gilman blackballed the band, despite the fact that before they had ever played the club Billie Joe and Mike had worked security as members of the collective that ran the joint. Yet, the deal with the major record company involved "mutual creative control," and the band *insisted* on creative control. They may have started recording for a major label, but they would continue to play the music they wanted to play. So, in order to maintain their compact with their fans, they had to sell out.

They needed people to have their backs when they were on the road, people taking care of the business end of being a successful band, so they could concentrate on playing their best music in the best way they could. At the heart of being an artist's manager is the idea that the manager takes care of all the things that would get in the way of the band making their art and bringing it to their fans. In order to bring their fans everything they could, every time, they had to "sell out." Elsewhere in this book, Mike says, "Did the Clash sell out? The Sex Pistols? They were on major labels."

Then there was the part of the punk ethos that said punks had to be underdogs. But suddenly, these punks who had been playing house parties a year earlier were all over MTV. Owing to a perfect storm of good timing, good music, and good image-making, their major label debut album, *Dookie*, sold five million copies and won a Grammy Award in its first year.

In the wake of the success of the Seattle branch of the punk family tree, the catch-all category "grunge," and then Green Day's epic rise, punk bands needed to come to terms with something that had never occurred to them before: the possibility of success. The sheer amount of adulation that *Dookie* received defied all punk logic and philosophy, as far as the arbiters of cred saw it. Ever since Johnny Lydon first sang the line "No future for you," punk bought into the idea. "No future" defined the 1977 wave of the movement in terms of the songs, the musicians, and their fans: why just be a loser when you could be a loud, obnoxious, in-your-face loser? That ethos didn't address something key, however: what happens when the losers win, and how do they manage it?

People identified with Green Day, and still do. A large part of the band's success is that fans continue to identify with them, and with each fresh salvo, they get more fans. Their shows are intergenerational, with grandparents bringing their grandkids to see the band. One college-age guy told me that in junior high everyone knew the lyrics to "Basket Case." Several years on, another crop of high school students used "Good Riddance (Time of Your Life)" as the theme song to many proms and played it at graduations almost as much as Sir Edward Elgar's "Pomp and Circumstance," ignoring the irony that drips from every note.

This also speaks to the band's dynamism—consider the differences between those two songs. "Basket Case" deals with anxiety at 120 snarky beats per minute of electric guitar and bass crunch with supersonic drumming. "Good Riddance (Time of Your Life)" deals philosophically with change, using just an acoustic guitar with violins. Those are dynamics, both musical and attitudinal. And only three years separate the two recordings. That, folks, is called dynamic artistic growth.

Where Billie Joe frequently espouses embracing chaos, what he is actually embracing is change, and most of Green Day's fans are generous enough to let the band change and grow with them. In the time between making *Dookie* (if you'll pardon the expression) and recording *Nimrod*, the band went through the kind of heavy-duty life changes that many twentysomethings do, and have done for generations. They got married. They had kids. They went from being kids obsessed with pot and poop to being adults, family men, and artists concerned with the state of the union while still managing to keep, and in some cases increase, their credibility with their audience. They do this by always writing from the heart and keeping their hearts in the here and now. They are involved in the same problems and pleasures that affect their fans. And that is why those fans *are* fans. While Billie Joe claims to write for no one but himself, a lot of people feel the same thing he does, or something similar enough that the songs resonate.

So, the dynamics affect everything the band does, for better or worse. For better certainly includes the growth of their political consciousness. For worse includes some of the albums made in the throes of addiction and strife. It allowed them to grow as musicians and thinking people, to grow into their own independent selves with their own ideas, and to stubbornly maintain the courage of their convictions. It allowed them to express, with clarity, what they feel at any given time of their lives, from the ennui of living in the nothing-doing areas of the East Bay to their rage at the country's leaders. They went from pot and poop to politics, but never from the viewpoint of "no future." As soon as they had kids, the questions became: "How do we maintain hope for the future? How do we instigate change in the future?" And with a big voice and a big platform, their music attacked these conundrums, loudly and forcefully.

As Larry Livermore points out in this book, Green Day are one of the very few bands in the Rock and Roll Hall of Fame to have done their best work in this century. They have a way of rebounding when people think they're through. When people wrote them off as a ship that had sailed in the mid-2000s, they surprised everyone by making not only one of their best albums, but one of the best albums in rock history, *American Idiot*. After the ill-conceived trilogy of albums, *!Uno!*, *!Dos!*, and *!Tré!*—their first, second, and third original recordings not to at least go gold—they have come back with another great album, *Revolution Radio*, that is getting the band all kinds of attention. That is another of the band's dynamics—you cannot write them off.

There are other dynamics you will discover in this book. There are interpersonal dynamics within the band, how they have changed over the years; family dynamics, how the families the band members grew up in and the families they have created have altered their lives; and dynamics of place, how they remain loyal to the East Bay. If you read between the lines, these dynamics all intertwine.

It is the rare rock band that has something to say and an audience to listen to it after twenty-five years. For one thing, most don't last that long. But when they do, a sense of creative lethargy seems to creep into the music. Since their first shows through the current tour that will keep them on the road for over a year, that has never seemed to be a problem for Green Day. Even their lesser efforts are that way because of being overambitious. It will be interesting to see what they have to say ten years from now. There are a lot of people who will be listening.

Hank Bordowitz
Ridgewood, New Jersey
January 11, 2016

Part 1

Longview

Where Green Day Fits In in the Scheme of Things

1

Time of Your Life

A Green Day Timeline

Just so the rest of the book makes sense in terms of the order in which things happened, this is a timeline of Green Day events. Most of these items will be dealt with in far more detail in the pages that follow.

October 28, 1947—Larry "Livermore" Hayes is born in Detroit, Michigan.

July 11, 1969—John Kiffmeyer is born in El Sobrante, California.

August 18, 1969—Elliot Cahn, as a member of Sha Na Na, precedes Jimi Hendrix as the penultimate act of the original Woodstock Music and Arts Festival.

February 17, 1972—Billie Joe Armstrong, the youngest of six children, is born.

May 4, 1972—Michael Ryan Pritchard is born to a heroin addicted mother. He is put up for adoption.

June 17(+/–), 1972—Michael Pritchard is taken in as a foster child by Cheryl Nasser and Patrick Pritchard. Eventually they formally adopt him.

December 9, 1972—Frank Edwin Wright III is born in Germany (his father was in the military at the time).

November 11, 1973—Jason White is born in North Little Rock, Arkansas.

1977—Billie Joe Armstrong records his first single, "Look for Love," for Fiat Records, owned and operated by the

One of those key moments in the lives of Billie and Mike was the day they discovered the all-ages punk shows at 924 Gilman St.

Green Day retrospective collage. How many album covers can you find?

people who ran the local music store. This led to a mini-tour of northern California.

1979—Billie Joe Armstrong gets his first guitar.

1979—Mike Pritchard's parents divorce. After a brief stay with his father, he moves to Rodeo, California, to live with his mother and sister.

September 1982—Billie Joe Armstrong and Mike Pritchard meet at Carquienez Middle School. They become fast friends. Billie Joe teaches Mike how to play the guitar, and they spend a great deal of time jamming.

September 1982—Andy Armstrong, Billie Joe's father, dies from esophageal cancer.

1985—Larry Livermore forms the Lookouts with fourteen-year-old bassist Kain Hanschke and twelve-year-old drummer Frank Edwin Wright III, known—probably because of that III—as "Tre."

1987—Billie Joe and Mike start playing with drummer Raj Punjabi and bassist Sean Hughes.

1987—Mike and Billie Joe discover the all-ages punk shows at 924 Gilman Street. They send in demos but do not get booked because the arbiters of taste at the club decide they are not punk enough.

September 1987—Billie Joe, Mike, and Sean all transfer to Pinole Valley High School. They name their band Sweet Children, abandoning previous naming attempts like Condom and Desecrated Youth.

October 17, 1987—Sweet Children play their first gig at Rod's Hickory Pit, the restaurant where Billie Joe's mother waited tables and Mike occasionally worked as a busboy.

Late 1987—Both Punjabi and Hughes quit the band. Mike takes up the bass. He starts practicing his bass in school. Unplugged, the instrument makes a sound like "dirnt, dirnt, dirnt" as he did. This earns him the nickname "Mike Dirnt."

1988—Mike and Billie Joe meet John "Al Sobrante" Kiffmeyer, former drummer of local heroes Isocracy. Kiffmeyer joins the band, now a trio of Billie Joe on guitar, Mike on bass, and Al Sobrante (a riff on the neighboring East Bay town of El Sobrante) on the drums.

November 28, 1988—Sweet Children play their first show at 924 Gilman Street.

December 1988—Sweet Children travel 200 miles north to play a party for a bunch of friends of Frank Edwin Wright III, drummer for the Lookouts. In his role with the Lookouts, Frank had become known as "Tré Cool." Lookouts leader Larry Livermore, who also ran the band's record company, Lookout! Records, is very impressed, and he asks Sweet Children to make records for the label.

1988—Sweet Children record *1,000 Hours*, their first Lookout! EP. Just before the record is pressed, they decide to change their name to Green Day, much to the consternation of Larry Livermore.

April 1989—*1,000 Hours* is released.

December 1989—Green Day record their first full album, *39/Smooth*, during Christmas break. The record comes out in early 1990.

February 17, 1990—Billie Joe drops out of high school.

April 20, 1990—Green Day record the *Slappy* EP.

June 1990—Mike graduates from Pinole Valley High School. Later that day, the band leave on their first tour of the United States. In some areas they play in fans' homes. In some places (like Minneapolis) they manage to book several dates.

July 4, 1990—Billie Joe meets Adrienne Nesser at one of their Minneapolis shows.

July 5, 1990—As Sweet Children, the group spend a few hours in a Minneapolis recording studio and cut a four-song EP for Skeen Records (Skeen 010).

July 10, 1990—The Lookouts record their final album, *IV*, at Art of Ears Studio in San Francisco. Larry Livermore invites Billie Joe to play guitar on the session.

July 1990—The Lookouts break up.

Summer 1990—Green Day release *Slappy*.

August 1990—The *Sweet Children* EP is released.

September 1990—Kiffmeyer quits the band in favor of attending Humboldt State University to study business. He has already started teaching Billie Joe and Mike how to take care of business as a band.

November 1990—Billie Joe and Mike jam with Tré Cool, now the former drummer of the Lookouts. He becomes Green Day's new drummer.

Spring 1991—Green Day record their second album (the first with Tré), *Kerplunk*. Critics and fans really like the album, and suddenly the band is selling out venues across America.

October 25, 1991—The band begins a self-booked tour of Europe in Osnabrück, Germany.

January 10, 1992—The European tour ends in Bremen, Germany. They had played in the Netherlands, Denmark, Lithuania, Poland, Czechoslovakia, Austria, Spain, England, Scotland, Northern Ireland, Wales, and Belgium.

Early 1992—The buzz about this indie band reaches the ears of major record companies, who come a-callin'. The band is adamant about controlling their music and image. This becomes a sticking point with many of the majors.

April 1993—They meet attorney (and former guitarist/vocalist) Elliot Cahn and his partner Jeffrey Saltzman on the recommendation of one of their roadies who "knew someone" at their firm. The attorneys already represent bands including Mudhoney, Primus, and the Melvins. Green

Day become legal clients and eventually sign a contract with the duo's management business, Cahn-man.

Summer 1993—The band signs a deal with Warner Bros.–owned label Reprise Records.

September 23, 1993—Green Day play their "final" show at Gilman Street. They are reviled for going to a major label. It would be over a decade before they play the venue again.

Late Fall 1993—The band spends five weeks recording and mixing its major label debut, with the working title *Liquid Dookie.*

Winter 1994—Green Day make their first video, for the song "Longview," in their shared living space.

Winter 1994—The band tours as opening act for Bad Religion.

Their first show in New York City's big arena.

February 1, 1994—Reprise Records releases *Dookie*. It quickly sells through its first pressing. At the same time, the single and video for "Longview" go out to radio and television.

March 14, 1994—Reprise releases "Longview" as a single.

March 16, 1994—Green Day play *Late Night with Conan O'Brien*. Two days later, they are on the *Daily Show*, and they play *MTV 120* three days after that.

April 1994—Mike and Tré marry their girlfriends, Anastasia and Lisa (in separate ceremonies).

June 1994—After a somewhat contentious long distance relationship, Billie Joe Armstrong proposes to Adrienne Nesser.

July 1994—Billie Joe and Adrienne get married.

August 5, 1994—Green Day join the Lollapalooza tour, which plays until September 5, with one short hiatus for . . .

August 14, 1994—The band plays Woodstock '94.

September 8, 1994—Green Day go to the MTV Music Awards with three nominations. They didn't win any, and it will take another four years until they do.

September 9, 1994—Boston radio station WFNX makes a serious mistake about the size of crowd Green Day would draw for a free concert at Boston's Hatch Shell. The promoters expect around 10,000 people. Over six times as many show up. When police and promoters pull the plug twenty minutes into the show, a full-scale riot ensues and spreads out into the streets of downtown Boston.

A show close to home at a much bigger venue than 924 Gilman.

February 28, 1995—Adrienne gives birth to Joseph Marciano (Joey) Armstrong.

Spring 1995—Green Day make the video for "When I Come Around." This marks Jason White's first performance with the group; in one scene he is kissing his girlfriend.

August 25, 1995—Green Day begin their first world tour as major label headliners. They take the queercore band Pansy Division—fellow Gilman and Lookout! alums—as their supporting act.

October 10, 1995—Despite a very active couple of years on the road, Green Day somehow manage to record a new album. They release *Insomniac.*

January 19, 1996—Green Day embark on a world tour, starting with two nights in Osaka, Japan.

March 27, 1996—Claiming exhaustion, the band cancels the rest of their dates for that year. They make some television appearances later that spring but take the rest of the year off from the concert stage.

December 20, 1996—Estelle Pritchard is born to Mike and Anastasia.

Winter/Spring 1997—Green Day hibernate in the recording studio for four months, thrashing out their next move after their sophomore album does not do as well as their debut (admittedly, a tough act to follow).

October 14, 1997—After spending much of September making up shows in Asia and Europe, the band releases *Nimrod.* They appear on the *Howard Stern Show* in the morning and on the *Late Show with David Letterman* that night.

October 17, 1997—"Good Riddance (Time of Your Life)" is released as a single.

October 1997—The band starts the *Nimrod* tour, which takes them around the world, including dates in Australia. Over the course of 1998, they play 120 shows.

Late 1997—Billie Joe, Jason White, Doug Sangalang, and Jim Thiebaud launch Adeline Records. It becomes home to many Green Day friends and side projects.

March 28, 1998—Green Day appear on the long running Australian TV show *Recovery.* Although scheduled to only be interviewed, they commandeer the house band's instruments and play a short set, much to the host's consternation.

May 14, 1998—The final episode of the hit comedy series *Seinfeld* ends with "Good Riddance (Time of Your Life)."

September 10, 1998—Green Day earn an MTV Video Music Award (a "Moonman") for "Good Riddance (Time of Your Life)."

September 12, 1998—Jakob Danger Armstrong is born.

December 31, 1998—Green Day end the year on MTV's New Year's Eve Party in Times Square.

1999—The band go on a short hiatus to recuperate, reflect on a dozen years as a band, and write new songs. They play a couple of parties and benefit shows, but overall they play only about 4 percent of the number of shows they did the previous year.

October 30–31, 1999—Green Day join Neil Young, Pearl Jam, Sheryl Crow, Billy Corgan and James Iha, Tom Waits, Lucinda Williams, and Brian Wilson in a benefit for the Bridge School, playing an "unplugged" acoustic set.

June 23, 2000—The band joins the Vans Warped Tour, which lasts through July.

October 3, 2000—The band releases the album *Warning*, which is met with critical brickbats and fan indifference. However, it leads to a barrage of media appearances, including David Letterman, Howard Stern, and some local radio interviews.

October 18, 2000—Green Day embark on a world tour that lasts sporadically through August of 2001, including several festival dates and opening shows for Blink 182 on the Pop Disaster Tour.

November 7, 2000—George W. Bush is elected as the president of the United States.

September 11, 2001—Al-Qaeda operatives fly two passenger jets into the skyscrapers of the World Trade Center, ultimately destroying about a square mile of downtown New York City. Another plane flies into the Pentagon in Washington D.C. A fourth airplane, slated to strike the White House, is forced down by passengers and crashes into a field in Pennsylvania.

November 13, 2001—Reprise releases a greatest hits collection, *International Superhits!*, on both audio and video.

July 2, 2002—Reprise releases a compilation of B-sides and other rarities, *Shenanigans*.

Going on tour with Blink-182 proved less than a disaster for Green Day, as they reached a new audience.

July 20, 2002—Green Day play what would be their last show for over two years at the Distortion Festival in Nottingham, England.

September 30, 2003—A band called the Network release their debut (and to date only) record, *Money Money 2020*, on Adeline Records. While the band plays a version of synthpop, the vocals are unmistakable.

November 2003—Green Day go into the studio to record *Cigarettes and Valentines*, the follow-up to *Warning*. They complete tracking and mixing the album, leaving the recordings in the studio to come back and work on mastering them. However, when they come back to the studio, the tapes are (allegedly) missing.

November 4, 2003—Iggy Pop releases the album *Skull Ring*. Green Day backs one of punk's founding fathers on the songs "Private Hell" and "Supermarket."

December 2003—Rather than re-record *Cigarettes and Valentines*, they decide to go in a different direction and begin the process of writing and recording once again.

February 1, 2004—More than 144 million people hear Green Day play a cover of "I Fought the Law" during the Super Bowl in an ad for iTunes.

Summer 2004—With the new album almost complete, they film a video for the first single, the title track "American Idiot."

September 7, 2004—The single "American Idiot" is released, along with the video.

September 21, 2004—The album *American Idiot* comes out. On the strength of the single and many amazed reviews, the album enters the charts at No. 1. Again, a media blitz follows. They do *Sessions @ AOL* and make appearances on *Late Show with David Letterman*, *Jimmy Kimmel Live!*, *Last Call with Carson Daly*, *Later with Jools Holland*, the MTV New Year's Eve celebration (once again), the *Manchester Evening News* and *Top of the Pops* in England, *Fritz Radio* and MTV in Germany and Italy.

October 16, 2004—The *American Idiot* Tour kicks off in earnest. Green Day begin by playing arenas, but by the second leg of their European tour in June, they are playing stadiums, including two nights at Milton Keynes National Bowl in England and one night each at the American football stadiums of the New York Giants and the New England Patriots.

August 1, 2005—The band rescinds Lookout! Records' rights to their pre-*Dookie* recordings owing to breach of contract and unpaid royalties.

August 28, 2005—Green Day wins seven MTV Video Music Awards, including Video of the Year and Viewer's Choice, in the aftermath of tropical storm Katrina passing over the Miami area.

November 15, 2005—The first "official" live Green Day album, *Bullet in a Bible*, is released. It is drawn from the two shows at the Milton Keynes National Bowl.

December 6, 2005—Green Day opens the *Billboard* Music Awards, playing "Holiday." Then they go on to win the pop group, *Billboard* 200 album group, Hot 100 group, and modern rock artist of the year awards. Billie

Joe Armstrong presents the Century Award, *Billboard* magazine's highest honor, to Tom Petty.

May 19, 2006—During a quiet year for Green Day, Billie Joe takes a trip to Atlantic City, New Jersey, where the show *Decades of Rock* salutes Elvis Costello. He joins Elvis on several of each other's songs, as did Fiona Apple and Death Cab for Cutie.

September 25, 2006—The tropical storm that interrupted the festivities at the 2005 MTV Video Music Awards became a full-fledged hurricane as it crossed the Gulf of Mexico, where it devastated New Orleans. Nearly a year later, there is still a lot of work to be done, but the New Orleans Superdome, which had acted as emergency housing for thousands, once again opens as a football stadium, as the Saints play their 2006 home opener. To honor the occasion and raise funds for the people who were still homeless after the flooding, Green Day and U2 collaborate on a single for charity, a cover of the Skids' "The Saints Are Coming," and introduce it during the pre-game ceremonies.

May 23, 2007—The band plays John Lennon's "Working Class Hero" on the season finale of the music performance TV series *American Idol.*

June 12, 2007—The album their version of "Working Class Hero" came from, *Instant Karma: The Amnesty International Campaign to Save Darfur,* is released.

July 27, 2007—*The Simpsons Movie* opens. The film includes Green Day playing a punk version of Danny Elfman's theme to the show (Elfman being a former SoCal punk himself with Oingo Boingo).

October 2007—While Green Day have been ensconced in the recording studio for months working on their follow-up to *American Idiot,* a Myspace page for a group called the Foxboro Hot Tubs appears. While there is very little information on the page, the lead singer's voice bears a remarkable resemblance to Billie Joe.

December 2007—The Foxboro Hot Tubs six-track EP becomes available for free download.

May 20, 2008—Reprise releases the debut album by the Foxboro Hot Tubs, *Stop Drop and Roll!!!* The band does a short club tour.

October 11, 2008—Mike's son Michael Brixton Pritchard is born.

March 24, 2009—Reprise Records and Green Day begin an aggressive re-release program of the band's records with *39/Smooth* and *Kerplunk.*

Over the course of the next year, all of their albums get releases on 140-gram vinyl. *39/Smooth* comes with 7-inch versions of *1,000 Hours* and *Slappy*. *Kerplunk* comes with a 7-inch version of the *Sweet Children* EP. The program also features a boxed set of the band's singles.

April 7, 2009—Green Day play a series of club and small theater dates throughout the Bay Area, performing their forthcoming new album, *21st Century Breakdown*, straight through.

May 15, 2009—The Bruce Vig–produced *21st Century Breakdown* is released.

May 16, 2009—Green Day are the featured musical guests on *Saturday Night Live*. Two days later, they appear on *Late Show with David Letterman*, and three days after *that* they perform on *The Colbert Report*. The following morning, they play on *Good Morning America*. After a short junket to appear on Japanese TV, the band appears on *The Tonight Show with Conan O'Brien* and *Last Call with Carson Daly*.

July 3, 2009—The *21st Century Breakdown* Tour kicks off in Seattle, Washington. The North American leg of the tour keeps the band on the road all summer.

September 4, 2009—*American Idiot*, the musical based on the Green Day album, opens at the Berkeley Repertory Theater.

September 13, 2009—Green Day play "East Jesus Nowhere" at the MTV Video Music Awards. The video for "21 Guns" takes home three Moonmen.

September 28, 2009—The European leg of the *21st Century Breakdown* Tour begins in Lisbon, Portugal, and continues well into November.

September 22, 2009—Green Day play "21 Guns" at the American Music Awards. They win the award for Favorite Alternative Artist.

December 4, 2009—The band begins the Antipodean and Asian Leg of the tour, playing through most of January.

January 31, 2010—Green Day and the cast of *American Idiot* play the 52nd Annual Grammy Awards. Nominated for three awards, the band wins Best Rock Album.

March 24, 2010—Previews begin for *American Idiot*, the Green Day Musical, on Broadway.

April 20, 2010—The original cast recording album of *American Idiot*, featuring the band, is released.

April 22, 2010—The band plays at the opening night of *American Idiot* on Broadway.

May 6, 2010—They play four songs on *Late Night with Jimmy Fallon.*

May 29, 2010—Green Day opens the second European leg of the *21st Century Breakdown* Tour. It runs through the Fourth of July.

June 8, 2010—The Green Day edition of the video game *Rock Band* is released.

June 13, 2010—Flying to New York immediately after a performance at the Novarock Festival in Austria, the band takes a few days in America so they can attend the Tony Awards. They play "Know Your Enemy/Holiday." *American Idiot,* the musical, is nominated for three awards and wins two of them. They continue their European tour three days later.

August 3, 2010—After a month off, Green Day play the second leg of their North American tour. It runs through early September.

September 10, 2010—Green Day play at the Stand Up to Cancer concert in Los Angeles.

September 13, 2010—The band plays "Last of the American Girls" on *Jimmy Kimmel Live!* with the cast of *American Idiot.*

October 8, 2010—The band plays a short South American tour.

October 28, 2010—Fresh in from a show in Lima, Billie Joe takes on the role of St. Jimmy in *American Idiot.* It boosts ticket sales mightily.

November 29, 2010—Mike's daughter Ryan Ruby Mae Pritchard is born.

January–February, 2011—Billie Joe reprises his role as St. Jimmy on Broadway.

February 13, 2011—The original cast recording of *American Idiot* wins the Best Musical Show Album at the 53rd Grammy Awards.

March 21, 2011—The band releases the double-CD live recording *Awesome as F**k.*

April 24, 2011—After 422 performances, *American Idiot* closes on Broadway. The band plays a surprise ten-song concert after the show.

August 11, 2011—Green Day begin test driving the new material they had begun to write at a 250-seat gig for friends, family, and fan club members at the Tiki Bar in Costa Mesa, California.

September 23, 2011—They play a similar show at 1-2-3-4 Go! Records in Oakland, California.

October 23, 2011—Billie Joe plays "Good Riddance (Time of Your Life)" at the Mark Twain Prize ceremony.

October 27, 2011—The band plays another test run of the new material in New York City at the tiny Studio at Webster Hall.

November 1, 2011—They offer yet another audition of the new material at the Mezzanine in San Francisco.

November 17, 2011—Once more for the middle of the country, Green Day try out their new material at Red 7 in Austin, Texas.

December 9, 2011—The band fills in for an absent Jane's Addiction at Live 105's Not So Silent Night holiday concert at the Oracle Arena in Oakland, California.

2012—Jason White, long time sideman for the band, becomes a full member of Green Day.

February 14, 2012—Billie Joe announces that they "officially started recording" their next project.

April 11, 2012—Billie Joe tweets his followers about the scope of the new project, announcing that it will be three separate albums, *¡Uno!*, *¡Dos!*, and *¡Tré!*, to be released in September, November, and January, following a similar path to Guns N' Roses' *Use Your Illusions* albums (although GN'R released both on the same day). They would later announce not one but two documentaries in the making: *¡Cuatro!*, about the making of the trilogy, and another using pre-*Dookie* footage of the band.

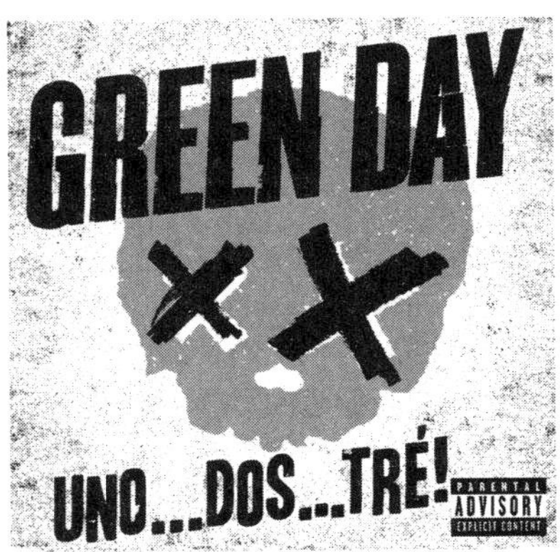

Three albums for the price of . . . three albums, *¡Uno!*, *¡Dos!*, *¡Tré!*.

April 14, 2012—Billie Joe inducts the selfsame Guns N' Roses into the Rock and Roll Hall of Fame.

August 6, 2012—They play the last of the secret shows, at Echoplex in Los Angeles. This one is also to tweak their chops for the forthcoming buttload of touring.

August 16, 2012—Green Day begin a short tour of Japan and Europe.

August 20, 2012—A Green Day version of the game/app *Angry Birds* is released. It is available for four months, and they are portrayed as pigs, naturally (c.f. Kevin Lyman's foreword).

September 6, 2012—The band plays "Let Yourself Go" at the MTV Video Music Awards.

September 13, 2012—They play "Oh, Love" on the season finale of *America's Got Talent.* The next day they play four songs on *Good Morning America.*

September 21, 2012—Green Day play the iHeartRadio Music Festival in Las Vegas. As the show's producers flash a signal that the band's time is almost up, Billie Joe throws a full-blown tantrum, using the word "fuck" and variations thereof a couple of dozen times a minute. He then smashes his guitar and walks offstage.

September 22, 2012—The band announce that Billie Joe has gone into rehab. This requires them to cancel a bunch of shows. It also impinges on the promotion of the trilogy, which suffers in terms of sales.

September 23, 2012—On the heels of Billie Joe going into rehab, the first album of the trilogy, *!Uno!*, is released.

November 13, 2012—The second album of the trilogy, *¡Dos!*, comes out.

December 11, 2012—The third album of the trilogy, *¡Tré!*, gets an early release.

March 10, 2013—With Billie Joe out of rehab, the band commences touring. They play for a month across North America.

May 22, 2013—Green Day begin a European leg of the tour that lasts most of the summer.

June 1, 2013—The band sets an attendance record at London's Emirates Stadium, selling 60,000 tickets.

September 24, 2013—The video documentary *¡Cuatro!* is released.

February 20, 2014—The band plays for a couple of weeks in Australia.

March 14 and 15, 2014—The Foxboro Hot Tubs play two shows at the annual South by Southwest music conclave.

April 19, 2014—Living a lifelong dream of being a member of the Replacements, Billie Joe fills in for an injured Paul Westerberg during the band's reunion gig at the Coachella Valley Music and Arts Festival. Also on this day, which is Record Store Day, Green Day release an album of demos and alternate versions of *¡Uno!*, *¡Dos!*, *¡Tré!* songs called *Demolicious.*

December 7, 2014—Jason White is diagnosed with tonsil cancer.

December 16, 2014—The Rock and Roll Hall of Fame announce that Green Day will be among the inductees in 2015.

April 16, 2015—In anticipation of their induction into the Rock and Roll Hall of Fame, Green Day play a show at the Cleveland House of Blues. For part of the show, John "Al Sobrante" Kiffmeyer plays the drums on some old Green Day and Sweet Children songs.

April 18, 2015—Members of Fall Out Boy induct Green Day into the Rock and Roll Hall of Fame.

May 17, 2015—Now firmly established in the rock and roll mainstream, Green Day play at 924 Gilman Street to raise funds for AK Press.

April 23, 2016—To celebrate the Tribeca Film Festival screening of *Geezer*, which stars Billie Joe, he plays a short set with Tré, Jesse Malin, and Joan Jett at the screening after-party.

August 11, 2016—"Bang Bang," the first track from *Revolution Radio*, is released with a lyric video.

September 6, 2016—The title track to *Revolution Radio* is released.

Another album, another tour—on the road with *Revolution Radio*.

September 23, 2016—The song "Still Breathing" from *Revolution Radio* comes out.

September 26, 2016—Having already postponed several dates due to a wicked case of the flu that rampaged through the Green Day camp, the band begins a series of warm-up club and theater shows, starting at the Newport Music Hall in Columbus, Ohio. Through the course of October, they will play shows at Starland Ballroom in Sayreville, New Jersey; the Tower Theater near Philadelphia; the House of Blues in Boston; the 9:30 Club in Washington, D.C.; Rough Trade Records in Brooklyn, Webster Hall in New York City; the Palladium in Hollywood; the University of California Theater in Berkeley; the Aragon Ballroom in Chicago; the Filmore in Detroit, Michigan; and the Pageant in St. Louis, Missouri. They had to cancel a show at the World Cup of Hockey.

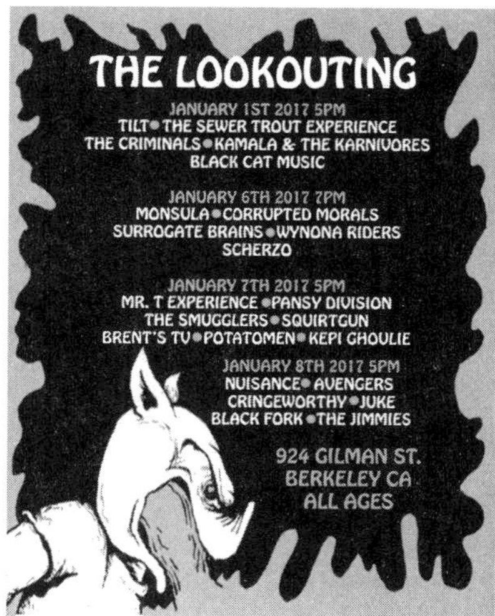

A bunch of bands getting nostalgic about a label that may have forgot to pay them but did get their names out there.

October 7, 2016—The *Revolution Radio* album is released.

December 31, 2016—The Green Day Experience light show is one of the main features of New Year's Eve on the Las Vegas Strip.

2

Stuck with Me

Who's Who in the Green Day Universe

If there ever was a more tightly bound unit than Green Day, it is tough to think of one. They are more like a gang than a band—endlessly in each other's corner, supportive and staunch even in some of the most trying circumstances. As Craig Marks observed in *Spin*: "The devotion the members of Green Day show to one another reminds me of kittens raised in the same litter who adoringly lick each other clean. Green Day finish each other's dick jokes, stick up for each other's parents, and share the same noisy electric razor for instant misshapen buzzcuts." The band has done well by their egalitarian ethic, even in the hard times. The idea that everyone is an equal member gave Tré and Mike the ability to beef when Billie Joe began to act overly important. This camaraderie kept them together when other bands might have imploded.

One of the glues that bind them is their working class upbringing and the type of loyalty it inspires. Billie Joe was raised in a home with a single mom and five siblings. Mike's birth mother was a heroin addict, and his adoptive parents divorced. Tré's father had his family living in a house with plastic sheeting for windows. In some instances, these origins and upbringings could have created issues when they hit the rock and roll lottery with *Dookie* and then again with *American Idiot* and *21st Century Breakdown*. With Green Day having total worldwide sales in the neighborhood of seventy-five million copies, you would think they'd own yachts, and you'd be dead wrong. For a long time, Billie Joe rode the BART. He spent his honeymoon in Berkeley, California, at the Claremont Hotel, as opposed to somewhere a little further away from home and more exotic. Their biggest vice, beyond the obvious chemical ones, is vintage automobiles. Whereas eighties rockers the Brains (and later Cyndi Lauper) observed that "money changes everything," Green Day would seem to call bullshit on that. And beyond everything else, they like to keep celebrities at arm's length.

This loyalty extends to their team. Many of the people they work with—like Jason White, who goes back far enough to have been in the "When I Come Around" video—date back to the Gilman days. Billie Joe has claimed that his friends are the biggest influence on his life. So here, if you will, is the roster of team Green Day, including a few retired numbers and some people who are exceptions that prove the point.

The Band

As you find out more about the members of the band, you realize just how much they have in common. Beyond the geography, there are similarities in their upbringing: their socioeconomic status, the somewhat laissez-faire style of parenting in their homes, and the disaffection for living in a boring zone in a really happening area. Then there is music, always a cornerstone in all their lives.

Billie Joe Armstrong

Billie Joe Armstrong was born in Oakland, California, on February 17, 1972, the youngest of six siblings. He grew up in the East Bay hamlet of Rodeo. His father was a jazz drummer who made his living driving a truck. His mother waited tables at Rod's Hickory Pit, a barbeque restaurant in nearby Vallejo that has since opened branch offices in El Cerrito and Walnut Creek.

When he was five years old, his parents took the family to Fiatarone's Music in nearby Pinole to explore getting music lessons for all the Armstrong kids. The owner, James Fiatarone, spotted star quality in young Billie Joe right away. In a quid pro quo deal, Fiatarone agreed to give Billie Joe lessons if he could record the youngest Armstrong. The record was called "Look for Love," recorded at Fantasy Studios. His father would take Billie Joe and other Fiatarone students on monthly gigs to perform for people in nursing homes and other venues. "It makes people happy when I sing," the precocious five-year-old Billie Joe said in an interview on the B-side of the single. Singing also gave him quality time with his father.

At Green Day's induction into the Rock and Roll Hall of Fame, he recalled his home life, thanking his mom and his siblings for all the music in the house. His oldest brother, Alan, had a home of his own by the time Billie Joe began to appreciate music and turned him on to British Invasion bands like the Beatles, the Stones, and the Kinks. Billie Joe recalled watching Showtime late at night when he slept over and seeing Alice Cooper at midnight. His sister Marci introduced him to Elvis's music. His other sister, Hollie, exposed him to bands like Kool and the Gang. His brother David introduced him to Led Zeppelin, Van Halen, Mötley Crüe, Def Leppard, and Cheap Trick—the music that he and Mike would later jam on when they started playing. His sister Anna had a large collection of contemporary (in the seventies and eighties) punk, turning him on to albums like *Horses* by Patti Smith, and Billie Joe claimed all of this different music "turned my world inside out."

Billie Joe's father was dying of cancer in early September of Billie Joe's tenth year, just as he was entering fifth grade. As he was coming to grips with losing his father, he met Mike Pritchard, and the two immediately hit it off. Billie Joe taught Mike to play the guitar, and before long they spent their entire afternoons after school making music. By the time they were fifteen, they were playing with other local teens in a band called Sweet Children. They played their first gig at the barbeque restaurant where Billie Joe's mother worked, and they were good enough to play there again. They started to play locally and even set up in the school courtyard to perform.

Along with Hillcrest Elementary, Armstrong attended Carquinez Middle School and John Swett High School, both in Crockett, California. He transferred to Pinole Valley High School in Pinole, which is where Mike went. While in high school, Sweet Children changed personnel pretty frequently. By junior year of high school, the lineup had boiled down to a trio—Billie Joe on guitar and vocals, Mike taking up the bass, and drummer John "Al Sobronte" Kiffmeyer on drums. This outfit caught the attention of Lookout!

It was too late for the trilogy albums, but fans turned out in droves to see the newly recovered Billie Joe Armstrong and his mates.

Records owner Lawrence Livermore, who signed the band to his label. To avoid confusion with another band, Sweet Baby, they changed their name to Green Day on the eve of their first record's release. On his eighteenth birthday (February 17, 1990), Billie Joe left Pinole Valley High to pursue his musical career.

In 1990, Armstrong met Adrienne Nesser at one of Green Day's early performances in Minneapolis, Minnesota. They married on July 2, 1994, and very soon after the wedding, they discovered Adrienne was pregnant. Armstrong's son, Joseph Marciano Armstrong, was born on February 28, 1995. Billie Joe's second son, Jakob Danger, was born September 12, 1998. At the time of this writing, Joey plays drums in a Berkeley-based band called SWMRS. Jakob is a guitarist and singer/songwriter who released his first material online in 2015; it features SWMRS drummer Joseph Armstrong and bassist Sebastian Mueller and was produced by Billie Joe. He has since been signed to Burger Records, an independent label based in Fullerton, California.

Mike Dirnt

Michael Ryan Pritchard was born in Berkeley, California, on May 4, 1972. His birth mother was an off-again, on-again heroin addict and put her son up for adoption. At six weeks old, Michael was put into the foster home of Cheryl and Patrick Pritchard in El Sobrante. They adopted him formally some time later. While he excelled in school, he missed a lot of it due to chronic conditions, including a heart problem, which were attributed to his birth mother's addiction. His adopted parents divorced and initially he lived with his father but eventually moved to Rodeo to live with his mother and sister.

Upon starting school at Carquinez Middle School in Rodeo, he met Billie Joe. "I remember the first conversation we had in Mrs. O'Connor's class," Billie Joe recalled to NPR's Terri Gross. "I met Mike and he came over to my house all the time. We became really close. My father was dying of cancer, and Mike came into my life at the same time."

Billie Joe taught Mike how to play the guitar, and they spent hours learning to play the hard rock of the day. They formed a group with Jason Andrew Relva (J.A.R.) on the bass and Raj Punjabi on the drums. As happens with groups during school, there was a lot of turnover, with the only constant being Billie Joe and Mike. During one of these periods of change, Mike took up the bass. He would bring it to school and practice during lunch and other periods of down time. Because of the sound the bass made when it wasn't plugged in, his classmates started to call him "Dirnt."

When Billie Joe and Mike started attending Pinole Valley High, they discovered 924 Gilman and hooked up with drummer Sean Hughes, forming a trio called Sweet Children. While they didn't play the club during the time Hughes was in the band, Mike and Billie Joe did work as security guards. Hughes left and was replaced by John Kiffmeyer. A little older and more experienced, Kiffmeyer helped them get gigs, including several sets at Gilman.

In 1994 Mike married his first wife, Anastasia. His daughter Estelle was born in April 1997. Anastasia and Mike divorced, and he married his second wife, Sarah, in 2004, but the marriage didn't last, as Mike was spending so much time in the studio recording *American Idiot.* He married his current wife, Brittney, in 2009, and they had two children: a son, Brixton, and a daughter, Ryan. Brittney was diagnosed with breast cancer in 2014. By 2016, she was in remission.

Mike learned how to play drums so he could better communicate with Tré. Mike played drums and Tré has played bass on recordings still unreleased to this day. During practice, the three members of Green Day frequently switch instruments. Mike says he does not necessarily want to be the fastest bassist; he'd rather be the catchiest. He is a classic movie buff.

Tré Cool

Frank Edwin Wright III (hence the childhood nickname "Tre," later to become "Tré") was born in Frankfurt, Germany, where his father was stationed, on December 9, 1972. When Frank Senior was demobilized, he moved his family to a remote part of California called Willits. The home was ramshackle, with plastic sheeting for windows and no indoor plumbing or electricity. In grade school, Tré learned the violin. In high school, he claims to have lost a testicle in a unicycle accident—one of his professional aspirations was to be a clown, and he went to clown college for a short time.

The family's closest neighbor—several miles away—was Larry Livermore. Tré's father had built Livermore's house. Tré would go over there on occasion, and Livermore had a drum set, which Tré found fascinating. According to Livermore, Tré was a natural. Livermore taught him a few things, and when Tré was twelve years old, he joined Livermore's band, the

Lookouts. "The first show I ever went to was one I played in," he told Craig Methieson of the *Sydney Morning Herald.* "There were 200 people there and it was at a pizza parlor."

After the Lookouts! broke up, Livermore recommended Tré to Green Day, who had just lost their drummer. Tré was not the first post-Kiffmeyer drummer, but none of the previous ones worked out, as they variously burned out, bombed out, and dropped out with Spinal Tap-like alacrity. Billie Joe had seen Tré perform, of course: the first time he experienced Tré onstage, the singer recalled, the drummer was wearing a tutu and a swimming cap.

After Tré joined the band, there was a time of adjustment. On the one hand, he had far more experience and was a step above all the band's previous drummers. It kicked up the musicianship in the whole band. Mike recognized that he had to build his chops or Tré would leave him in the dust.

On the other hand, Tré had to deal with some of the changes that came with playing in this new band. He needed to get used to Green Day's no-nonsense, no-frills musical direction. He cut down on the number of drums in his kit. "It took me a while to get it: Play the song, not the instrument," he told *Rolling Stone*'s David Fricke. "I started figuring out how to make the band a stronger unit, to make it jump."

He has been described as looking like animator Tim Burton's idea of a rock drummer, with bugged-out eyes and hair that changed color and shape often. As with Led Zeppelin, there is a shark incident involving Green Day, and it belongs to Tré, who caught a shark during a fishing trip. While the shark was still alive, it frightened Tre, so he hit it repeatedly with a baseball bat. No groupies were hurt in the incident, or even involved.

Tré was a DJ while he was in high school, dropped out as a sophomore, and earned a GED. He was taking courses at the clown college, but had to give that up as the band became more and more successful.

Tré was the first member of the band to become a father, and his daughter Ramona was born in 1995. He married her mother, Lisea Lyons—a photographer and artist—three months later. A year after that, they divorced, and Lisea moved to New York. In 2000, he married his second wife, Claudia. They had a son, Frankito (Spanglish for "little Frank," as opposed to Frank IV). Billie Joe is Frankito's godfather (as Tré is the godfather of both Joseph and Jakob Armstrong). By 2003, Tré and Claudia were divorced. He married Sara Rose Lipert early in 2014.

Jason White

It's tough to decide whether to put Jason in this section or the next. He has been a friend of the band since the beginning and toured with them for close to twenty years, and he became an "official" "full" member of Green Day for *¡Uno!*, *¡Dos!*, and *¡Tré!*. Currently his status is somewhat murky, albeit important. He was born on November 11, 1973, a year after the key three members of the band.

A member of Pinhead Gunpowder, the Network (allegedly), the Foxboro Hot Tubs, and of course Green Day, Jason has belonged to a dozen or so bands over the years. Originally from Little Rock, Arkansas, he landed in the Bay Area after he replaced Monsula's guitarist, who had to leave their tour when the band played the Arkansas state capital. White stayed on for the remainder of the tour, which ended on the band's home turf. He played with a number of bands and became friendly with Green Day, joining Billie Joe's side project Pinhead Gunpowder in 1994.

As mentioned earlier, White is in the video for "When I Come Around" (that's him and his circa 1994 girlfriend necking on a car hood at around 1:50 into it), and when he sat in on guitar for the video of "Wake Me Up When September Ends," he became the first non–Green Day member to play in one of the band's clips. He is also on second guitar in the videos for "Working Class Hero," "Jesus of Suburbia," "Last of the American Girls," "21 Guns," and "East Jesus Nowhere." When Billie Joe formed Adeline Records in 1997, White helped run it.

In 1999, he joined the band onstage during two benefit concerts for the Bridge School. As Green Day's music became more complex, it was harder to sound anything like the recording without a second guitarist, so they asked White to join them on the road, which he continued to do through the *Revolution Radio* Tour. He joined the band as a full member while the band was making the *¡Uno! ¡Dos! ¡Tré!* trilogy. When asked about how White's presence in the studio affected the band, Billie Joe told *Guitar Player*'s Art Thompson: "I wouldn't even consider that the way we record is as a three piece band anymore. I had to break out of the limitation of being in a trio because there are only so many things you can do with three people, at least for our particular style of music." White fit right in. Their musical backgrounds were compatible, Billie Joe's and his style of both playing and singing meshed, and there was the all-important Gilman connection. They were all part of the same scene, and they already knew each other before they ever played together.

White is married to Janna White and has two children. Around the time of the birth of his second child, White was diagnosed with tonsil cancer, for which he was treated.

Former Members and Side Guys

Between John Kiffmeyer and Tré, there were a number of potential drummers that went the way of the drummers from Spinal Tap. This section deals with the people who played with the band and in hindsight made a difference, the players who fattened up the trio so they could become a group that could fill a stadium, the side guys past and present, and the former Sweet Children who come up when the band's history is discussed.

John (Al Sobrante) Kiffmeyer

Several years older than the members of Green Day when they came around to Gilman Street, Kiffmeyer was playing with the band Isocracy. During the Sweet Children years, Billie Joe and Mike had worked with a series of drummers, and when Isocracy broke up, Kiffmeyer became the penultimate one. Beyond bringing a big beat to the band, Kiffmeyer knew his way around the punk/underground rock scene, and he became the band's Sherpa, calling friends to start getting more gigs. One of those calls was to Larry Livermore—member of the Lookouts and founder of Lookout! Records—who was so impressed by the band's live show that he signed them to the label.

Aside from his drumming, Kiffmeyer was studying journalism at Contra Costa Community College, where his edition of Sweet Children played their first gig together. He recorded the *1,000 Hours* EP, the *Slappy* EP, the *Sweet Children* EP, and the full-length *39/Smooth* album with the group.

His exit from the band has become rock and roll folklore. After a couple of years at the community college, he was accepted at Humboldt State College. Where Contra Costa was in the heart of the East Bay, Humboldt was hours away. He never told the band he was leaving. He was just gone. Livermore introduced the band to Tré Cool, formerly of the Lookouts, and he became the group's drummer.

Kiffmeyer joined several other bands later on, including the Ne'er Do Wells and the Ritalins. He kept his hand in music, managing one band and producing a record for another. He married independent filmmaker and professor Greta Snider, and he became a specialist in filming green-screen effects for commercials.

The weekend they were inducted into the Rock and Roll Hall of Fame, his former bandmates invited Kiffmeyer to play a set with Mike and Billie Joe (Tré graciously sat it out), performing music from Sweet Children- and *39/Smooth*-era Green Day.

Raj Punjabi

Raj went to school with Billie Joe and Mike and played drums in some of their early bands. These days he is in the marijuana business and was in the news for trying to get the Columbia County Planning Commission in Washington (where pot is legal) to allow him to create a 24,000-square-foot indoor marijuana farm.

Timmy Chunks

Timmy toured with Green Day, performing on guitar and backing vocals from 1997 to 1999. He served as a guitar technician on *Warning*. Timmy is the founder of Chunksaah records—now of Asbury Park, New Jersey—which was started in 1993 in New Brunswick, New Jersey, by the Bouncing Souls so that they could release their own recordings. Other artists who have released records on Chunksaah include the Mighty Mighty Bosstones, the Arsons, and the Loved Ones. Timmy wrote several songs with the Bouncing Souls, as well.

Mike Pelino

Mike toured with Green Day on guitar and backing vocals during the 2004–05 tour. Another Lookout! Records alumnus, he was a member of the Enemies. He signed on to join one leg of the *American Idiot* tour but stayed for the whole thing. Beyond his music-playing activities, Mike was a key player in starting one of the first contemporary music radio stations in Shanghai, China. Mike appears in the Green Day movies *Heart Like a Hand Grenade*, *Comp'd: Green Day*, and *Bullet in a Bible*, as well as the 2007 documentary *924 Gilman* and a 2005 episode of *Access Hollywood*.

Jeff Matika

Jeff began playing guitar and doing backing vocals for Green Day on the 2009 *21st Century Breakdown* tour. A friend of Jason White's from his days in Little Rock, Arkansas, Jeff also hosts an eponymous show on the Green Day fan site Idiot Nation.

Garth Schultz

Garth played brass on tour with Green Day from 1997 to 1999. He had previously played with his brother in the Skeletones and in the punk-ska band Goldfinger. He says his best times on the road were with Green Day. He fondly remembers touring in Italy and taking the opportunity to visit the Vatican. Prior to his time with Green Day, Garth served as a member of the US Marine Corps at Camp Pendleton in California, in Japan, and in the Persian Gulf theater of war. When he finished that very different kind of tour, he took advantage of his GI Bill benefits and went to college. As of this writing, he works for River City College as an advisor and takes a particular interest in advising returning GIs.

Gabrial McNair

Gabrial played trombone and sax from 1999 to 2001, both on tour and on the *Nimrod* record. Another 1973 baby (born on September 8), he also plays guitar and was a drum major in high school. An alumnus of the California Institute of the Arts, he has a band called Oslo and a long (predating his work with Green Day) working relationship with Gwen Stefani, starting with his work with No Doubt in 1993 and continuing into her recent solo career.

Kurt Lohmiller

Kurt played trumpet, percussion, and did backing vocals for Green Day between 1999 and 2004. In one of the many live video versions of "Boulevard of Broken Dreams" on YouTube, you can see him standing behind a timpani and singing.

Ronnie Blake

Ronnie toured with Green Day, played trumpet and percussion, and contributed backing vocals between 2003 and 2005. Born on May 23, 1972, and hailing from Fullerton, California, Blake attended Cal State Northridge and has a master's degree in music from the California Institute of the Arts. His kudos include the International Trumpet Guild's Mock Orchestra Audition in 1992, the Dolo Coker Jazz Scholarship, and Outstanding Trumpet Player in the Pacific Coast Jazz Festival honors. In addition to Green Day, Ronnie has worked with artists including Aaliyah, Ben Harper, Dr. Dre, and Big Bad Voodoo Daddy. He appears in the Green Day film *Bullet in a Bible.* Blake also runs a website called Hispeedhorns.com, which arranges and adds horn parts to recordings for producers or bands that want them. As of this writing, Blake is working on a solo album.

Jason Freese

Jason plays saxophone, piano, and trombone on the road with Green Day. Born on January 12, 1975, he has also worked with the Goo Goo Dolls, Weezer (both bands also overseen by former Green Day manager Pat Magnarella), and his own band, the Vandals. He also plays for the children at the school where his wife Amy works.

Controlling Interests

The musical entity Green Day consists of three musicians, but as we'll see in coming chapters, it takes more than a band to become a phenomenon like Green Day. There are also the people who actually keep tabs on the group's business (so they don't have to), who work with them in the studio doing the technical stuff that can mean the difference between a hit and a miss, among other things. These are some of the people who have helped—and some who are still helping—make Green Day the band they are.

Andy Ernst

As the owner of Art of Ears studio, Andy Ernst wound up producing a lot of punk rock records. A musician himself, Ernst had played in bands that were featured on the *Jackass* soundtrack, and he shared stages with bands including the Commodores, the Greg Kihn Band, Clover (during Huey

Lewis's tenure in the band), and Tower of Power. In addition to producing *1,000 Hours*, *Slappy*, and *39/Smooth* with Green Day, he produced records for Screeching Weasel, AFI, Malo, and Rancid, among many others.

Elliot Cahn

While matriculating at Columbia University in the late sixties, guitarist and vocalist Elliot Cahn began singing harmony as part of the Kingsmen, one of the school's a cappella glee clubs. Several members of that glee club discovered a common fondness for vocal music of the fifties and started playing as Sha Na Na in 1969. By that summer they were the penultimate act at Woodstock, playing Monday morning for the hardcore few who had mostly stayed to see the closing act, Jimi Hendrix. Sha Na Na were given a check for $350, which allegedly bounced. However, their appearance on the three-album set and in the movie helped them kick off a fifties revival that led to such cultural phenomena as *Grease* (they played half a dozen songs in the movie as Johnny Casino and the Gamblers) and *Happy Days*. In 1977 they got their own TV variety show, which lasted for four years.

Along with Cahn—who played rhythm guitar, did some of the arranging, and of course sang—there were eleven original members, including Henry "Shannon" Gross and several who went on to careers in music, medicine, business, academia, and law. This is the direction Cahn took after four albums.

He moved to the Bay Area, finishing off his bachelor's degree, a law degree, and a Master of Jurisprudence degree at Berkeley. After several years cutting his legal teeth, he started to ply his law degree in the music business in 1975 after answering an ad from the office of Michael Krasner. He got the job and began working on merchandising deals for the likes of Santana and Journey. "It was just dumb luck," Cahn told *SF Weekly*. "There aren't any jobs in music that get advertised."

By 1989, Cahn was ready to have his own name on the office door. At the time, he was carpooling with another rocker-turned-lawyer, Jeffrey Saltzman. When the opportunity to manage the metal band Testament came his way, he brought Saltzman in to help. Together, they became Cahn-Man Management.

In 1993, Green Day were advised to see Cahn as the record companies started to come calling. Between their legal and management businesses, the law firm or Cahn-Man represented artists including Primus, Rancid, Exodus, and the Offspring. As Cahn recalls it, one day Green Day just walked in the door. Cahn-Man signed Green Day to a four-year management contract and negotiated their deal with Reprise.

Leveraging the relationship with Green Day, Cahn-Man started 510 records, a company funded and distributed by MCA. As music supervisor for the film *Angus*, Cahn used Green Day's previously unreleased song "J.A.R. (Jason Andrew Relva)" without clearing it with the band.

Perhaps Cahn's biggest mistake was not taking into account the fierce loyalty the band had for the people around them. The band wanted to license merchandising rights for Green Day to one of those friends, but Cahn-Man sold the rights to one of the biggest merchandisers in the world, Brockam.

Whatever the last straw was, by the time *Insomniac* was released, the band had grown disenchanted with Cahn-Man. They were tired of being treated like resources and disinclined to be anyone's cash cow. The longer they stayed with Cahn-Man, the more like this they felt, so they fired them. Cahn-Man filed suit, and the issue was settled out of court.

Randy Steffes

Manitoba-bred Randy Steffes grew up in the town of Beausejour. After working in a Winnipeg-based punk band through the late eighties and into the nineties, he went to work for Green Day, filling such roles as guitar tech, sound man, and road manager. When the band split with Cahn-Man, they needed to get away from what they felt was self-serving corporate management, and they became one of the very few self-managed bands on a major label. Wanting to choose someone within the band "family" as management liaison, Green Day appointed Steffes as the de facto manager of the band. "I've worked for the band and they trust me," he told MTV News.

Steffes held this role in the band from October 1995 through August 1996, when the band signed with Triad Management. Triad was a corporate heavyweight, but it was also in the Green Day family. The company was owned by Bob Cavallo, father of Rob Cavallo, who produced *Dookie* (and went on to produce the majority of Green Day's albums).

Pat Magnarella

Pat Magnarella grew up among the small towns in upstate New York. He played piano and worked in some punk bands in high school but had no ideas about making his living in music. He went to college at the

University of Florida, thinking he was going to be a professional golfer, but he soon realized that wouldn't work out either. While deciding what course of study he wanted to follow, he became the chairman of the school concert committee, overseeing a big budget to put shows into the school's 2,500-seat auditorium and a 600-seat club. Spending the school's money, he became acquainted with performing arts agents in New York and Los Angeles while phoning them about their acts. He found that he enjoyed it, moved to New York City after graduation, and found a job in the mailroom at American Talent International.

Magnarella moved up a couple of rungs, becoming an assistant in the rock department at one of the bigger agencies, International Creative Management. A year later, he became an agent at Venture Bookings, a company run by one of the agents he used to deal with at Florida State. Venture was pretty much alone in booking new, burgeoning alternative acts like Soul Asylum, the Replacements, 10,000 Maniacs, Living Colour, Hüsker Dü, Violent Femmes, the Meat Puppets, and Nick Cave, among others. After four years, Venture became enormously successful and merged with Triad, spurring a move to Los Angeles. Suddenly, Magnarella became the guy on the other end of the phone, booking bands like the Goo Goo Dolls and Weezer on the college circuit. In 1996, he was enlisted to manage Green Day after a year during which they managed themselves. He managed them until the summer of 2017, shortly before this book went to press. Magnarella went from Triad to the powerful film and music management company Mosaic Media to finally hanging his own single as Pat Magnarella Management in 2004.

PMM has expanded into representing professional action sports athletes, including surfers and skateboarders, and fine artists. Magnarella has managed Green Day, the Goo Goo Dolls, and several other musical artists, and also deals in film and theater. He also ran Pat's Record Company as a joint venture with Universal through 2007, and Billie Joe's Adeline Records.

As Green Day entered the Rock and Roll Hall of Fame in 2015, the band thanked him. "[You] have very thick skin," Mike said from the stage as he accepted his "Rocky." "You're very patient, nobody in the world would have let us be ourselves the way you have. We truly appreciate you."

Jonathan Daniel

As a student at UCLA, Daniel played bass in a 70s hair metal band Candy with Izzy Stradlin, booking Izzy and Axl Rose's band Hollywood Rose first

Green Day A&R and Producer Rob Cavallo.

Yodel Anecdotall/Yahoo! Inc./Wikimedia Commons

gig at Madam Wong's. He and partner Bob McLynn started Crush Management in 2003, stumbling upon Fall Out Boy, and along with new clients Green Day, represent FOB, Sia, Train, and others.

Rob Cavallo

Born on March 21, 1963, in Washington, D.C., Rob Cavallo was pretty much brought up in the music business, as his father owned the Cellar Door, a small but renowned club that featured such artists as Miles Davis, who's fusion-era masterpiece *Live Evil* was recorded there, as was Neil Young's *Live at the Cellar Door.* The club was sold in 1981. More lucratively, Bob the elder managed artists ranging from the Loving Spoonful to Weather Report to

Prince. He moved his family to Los Angeles when Rob, the younger, was ten years old. His father's management company, Third Rail, managed Green Day, among many others.

Shortly after the move to LA, Cavallo discovered his father's Beatles records and began playing the guitar. "I had to know how they were making those sounds, and it made me so insane," he told an interviewer for Guitar Center's website. He began his personal vision quest to learn how they did it. By the time he felt he had learned the secret, he had also learned how to play all the Beatles songs (and the catalogs of Led Zeppelin, the Rolling Stones, and the Who as well) on guitar, bass, drums, piano, and a host of other instruments. He studied the art of productions and the science of sonics. He vivisected fifty years' worth of popular music to figure out what made it tick.

His father encouraged young Rob's interest in music, bringing him to the recording studios where clients were cutting records. He also bought his son a four-track tape recorder, which allowed Rob to learn some of the nuances of making multitrack recordings. Rob also played in cover bands throughout high school.

After graduation and as he attended the Grove School of Music, he began working with legendary engineer George Massenburg, helping to maintain the studio, fix the equipment, and assist Massenburg on recordings by Linda Ronstadt and others.

In the mid-eighties, perhaps via his work with Massenburg (who also recorded Fleetwood Mac) or through his father, he made the acquaintance of Warner Bros./Reprise Records president Lenny Waronker. The Reprise exec recognized a kindred spirit—someone who was at home in the studio as well as "doing business"—and offered him a position in the A&R department. One of his first projects was the eponymous debut recording by LA fuzz band the Muffs, an album that became a favorite of a young musician from Berkeley named Billie Joe Armstrong. Cavallo was among the people trying to get Green Day to sign to their record company, and he helped get Green Day to agree to record for Reprise. He went into the studio with his new band, and together they recorded *Dookie.*

In addition to recording most of Green Day's Reprise albums, Cavallo rose through the ranks of Warner Bros., becoming a company vice president and staff producer and eventually earning an appointment as Warner Records chairman. He continued to produce, recording hits with the Goo Goo Dolls, Kid Rock, Paramore, and My Chemical Romance. He recently started a joint venture with veteran executive Abbey Konowitch and Video

Games Live founder Tommy Tallarico called Rockmania Live in order to, according to the company Facebook page, "create a global music franchise similar to Cirque du Soleil or Blue Man Group." They create multimedia symphonic rock presentations of classic albums by artists like Led Zeppelin, the Who, and Pink Floyd.

At Green Day's Rock and Roll Hall of Fame induction, Billie Joe said of Cavallo: "I really feel like you're a brother. We're kindred spirits in the fact that we can sit around and play songs all day long together, and to speak in that language."

Lawrence Livermore

Larry Livermore was born Lawrence Hayes in Detroit, Michigan, on October 28, 1947, and he lived in the Detroit area throughout high school. In his blog he calls this his "MC5-Stooges-White Panther Party era." Livermore moved to the Bay Area to attend Berkeley just as the first (second?) wave of punk hit in 1977. He didn't finish Berkeley until 1992, but he did start a zine called *Lookout!* and became a fixture on the Bay Area punk scene. He moved to Spy Rock, California, in the mountains about 150 miles north of San Francisco, "in search of something real." That reality involved living in a house with no electricity besides a solar panel and spending his time "fending off bears and crazed pot growers." Getting into the DIY spirit of punk, he started his own band with sixteen-year-old bassist Kain Hanschke and twelve-year-old drummer Frank "Tre" Wright. He borrowed the name of the band—the Lookouts—from his zine.

Like so many in the East Bay punk scene, Livermore wore many hats. In addition to putting out *Lookout!*, he wrote for the notorious zine *Maximumrocknroll* for seven years. He gave Tre Wright his first drumming gig and his stage name, redubbing him Tré Cool when he joined the Lookouts. Livermore became a main mover and shaker at 924 Gilmore Street. He had a hunch the East Bay punk scene would become something big long before Green Day got famous. "With both Operation Ivy and Green Day, I knew within thirty seconds of the first time I saw them that they had the potential to be great and I wanted to do a record with them," he told Rob Harvilla of the *East Bay Express*. "I knew the bands we were seeing at Gilman were as good, or better than anything I was hearing on the radio or seeing in other clubs, so I thought if there was any justice, some of them would make it big."

With partner David Hayes and some money put aside from his welfare checks, Livermore started Lookout! Records in the grand DIY tradition of putting out recordings by his band and others, many of them associated with Gilman. In 1982, he broke up the Lookouts. Hayes left Lookout! to form his own company in 1989. When Green Day got huge, Livermore finally realized he would not have to go back on welfare any time soon, especially since Green Day left their Lookout! recordings with Lookout!. In 1992, Livermore began to get restless, so he and Patrick Hynes founded the band the Potatomen, and they released several records. By 1997, he found that running a record company that had grown way beyond its beginnings was no longer fun. He actually sided with the Gilman's concern that the overexposure of the Bay Area punk scene—and the attempt by record companies to catch Green Day's lightning in a bottle—would ruin everything he found beautiful and special about the East Bay punk community. He and his partner sold Lookout! to employee Chris Applegren.

Livermore put *Lookout!* magazine to rest in 1995 but continued to write. He had a column in *Punk Planet* and another in *Absolute Zippo*. He still dabbled in the record business and put out the 2012 compilation *The Thing That Ate Larry Livermore*. The compilation included Emily's Army—now called SWMRS—a band that featured drummer Joey Armstrong. Livermore published his first memoir, *Spy Rock Memories*, in 2013, and his book on Lookout! Records, *How to Ru(i)n a Record Label*, in 2015.

Kenny Butler

Kenny Butler has been Tré's drum technician since *Nimrod*. He became a roadie as a way to get into shows. He would hang out at a concert as the band and crew unloaded equipment, and then he would find something to bring in, gaining entrance for himself. Eventually, one of the bands hired him, and he became an official roadie.

As Green Day were getting ready to go on tour to support *Dookie*, they—having a bigger budget than before—decided they could afford a small crew. One of Butler's friends was recommended for one of the live sound engineering positions, and Butler tagged along when the friend went to meet the band. They all hit it off, and while Butler had commitments for that tour, he started working with Green Day in 1997.

Bill Schneider

Bill Schneider has been in the Green Day camp almost since the beginning. As a member of Monsula, their paths must have crossed at 924 Gilman.

Schneider is the Jason White connection, as well. He has played bass in Pinhead Gunpowder, Billie Joe's side project, since 1990. At various times he has worked as Billie Joe's guitar tech and as Green Day's band coordinator. When the band is on the road, he is the man on the spot, keeping an eye on the pit. When Billie Joe dives or wanders into the audience, Schneider is the one who sees that Billie Joe gets back onstage.

On his own, he has played bass, guitar, and keyboards; he has composed music, taken photographs, and done graphic design; and he has worked with such non-punks as Madonna and Bette Midler. He also has a lot of retail experience in musical instruments as owner of the Univibe Music Shop in Berkeley. When Billie Joe decided to open Broken Guitars in Oakland, he brought on Bill as a partner.

Mitch Cramer

Mitch Cramer segued into the Green Day camp while he was still working as a representative for Goldenvoice, the company that produces the annual Coachella Festival, among other tours at other venues. He served as production manager for Green Day for nine years. During that time, he also worked with the band via Third Rail Management during down time. At Third Rail, he handled all daily responsibilities for Green Day, including working with Reprise and the band's accountant and attorney, coordinating with the band's publicist and overseeing press approvals, coordinating an overhaul of the band's web site, hiring staff to redesign the band's fan club, working on endorsement deals and merchandise ideas and approvals, and handling all artist's requests, regardless of their nature or who sent them.

But Cramer was mostly the man in charge of logistics when Green Day were on the road, and in this role he coordinated travel and secured all necessary visas and immigration documents, dealt with tour accounting and promoters regarding money for the shows, worked within the band's budgets, made sure the band was in the right place at the right time, coordinated all press with the record label and journalists, and hired vendors and crew. He still does this with many other artists, and when he is not on the road, he lives in Nashville, Tennessee.

Kevin Lemoine

If you have enjoyed the sound at Green Day shows, thank Kevin Lemoine. As the Front of House engineer, Lemoine is responsible for the sound that the audience hears, as he mixes the band live, in real time. He started learning his way around soundboards when he helped set up some gigs and haul the equipment for a band some of his high school friends played in. Seeing Kevin's affinity for equipment, one of the older sound engineers began to show him the ropes of live audio engineering. He explained the intricacies of the audio mixer and the function of each knob, button, and slider. By the time he was in his late teens, he was mixing live sound in clubs.

By the time he was twenty-one, Lemoine was doing sound at the Continental Club in Austin, Texas. He parlayed that into road work by asking the bands that played the club to think of him when they needed someone to mix sound for them. One of those gigs took him on the Vans Warped Tour. There he met Green Day, and he has done front of house work with them throughout this writing.

Butch Vig

Bryan David Vig was born on August 2, 1955, in Viroqua, Wisconsin—a small dairy farm town about equidistant from Madison, Wisconsin, to the east and Dubuque, Iowa, to the south. His father was a doctor, and his mother taught music. After studying piano for six years, he saw the Who's Keith Moon blow up his drum set on the *Smothers Brothers* television show and was inspired to buy a sixty-dollar kit of his own.

Vig attended the University of Wisconsin at Madison. While in school, he created the soundtracks to several low-budget movies, the best known of which is probably the horror flick *Slumber Party Massacre.* In addition, he played drums for a bunch of garage bands and ended this run with the band Spooner. He met classmate Steve Marker and helped set up a recording studio in Marker's basement. They started a small label, Boat Records, to put out the self-produced Spooner records and recordings by other local bands they liked. By 1984, they outgrew the basement space and opened the more professional Smart Studios, and all the while Vig drove a cab by day and gigged with Spooner at night.

When Spooner ran out of steam, Vig formed two bands—Fire Town, with two of his old Spooner mates, and First Person, with Marker. After Fire Town released their first independent record, they were signed to Atlantic. The Atlantic record vanished without a trace, and the band broke up. After a brief Spooner reunion, Vig set to work as a full-time producer. He produced Killdozer's *For Ladies Only* at Smart, garnering attention in the rock community. Nirvana went to Smart to record demos for the follow-up to their indie debut *Bleach.* When the time came to record the actual album, the band called on Vig to produce their major label debut, *Nevermind.* That album's success, along with his work on Smashing Pumpkins' *Gish,* set his producing career on fire. His reputation was further solidified with his work on subsequent Smashing Pumpkins albums, more Nirvana projects, and work with groups including L7, Chainsaw Kittens, Sonic Youth, and Nine Inch Nails.

Having produced, by his own count, a thousand bands that were just guitar, bass, and drums, Vig got the yen to try something different and get back into flexing his playing muscles. With Marker and Scottish singer Shirley Manson, he started Garbage, a band that turned into a hit-making entity in its own right, earning several Grammy nominations, an MTV Europe Music Award, and selling around seventeen million albums all told.

While producing *21st Century Breakdown,* Vig noted certain similarities between Green Day and Nirvana. "I saw the same thing in Kurt," he told *Rolling Stone*'s David Fricke. "When he played, it was like he was free. And Billie Joe has told me that: 'When I'm onstage, I'm free. I'm not thinking.' . . . When they lock in, they play like no other band I've worked with."

Chris Dugan

Chris Dugan was born on May 11, 1973, a few days after Mike's first birthday. In high school he played drums in several bands and learned rudimentary recording skills to stay relevant and busy. One of the bands he recorded was the Frustrators, Mike's side project. He and a partner opened Nu-Tone studios in 1995, and it became a favorite of the East Bay punk scene. He started working at Studio 880 in 2002 and released a recording with his own band, the Effection, called *Soundtrack to a Moment* on Adeline. The connection between the Frustrators and Studio 880 put him on Green Day's radar. When they bought 880 and renamed it Jingletown Studios a year later, he recorded the mysterious band the Network and tracks on Iggy Pop's *Skull Ring.* He engineered every project Green Day has done since *Warning,* winning Grammy awards for his engineering work on *21st Century Breakdown* and the Original Broadway Cast Album for *American Idiot.* He also worked on the album by the Foxboro Hot Tubs, and Billie Joe and Norah Jones's *Foreverly.* Dugan's work in photography and video projects with the band are frequently featured on the Green Day website. He had his first film audio experience on the movie *Geezer,* capturing the sound on the live music scenes.

The Fans They Call Onstage

Over the years, Green Day must have had over a thousand people from the audience come up and play with the band, sing with the band, or take over for the band after Billie Joe taught them Operation Ivy's "Knowledge." Someone compared the process to getting to play the TV game show *Let's Make A Deal*—the more outrageous an audience member's look or approach, the more likely he or she was to be picked. Although the band leans toward a working-class egalitarianism with much of what they do, the people who get onstage are most likely going to be in the front of the venue. This does, of course, include people in the pit and people who manage to work their way down from the cheaper seats.

At Lollapalooza in 2010, Dan Michie got pulled up onstage to sing "Longview." His rendition was so notable it was covered by MTV News. "There's no words to describe it," he told MTV's James Montgomery. "If you've ever seen 80,000 people before, that's one thing, but seeing them look back at you, that's something that doesn't even seem real." He ran around the stage and didn't miss a beat. Billie Joe was so impressed that he gave Dan a guitar and arranged for a car to drive him home.

Dave Wasierski and a bunch of his buddies took the eighty-mile drive from his hometown of Olivia, Minnesota, to Minneapolis to check out the Vans Warped Tour in 2000. About halfway through Green Day's six o'clock set, Billie Joe started calling for a guitarist. Dave played guitar in a band, and his friends were all pointing at him. "You?" Billie Joe said, pointing at him. "You play the guitar? Can you play three chords? Really?" Dave's posse assured him that Dave could, and he was hoisted out of the pit and onto the stage. Billie Joe strapped his guitar onto Dave, gave him a kiss, and told him the chords, and Tré and Mike launched into the song with him. When the song was over, Billie Joe insisted Dave stage-dive into the pit, and, as the band kicked into "Basket Case," he did. After the set, he got his picture taken with Billie Joe.

One young man named Sam (who calls himself Clover on the Green Day Authority boards) who managed to get onstage recalled the experience, saying: "Billie Joe put the spotlight on no less than six people, one of them a guitarist. This guitarist in particular was pulled onstage to play Green Day's famous rock opera, 'Jesus of Suburbia.' As soon as I heard this, I told myself that it was going to be me that would be onstage." He made a sign that, on one side, read, "ME+GUITAR = JESUS OF SUBURBIA." On the other side it read, "AND . . . I'M F*I*ING [sic] AWESOME TOO." He took it to a show in Hamilton, Ontario. Every time a member of the band came to the side of the stage where he was sitting, he held it up. After "American Idiot," Billie Joe pointed at him.

> Billie Joe: You plus guitar equals "Jesus of Suburbia." Is that what you are saying?
>
> Sam: Yeaaaaaaaah!
>
> Billie Joe: Can you really play?
>
> Sam: Yeaaaaaaaah!
>
> Billie Joe: Swear to God?
>
> Sam: Yeaaaaaaah!
>
> Billie Joe: All right. Get your ass up here, kid. Let's go.

After making sure he had not done this before, the 17,000 people in the hall yelled and booed, and Billie Joe put a black Les Paul Junior (Billie Joe's instrument of choice) on Sam's shoulders and handed him a guitar pick. Billie Joe suggested he turn up the volume, which he did. He then told Sam to keep an eye on Tré. Tré counted the song off, and Sam started playing. He didn't stop for seven minutes.

"For seven minutes," Sam wrote, "I got to play with my favorite band. It doesn't get any better than that." The next morning he was mentioned in a review of the show in the *Toronto Sun.* The band even posted a picture of Billie Joe with his hand on Sam's head on their website. As with thousands of fans—a small minority but still a lot—Sam got to be a member of Green Day for seven minutes that would last him a lifetime. No, it doesn't get much better than that.

This behavior continued on into the *Revolution Radio* tour in 2016. During a show at Chicago's Aragon Ballroom, while the band played preliminary club dates to warm up fans for the album and the band for the much larger shows to follow in 2017, a fan named Thomas Bulvan also attracted Billie Joe with a sign. His read, "I can play every song on *Dookie*." Security hauled him onstage, Billie Joe strapped Blue around the young fan's neck, and off they went. If Billie Joe ever needed an understudy, Thomas Bulvan could be it. He played the song perfectly, and when Billie Joe stuck a mic in his face, he sang it perfectly. He leaped, did splits, and was all over the stage and equipment. And when the song was finally over and Billie Joe took Blue back, he did a stage-dive into the pit.

Sometimes, an audience member doesn't even wait to get called. Mike recalled a show in San Francisco where a fan did a dangerous dive into the audience, jumping from a twenty-foot-high balcony and crowd-surfing to the stage. "It was fucking amazing," he said. "The crowd caught him; it was crazy! A friend [of mine] who was a stuntman said he couldn't do it better himself."

Having reached the stage in such an astounding fashion, Billie Joe handed the fan a guitar and had him play "Knowledge."

3

I Was Here

The Punk Rock Continuum and Green Day's Place in It

What Becomes of Old Punks?

Very few sights rival the pathos of an old punk. When the firebrands of the class of '76, the musicians recognized as the original "punks," hit the stage these days, the shows take nostalgia out for a walk, giving our sense of revolution a bit of air before we stuff it back into our iPods, where it screams through headphones to get out, but only we can hear it.

- Two-tone ska artists like the Selector and Bad Manners continue to capitalize on the third wave they influenced nearly four decades ago.
- The Sex Pistols have turned cabaret, bashing out "God Save the Queen" in Las Vegas casino show rooms.
- Bob Geldof took on the cause of African starvation, initially through his musical pursuits and then over them.
- Tom Robinson has a BBC talk show.
- The Gang of Four work on Internet music sites and teach at universities where long sleeves and ties cover their tats.
- Conservatory-trained Joe Jackson and the artist with whom people forever confused him, Elvis Costello, both record for *classical* labels.
- Electronica musicians regard Suicide's Martin Rev as their patron martyr, while Rev's late partner Alan Vega made a name for himself as a painter.
- The Jam's Paul Weller took his Who-influenced, post-mod roots back to the Tamla-Motown from whence they came and invented post-blue-eyed-soul.

Even the punks that survived had to *grow*, and this was sometimes painful, both for the artists and the audience. U2 went through their electronic dance phase, coming out of it sounding suspiciously like classic rock (in the best sense of both words). Wire metamorphosed continuously, temporarily disbanding when they hit creative roadblocks.

As the acknowledged granddaddy of punk, Pete Townshend said during an interview for now defunct webcaster MCY.com that you must recognize your current position in life: "I have to accept that if I write songs today, they are songs that are written by [a] very mature, very stable, serene, contented, balanced man. What a yawn!"

Ironically, one of Townshend's spiritual children, Billie Joe, echoed this sentiment in *Rolling Stone*, saying, "I felt like I was too old to be angry anymore . . . It's sexy to be an angry young man, but to be a bitter old bastard is another thing altogether."

Fresh off a win for Album of the Year at the 2005 Grammy Awards—for one of the most mature, politically and personally astute rock recordings in many moons—Green Day earned grudging respect among critics, the music industry, a new coterie of fans, and even their peers. This band made their reputation with songs about chronic masturbation from albums named for shit and segued into recording one of the best-heard repudiations of the state of politics and America. They demonstrated the range and scale of what punk rock can accomplish and what it has become, how things grow, how they change, and what remains.

But where do they fit in with all of this? What is their part in the grand scheme of punk? There are those that argue that Green Day have nothing to do with punk. Do they have a case?

Punk—The Early Years

Johnny "Rotten" Lydon once defined punk as musical honesty. One of the first uses of the word "punk" to describe music came from the godfather of music journalism, Lester Bangs. He and fellow travelers at *Creem* Magazine began using the word to describe the garage band sounds of the Seeds, the Sonics, and the Count Five, and the word came to encompass the sounds of the MC5 and the Stooges as well. This confused occasional *Creem* contributor and famous beat author William S. Burroughs, who said, "I always thought a punk was someone who took it up the ass."

When the Ramones came around, it was the only word for them. Unlike New York scene progenitors like the New York Dolls, whose appearance—dressing in heels and dresses with lots of makeup—got them lumped in with glam bands, the Ramones' three chords played loudly and sloppily at

The Ramones were the progenitors of modern punk two generations before Green Day. Joey Ramone thought Green Day was "cool."

breakneck speed, along with their singing about sniffing glue and other teen avocations, was both a throwback and a revelation. At a time when the prevailing popular recording artists like REO Speedwagon, Jackson Browne, and the Eagles filled the rock airwaves with music that relied on slickness, the Ramones were all about energy.

That energy was inspirational. No band since the Beatles encouraged more people (including Green Day) to pick up electric guitars and play, especially in England, the destination of a pilgrimage many East Coast bands made on their own dime during the '70s. "At our soundcheck at Dingwalls," the late Joey Ramone recalled to Mat Snow in *Q*, "all these kids—Johnny Lydon, Joe Strummer—were there telling us we were responsible for turning them on."

The effect was galvanic. Bands like the Clash (Strummer's group) and the Sex Pistols (for which Lydon changed his last name to Rotten) started playing a club scene in the UK that was created just for the new English punks. The Sex Pistols and the Clash were largely about politics and anarchy, but it didn't take long for bands with more prurient—or at least personal—themes to show up. For example, one of the first, the Buzzcocks, true to their name, would sing about masturbation and other glorious teen activities.

The Many Faces of Punk

The energy of punk became a catalyst that linked hundreds of bands making incredibly diverse music—it covered groups from the Circle Jerks and Black Flag to the Talking Heads and the B52s. It was the West Coast bands, for the most part, that made "cred" an important part of punk. Elements of cred included a DIY ethic and a large dose of nihilism. Where the Sex Pistols had wanted to provoke change in society, Black Flag wanted to tear it all down.

The arbiters of "cred," mostly the bands themselves and the fanzines that covered them, saw themselves as guardians of the purer faith. Berkeley zine *MaximumRocknRoll* laid out some of the dos and don'ts of what maintained punk cred in their pages: a band with a clip on MTV can't be punk, and any band from a punk scene that signs to a major label has sold punk out. If a band hit it big, they were suddenly no longer punk in the eyes of these hardcore fans. For example, X went from being one of the lynchpins of LA punk to virtual outcasts on the scene when they signed with a major record company. When Green Day did, one *MaximumRocknRoll* stalwart was so furious that he picketed a Green Day show in Petaluma, California.

The members of Green Day recognized this as one of the perils they faced going the major label route: the arbiters of punk might never accept them as punks again. Green Day chose to color outside of those lines, to dare to be both punk and popular. But they also echoed Lydon's definition of punk. They would not sign a deal that would take away their artistic control. They wanted to maintain their "musical honesty." Finding mainstream popularity was not an end they had in sight when they started playing. It was not an end they were reaching for when they toured extensively and intensively for all those years.

Punk had become like a mole—it spent so much time underground it could not conceive of coming into the light or that anyone would want it to. The high cabal of punk cred essentially said that it was not punk to rise above the underground. The folks who felt they defined punk did not *want* punk to reach the masses. They wanted it for themselves.

The Clash's Joe Strummer: "When Green Day come out of my radio, let me tell you, it sounds a lot better than the rest of the shit coming out of it."

However, it was inevitable that punk would be subsumed into the greater mainstream of rock. Most of the early punks saw it and either changed or went from being angry young men to bitter old bastards, as Armstrong observed. It took a lot for many of the early punks to come to grips with this. "We're just a band and we release records," Strummer said to *Melody Maker*'s Chris Bohn upon the release of *London Calling*, "and that's the fact of the situation, I'd say, but people think they've got to swallow all the bullshit with it."

Pop Go the Punks

By the early eighties, bands that began as punks (and "new-wavers," as those in the record industry tagged them because they did not like the Burroughsesque connotations of the word "punk") began to infiltrate the pop charts. Groups like Blondie, who—like the Ramones—broke out of

New York's CBGB, had massive pop hits. Bands like the Offspring were able to sell millions of records via an independent company, as were transplanted East Bay homeboys NOFX. Bands that started out indie, punk, and DIY—like Hüsker Dü, the Replacements, and Sonic Youth—all went over to the "dark side," signing contracts with major record companies. This is the environment in which fourteen-year-old Mike Pritchard (later Dirnt) and Billie Joe Armstrong started playing music together. When they began recording in the late eighties, they had developed a sound that mixed the marrow of punk with the heart of the Beatles. In their wake, a fresh wave of pop punk artists started to flourish.

Of course, there were detractors. When they signed to Reprise Records for their third album, some of their old friends and fans—like the former followers of X—rejected them as sellouts.

"Selling out is compromising your musical intentions," Mike told Jim Testa of *Jersey Beat*. "There are a couple of people out there who really have it in for major labels, but will they back it up? Will they throw away their Buzzcocks albums and their Sex Pistols albums, their Generation X, all that shit? I don't think so."

"We were never really in that whole PC punk clique," Billie Joe further opined to Jonathan Gold in *Spin*. "I guess if I wanted to be in a clique, I would've probably gone out for the baseball team in high school."

To Green Day, punk had less to do with how they sounded and more to do with how they acted and lived. They regarded their personal punk ethic, in part, as making their own rules, musically and personally—that and occasionally soaking down an audience with beer and then mooning them. In their early experience, punk was music a person could ride a skateboard on a half-pipe or mosh to music from groups like the Dead Kennedys and the Circle Jerks.

However, Johnny Lydon expressed righteous anger at the very idea of Green Day being punk to Randall Roberts of the *LA Times*: "I can't stand them . . . They haven't had to go through the violence, and the hate, and the animosity that us chaps way back when had to put up with. We had to fight for every single footstep."

Lawrence Livermore, the former owner of Lookout! Records, the indie that brought Green Day and many other nuvo-punk bands into record stores everywhere, sees it differently. "The whole gist of original punk was to annoy, outrage and shock people," he told Alec Foege of *Rolling Stone*. "That's not the main thing of Green Day. They sing simple, cool love songs with a lot of energy."

What Lydon also seems to not take into account is that when the Sex Pistols were burning bright—when the class of '76 bands like the Sex Pistols, the Clash, and the Ramones were doing their punk thing—the members of Green Day were truly "sweet children": they were four years old. They are not the second coming of punk; they are the second generation.

And despite what Lydon says, Billie Joe would contend that they certainly had their share of adversity. They grew up in lower middle class families and had to fight it out just to get equipment. They toured in rusty vans and graduated to a book mobile, playing to empty clubs. They endured road food and the "liquid dookie" that could follow in its wake. They suffered the brickbats that their peers from Gilman Street and outsiders like Lydon continued to throw at them.

"I realize how shit on we were by our own community," Billie Joe told Matt Hendrickson of *Details*. "I get so mad that when I run into these people in the street, they're lucky I don't have a fucking knife in my boot."

However, a main ethos of punk—the desire to move bodies and minds through honest music—has never left them. Initially, they turned their angst inwards, making fun of themselves rather than blaming "society." Twenty years on, they added the political element to their palate, a move the first (second?) wave of punk rockers should have reveled in. Indeed, some, like blogger Nicky Smith, contend that "Green Day's greatest achievement was crippling punk fascism."

"I still love punk," Billie Joe told Craig Rosen of *Billboard* in 1997. "I'm only 25 years old, and I still love it. I don't want to abandon it. It made me who I am."

For Green Day, punk took on all the earmarks of a religion. There was the community, and the spirituality in that community, that made things like Gilman happen. It has factions that argue and fight about just what punk is. It offered them self-discovery, sanctuary, and some sort of salvation. "I think it has a lot to do with burning down the establishment to create something new," Billie Joe told *Out* a decade later. "It's something that's supposed to empower you."

Beyond Gilman, however, the idea of punk has been something of a mixed bag for Billie Joe. On the one hand, it is the way he chooses to live. To him, and the rest of the band, this transcends a musical direction. It transcends the nihilism that more austere punks see as a given. The members of Green Day regard punk as more of a mindset. On the other hand, Green Day has musically transcended their punk roots.

"When we started out as a band, we played punk rock, the music," he told *New York Rock*. "We're just as much punk as we used to be . . . We didn't start the band to cash in a lot of money. When we started out, punk was probably the most unpopular music around."

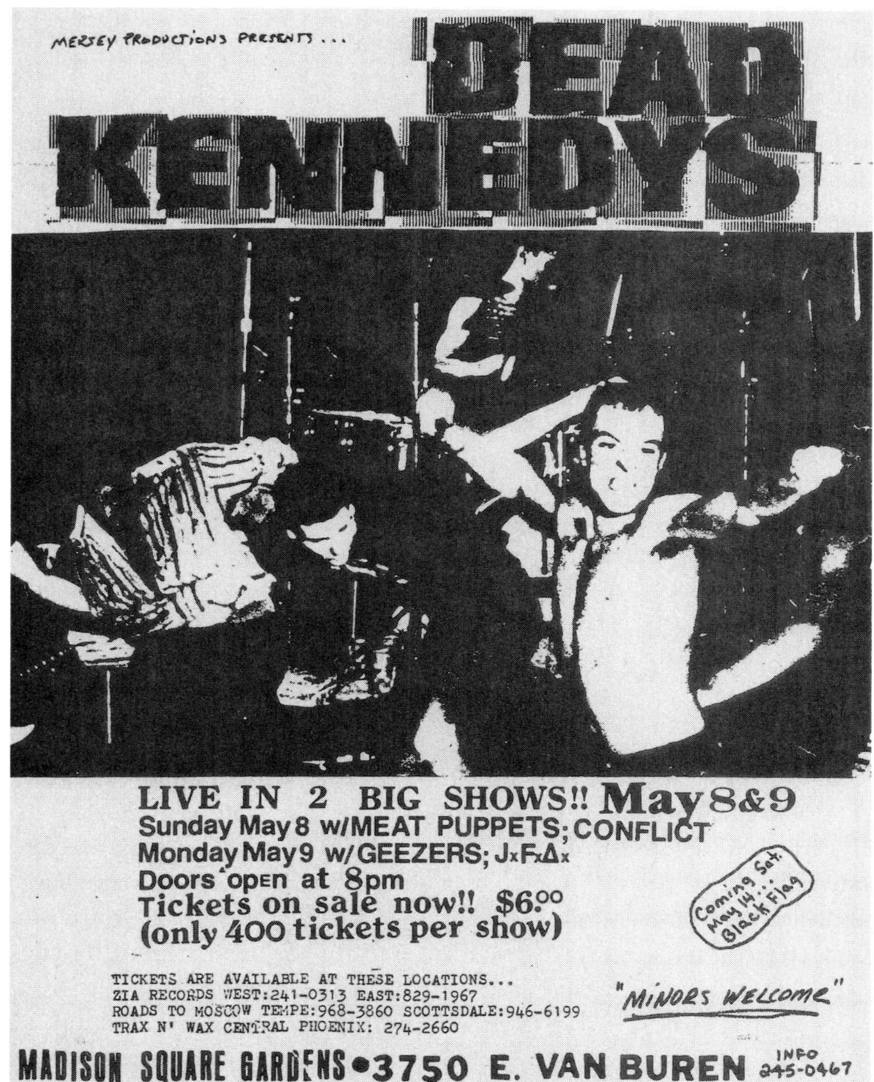

Jello Biafra and the Dead Kennedys rode the second wave of punk with songs that urged listeners to tear it all down.

Another aspect of punk that the band celebrates is that every generation has its punks, whether they're called that or not. Ultimately, the punks that carry the flame have to pass it on. If they don't, the next generation will simply take it from them. Punk carries on.

Cole Becker of the young indie band SWMRS agrees with the idea of punk as an ideology more than as a musical sound. "Everything is always going to come from a very punk spirit," he told *Upset* magazine's Ali Shutler. "What we like about punk is that it's very activist and very visceral." Of course, the first two SWMRS albums were produced by the drummer's dad. The drummer is Joey Armstrong, and his dad is Billie Joe.

Green Day's music—and "pop punk" (a phrase that Billie Joe wants to wipe out of the English language) in general—is, of course, popular now. And, according to data analysis company Polygraph, which ran a study based on playlists with the word "punk" in them on Spotify and YouTube, Green Day occupy the No. 1 position among punk bands. Over half of the "punk" playlists had music from Green Day on them. The Sex Pistols did not even appear in the top ten playlists. Matt Daniels, who conducted the study, concluded that then new bands kept the current generation's punk flame burning, in the same way the Pistols, Black Flag, the Dead Kennedys, the Buzzcocks and earlier generations of punks had in their time. He even went so far as to say that Green Day did not need the hyphenated label of "pop punk." As far as this generation is concerned, they are the real thing.

In 2015, their Rock and Roll Hall of Fame induction but a month old, Green Day played a "secret show" at 924 Gilman. It was a gathering of the tribes of sorts, a bunch of people who came up through the all-ages club rallying to celebrate a twenty-fifth class reunion. Green Day played to a club packed with grown-up punks. "That was so emotional," Billie Joe told Brian Hiatt of *Rolling Stone*. "Looking out in the crowd, you see familiar faces that once had piercings and dyed purple hair, and now it's covered in gray." In the crowd were former punks who had turned the punk experience into jobs as teachers and professors, artists and authors, all who discovered their ability to express themselves as punks and through punk, old punks who grew up gracefully.

4

Hitchin' a Ride

Some Artists Who Proudly Claim Green Day as an Influence

It is likely that only Elvis and the Beatles inspired more people to pick up a guitar (or bass or set of drum sticks) and join a band than Green Day. And they influenced two generations worth of players, the first inspired by the raw simplicity of *Dookie* and the second spurred on by the power of *American Idiot.* Here, then, is a far from complete list of about seventy bands that claim Green Day as an influence, at least. Some of them are famous, and some of them have great stories. (Some have both.) As of this writing, all of them are working musicians who acknowledge that they are beholden to Green Day.

- **5 Seconds of Summer** namecheck Green Day on the song "Long Way Home" and said they were brought up in the age of Green Day, acknowledging their influence.
- **20 Eyes** keyboard player Wolf Bradley told *Random Length*'s Mike Botica: "Green Day came out with *American Idiot,* and I was like 'That's what I love. That's the thing.' My first concert was Green Day, and from then on in, they were my favorite band ever." (Interestingly, Wolf's mother was in the Whigs, a band roughly in with the New Wavers of the eighties.)
- **Lee Aaron** started her musical career playing "alt-rock" under the influence of Green Day (and others).
- **AFI** thank Tré Cool on their album *The Art of Drowning.*
- **All Time Low** lead singer Alex Gaskarth, on the We Love DC website, told writer Mike Darpino that Green Day is one of his favorite bands.
- **Arcane** claim Green Day, alongside Taylor Swift and Arcade Fire, as an influence.
- **The Ataris** list Green Day as one of bands that influenced them in making their album *Anywhere but Here.*

- **Bad Religion** guitarist (and founder of Epitaph Records) Brett Gurewitz says Green Day is one of his favorite bands. Bad Religion thank Green Day on their album *Stranger than Fiction.*
- **Frankie Ballard**, chart-topping country artist, has Green Day's entire *Dookie* album on his iPod.
- **The Baltic**'s singer/guitarist Adam Dankowski told Bethany Ao of the *Denver Post* that his first show was a Green Day concert. "I cried during '21 Guns.'" The rest of the band claim them as an influence, too.
- **Bayside**'s bassist Nick Ghanbarian told Ryan McGonagal of the *Daily Slice* that "we all look up to bands that we grew up on like Green Day and Bad Religion and stuff like that . . . it's the reason I picked up a bass, early nineties."
- **Big Scary** drummer Jo Syme confessed to *Tone Deaf*'s Nick Reid that she "was loving" Tré Cool as she learned to play the drums.
- **Blink-182** thank Green Day on their record *Enema of the State.*
- **Bob Moses,** the electronic duo of Jimmy Vallance and Tom Howie, share a love for post-punk bands, such as Green Day.
- **Breakmouth Annie** cites Green Day as an influence along with some of Green Day's influences, like the Clash and the Ramones.
- **Jack Bruno** (a.k.a. Raw Fabric) said that he decided music was his thing after his mom took him to a Green Day/Blink-182 Pop Disaster Tour show in 2001.
- **Car Seat Headrest** (a.k.a. Will Toledo) taught himself to play guitar by practicing Green Day songs.
- **Josh Carter**, late of the Smoking Popes, says Green Day had a big influence on his career.
- **Amyra Dastur** was inspired by Green Day.
- **DCO** claim Green Day (and Blink-182) as an influence.
- **Dead Man's Hand** bassist Jeff Kent says he is inspired by bands with prominent bassists, like Green Day's Mike Dirnt.
- **The Donnas** thank Green Day on *Turn 21.*
- **Melina Duterte** (a.k.a. Jay Som) learned how to play guitar using Green Day tabs.
- **The Ergs!** guitarist Mikey Erg told *Westword* that he is "definitely influenced by old Lookout! Records bands like early Green Day."
- **Fall Out Boy** bassist Pete Wentz, as he inducted Green Day into the Rock and Roll Hall of Fame, said: "No one else can do anything the way Green Day does. When *Dookie* broke, I remember thinking 'this is a band that speaks to me, that sounds like me, that looks like me and they're

played on the radio and MTV. They made an odd kid feel like I had a foothold in pop culture."

- **Newton Faulkner**, speaking to *What's on Stage*, said: "[I] played bass in a Green Day cover band. *Dookie* was probably the first album I bought." Faulkner had a few chart-topping hits in England and later starred as Johnny in a London company of the musical *American Idiot.*
- **Fidlar**'s Zac Carper received some personal help from Billie Joe when Carper started dealing with his own addiction problems, but long before that, the first song that Zac learned how to play was "Good Riddance (Time of Your Life)."
- **Florence and the Machine** lead vocalist Florence Welch told *Rolling Stone*: "The first CD I ever bought was Green Day's *Dookie.* It was my first clue that there could be a whole identity around the music you liked." Before her success with the Machine, Welch and producer and artist Dev Hynes cut an acoustic version of *Nimrod.* "Later, I met Billie Joe Armstrong, and he told me he liked it," she said of that recording. "My 13-year-old head was exploding somewhere in the past."
- **Foo Fighters** have Billie Joe listed first on the thank you list of *One by One.*
- **Ezra Furman** discovered punk rock through Green Day (and the Ramones).
- **Robbie Gold**, singer/songwriter, claims Green Day as one of his major influences.
- **Good Charlotte** claimed Green Day as an influence on MTV News and thanked them on *The Young and the Hopeless.* Guitarist Benji Madden has a Green Day sticker on one of his guitars and has said that he has been a Green Day fan for years.
- **Goodnight, Texas** guitarist Avi Vinocur bought *Dookie* when he was nine years old. It was the first CD he purchased with his own money, and it inspired him to pick up a guitar.
- **Oscar Isaac** (yes, the *Star Wars* actor) was the front man for a ska-punk band called the Blinking Underdogs that once opened up for Green Day.
- **Kaiser Chiefs** former drummer Nick Hodgson said that Green Day, by being so punctual and polite, taught them manners. He told Contactmusic.com: "We thought they would be real rock and roll divas until we went on tour with them from Ireland to Scotland. The manager told us we had to get off the tour bus when we boarded the ferry and we

said, 'I bet Green Day don't have to.' But when we got off the bus we saw that Green Day were the first off, sat in a café at 6 AM."

- **Lady Gaga**'s first album was *Dookie*. "I remember when I bought [it]," she told *NME*. "I just wanted to lick the pages from the booklet! That particular album, I mean, it is iconic."
- **Lasting Effect**'s guitarist Brandon Leavell cites Green Day as the band that really got him into music.
- **Lost In Society** bassist Nick Ruroede says that listening to *American Idiot* got him into music and playing.
- **Louden Swain** (of *Supernatural* fame) say they started out in a garage band influenced by Green Day.
- **The Maine**'s rhythm guitarist Kennedy Brock says he was motivated by his friends listening to Green Day.
- **Maple Hill** said they admire Green Day.

Pop Disaster Tour mates gave Green Day a big thank you in the *Enema of the State* notes . . .

- **Mayday Parade** drummer Jake Bundrick grew up listening to Green Day and calls them one of his favorite bands.
- **"Arthur McBarfson**," founder of Get Loud Records, recalls buying an old electric guitar in the fifth grade and learning *Dookie* from end to end, beginning his lifelong love of punk rock.
- **Andrew McMahon**'s second band was a Weezer/Green Day tribute band called Tweezer.
- **Mest**'s Tony Lovato thanks Billie Joe in the *Destination Unknown* liner notes for inspiring the creation of so many great bands.
- **Minority 905** released a video covering all of Green Day's hits in ten minutes.
- **Haythem Mohamed** picked up the electric guitar after hearing someone play some Green Day.

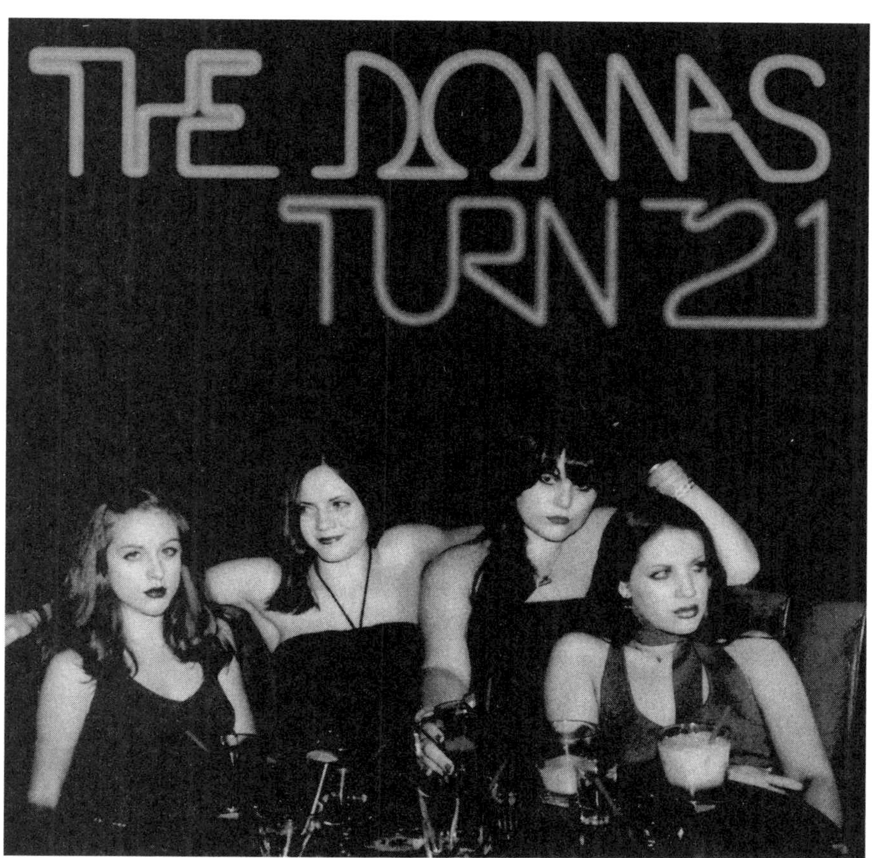

. . . as did the Donnas on *Turn 21.*

- **Nap Eyes** singer/guitarist Nigel Chapman cited Green Day as an influence, along with the "Johnny Appleseed Song," Joni Mitchell, and Neil Young.
- **Neck Deep**'s Ben Barlow looks up to Billie Joe as a legend and the last word in punk.
- **New Found Glory**'s official bio cites Green Day's influence on the song "Radiosurgery."
- **NOFX** thanks them on *Punk in Drublic* and gives them a shout-out on "Jesus" from *Frenzal Rhomb.*
- **Our Untold Story** founder, composer, singer, and guitarist Xander Turian cites Green Day as one of his main artistic influences.
- **Pierce the Veil**'s Vic Fuentes speaks of his undying love of Green Day.
- **Plainsunset**, recording artists from Singapore, all met in school, heard *Kerplunk*, and decided to form a band.
- **Rancid** thank both Billie Joe and Adrienne Armstrong on *Let's Go.* Billie Joe also wrote the song "Radio" on that album.
- **Rat Boy** claims Billie Joe is beyond an influence and one of his heroes.
- **Reckless Serenade** drummer Matt Ruggiero says the first song that he learned on the drums was by Green Day.
- **Ricky Reed,** although a producer of pop acts like Jason Derulo and Meghan Trainor, grew up in Oakland's punk scene, listening to Gilman bands like AFI, Operation Ivy, and, of course, Green Day.
- **The Regrettes** bassist Sage Nicole says she will love Green Day forever, as they have helped her make it through the day since she was eight years old.
- **Rosedale** guitarist Mike Liorti recalls enjoying Green Day because it was in his brother's collection and says the band was his entrance into punk rock.
- **Scarlet Avenue**'s Amos Ang recalls his father buying him and his brother a Green Day concert DVD that they played along with until he and his brothers had it memorized. Ang says they played it all the way through for their father every night for the better part of a year.
- **Sharp Shock** singer/guitarist Davey Warsop cites early Green Day as an influence.
- **Simple Plan**'s lead guitarist Jeff Stinco said that Green Day pushing their music and taking on large themes made Simple Plan want to find a way to do that themselves. In the video for "Shut Up," bassist David Desrosiers has an *American Idiot* sticker on his bass.

- **Jamie Skinner** is an English singer/songwriter and performer who has seen Green Day play fifteen times over the course of the last seven years.
- **Gina Sobel** is a classically trained flautist who plays both jazz and rock, but she loves Green Day.
- **Sum 41** thank Green Day on *All Killer, No Filler* and namecheck them in the "Still Waiting" video. Vocalist and guitarist Deryck Whibley says that the "Basket Case" video immediately made him a fan.
- **Tacocat** drummer Lelah Maupin says that Green Day was the first band that made her care about music.
- **Take the Stage** drummer Shanne Garcia recalls that Tré was the main drummer he learned from while watching music on TV.
- **Tegan and Sara** call Green Day a major influence on their writing. Tegan recalls playing *Dookie* incessantly and that it made her want to play the guitar.
- **Thunderpussy** bassist Leah Julius's brother was in a punk band and *sold* her a copy of *Dookie*, her first CD.
- **Twenty One Pilots** drummer Josh Dun's family forbade video games and rock in their house. "I'd hide albums like Green Day's *Dookie* under my bed," he told *Rolling Stone*'s Andy Greene. "Sometimes they'd find them and get real mad."
- **Violent Soho**'s guitarist James Tidswell recalls growing up and constantly listening to *Dookie.*
- **We Are the Movies** guitarist Tim Waters recalls listening to only Green Day for a couple of years and that the music inspired him to buy a guitar.
- **Weezer** namecheck Green Day on the *Pinkerton* song "El Scorcho": "I asked you to go to the Green Day concert . . . You said you never heard of them." Rivers Cuomo says he learned how to write songs by listening to Green Day.
- **Nick Woods** of Direct Hit! remembers his cousin playing Green Day, the first real punk band he ever heard.

5

Let Yourself Go

Green Day and Their Fans

Being in a band, you have to be a fan first," Billie Joe told one of his heroes, Paul Westerberg of the Replacements, and writer Steve Kandell in *Spin*. "So when you meet people who have something to say about how some song affected them, those are the people I connect with. I am still that person myself." He noted that his sister had taken him to see the Replacements when he was fifteen, and now his fifteen-year-old son was also a big fan.

Lots of bands pay lip service to their fans. Some actually like them but find it hard to interface. While Green Day's members can be a bit reticent to fans who approach them on the street, they do continually invite them onstage with them. The feeling goes both ways. There is a tremendous bond between Green Day and their fans. Green Day understand where their fans are coming from because they identify with them—they were and continue to be fans of their favorite bands. Their fans feel the understanding and affection.

Not only are Green Day fans passionate, they are loyal. A Green Day audience includes people from age seven to seventy, from the kid who got turned on to them by an older sibling to the fans that saw the Ramones play in their late twenties, bought *Dookie* in their forties, and got revved up to *Revolution Radio* in their sixties.

This loyalty also cuts both ways. It is one of the hallmarks of the band on both a personal and professional level. Personally, they have played together for close to thirty years and *still* hang out together when they aren't working. Professionally, the loyalty manifests in the dialogue they maintain with their audiences.

Rolling Stone's Alec Foege captured a scene from the *Dookie* days that speaks volumes for Green Day's relationship with their fans:

> Billie Joe . . . stands aloof outside the student union at the University of Regina . . . a small group of smiling girls in their mid-teens gathers around the slightly built singer. "I just wanted to tell you, says [one], pausing, breathless, "That your lyrics really speak to me."

> "Can I give you a hug?" says [another] with a squeal. Billie Joe shrugs his shoulders and then sheepishly obliges. The others catch on; soon each braves a squeeze.

Of course, this has a flip side. Some fans are like the people you know who value others on a superficial level. These are the fans that feel that, because they bought a ticket or an album (or even both!), they have the right to demand backstage passes or get offended when the members of Green Day (almost always politely) turn down the offer of a drink when they are recognized.

While scenes like this play out occasionally (there are a few more in the book), for the most part, Green Day's music resonates with their fans in a large and personal way. People like to sing along with it in cars. Fan and writer Tanya Elder of the GreenDayMind blog, recalling an experience she had on a bus, said: "I heard the strains of '21 Guns' coming out of a set of earphones. In the seat in front of me was a little girl, probably around nine, blasting the song and singing along with it, which usually bothers the hell out of me on a bus or a subway. But in this case I thought to myself, 'Wow, she's listening to Green Day so young,' and I wondered where the band would take her on her musical life and journey."

Green Day as a Connecting Event

As a mother-son bonding experience, a mom took her eleven-year-old son to see Green Day play. As the boy had gotten older, they seemed to do less and less together, so she took him to Central Park's Summerstage to see the band do some songs for *Good Morning America*. They left their apartment before sunrise and got in the long line to get into the venue, barely making it. Two hours before the band was supposed to play the show, they started to do a soundcheck, a mini concert in itself. She noted:

> There were people of all ages there, big and small, young and old, of all ethnicities, from all over the Tri-State area. The crowd was into it the entire time, waving, singing along, and even forming a mosh pit in the middle of the crowd. At one point . . . Billie Joe Armstrong had a little girl, maybe six or seven, go up on stage and dance while he did his magic on the electric guitar. The little girl danced and waved and jumped as if she was born to it . . . He reached out to the audience to see who would sing on stage . . . and after a few tries it was a young, excited African-American girl who, as she caught her breath, rocked to the vocals without pause or faltering as Billie Joe watched in awe.

Green Day can change their fans' lives.

Cristycroad/Wikimedia Commons

For a while, after the onslaught of *Dookie*, the band found it hard to deal with all the adulation. They went from being a purely local phenomenon to a band with a small but loyal underground following that allowed them to sell a thousand tickets in New York. They would crash on the couches and floors of their fans in the US and Europe, sometimes playing to a dozen fans, other nights playing to hundreds. Perhaps 40,000 had seen fit to purchase their records. Then, by 1994, millions of people had Green Day records. One of the things that really troubled the band at this time was the loss of the intimate relationship with their fans. How do you create intimacy with ten million people?

It took a radical rethink to revise their approach, but after the hoopla about *Dookie*—as they went from selling ten million albums to a more manageable two or three million and got to play at theaters rather than coliseums—they began to regroup and restage their show. From that point on, it grew more organically, so when they started playing larger venues again, they had grown into them. This allowed them to figure out ways to jump into a mosh pit at a stadium or walk out into the crowd (or, with proper staging, *seem* to walk out). Fans were invited onstage to play instruments, sing, dance, or cross-dress (for "King for a Day"). To an extent, the equilibrium returned.

And with *American Idiot* they managed to attract a generation of fans who might know "Longview" or "Basket Case" but weren't even born when *Dookie* ruled. They continued to make music that spoke not only to their generation but also to members of every generation, and their fan base grew. At the filming of a "Decades" program for Elvis Costello, the biggest response to any of the guest musicians, including Death Cab for Cutie and Fiona Apple, was for Billie Joe. He came out to the type of Jersey welcome that used to greet local boy Frank Sinatra, ruling Brits the Beatles, and hometown hero Bruce Springsteen. It was as loud, or louder, than the response to the show's star. The same kind of reaction rose from the cheap seats when the band came out in Cleveland, Ohio, to be inducted into the Rock and Roll Hall of Fame.

Some Celebrity Fans

When Bruce Springsteen was promoting his autobiography, *Born to Run*, he did a Q&A on Facebook. Someone asked who he listened to, and he said he had an iPod full of stuff. Asked what was on it, the first thing he came up with was Green Day, saying: "Green Day, they make great records and they're always thoughtful and intense and they have a band that plays great together."

Green Day have always been a little bit leery of the whole Hollywood celebrity thing. It is one of the reasons they still live in Oakland (though they do own homes elsewhere). When Billie Joe played St. Jimmy on Broadway, lots of famous people who were anxious to meet him worked their way backstage. Among them were Lady Gaga and, still a couple at the time, Tom Cruise and Katie Holmes. The one that got Billie Joe really excited, though, was Michelle Pfeiffer; he confessed to having a major crush on her in his teens. He was even more impressed when Chita Rivera, having seen *American Idiot* during its initial run in Berkeley, came backstage.

Facebook founder Mark Zuckerberg is a also big fan of Green Day. When *21st Century Breakdown* came out, he posted to his tens of millions of Facebook friends, writing: "New Green Day album out this weekend. I've been waiting for this for years." When he was introducing the Spotify Facebook feed at the 2011 F8 conference, he used Green Day as an example, showing them in a friend's Spotify feed, and tweaking him a bit because he seemed to come to the band somewhat later. Billie Joe played at the wedding party when Zuckerberg married Priscilla Chan. "He's kind of a Green Day fan, in almost a nerdy kind of way," Billie Joe told Bravo's Andy Cohen. "[It] was really endearing." One of the things that Billie Joe likes about Zuckerberg is reflected in his own lifestyle. He feels like Zuckerberg lives like the band does, comfortably but not too ostentatiously, in a way befitting any guy of his age.

Tennis superstar Serena Williams is also a big fan. She has had problems with stalkers since 2002, but in the case of Green Day, she confessed in the *Belfast Telegraph*: "I'm a bit of a stalker. I don't know how many [Green Day concerts] I've been to, maybe too much [sic]. It's got to the point where I know the run of the show . . . If I were them, I'd kind of watch out for me." To which Billie Joe responded in *Q*: "She really comes to the gigs. When I know she's there I like to play some songs that are a bit more rare, because she's one of those fans that's into album cuts." Adrienne has been known to send Williams pictures of the band playing shows she missed. A guitarist as well, Williams owns a blue Stratocaster, to match Billie Joe's ubiquitous Blue.

6

Nobody Likes You

Green Day and Their Detractors

"If there's ever been a band that took a shit on the punk movement while claiming to be punks (and earning a fortune), it's Green Day," David Reidel wrote in the *New Haven Advocate.*

While Green Day has surely influenced much of the rock and even popular music that will follow them, there are those who . . . have their problems with the band. As Luke Kuzava of the *Santa Fe New Mexican* wrote around the time of *American Idiot,* "Green Day is an easy band to love and an even easier band to hate."

Selling Out

While the band's history is heavily invested in the all-ages Berkeley venue 924 Gilman Street, their relationship with the club has often had what the Buzzcocks might have called a different kind of tension. Early on in their career, when Sweet Children attended shows and got caught up in the whole Gilman Street vibe, they got no traction as a band. Part of the problem was that one of the founders of the club—punk icon Tim Yohannon, who was also one of the founders of the Berkeley punk zine *Maximumrocknroll*—rejected Green Day's audition demos for the club out of hand with two words: too poppy.

The subject of Gilman in general and Yohannon in particular galled the band, and they tried to avoid the topic with the press. Not mentioning Gilman Street in interviews was more for the protection of the scene than an expression of the band's disaffection. There was a pervasive fuck-the-major-labels attitude, and it was writ large on the walls of 924 Gilman. In a lot of ways, it was like the East Bay punk scene didn't want to belong to any club that would have it as a member. Initially, this came as something of a shock to the members of Green Day, but even as early as 1994, they had started to become philosophical about it.

But the fact is that in the five formative years that they played the venue—between John Kiffmeyer joining the band (and lending them a little more punk cachet) and late November of 1993—they played less than forty gigs there. This from a band that spent hundreds of days at a time on the road. Yet many at Gilman seemed to take their major label affiliation and all its trappings as a personal affront.

"People are prepared to dismiss a lot of crazy things that have happened in the history of rock 'n' roll," Billie Joe told Ian Fortman. "From Michael Jackson being accused of being a child molester to Axl Rose being a racist, but we'll be getting asked about being 'sell-outs' for the rest of our lives." Rather than dwell on this, they put it behind them and moved forward.

Not that the reactions were solely from the Gilman crowd. Yohannon, for example, as the publisher/editor of *Maximumrocknroll*, represented an even broader constituency. For many in the punk community, the zine was the arbiter of cool. Early on, Yohannon dismissed the band as soft, criticizing them for writing about girls rather than more punk concerns. Similarly, other influential zines like Gerard Cosloy's *Conflict* never had a kind word for Green Day.

In the best artistic tradition of addressing detractors, Green Day addressed Yohannon in song. The specific song, "Platypus (I Hate You)" from *Nimrod*, has such inspiring lyrics as "It's time to quit/You ain't worth shit." And while the worthless person in question is never mentioned by name (though his circumstances—dying of cigarette-borne cancer—gives a huge hint), Billie Joe tweeted "Platypus was written for Tim Yohanon [sic]. And I pray to god I misspelled his name. Rest in shit you fucking cunt." Can't get more specific than that.

Ultimately, it didn't matter. Nicky Smith, in an article entitled "Green Day Crippled Punk Fascism," wrote, "Green Day might've been banned from Gilman St. but they made out fine professionally—they became so popular that *Maximumrocknroll*'s opinion was irrelevant and Cosloy's disapproval was pissing in a wildfire."

Critique and Vitriol

This, of course, never stopped the critics. While much of the actual constructive criticism will be dealt with in the section covering the group's recorded output, there are those that spit vitriol for the sake of spitting vitriol.

John Kays, for example, took enormous glee in tearing up *21st Century Breakdown* in the *News Blaze*. He suggested that Joe Strummer, more than turning in his grave, was trying punch his way out of his coffin so he could smack Green Day around. He savaged the lyrics as "bumper sticker slogans," and made fun of their playing, writing: "I am brutalizing this record. I'm Spartacus in the arena with it. Didn't know I could be so cruel."

Much of the more febrile criticism comes from people talking about how much money the band makes, as if the band set out to become so wealthy. Carter Maness of the *New York Press* prefaced an article (subtitled "A timeline explaining how Green Day got famous and turned awful") tracing Green Day's path to the Broadway opening of *American Idiot*, writing, "Let's wander through the years of stacking dollars as Green Day readies its jock jams for the world's biggest stage and another huge payday."

As with the comment about "jock jams," some of the criticism gets leveled at their audience in quasi-sociological observations. Early in her career, critic Debbie Sprague commented via Amazon on how Green Day and other "pop punk" bands "finally brought skate-rock into the world of John Q. Mallrat." A lot of this criticism deals with whether Green Day is "punk enough" and questions the group's "cred" because they had the temerity to become popular, sell millions of records, and sell out large concert halls and stadiums. It makes Billie Joe's observation very early in the band's transition to a major level seem both ironic and prescient: "I hope it doesn't get too out of hand, because it's kind of sketchy," he told Peter Howell of the *Toronto Star*. "We're not that kind of band."

A lot of the reviews for *American Idiot* marveled that the band had anything left at all after the perceived misfires following *Dookie*. They took a tone to the effect of "who expected anything like this from Green Day?" To which Tré responded, "Oh, yeah? Well they can just . . ."

More insulting to Rob Cavallo and Butch Vig are the potshots at how Green Day's records sound, like Maness's comments that "third floor joints in Koreatown have better production values" than *Warning*, or that they compress the guitars so much on *Insomniac* that it "could cause toothaches." *Salon*'s Stephen Deusner accused the band of sounding "studiously antiseptic" and said that "Oh, Love," the first single from *¡Uno!*, "is simultaneously anthemic and inconsequential."

Musician Haters

Some of Green Day's peers have lost faith in them, too, for any number of reasons including those above. Many of their punk and pop punk progenitors felt that Green Day had ripped them off and somehow "won" by doing this. One of the more balanced reactions came from Dashboard Confessional's Chris Carrabba in *The Onion*'s A.V. Club interview: "I'll be the first to admit that, like, when Green Day got popular, that was my problem that I didn't like them anymore. But I never pretended that I never liked Green Day. That's crazy."

When *American Idiot* came out, the Killers' Brandon Flowers reproached Green Day for being opportunists. He asserted that the band had taken advantage of "calculated anti-Americanism" with the title track. He thought it was "really cheap."

As Billie Joe lashed out at Yohannon in song, so did Jawbreaker's Blake Schwarzenbach take on Billie Joe with a "secret," untitled acoustic track that ends his band's own major label debut (and final album) *Dear You*. The story has it that the band's bassist, Chris Bauermeister, was partying with Billie Joe when the latter announced, "I'm fucking crazy." A bemused Bauermeister brought this story back to Schwarzenbach, who wrote, "Now everyone tells me they're crazy/Crazy people aren't so fucking boring."

The issue of "who's a punk?" frequently begins and ends with Green Day, as they are the biggest targets and therefore the easiest to hit. The Black Crowes' Chris Robinson railed against the band, saying: "This big resurgence with Green Day and all that . . . pretending they just invented punk rock again—what's so fucking genius about that? Good, so now we've gone back to three chords again."

The biggest detractors have been the second- and third-generation punk rockers, the class of '76 and the mid-80s punks like Bill Stevenson, who played the drums with late 70s LA hardcore heroes the Descendants. He found it confounding that he would turn on a radio and hear Green Day ten times a day, and think how much they sounded like what he had been doing for years. It made him doubt the truth in that music. And he took it personally, according to Ian Fortman, saying, "It kind of hurt my feelings."

Some of the biggest decriers of Green Day are the "original" members of the Western European punk movement. Part of the reason might be the band's early attitude. As the *New York Times* Jon Pareles noted early on in Green Day's career, "Punk prevails not as revolutionary music—the hope of its British wing—but because it's bratty."

Some of those artists, like Northern Ireland's Stiff Little Fingers, agree with Stevenson that they cannot understand how come these latter-day snot rockers could sell millions of records and fill arenas and stadiums while they can barely sell out clubs. They could hear the same radio and television outlets who refused to play them when the music had just begun, yet all these years later they were lavishing that attention on Green Day and their ilk. Similarly, the Buzzcocks' vocalist and guitarist Steve Diggle likened what Green Day do to "acting out a pantomime."

One of the major voices of dissent when it comes to Green Day is Sex Pistols vocalist John "Johnny Rotten" Lydon. Never one to hold his tongue when he could lash out, he had choice words for Green Day when he was on his fellow Pistol Steve Jones's English radio show, "Jonesy's Jukebox,"

Johnny "Rotten" Lydon of the Sex Pistols and Public Image Ltd. called Green Day "sticky tape on a duck's arse," whatever that means.

calling them "silly fat kids," and "sticky tape on a duck's arse" (an interesting image, but what does it mean?). In 2006 he insisted that Green Day would have floundered and drowned in the audiences' spit during the heyday of punk. Some six years later, he had mellowed his opinion a little. While he still doubted Green Day's credibility and credentials as punks, he told Hitfix.com's Katie Hasty: "They're imitating a thing that they clearly don't understand. We're all for equal opportunity. We view them as that. They rate the Pistols very highly, and I have no animosity. But I don't like to see it watered down like that."

Dave Hilson of Tokyo's *Daily Youmiuri* summed up this line of thinking in a sort of left-handed compliment to the band, circa 2002: "Say their music is 'snot rock.' Call them faux punks or juvenile. Complain that they don't have the talent of a band like the Clash or the angst and attitude of groups like the Dead Kennedys or Black Flag. But those bands aren't around anymore, and Green Day are almost all we've got."

With typical bravado, Billie Joe responded to these kinds of statements to Neala Johnson of Australia's *Courier Mail*: "I'm going to be playing music no matter what. You can throw rocks at me, but I'm still gonna be playing my guitar."

7

The Instrument That I Want

The Guitars, Basses, Drums, and Everything Else That Green Day Play

The 10,000 Guitars of Billie Joe Armstrong—Gibson Electric Division

Billie Joe likes to name his special guitars. While the name of his first guitar (if it even had one), a bright red Hohner acoustic, is not common knowledge, the name of his first electric guitar is. It is a Fernandes version of a Fender Stratocaster, and like so many of his instruments, he named it for its color: Blue. It previously belonged to his guitar teacher, George Cole, who allegedly got it from a member of Santana. Blue acquired a patina of electrician's tape around the large cutaway when Billie Joe dropped the guitar at a gig after someone knocked into him. The guitar got a nasty crack in it. He also has a Fernandes Les Paul, which he refers to as "Blue's cousin Les."

He has dozens of other Les Paul variations, predominantly from the company of origin, Gibson. These include one made by the Gibson Guitars Custom Shop, several Les Paul Standards and Specials, and a wide array of Les Paul Juniors. He bought his first Junior—a 1956 sunburst model—at a guitar show in San Rafael, California, in 2000. He called it Floyd. "I could tell right away it was special," he told Gibson's Courtney Grimes. "At the time I was playing mostly Fenders, and the Junior was a completely different guitar from anything I had played before . . . It is perfect for my style of playing." Now, he claims to have twenty Juniors from the 1950s alone, one of each model Gibson made during those years. "Floyd is still my favorite, but I recently bought a '56 Les Paul Custom Black Beauty and it's a close second," he told Michael Leonard of Gibson.com. "I have about 30 vintage Les Pauls now and I love them all."

Floyd also inspired the Billie Joe Armstrong Signature Les Paul Junior. Introduced in 2006, it has pretty much everything Floyd had along with all the things Billie Joe wished it had, like a slightly narrower neck to make it easier to grasp. He had Gibson modify the original vintage pickup, proprietary to the signature instruments, to give his sound even more punch and less hum.

Another Billie Joe Armstrong signature instrument is a version of the 1959 Les Paul Junior with the double cutaway body. This one also has the slimmer neck and modified pickups, along with the Adeline Skull logo hot stamped on the pick guard in silver. It comes in a soft black case with leopard spot lining.

Among the other named instruments in his arsenal are a white '56 Junior he calls "Whitey," a yellow '59 named "Cornel Mustard," and a black '55 he calls, naturally, "Blacky." On *21st Century Breakdown,* he also used a Slash Signature Les Paul and a Jimmy Page Signature Les Paul.

Some of the other Gibson electric guitars in his collection he uses are an ES-335 "Chuck Berry" semi-acoustic with a piezo pickup built in for a more acoustic sound; an ES-135; an ES-137 Classic and Memphis Billie Joe Armstrong model; SG Special, Junior, Standard, and Celebrity models; an Explorer; a Flying V; a 1965 Melody Maker Pelham; and a BB King Lucille Model.

The 10,000 Guitars of Billie Joe Armstrong—Gibson Acoustic Division

In terms of acoustic guitars, he used a Gibson J-180 to record "Good Riddance (Time of Your Life)." This instrument was a favorite of Phil Everly of the Everly Brothers. As Billie Joe continued to use it, he got a signature version of that instrument as well. He used that one on the recording of *Foreverly,* his take on the brothers' *Songs Our Daddy Taught Us,* recorded with Norah Jones.

Billie Joe came by one of those acoustic guitars in an interesting way: "In Green Day's '21 Guns' video, Billie Joe Armstrong is playing my Gibson acoustic," producer/engineer Chris Lord-Alge told Gibson's Anne Erickson. "It was a prototype Gibson made that was given to me, and he liked it so much that I gave it to him, and Gibson made a signature acoustic of it. I begged him to give me one and he never did!" Billie Joe did, however, give him one of the black Les Paul Juniors.

Billie Joe Armstrong with one of his beloved Gibson Les Paul Juniors. He is alleged to own hundreds of them. *Sven-Sebastian Sajak/Wikimedia Commons*

Acoustic guitars have always been a part of Green Day's instrumental retinue, a part of their touring equipment even before the bookmobile. On the back cover of *Kerplunk*, there is a picture of Tré holding an acoustic guitar from a show in Tucson, Arizona, that was shut down because of noise complaints when they played amplified. In the instances when something like that happened—not rare, as many of the early shows were booked by kids no older than they were, and almost certainly unfamiliar with zoning and noise statutes—"we would have an acoustic there and still be able to play," Billie Joe told Gibson's Andrew Vaughan.

Billie Joe's collection includes quite a selection of other Gibson acoustic guitars. These include a 1968 Limited Edition J-45 Ebony and a more standard J-45; an Arlo Guthrie LG 2¼; a vintage ES-120 TD; a Hummingbird; and the J-200 he used to record "Wake Me Up When September Ends."

The 10,000 Guitars of Billie Joe Armstrong—Fender Electric Division

But Billie Joe uses a slew of Fender guitars as well. Up until the time of *Dookie*, most of the guitars he played were Fenders, or modeled after Fenders (like Blue). A fan of Telecasters, he had his guitar tech put together a hybrid of the Telecaster and the Junior—a Tele body, pick guard, and neck with a single Seymour Duncan pickup and volume control. He also plays a standard Telecaster, a 1975 Custom Telecaster Deluxe, a '72 Classic Series Tele Deluxe, and the granddaddy of the modern Telecaster, a '52 Esquire (similar to the one Bruce Springsteen plays). While Blue, the Fernandes Strat, will always occupy a warm space in Billie Joe's heart and left hand, he has several of the Fender Stratocasters as well. These include a white 1962 (so, Pre-CBS) Strat, a Custom Shop Strat, a Buddy Guy Signature Polka Dot Strat, and a Standard Strat. He is apt to put a humbucker pickup into his Strats. He also plays both a Jaguar and a Jazz Master.

The 10,000 Guitars of Billie Joe Armstrong—Gretsch and Beyond Division

Another electric guitar brand that Billie Joe seems fond of is Gretsch. Models he owns include a G117, a G5420T, a G6123 "Monkees" model, a 6210 Chet Atkins, a Brian Setzer Hot Rod, an Anniversary 65, and a White

Falcon. There are also some true oddities in his collection, like a relatively rare 1967 Martin GT-70, a semi-hollowbody instrument with DeArmond pickups made during Martin's brief foray into electric guitars. He uses an Australian instrument, the Maton MS 5500; a Harmony H59 Rocket; an Ibanez RX20, a Rickenbacker 330 (modified with only one volume control) and 360; a Guild G50 and D50; an Alvarez Yairi; and Taylor 514C acoustics.

He puts these guitars (predominantly the electrics) through a variety of amplifiers, including a Custom Park 75, an Orange OR-120, a HiWatt Custom 100, a Gallien-Krueger 250, as well as Marshall Plexi 1959SLP and JCM800 heads (the former augmented with a "crunch mod"). All of the heads run through a pair of Marshall speaker cabinets. He also uses one-piece amps like a Fender Vaporizer and a 1958 Twin 5F8-4. This collection may have been winnowed down recently as his new shop with Bill Schneider, Broken Guitars, featured some refugees from his collection.

Mike Dirnt—Keeping it Simple

If Billie Joe's tastes run to Les Paul Juniors, Mike's instruments are even more basic: he almost exclusively uses Fender Precision basses, especially his signature model. He has an Ampeg SVT cabinet with a Fender Bassman head, as well as a Mesa Boogie MB2000. "They're half tube and half solid state," he told *Guitar World*. "I wanted to custom make my own sound, and Mesa Boogie was really willing to work with me. They made me 6 × 10 [six 10-inch speaker] cabinets, and we put those on top of a 1 × 18."

Tré's Cool Kits

Tré has played on drum kits by Ludwig and SJC Custom, with a 7 × 14 mahogany snare and Remo heads, a 9 × 13 rack tom-tom, 16 × 16 and 16 × 18 floor tom-toms, and a 15 × 24 bass drum. His hi-hat cymbals are 14-inch Dyno Beats. He uses two crash cymbals, a 19-inch Zildjian K Dark medium thin crash, and a 19-inch medium thin crash. He has a 22-inch Ping ride and a 20-inch K Crash ride. Tré maintains pretty much every cymbal he has ever owned, and he will vary them, especially while recording. During the recording of *Nimrod*, for example, Rob Cavallo recalled to *Rolling Stone*'s Alec Foege that "Tré changed the sound of his cymbals on almost every song."

Jason White's Jams

Jason White also favors Gibsons, playing a double cutaway '50s Les Paul Junior and a Gold Top Les Paul Standard. He also likes the ES-335, modified, like Billie Joe's, with a piezo pickup to sound more acoustic. For a more jangly sound, he opts for a Silvertone with lipstick-tube pickups. He plays these through two Marshall heads, modified similarly to Billie Joe's.

8

Welcome to Paradise

The East Bay Environment That Shaped the Band; or Not Their First Rodeo

Rodeo, California, comprises about 4.6 square miles on the coast of the San Pablo Bay, a northern extension of the San Francisco Bay. It started off as a shipping outpost for local cattle during the 1800s (hence the name). Cattle drives ran through the town to the shore of San Pablo Bay, loaded the cattle onto ships, and sent them off to the slaughterhouses up until the early years of the twentieth century. Because Rodeo is a small town, the railroad that cuts through (running parallel to Christie Road and featured in the song of the same name) does not even stop there. It is far enough from San Francisco to make it a perfect place for oil refineries. The first oil refinery was built in the town in 1896 and is still in operation. In 2010, about 8,679 people lived in Rodeo.

In many ways, Rodeo operates like a company town for the refineries, with little boxes for the workers to live in, in addition to being a bedroom community for Oakland, Berkeley, and San Francisco. American flags fly from the front of the homes. By all appearances it is a quiet suburban community. Looks can deceive, though. A local grocery store serves as a nexus for the amphetamine trade. And then there are the refineries themselves, which are never really pleasant to be close to. However, the elementary school Billie Joe attended was practically across the street from one of them.

Despite its proximity to the thriving university town of Berkeley, Rodeo is secluded enough that people who live there can feel isolated, especially if they do not have a car. From a town like Rodeo, even catching a train first involves a significant drive. For example, to get to Vallejo—the location of Billie Joe's mom's place of business, Rod's Hickory Pit, which is about ten miles further away from the cities of Berkeley and Oakland—would take about fifteen minutes by car. It could take around two hours by mass transportation.

So, on the one hand, this is a very staid, quiet area. As a longtime resident once said, it is the unhippest place in the Bay Area. "I didn't really have anything to be proud of, living around here," Armstrong told *Rolling Stone*'s Alec Foege. "I lived around American pride and stuff with all these hicks and shit, but they really don't have anything to be proud of living out here. There's nothing here."

On the other hand, it is reasonably close to one of America's key areas of twentieth-century cultural agitation. The Haight in San Francisco is where the free love movement of the sixties, acid rock, and arguably thrash metal was born. Berkeley gave the world the free speech movement. A lot of radical ideas came out of the Bay Area; it makes places like El Cerrito, Pinole, El Sobrante, and Rodeo a study in juxtaposition.

Musical Hotbed

For all its "unhipness," the East Bay has produced an impressive number of creative people. Bay Area hip hop crew the Heartbreak Gang, Primus guitarist Larry La Londe, Possessed singer Jeff Becerra, pop singer Jocelyn Enriquez, and rapper Young Bari all attended Pinole High, the same high school that Billie Joe and Mike went to. Students who attended nearby high schools included Kirk Hammet of Metallica, Les Claypool of Primus, and many others.

Early on, Green Day may have captured and channeled the element that unleashes all this creativity—ennui. The most exciting place to hang out when they were in high school was the bowling alley, which was one of the things that made 924 Gilman so enticing. As former Pinole student Becerra told *SF Weekly*'s Jessie Schiewe: "People just wanted to hang out, get fucked up, and play music together. There was nothing else to do."

"We grew up in small suburbs in the Bay Area, and we were all kinda small town kids," Mike told Neil Perry of *Kerrang!*. "You could either be a big guy and play sports or be a little skinny guy and get a guitar and go, 'Wow, cool!'"

There is a ubiquitous video of Green Day playing the 1990 Pinole High School Foreign Foods Day in the school's mall (also known as the quad or courtyard to Easterners). The majority of the Pinole High School students in the eighties and nineties where white. That has changed in the years since Mike and Billie Joe attended. Now they are mostly African American and Hispanic, and hip-hop rules, but the school's musicality continues. While individual music lessons fell victim to funding cuts, the school still manages to employ two full-time music teachers and offers courses in guitar, jazz, piano, marching band, symphonic band, and concert band. Even students who never took a music class at Pinole still seem to be affected by the musical nature of the place. The campus sports a speaker system that anyone can use, making it something of an open mic. Part of the reason for the school's

Rumors of Gilman's death have been greatly exaggerated.

musicality and quality was that in an environment with so many musicians, competition would be fierce. A brief YouTube search for Pinole High Music proves that. (Try it!)

Another element that helped power Pinole's music was Fiatarone Music, the selfsame place where Billie Joe had singing lessons and for whom he recorded at five years old. He was but one student who wound up at Pinole and frequented the Fiatarone's store.

Loyalty

Nonetheless, while they may not have high regard for Rodeo, the members of Green Day continue to live in the East Bay, making it their home base. They all currently reside in the more urban enclave of Oakland, although Billie Joe also has a home in New York City. The place they most wanted to stay away from was Los Angeles. "We stay close to home in Oakland," Billie Joe told the *Sydney Sunday Telegraph*'s Kathy McCabe. "If you don't want to be bothered, don't go somewhere you're going to be bothered—and it's pretty easy to see there are certain people who seek that out, who pursue that shit because it makes them feel important. For a lot of musicians Hollywood is an elephant's graveyard where they can still feel important."

"There is something that keeps us in check—it's called the East Bay," Mike added to this thought to Perry one evening before the band played a homecoming concert. "We're in it right now, and there'll be 2,000 of those assholes—our closest friends—out there later keeping us in check!"

Community has always been an integral part of Green Day. Many songs are named for friends of the band. "J.A.R." stood for Jason Andrew Relva, a friend of the band (and a former Sweet Child) who died young in a car crash. "Brain Stew" was the nickname of James Washburn, who sported a Mohawk when the band met him and segued into working on cars, another of Green Day's avocations.

Many of the locations in songs have real-life corollaries in the East Bay. "Tight Wad Hill" had a good view of the high school football field, and those who did not want to pay to get in the game, or wanted to do drugs during the game, would go up there. It is a favorite hangout for tweakers. Similarly, "Welcome to Paradise" celebrates the Oakland factory space on West 7th Street where several of Billie Joe and Mike's friends squatted. Starting in their late teens, they both lived there, as well. As previously mentioned, the tracks by Christie Road continued to be a party place until the Santa Fe Railroad Police shut it down.

Similarly, Green Day wear their East Bay influences on their sleeves and other parts of their T-shirts. They still have kids come onstage during shows so they can teach them Operation Ivy's "Knowledge," which must bring some royalties to that late band's Jesse Michaels. Michaels also did the artwork on some of Green Day's earlier records. Billie Joe calls Operation Ivy

An old-fashioned punk rent party to keep the lights on at 924 Gilman St.

Some of Green Day's formative political ideas came from seeing bands like the Dead Kennedys at Gilman.

one of Green Day's great inspirations and equates Michaels as the punk-rock version of beat author Jack Kerouac, another late Bay Area resident albeit not a native son.

The band also helped inspire members of their community. When they met Mike Olyphant outside of a club and offered him a toke, he was a spoken word artist. They motivated him to form the band Fetish and would enjoy hanging out at the band's warehouse home and practice space. "It wasn't so much what they were doing," Olyphant told Foege, "it was how they treated me. They were really, really considerate."

On Green Day's first tour as a major label act, they took local queercore band Pansy Division on the road with them throughout America, and they took another local group, the Riverdales, with them throughout Europe and on another North American tour. Billie Joe produced an album for the Riverdales, as well. Both opening acts, not so coincidently, were on Lookout! Records at the time.

¡Dos! featured a member of a more current band trying to rock its way out of Rodeo. Billie Joe caught the Mystic Knights of the Cobra playing a set at Gilman. He told the *Alternative Press* they were "doing stuff that's far more creative than anything I've seen in a really long time, and they're from this shit town that I'm from."

Berkeley

Green Day friend Aaron Cometbus's eponymous band advertises a Gilman date.

For some people this loyalty to their home area is a mystery, a "come on, Jed, you gotta move away from there" moment almost equal to the political stance they started taking around the time of *Warning*. Where did this come from? And the answer to both of these questions is Berkeley. As Billie Joe told the *Advocate*'s Kurt Reighely, "Being from the Bay Area . . . it's all about the alternative lifestyle. Punk rock was about being an individual and coming to your own conclusions."

"As far as getting into punk was concerned," Tré added for Perry, "it was just, well here's some kids with just as crappy equipment as we've got and they're making great music and playing gigs. It was kind of the classic realizations of 'Hey, we could do this.'"

The key thing that led to this realization was when they all found their way to 924 Gilman Street.

9

Gilman Street Serenade

Where Green Day (and So Many Others) Cut Their Teeth

No Drugs

No Alcohol

No Fighting

No Racism

These words are printed large on the entrance to the all-ages club run by the Alternative Music Foundation. They are the essential bylaws of the foundation, and all people who attend shows there are expected to respect those rules.

Opened in 1986, the Alternative Music Foundation was the brainchild of Tim Yohannon and Victor Haden, both of whom wanted to promote independent music and art to an all-ages audience. Haden had scouted a space that would serve their needs in an industrial area of Berkeley, right next to a canery. It didn't take very long after opening before it was better known by that space's address: 924 Gilman Street. Yohannon had a little political leverage, having worked with the Berkeley Citizens' Action Group helping their candidates become the majority members of the city council, and was able to get the city's support for the venue, including the blessing of Berkeley's mayor. They rented the space for $2,000 a month and started off presenting shows on Friday and Saturday nights and a matinee on Sundays.

The story goes that, at Pinole, freshmen Mike and Billie Joe were approached by an upperclassman with a brightly colored Mohawk. He handed them a flyer for a punk rock show at Gilman, which the younger boys had never heard of. He offered to take them there that night, and they were hooked. The headlining band that night was Isocracy, featuring drummer John "El Sobrante" Kiffmeyer.

Run by volunteers (including Billie Joe and Mike, who, despite their slight stature, worked security), the club offered a sense of community to the members of the scene. Because of this, rules were obeyed (for the most part) and hardcore shows at Gilman were far safer than the ones in the bars. As one of the early volunteers recalled, "There was something in the air . . . back then, a good feeling or a sense of pulling together, and unity among people who just wanted to see [bands in a place] that was free of sexism, homophobia, racism, and especially violence." The music also reflected these values.

During his speech at Green Day's Rock and Roll Hall of Fame induction, Billie Joe described the club as a "Romper Room for degenerates," and said, "It was so great . . . We got to watch our friends' bands and they got to watch us play."

The club closed for a time in 1988, after vandalism, a dwindling number of volunteers, and a 16,000-dollar settlement in a lawsuit by an injured slam dancer took their toll on Yohannon. However, some of the core volunteers started to relaunch the venue. They raised ticket prices slightly, put out a newsletter, cut back the number of shows to five a month, and hired a professional security guard to take care of the problems that the skinny kids like Billie Joe and Mike could not. As Yohannon had booked most of the shows, that fell to volunteers, as well. Membership cost two dollars a year and made a person part of the collective that controlled the club.

The people at Gilman were diverse: hardcore anarchists mingled with nihilists. People from UC Berkeley made decisions with unreformed hippies and of course young punks like Billie Joe and Mike. "It wasn't macho, it wasn't muscular, it wasn't spikes and leather," Billie Joe told *Rolling Stone*'s Alec Foege. "The main thing was that it was really silly. The first time I ever saw him play, Tré Cool was wearing a tutu and an old-woman swimming cap."

It was a place where they learned a lot. They learned about working together, about how a collective works. They learned about punk rock by absorbing it through their pores. They learned about political dissent, that it was okay to say bad things about people who you thought were bad leaders. Another of the lessons was to be bold and say what you wanted to say clearly. It was reflected in everything from the music to the flyers advertising shows: a tank with Ronald Reagan's head grafted on top shooting at a crowd led by Mahatma Gandhi, elaborate drawings featuring barbed wire and skeleton fists, lots of images of Death doing outlandish things in comics and cartoons, along with more traditional images like pictures of the bands.

Initially told by Yohannon that they were not hard enough, Green Day (or, as they were known then, Sweet Children) came back with Isocracy's drummer and a much more driven sound. Under the new regime, Sweet Children played their first show at Gilman on November 8, 1988. All told, they would play around forty shows there, including the New Year's Eve show in 1990. They played what was supposed to be their last show at Gilman on Christmas Eve, 1993, while hard at work on *Dookie*. The word had already spread through the punk community that they were working on a major label record. Very few people showed up to the show. Green Day was effectively being shunned by their own community.

Blackballed

When Green Day signed their major label contract with Reprise, the board passed another rule: no major labels. As longtime volunteer and board member Jesse Townley admitted to Thebaybridge.com's Roman Gokhman: "I'm one of the primary people who passed the 'no major labels' ban at Gilman in 1994—mostly in response to Green Day's huge success. We did not want to become the minor leagues for major labels."

However, even before the blackball and even before *Dookie*, Gilman was becoming uncomfortable for Green Day. As their popularity grew, people from outside the Gilman cabal started to come to see them. They began to feel like pariahs, like they had become homeless as a band. After spending much of their teenaged years devoted to the club, they had to move on and spent more time on tour than at home.

As far from the event as 2011, it rankled Billie Joe. "On a certain level, that's always been a love-hate thing with me," he told Matt Hendrickson of *Details*. "The only thing we did was realize our potential and push it. I did get nostalgic for the old days at one point, but now? No fucking way."

Despite the formal snub for having the temerity to sign a major label contract and then displaying the bad manners of becoming successful playing punk rock, the members' side projects continued to do shows at the venue—Billie's (very) on-again/off-again project Pinhead Gunpowder played, as did Mike's band the Frustrators.

One of the Pinhead Gunpowder gigs brought some new music from their hometown to their attention. On the bill was a Rodeo band known as Mystic Knights of the Cobra, a theatrical band with elements of rap, punk, costumes, two women lead singers, and barely controlled chaos. "That was really inspiring," Billie Joe told the *Alternative Press*, "It was just fun to watch." One of their singers, Lady Cobra, wound up rapping on the *¡Dos!* track "Nightlife" and having the next track named after her.

Green Day proper did not do a gig in the small venue of their youth until shortly after they (gasp!) got into the Rock and Roll Hall of Fame. They did, however, donate an old sound system to the club. As of this writing, the club continues to use it.

Even so, during the band's induction into the Rock and Roll Hall of Fame, Billie Joe closed out his speech with a shout out to the all-ages club, saying, "We are so fortunate to have played there."

Rumors of Gilman's Death Have Been Highly Exaggerated

Lots of iconic rock places fail. New York City is full of examples of bygone celebrated clubs and concert venues. The original Max's Kansas City is now a grocery store. The Bottom Line is owned by NYU, as is the former space of the Palladium, now an NYU dorm. By the nineties, CBGB had become something of a scenester mecca. This, in large part, drove away its core audience. As the Bowery, like almost all of Manhattan, became a place where only the very wealthy and the very lucky (who found rent-controlled space) could live, they closed down in the face of crushing real estate prices.

Neighborhoods change. When the Gilman Street Project launched, it was in a seedy industrial area, with little going on there except for the club itself on weekends and after business hours when the venue was open. By 2010, in part due to the influence of institutions like Gilman and the even earlier Ashkenaz Music and Dance Community Center (which opened in 1973) on the neighborhood, the existing industrial tenants like the welding supply company and the canery were surround by businesses like coffee shops, a Chipotle, a brewery, two wineries, bistros, ski shops, an Office Depot, and that hallmark of gentrification, a Whole Foods store. Even the Berkeley Repertory Theater, where the theatrical version of *American Idiot* was workshopped and played through the fall of 2009, before starting its year on Broadway, is less than three miles from Gilman. Needless to say, in this area without rent control, the monthly nut of running Gilman rose. Precipitously. To the tune of $31,000 a year.

Of course, the cost of doing business for the not-for-profit club got bumped up every year since the club opened, and they always managed to find the money. This time it was different. As a message on the 924 Gilman Street website put it, the new rent reality was "the equivalent of having 20 years of rent increases into one."

So Green Day's music was at the heart of a February 2016 benefit for Gilman, both to keep it running and to raise funds so that the collective running Gilman could eventually buy the building they were in. The odd thing was that Green Day, while they were at the show, were not playing it. Instead, "A Tribute to *Dookie*" had fourteen local acts performing a track from the seminal pop punk record, each in their own idiom. Oona Garthwaite of Marston did an ethereal dream rock version of "Burnout." Other versions included a mariachi take on "Having A Blast," a gospel-impelled "Longview," and a ten-minute-long theatrical reading of "Basket Case."

Another irony of the concert was that it was held in the Fox Theater (a favorite venue of Green Day) because Gilman was just not big enough to make the show worthwhile. While no member of Green Day picked up an instrument, Billie Joe did make a speech to the assembled about the importance of Gilman. The mayor of Oakland proclaimed the day Green Day Day, and, looking at the band, said, "This is why I went through the election process! Just to do this."

Integrity

Gilman inspires this kind of loyalty because it has always lived up to its opening credo. It never sold out, except for capacity concerts. While the Green Day connection brings in some of the curious as they tour the Bay Area, it is far enough away to discourage a casual trip. They rarely sell Gilman merchandise away from the venue, although you can now buy Gilman goods from its website. You can't go to Abercrombie or Hot Topic and buy a Gilman T-shirt. You have to go to Gilman. "Gilman is just a place that has deep values and beliefs," Billie Joe told *Rolling Stone*'s Foege. "Being at a Gilman meeting, you feel like calling each other 'comrade.' It's a socialist way of looking at rock and roll music. It's a community."

That word again.

Not that Gilman is always a punk paradise. Over the years there have been problems. In 1994, ex-Dead Kennedys' leader Jello Biafra was beaten on in the pit at Gilman. He sustained injuries severe enough that he had to cancel a spoken word tour to recover.

In 2014, the collective nearly split in two when a New Jersey band, Joy Ride, performed a song with the refrain "You're such a bitch," and encouraged the audience to sing along. This offended the sound person, who cited this as a violation of the no racism rule, which had expanded to include sexism and generally overbearing conduct. This led a faction of members to call for a boycott of the club, saying that it had started resting on its ethical laurels by not enforcing the rules.

A couple of the incidents cited by the boycotting faction were perpetrated by bands that included former booker Mike Avilez. His band Guantanamo Dogpile featured women in burkas while members of the band took on the role of Muslim extremists. Was this theater or did it break the no racism rule? Clearly several Middle Easterners took offense at it. This all made former Operation Ivy front man Jesse Michaels sigh. "We are all aware of what is written on the wall, but the argument that Gilman once followed those rules absolutely or anything close to perfectly is false."

However, despite everything, as of this writing, Gilman keeps on keeping on. It offers a safe place for children of all ages to enjoy a show. It encourages musicians to play, artist to create. "Gilman's influence extends far beyond just music and it definitely goes beyond punk rock, which is the most generic description usually given to the club," longtime booker Jay Unidos told Aidin Vaziri of Gibson.com. "Gilman has helped to shape generations of Bay Area youth. It is a place where people who grew up with or in the place now bring their children."

Billie Joe's children have certainly been there. Joey's band SWMRS headlined an all-day punk fest at Gilman on the weekend the Super Bowl took place in nearby San Jose, an alternative alternative to the most-watched sporting event in America. The Gilman Street collective keeps on keeping on.

"It was a fun scene," Mike told David Friedman of *News Times*. "It was a place where everybody came together for music. Once you got in there . . . everything was dropped. It was all about the music."

And Larry Livermore is grateful for that. On his blog he wrote, "Thank you to Green Day, to Gilman Street and the East Bay, to all of you who found each other and banded together to create a scene, a culture, and a music that transformed our lives and will continue to reverberate through the ages."

When Green Day played their short set at their Rock and Roll Hall of Fame induction, the screen behind them displayed a mixture of fliers from the bands that they came up with at Gilman and other East Bay venues. Livermore was in tears, and he later wrote that "Green Day's hearts and minds had never strayed to terribly far from home."

10

Tight Wad Hell

The Business of Being Green Day

All by Myself

Initially, Green Day managed themselves. They booked all their own shows, made a handshake deal with Larry Livermore to become recording artists, and toured extensively throughout North America and Europe all on their own. And they were in their late teens when they did it.

Eventually it got to be too much for the band to take care of their business and their music. Their fan base had grown to the point that they could no longer play the small "punk" venues around the country without alienating their growing coterie of devotees. And then these nineteen-year-olds had to deal with the kind of promoters who booked the bigger venues and found those promoters taking advantage of their youth and inexperience. "You have to have the right people on your side," Mike explained to *Jersey Beat*'s Jim Testa. "We had been trying to do it by ourselves, and it just wasn't working. . . . So we decided if that's what it's going to take, we might just as well take it all the way."

You Ain't Nothing but a Cahn-Man

They signed with Elliot Cahn and Jeffery Saltzman's Cahn-Man Management in April of 1993. Mike maintains that they learned about the promoters via one of their roadies, who knew another band working with Cahn-Man. According to Cahn, Engine drummer David Hawkins brought them in.

Cahn-Man circulated the group's demo as well as the previous albums. At that time, any independent record that sold over 20,000 copies pinged on the major label A&R departments' radar. Green Day had sold, between their first two albums, closer to 60,000. So, when the demo arrived, there was a lot of interest.

They hired a manager to put a layer of insulation between them and the "bullshit" that artists on the road to success often face, and to help them make good decisions along that road. There are choices to be made, they bring their choice to the manager, and it is up to the manager to take care of it. Indeed, many record companies, especially the big ones, will not allow an unmanaged band to stay that way. If A&R is going to sign a band, they want to have that professional buffer between them and the artists. They do not want crazed musicians running amok in their halls, collaring their employees, and asking people who probably don't know the answer why their record isn't selling in Chicago. It gives the band freedom to create and play. In rock and roll, a trustworthy manager is golden.

"I personally don't like the business aspect of our music," Mike told Testa. "I don't think I could handle balancing the books if we ran our own record label. . . . We like touring a lot more than we like staying home and taking care of our business affairs."

Getting a Reprise

Thus, the band signed to Reprise records, a division of Warner Bros. It had little to do with whether they were being punk. They had outgrown Lookout! Records, and the band and Larry Livermore knew it. Their decision had everything to do with distribution and getting their records to their fans, and everyone involved realized it was nothing personal.

Two things involving Lookout! Records happened immediately. The group promised that Larry Livermore's label could put out the records they had recorded for Lookout!—*1,000 Hours*, *39/Smooth*, *Slappy*, and *Kerplunk!*—for as long as the label wanted to. That was part of the deal with Reprise. Lookout! got Green Day a list of the people who ordered their records by mail and the independent stores that carried the records and created a mailing list. The group sent postcards to the fans and the stores asking to be kept in the loop about cool stores or radio stations in the fans' localities.

For their part, Reprise worked very hard to break this anomalous punk band in their midst. The label genuinely seemed to appreciate their work ethic. "They've been out there working their butts off," their project manager Geoffrey Weiss told *Billboard*'s Carrie Borzillo. "The band is adamant about its roots in punk. They really want to maintain that kind of base and are committed to the people that helped them get this far." Thanks to the joint effort of the band and the label, the debut single for Reprise, "Longview," debuted at No. 1 on the *Billboard* Heatseekers chart, an indication of the strength of their forthcoming album, *Dookie*.

The company also sent them to Germany, one of the band's European stomping grounds on previous forays. This European tour was forty shows, and while some of the venues were small, the band was the opening act for longtime German punk heroes Die Toten Hosen at a 10,000-seat arena. Green Day played nine shows with them for 80,000 people all told. On earlier European tours, the band had built a strong following, a foundation for Reprise to capitalize on. A show in Madrid was broadcast on Spain's Radio Nacional. British music television channel VIVA did a documentary on the European tour. Promoting *Dookie* in Europe, Reprise sent out a Green Day lunchbox containing a copy of the CD, a video tape, and other cool stuff—an expensive piece of swag for a new band.

By the time they hit Europe, Green Day had already sold around a third of a million copies of *Dookie*, which was three times as many copies as anyone at Reprise had predicted. In November, Green Day won the rookie-of-the-year honors at the Billboard Video Awards in Santa Monica, California—with "Longview" winning the Maximum Vision Award for the video clip that did the most to advance an artist's career—and also took home the award for Best New Artist Clip in the alternative/modern rock category. These were the first of many industry honors the band would go on to receive, and they weren't even there to accept them. In true Green Day form, they were playing a gig about twenty-five miles away in Dominguez Hills.

"The whole thought of going on to a huge corporation bothered us," Billie Joe told Borzillo, "but we're comfortable with it now." For Reprise's part, they were determined to work the record for a full year and were confident that they could break three or four tracks on the radio long before *Dookie* hit the Top 10.

Welcome to (Trouble in) Paradise

By 1995, Cahn and Saltzman had gone from modestly successful metal managers to representing one of the best-selling bands in the world. This gave them a certain amount of leverage, and they exploited it immediately. One deal they put together involved supervising the music for a film called *Angus Bethune*. By the time the film was released, the title had been shortened to

Angus, and the soundtrack included the Green Day song "J.A.R. (Jason Andrew Relva)," about a former bassist (from the Sweet Children days) and friend of the band who had died in a car accident at just twenty years old.

Cahn and Saltzman also launched their own label, 510 Records—named for their telephone area code in the grand tradition of 415 Records—which was distributed by MCA, who hoped that maybe a bit of Green Day magic would rub off on them, as then MCA President Richard Palmese told *Billboard*'s Craig Rosen, "I really believe Jeff and Elliot are in the position to successfully attract important artists whose careers we will develop together through MCA." The first band they signed did have Green Day cachet—the Dance Hall Crashers were formed by former Operation Ivy members Tim Armstrong and Matt Freeman, although they were long gone to Rancid by the time 510 signed them.

However, things were not going well between Green Day and Cahn-Man Management, a company the band might say was aptly named. They were spending a lot of time putting their newly found music business leverage to work. The managers were probably less than enthused that Green Day was going on the road to play at $7.50 a seat. At one point during their relationship, Billie Joe complained about "being conned" into playing Lollapalooza by their "management." Is it possible he meant Cahned?

Cahn-Man did several other things that displeased their client. Green Day signed with the company because they wanted managers to facilitate the desires of the band, not act unilaterally. But Cahn-Man liked the weight this band—which had an album that had already sold six million copies—gave them. As they were in charge of the music for the film *Angus*, Cahn-Man put Green Day's "J.A.R. (Jason Andrew Relva)" in the film, on the original soundtrack album, and it was released as the first single from the album. Then Cahn-Man leaked it to radio early, all without the band's permission. They licensed the band's merchandising rights to one of the biggest companies in the field, knowing that the band wanted the rights to go to some friends who were carving a niche in the business. The band felt that their management was ignoring them, that they had become a line on the ledger for their ambitious managers.

All by Myself—Take Two

Less than two years into their management contract, they left Cahn-Man. They knew there was going to be some upshot from this, and they were served with it late in August of 1995 via the Alameda County Superior Court. Cahn and Saltzman sued them for breach of contract and for owing them a great deal of money from the eight million copies of *Dookie* sold to date. The suit claimed that the band owed them $165,000 and 20 percent of all royalties from *Dookie*. The managers' attorney, David Phillips, claimed that there was no legal basis for canceling the contract, saying, "It's just another classic case of where memories are short." Eventually, the case was settled out of court.

The band once again went without management. Guitar tech Randy Steffes became their "liaison." There is a hysterical confrontation between Steffes and *Melody Maker*'s Andrew Mueller recorded in Mueller's book *Rock and Hard Places*. Steffes had created a daily sheet for the band and crew that he pinned to their production office at every venue they played. He called it "The Daily Whiner." When he came to meet Mueller and his photographer in an arena during this period, Steffes was riding around backstage on a Razor-like motorized scooter, his blond dreadlocks flying behind him.

Needless to say, taking care of business became a problem again. This became evident upon the release of Green Day's second album, *Insomniac*. "We didn't set up this record," Billie Joe told Tom Lanham of *RIP*. "We didn't do any promotion beforehand, we completely quit doing interviews, and basically we just wanted to go on into it. We weren't even sure if we wanted to do a video." They eventually did do a video for "Geek Sting Breath/Brain Stew." It was so nasty that MTV had to take it out of daytime rotations. People kept calling to complain about how disgusting they found it.

It was a time when many saw the band as a fading one, as will happen when a band sells ten million copies of an album. They make themselves a tough act to follow, even for their own follow-up. Once again, Cavallo produced. They made a much angrier album, and it sold several million copies. This would have been fine for some other band, but everyone seemed to expect this album to sell another ten million copies, so they branded it a "disappointment." Most bands would kill for sales that disappointing.

Touching the Third Rail

Clearly they were a band in need of direction and someone to take care of their business while they made their art. They wound up with signing with Atlas/Third Rail, a management company owned by Bob Cavallo, father of their Reprise A&R person and producer. They were placed into the care of Pat Magnarella. The change disappointed Steffes, but he took it with equanimity. He continued to work with the band.

Bob Cavallo (the elder) held legendary status and gravitas among managers. He had started as a club owner, and he signed on to manage acts ranging from the Loving Spoonful, the Mugwumps, and Little Feat to Earth, Wind & Fire, Weather Report, and Prince. He had hired Pat Magnarella the previous year likely for several reasons: He saw Magnarella as a younger kindred spirit. They both had started out producing concerts and went on to work as booking agents before moving into management. The younger Magnarella had been working extensively with alternative bands, and the ever-savvy Cavallo saw this as an opportunity to expand his empire.

When the *Insomniac* tour got scuttled somewhere in Germany, the band came back to Oakland to regain their strength and work on their next album. When it was time for that album, *Nimrod*, to come out, the band and record company definitely did some "set up" work. There was a guerrilla marketing campaign that sent *Nimrod* stickers to record stores (hey, kids, remember those?) so that they could put it over the faces on other posters. They started to work the first single, "Hitchin' A Ride," over a month before the album came out so that when *Nimrod* hit the streets the song would have been on the radio for seven weeks. They even set up the band to do interviews with high school newspapers and invited journalism students to shows to encourage interest from a younger audience. Green Day toured, and there were radio contests and finally a secret weapon: "Good Riddance (Time of Your Life)," the melancholy ballad, was released and found an audience Green Day would have been shocked and appalled to have even three years earlier—MOR (middle of the road, adult oriented) radio. It is probably still their most played song overall, especially if you include proms and graduations.

As they toured, the venues started getting smaller. Not to the pre-*Dookie* size—they were still playing theaters and the occasional arena—but certainly not the kind of venues that a band that had sold in excess of fifteen million albums should be playing. Part of this was the band's choice. One of the things that had exhausted them during the *Insomniac* tour was dealing with the rolling contradiction of playing large venues as a punk band. They needed to resolve this paradox. By the time *Warning*, their next album, came out, the band, management, and (reluctantly) their booking agent made some interesting choices.

The Road to *American Idiot*

Green Day had been on the road for over ten years by the time *Warning* came out. This meant that the fans who had followed them through the grimy club circuit as teens and stayed with them for their Saturn Booster ascent with *Dookie* in their twenties were now pushing thirty. It was time to attract a new, younger audience. Leading up to the release of *Warning*, they did this by cutting their show to half an hour and joining the Vans Warped Tour. This had a couple of quick effects. As soon as they signed on, the tour booked nine more venues. It also exposed Green Day to the new audience that they wanted. They spent 2001 playing theaters, amphitheaters, larger clubs (like the House of Blues), and the occasional arena. Then there was the masterstroke.

In Green Day's wake, a lot of younger bands rode the pop punk surf. One of the most successful of these bands was Blink-182, who played to exactly the fan base Green Day were looking to reach. So, the 2002 Pop Disaster Tour came about. While there is a lot more on this elsewhere in this volume, the key business coup of this tour was that Green Day played the first set every night and by most accounts blew Blink-182 off the stage. Now, having solidified their fan base with their always energetic, always kinetic shows, they had to set out to make an album that would capitalize on these inroads. Along with this, Reprise released a greatest hits collection for new fans and a collection of B-sides and other ephemera for older ones. It was a strategy that spoke volumes for how Reprise felt about the band. "They are what we used to call a career band," Warner Bros. Records Chairman Tom Whalley told *Daily Variety*'s Phil Gallo. "Great songwriting, great live act. They are reaching people all over the world."

Just how successful was the strategy? He told *Billboard*'s Chris Morris about an incident with a couple of his teenaged daughters' friends who came by the Whalley house but apparently did not have a firm grasp on what their friend's dad did. "They said, 'Do you know who Green Day is?' Like they knew something I didn't."

Again, the story of *American Idiot* is writ large elsewhere in this book, but it was the album they needed. On the strength of the first single, the title track, and incredibly strong reviews—pumped up by their widened fan base and the audacity of the project itself—the album was No. 1 in America, Canada, Japan, and Australia during its first week of release. The associated tour played to stadiums, and by this time Green Day were prepared to rock them. From the American tour alone, they grossed $36.5 million.

Pat's Record Company

Like Cahn-Man before him, Pat Magnarella took the opportunity to start his own label, Pat's Record Company. Also similar to Cahn-Man, the label was distributed by Universal, the larger corporation that now controlled MCA. Unlike Cahn-Man, it wasn't something he chased. Like so many things in Magnarella's professional life, he did good work, so opportunity came to him.

While Green Day was in the studio putting the final touches on *American Idiot,* Magnarella was approached by a friend in A&R about his own musical imprint. While that didn't work out, he was soon contacted by Universal. Now run by the founders of Republic Records—Monte and Avery Lipman—Universal didn't have to work too hard to convince Magnarella to make the deal.

The way he chose to operate the label, however, said a lot about why Green Day stays so loyal to him. He was being distributed and promoted by a major label, but he wanted to run his company like an indie. "I'm not going to be spending a million dollars on videos and half a million on pop radio," he told *Billboard*'s Melinda Newman. "We made (the company's first signing) Number One Fan's video for $4,000. In reality, it's a little indie label. There's no pressure on this deal for anybody. If we sign good bands and get lucky, good." Little wonder he sent Number One Fan out on the Vans Warped Tour that summer.

Lookout! Lookout!

Meanwhile, back in Oakland, Lookout! Records was having trouble. Larry Livermore had sold the company to some of his former employees and retired. "I was sick of it," he told the *East Bay Express*' Rob Harvilla, "partly because I was feeling like Lookout! was turning into something very different from what I had intended, and partly because it wasn't fun anymore."

With visions of a dozen new Green Days being signed with money furnished by the original Green Day's ongoing agreement with the label, the new regime started spending more money than they had. The result was that royalty payments did not get made. The company would send out statements with positive royalties on the bottom line, but no checks.

After a year or so of this, Green Day decided that they were being taken advantage of and took back their Lookout! catalog, which had long been Lookout!'s cash cow. "It's been over ten years, and really we're not the first band to do it," Mike told Harvilla. "I feel like we've more than honored our handshake agreement with Lookout!."

It was the nature of the agreement that pissed off a great many Lookout! bands. They all made the handshake, and up until the turn of the millennium, they all got what was owed them. "It wasn't [so much] about the money," Jesse Townley, the label's "Royalty Advocate" told Harvilla. "It was about living up to your promises. If it was about money, we wouldn't be in these bands. If it was about the money, Green Day would have pulled their records in '94."

What happened to Lookout! is a classic case of, as Livermore's book title describes it, *How to Ru(i)n a Record Label.* As he wrote in a blog post, "No matter how rich a band is, they shouldn't be expected to subsidize a failing label forever."

Breaking Down in the Twenty-First Century

While the trials and tribulations of making *21st Century Breakdown* are recorded elsewhere in this book, it was a record that took considerable effort. First, the band was charged with something they had not had to face since recording *Insomniac*: making a follow-up to an enormously popular record. This time, instead of breaking with success, they embraced it and put together another concept album-cum-rock opera. Green Day's business partners did a prodigious amount of advance work. The band had a much higher profile now, with the vociferous, opinionated *American Idiot* still fresh in fans' minds, even five years on.

Scheduled for a late spring release, the machine got cranking early. The album was announced at one of the music world's biggest forums when the band presented a Grammy Award at the February festivities. During the later days of March Madness, the song "Know Your Enemy" was featured during the opening moments of the NCAA Tournament broadcasts. In further sports connections, "See the Light," "21 Guns," and the title track were featured songs on ESPN. The single of "21 Guns" came out in mid-April, and rose to No. 1 on the Modern Rock charts, selling 87,000 digital downloads. Around the world, it became the most added song on radio.

The band tapped into new media as well. One of their promotional shows—in which they played the album all the way through on their home turf at Oakland's Fox Theater—was licensed to Comcast for their play-on-demand platform. A concert shot with thirteen high-definition cameras in Phoenix, Arizona, was made available on Verizon's V CAST for wireless and Fios TV customers. The Verizon website made a remixing platform available, giving fans the opportunity to do mash-ups of *21st Century Breakdown* songs, and turned it into a contest. They also gave away a ringtone of "East Jesus Nowhere." The band, record company, and management released a multilingual web presence for the band. Among other things, the site made the band's music and merchandise available by ecommerce.

Of course there was a major tour that travelled the world. "They are truly a global touring band," Live Nation CEO Jason Garner told *Billboard*'s Mitchell Peters. "Green Day has become one of those . . . touring powerhouses that can sell tickets from Stockholm to Paris to Kansas City to Toronto."

Three for Three

After another period of relative quiet and creativity, Green Day surfaced again in 2012 with not one, not two, but three albums worth of music, to be released over the course of five months. And still Reprise was on board, taking on the challenge of promoting three separate albums of Green Day music. One thing that helped was the amount of set up time the band gave their business partners. They announced the albums in early summer for an early fall release, giving Reprise a full season to get up to speed. "Having release dates and artwork enabled us to get everything up for pre-order from the minute the hype started," Warner Bros. Records UK Vice Chairman Jeremy Marsh told *Music Week*'s Tim Ingham.

The promotions ranged from free songs to a Green Day version of the social gaming sensation Angry Birds. "The game itself launches in full later in the year, and directly links to a retailer whenever the game pauses, generating a huge number of impressions," Marsh added. Using the web and other digital tools allowed the record company to reach out to fans who showed interest in the band during the release of *¡Uno!*, with the hopes of keeping sales up for *¡Dos!* and *¡Tré!*. The band appeared on the cover of *Rolling Stone* and *Spin* in the United States and *Kerrang!*, *Rock Sound*, *NME*, the *Sun*, the *Sunday Times* culture sections, *Q*, and *Mojo* in the United Kingdom. It also coincided with an English production of the play *American Idiot* touring the United Kingdom.

Just as the first album of the trilogy was released, Billie Joe had an epic meltdown at the 2012 iHeartRadio Music Festival and spent the rest of the year in rehab, messing up many of the planned promotions. The trilogy certainly sold fewer copies than any previous new Green Day recording.

Sorta Full Circle

Ironically, during the summer of 2016—just as Green Day were once again making a cicada-like emergence, showing up and making noise with the sudden impending release of *Revolution Radio*—a voice from their past reemerged as well. Jeff Saltzman, the Man in Cahn-Man, became one of three owners of a revived dive in their hometown. They turned Oakland watering hole Ye Olde Hut into the Rockridge Improvement Club, changing the shot-and-a-beer joint into an upscale bar dedicated to "craft cocktails." Saltzman seemed to think that at the time it was a more lucrative option than the music business.

As far as Tré is concerned, the business side of the music business equation is secondary. "We don't do it for record sales," he told Peters. "I don't think any record is going to do what *Dookie* did ever again, so you can't really compare the record to something that was that much a part of pop culture. We just wanted to keep going forward and opening new doors for ourselves musically and challenge ourselves as songwriters."

Getting involved in the mainstream of the music business was one of the most momentous decisions the band could have made back in 1993. While, in retrospect, signing with Reprise may have pissed off a few fans, it opened up new horizons that Green Day could not have even dreamed about at Gilman Street. "I don't regret signing to a major," Billie Joe told *Time* magazine. "It was the right thing to do and we had no problems."

I Fought the Law

Green Day Runs Afoul Legally

Chatting with Green Day one afternoon, Neela Johnson of Australia's *Courier Mail* asked how they deal with all the noise of everyday life. In true Tré fashion, he answered: "I like to break laws. Just little ones, not big ones, like speeding, running stop signs."

Apparently Tré does this with impunity, as he does not seem to have been caught. He even took a trip to Cuba before the embargo was lifted, admitting that, at the time, he probably broke a few laws by doing it. (What's the statute of limitations on that?) On the other hand, there have been some instances when members of the band, the band itself, or the business surrounding the band have found themselves calling their attorneys, or at least dealing with facets of the legal system.

Sued by a Cahn-Man

The first serious legal trouble Green Day ever had to deal with was the breach of contract suit brought by the managers who had helped them get signed to a major label. Awash in the leverage that representing a band that sold ten million albums can bring, Elliot Cahn and Jeff Saltzman played it for what it was worth. According to a variety of sources, they first used that leverage to become the "music supervisors" for the movie *Angus*, possibly because they could get Green Day for the soundtrack. They started their own record company, a joint venture with MCA Records.

When Green Day's single "J.A.R."—a track from the film soundtrack—turned up on certain modern rock stations weeks before it officially "went to radio," it was suspected that Cahn and Saltzman offered the early copies as an enticement to play the acts on their own label. Between the new record label, their legal clients, their other management clients, and all the other projects they had, Cahn and Saltzman didn't keep their eyes on what should have been their main priority: the group that got them all that influence in the first place. They started to act on the band's behalf for their own benefit and not for their artists; for example, they signed them up for the Lollapalooza tour without first consulting them.

Green Day fired the first salvo in trying to get their managers to pay attention, telling Cahn and Saltzman that they wanted to lower the firm's take from 20 to 15 percent. This was still a lot of money considering the kind of record royalties, publishing royalties, touring revenue, and merchandise sales Green Day were generating.

"We felt like we weren't being treated like people anymore but as assets," Billie Joe told *Rolling Stone*'s Alec Foege. "So we were just like, 'Fuck this.'"

The band officially severed relations with Cahn-Man with about two years left on their contract. Soon, Cahn-Man fired back, suing the band for breach of contract. The percentages change came up. Cahn-Man's attorney claimed Green Day was still contractually obligated to pay the 20 percent. Green Day's attorney Bernard Burk said that the percentages had been renegotiated, that contracts are often renegotiated as conditions change. If Cahn-Man "didn't see the road signs," Burk said of the split, "he was driving with his eyes closed."

Eventually, the matter was resolved out of court, but neither party was inclined to talk about the terms.

Moon over Milwaukee

When Billie Joe was less than pleased with an audience or his own performance, he was apt to wave his naked ass at the crowd at the end of a show. For a while this was all fun and games. Then, on November 21, 1996, that changed. Green Day had played a meh show at the Mecca Arena in Milwaukee, Wisconsin. Billie Joe mooned the audience, and after the show the local constabulary was waiting.

"I went backstage," Billie Joe told *RIP*'s Tom Lanham, "and this guy Jimmy who does security for us goes, 'Come on—there's a car waiting for you outside right now. You've gotta get out of here!'"

They ran for the car, and suddenly it was surrounded by the police (not the band). Billie Joe was cuffed and put into the rear of a squad car. They arrived at the police's home base, and the cops made Billie Joe empty all his piercings of jewelry and remove his belt and shoelaces. Billie Joe was booked and put into the holding tank.

As Lt. Christopher of the Milwaukee police department explained to MTV news: "Mr. Armstrong dropped his pants to his knees and exposed his buttocks to the crowd. The problem was he exposed himself to a crowd of about 6,000 people, including people as young as ten. That was our main reason for taking action." In the end, Billie Joe paid a fine of $141.85 and was released.

Over a decade later, Billie Joe's butt became an issue again. He and a companion were getting ready to board a Southwest Airlines flight from Oakland to Burbank. Apparently the airline was not up to speed on the style of low hanging pants—a style that Billie Joe happened to be wearing that day. As he was putting a bag in the overhead compartment, one of their flight attendants took exception to the look.

As ABC-TV producer Cindy Qui, who happened to also be on the flight, observed: "A flight attendant approached him and says, 'Pull your pants up.' He says, 'Don't you have better things to do than worry about that?' and then the flight attendant says again, 'Pull your pants up or you're getting off the plane.' Billie Joe replied, 'I'm just trying to get to my fucking seat!'" He and his compatriot were "escorted" off the aircraft.

Billie Joe tweeted about it almost immediately. Representatives from the airline got in touch with him and put him on the next LA-bound flight. Southwest delivered a press statement, saying: "As soon as we became aware of what had happened we reached out to apologize for this customer's experience. . . . We followed up with this customer and involved employees to get more details and, in our latest conversations, understand from the customer the situation was resolved to his satisfaction."

While this incident did not devolve into legal action, it very well could have. It did for another passenger who was removed from a flight on another airline for essentially the same reason. That passenger was actually arrested because his pants fell down as he was boarding. He, in turn, sued the airline.

"Green Day Accused of Ripping a Man's Face Off"

Not a crime of violence, the above clickbait headline led to a story in *TMZ* about one of the many intellectual property disputes Green Day has been involved in. The man in question was an artist named Dereck Seltzer. The face in question was a piece of art he created called "Scream Icon" that was plastered as street art all over the greater Los Angeles area.

In 2008, photographer, lighting designer, and video artist Roger Staub came upon one of the posters of the image on a brick wall at the corner of Sunset Boulevard and Gardner Avenue in LA. The poster, along with a great deal of the wall, was covered with graffiti and other posters and stickers. Staub took a picture of it and put it into his image collection.

The "rip off" in the headline came several years later when Staub was hired to create the video images shown during the *21st Century Breakdown* Tour. The song "East Jesus Nowhere" reminded him of this image. He set out to re-create the wall, with the image and all its graffiti, as well as change the color of it and paint a big red cross over it. He then had other people add on some images of their own; many used religious icons, which are further defaced as the video goes on. The video played behind every performance of "East Jesus Nowhere" on the tour, including the band's appearance on the 2009 MTV Video Music Awards. Seltzer sought the band out, telling them that they were using his image without authorization. They, allegedly, offered him concert tickets. Not quite the settlement he was looking for, Seltzer got a lawyer and sent Green Day a cease and desist request. The band ceased and desisted using the video.

Seltzer, however, went on to sue the band for copyright infringement. After all the evidence was in, but before the case got tried, Green Day's attorney saw that Seltzer and his attorney really did not have a case. For one thing, posters tend to be regarded as a "fair use" item once they are posted. Seltzer asked the court for a summary judgment based on the doctrine of "fair use," and the court agreed. Then Green Day requested the plaintiff (Seltzer) pay the legal fees, as they saw this as a nuisance suit. The district court agreed with that, also.

Less than happy about having their case thrown out of court, and then having the insult of having to pay the court fees, Seltzer and his lawyer bucked the case up to the next level and were heard by the Ninth Circuit Court of Appeals. They, too, saw the issue as fair use, but they decided that Seltzer was reasonable in bringing the case to court and dismissed the payment of lawyer fees, and all parties bore their own costs.

There have been other instances of lawsuits against the band for intellectual property theft. In 2006, Paul McPike, a grocery clerk from Oregon, claimed that he wrote the song "American Idiot" as a high school student, fifteen years before Green Day recorded it. McPike said it had been recorded during a live concert, and he maintained that the tape must have somehow wound up in Billie Joe's hands. "It was real disbelief every time I turned on the radio," he claimed, according to J. P. Gorman of *Cinemablend.*

Initially the US district court threw out the case, but the judge reconsidered, allowing McPike to build a better case. He was, of course, trying to get a piece of the album's action, and that's a lot of action.

Once again, the case disappeared.

In another case, a British band called Other Garden claimed that Billie Joe stole their song "Never Got the Chance" and used it as the title track on *Warning*. Green Day denied it, of course, and put both songs up next to each other on the band's website to let fans decide for themselves.

In the meantime, Other Garden contacted Green Day's publisher, requesting that they freeze any assets generated by the song. Ironically, both songs bore a striking resemblance to the Kink's tune "Picture Book" from the 1968 album *The Kinks Are the Village Green Preservation Society*. Colin Merry, Other Garden's lead singer, told MTV News, "It looks like the little bloke is going to get shafted, from my end." This case also evaporated without anyone determining who shafted whom.

Green Day has asked for their day in court, as well. Reprise filed a suit against a Mexican group called Panda, claiming that Panda plagiarized not the music but *the lyrics* for the Green Day songs "Dry Ice" and "At the Library." Reprise sought ten million pesos plus royalties, just a bit over half a million US dollars. Allegedly, Panda paid off.

Image Is Everything

Then there's the case of actor Morgan Weed. Weed was in the original Berkeley production of the musical *American Idiot*. A film crew took a lot of footage of the rehearsals for the show. When the show moved to Broadway, Weed was no longer part of it.

However, her image went on. A television ad was made from the footage taken of the rehearsals. These included several yards of Weed, particularly her singing "21 Guns." When she saw the ad, she realized she had signed nothing that would let the producers exploit her image like that. Especially since she no longer had a part in the show.

In a lawsuit, she claimed that the producers misused her image and reputation to the point that she was distraught at seeing herself in the promotional campaign. She felt the film damaged her reputation and jeopardized future projects. Because of the video, she suffered from headaches, sleeplessness, anxiety, and stress.

She went on to play Courtney Lawrence in the Broadway production of *American Psycho*, and other roles in theater and on TV, but the lawsuit seems to have disappeared without a trace.

DUI

Green Day recorded a song by Tré called "DUI" for the 1997 album *Nimrod*, but it didn't make it onto the final version. It was due to be released on the 2002 album *Shenanigans*, as well, but it did not make it onto that one either. This is probably just as well, though, since it might have gotten some ironic airplay less than four months later.

Very early on the morning of January 5, 2003, as the band was working on getting their act together and creating *American Idiot*, Billie Joe was arrested for being a liquid idiot behind the wheel of his black BMW convertible. He was pulled over for speeding, and when the officer came to his window to ask for his license, registration, and insurance, he smelled alcohol on Billie Joe's breath. The officer gave him a breathalyzer test, and Billie Joe rang the bell, blowing a .18, more than double the California legal limit of .08.

According to a Berkeley police spokesperson, Billie Joe was very cooperative. He did not try to trade on his celebrity. He was taken to jail and booked on a charge of misdemeanor drunk driving. The judge assigned bail at $1200, and later that morning he was bailed out.

Later that month, at his arraignment, he was sentenced to community service. His main thought about that in retrospect is "I definitely regret that." It would come back to haunt him sometime later.

12

Off the Wagon

From "Green Days" to Rehab

Mind-altering substances played a large part in Green Day's history. The band name itself, of course, refers to a day smoking pot. Then there certainly is the social element. For example, [Spunge] front man Alex Copeland told SoGlos.com's Alice Lloyd that one of his favorite moments in his two-decade career was "supporting and getting wasted with Green Day." Early impressions of the band noted that, aside from the marijuana from which their name arose, they didn't smoke cigarettes, and one *Rolling Stone* writer observed that they rarely consumed alcohol either. However, Larry Livermore—who, as owner of Lookout! Records, knew the band very early on—has another take on the latter. In an interview with Greenday.net, he recalled a gig when someone had bought the seventeen-year-olds in the band a lot of beer. "[B]y the time they went onstage, they were lucky if they could figure out which way the audience was, let alone hope to play their instruments, or even how to hold them," Livermore said. Yet they still played an outstanding set.

This might explain one of the reasons certain events progressed the way they did. The beer and pot never seemed to affect their performance. In the early days, drugs were as natural as pizza, ramen, and bad road food. In the time between *Kerplunk* and *Dookie*, Billie Joe and Tré lived in an industrial squat with a band named, in harmony with Green Day, the East Bay Weed Company. Given this, naturally a lot of pot was consumed. Billie Joe recalled the time for David Fricke of *Rolling Stone*, saying: "Dropout kids, people that felt like outcasts—they were coming into this scene. Things like scarification, bad tattoos, drinking booze, snorting methamphetamine—nobody thought of it as addict behavior."

Tré admitted that his inability to stay sober in LA was the reason he and Donnas drummer Torry Castellano fell out. Mike Dirnt remembered, in a 1995 *Rolling Stone* article, writing the bassline to "Longview" while "frying so hard on acid" and saying, "'Billie, check this out. Isn't this the wackiest thing you've ever heard?'" When he tried to recall it later, however, it took him a bit of time to re-create.

They recall several acid trips of note. During one, Tré pulled Billie Joe into a bathroom with him. He handed a surprised Billie Joe an asthma inhaler, saying it was rad. Another time they were staying at a young woman's house during one of the early tours. Tré and Billie Joe were on acid, sitting with her in her kitchen, when she had to leave the room. She admonished them not to touch the other door in the room. Which, of course, they did. They released the hounds, literally, getting trampled by a pair of huge Afghans. Mike told *Q*'s Ben Mitchell, "It was like something out of *The Dark Crystal.*"

LSD seems to be part of their vocabulary. When *Rolling Stone*'s Andy Greene talked with Billie Joe about his feelings regarding the Rock and Roll Hall of Fame induction and if he was still "coming down off the high of that night," Billie replied: "Yeah. It's sort of like a natural LSD. The whole thing was just surreal, but instead of LSD it was reality. We had a great time. It was just a wild weekend. There was so much going on."

No DARE in His Family

Since Billie Joe was the youngest of six children, with his father passed on and his mother working as many hours as she could as a waitress, it is easy to imagine the chaos in the Armstrong house. With five older siblings, it was very likely that Billie Joe was exposed to most of the ways teens could behave badly long before he was a teen and without the filters of parents.

The band got their name from pot, and Billie Joe was known through his high school days as "two dollar Bill" for selling loose joints for a couple of bucks a piece. The band has also admitted to using speed in the early days, before parenthood. As the band continued to get more famous and more affluent, drinking became the vice of choice, at least for Billie Joe. "Play a gig. That's where you can really release all your energy and stuff. And then you get done, and you get drunk," he told Jaan Uhelszki of the *San Francisco Chronicle.* "I'm a pretty heavy drinker. That's what I do. That's my agenda for the day. Which is not really that exciting. It's pretty much the same as anybody else. A person drives to work, work wherever they work, drive home, and they loosen up and hang out until they fall asleep and do the whole thing all over again the next day."

Part of the problem was that he could not quiet his mind. Ideas just never stopped. It kept him from sleeping (which—along with having an infant in the house—inspired *Insomniac*). Being perpetually overstimulated also gave him mood swings and led to blackout drinking—anything to quiet the perpetual noise of his river of ideas.

He often got his drink on before going onstage. The band had a long-time ritual of downing a shot of vodka before hitting the spotlight. Before that, however, much beer and other shots were consumed. There were beers onstage, and then more booze on the bus to the next show. This got especially bad during the *Nimrod* tour. Billie Joe called it "liquid courage." It got him loose and not caring about going balls to the wall.

Making *Nimrod* was a demanding, frustrating experience for the whole band. They were in the studio from noon until two o'clock in the morning. This went on for four months. Billie Joe was not the only one drinking. One line from the song "Walking Alone" says that the song's character—which presumably represents the band and their circle—is "too drunk to figure out they're fading away," referring to his childhood friends. The first time he ever played "Good Riddance (Time of Your Life)" live was as the encore to a show in New Jersey. In *Spin* he told his hero, Paul Westerberg of the Replacements, that he "had to pound a beer backstage to get up the courage."

It was around this time he realized he had a problem. He started trying to dry up in 1997. However, he didn't like the idea of "programs," like the organization that dares not utter its own name. It is hard to be "anonymous" when you are one of the biggest rock stars in the world.

He started to lose track of events and was becoming a blackout drinker. From one night to another, he might wind up on a stranger's couch, on a park bench, or in worse circumstances.

The Wages of Intoxication

"I had a tendency in my past to get caught up in partying too much or making bad decisions," Billie Joe confessed to *Detail*'s Matt Hendrickson. "In 2003, I ended up in jail with a DUI, and I definitely regret that."

In that instance, according to the *Smoking Gun*, Billie Joe was driving his black BMW convertible. He was pulled over by the police for speeding. The police smelled alcohol and gave Billie Joe a Breathalyzer test. Billie Joe's blood alcohol level came up as .18, more than twice the California legal limit of .08.

Three years later, this incident came back to bite him on the ass. A series of advertisements featuring the DUI mug shots of Billie Joe, along with actor Kiefer Sutherland and former NFL quarterback Steve McNair, ran in the *New York Times.* The ad was paid for by an organization of booze manufacturers opposed to laws that would make breathalyzers attached to the ignition of cars mandatory. The ad campaign worked to bait and switch the idea, pointing to tougher laws for "hard-core drunk drivers" like Billie Joe and fewer restrictions for those partaking in "moderate and responsible drinking prior to driving." While Billie Joe only had that one infraction (as opposed to Sutherland's four), perhaps the fact that he, as a high-profile celebrity, was caught was enough of a reason to land him on the list. Either

One of the few *¡Uno!, ¡Dos!, ¡Tré!* shows before rehab.

way, it looked very bad for everyone involved. It also worked, as both the alcoholic beverage lobby and the automakers fought the laws.

As early as *Insomniac*, Billie Joe was feeling the effects of his habits. His efforts at self-recovery just were not working. Before going onstage he was apt to drink a bottle of wine and a pot of coffee, and it was starting to get old. As the band started working on *American Idiot*, Billie Joe fled to the coast (in his case, the East Coast) for inspiration, landing in New York City and hooking up with his New York drinking buddies. By several accounts, vast amounts of red wine and numerous vodka and tonics were consumed, but this was not the inspiration Billie Joe needed.

During the recording of *American Idiot*, he was scheduling sessions around his hangovers. He was asked about the song "Before the Lobotomy," which he said was based on something he had read about a hyperactive child whose father forces him to have a lobotomy, but he reckoned that it also was a good metaphor for the "stupidification" of society, and his own bouts with getting stupefied by drinking.

Nearly every description of both the creation of the album and shows by the Foxboro Hot Tubs album involved gallons of booze and clubs just littered with cans of Pabst Blue Ribbon. Yet, as Livermore observed, even when they were blitzed they were functional. This armor started to rust around the time that the band recorded a show for MTV. When the shoot was over, MTV decided that it could not show the program before 10 p.m. Billie Joe was so out of it that they were afraid he would scare younger kids.

The night after presenting Robert Plant and Alison Krauss with the Best Album Grammy, the band met with Jacqui Swift from the *Sun*. She noted that they were looking more than a little tired. "We got to bed at 5AM," Billie Joe told her. Then he cracked open what she aptly described as "a hair-of-the-dog bottle of beer." A couple of months later, to Neala Johnson of Australia's *Courier Mail*, he said, "I like to drink 'til I pass out and urinate all over the floor." Then he laughed and said, "I'm just kidding. I don't. I don't drink."

To which Mike replied, "I don't urinate."

But he did drink, and he continued to talk about it. "Most of the stuff we've come up with, like bringing people up to sing or running around in drag, that's all from being liquored up," he told *Q* magazine. "There was a time when I was up to a six pack of beer and maybe a couple of shots. That's when you're really cooking in the middle of a tour."

The band became somewhat infamous with their drinking. Cheech Marin claims to have hung with the band and introduced them to the joys of

T&Ts—tequila and tonics. However, Cheech claims they called the beverage "the Cheech." "And then it started to spread," Marin told the *Daily Beast.* "People on the road, other bands: 'We had a Cheech over in Minnesota.'" When Billie Joe appeared on *Real Time,* he told Bill Maher, "We were trying to be the Cheech and Chong of punk rock for a while."

During the courtship period about making the Broadway show of *American Idiot,* director and cowriter Mike Mayer recalled spending a night drinking, eating steak, and then spending time in the studio with the band. The next day he was massively hungover. One of the things that was unusual about the show when it opened was that the audience was allowed to bring drinks back to their seats.

Similarly, the day after *21st Century Breakdown* was mastered, *EQ*'s Ken Micallef recalled them starting to drink. They polished off sixteen bottles of wine and forty beers, and then they rolled into a studio in Chelsea and jammed on the same song from 2:00 a.m. to 6:30 a.m.

Before a show at New York City's Irving Plaza during the 2012 tour, Billie recalled having a case of the heebie-jeebies about playing a small club in the big city. Between what he consumed backstage and what he drank during the show, he had polished off the better part of a six-pack. He woke up the next day across town at one of the small parks that dot the waterfront beside the West Side Highway. He told Fricke: "There are a lot of gigs where I definitely walk the line between what is control and what isn't. I like the feeling, like you're walking on air. It's like flight—and danger."

This fine line between control and bedlam would sometimes land on the side of bedlam. At a show in Peru during the *21st Century Breakdown* Tour, he launched into an anti-technology tirade that culminated with his wish that Steve Jobs would die of cancer. Within a year, Jobs had.

Early in September of 2012, Billie Joe took ill in Bologna, Italy, and the band had to cancel their show there. "We sincerely apologize to our fans," the press release read, "but unfortunately due to illness Billie Joe has been hospitalized, and we regretfully must cancel our performance in Bologna, Italy this evening. We are beyond devastated and will make it up to you when we come back next summer." The reason for the illness, according to the band, was dehydration.

Shortly before the release of the trilogy, Billie Joe spoke with *Billboard*'s Phil Gallo. Gallo asked him about the song "Amy," a tribute to the late Amy Winehouse. "She never got the help she needed," Billie Joe told him. "I know what it's like to go down a really dark path and I have had good people around me to help me survive." In retrospect, the discussion seemed somewhat prophetic.

iHeartRadio

The climactic episode of Billy Joe's tribulations with intoxicants came a couple of weeks later. On Friday, September 21, 2012, at the iHeartRadio Music Festival in Las Vegas, Billie Joe came onstage well "hydrated." By this time, he had added pills to the mix. These prescription medicines were mostly to help with the anxiety and insomnia that has haunted him for most of his adult life. "[I] started combining them . . . My backpack sounded like a giant baby rattle," he told Fricke, referring to the bottles of pills he carried around.

As Billie Joe proceeded to pound some beers, Mike became very concerned, due to the usual anxiety he felt before every show and the fact that they had been sitting in their green room for hours. Recalling the moments just before the iHeartRadio concert, Mike told Fricke: "I took him aside and told him, 'Dude, you've got to fucking lay off the sauce.' And the minute I walked onstage, I thought, 'This is not gonna be good.' We're known as a pretty tight band. He couldn't play guitar."

"Mike was fucking pissed," Billie Joe concurred to Fricke. "'You're scaring me. You're fucking up your life. You're fucking up everybody else's life. You need to get your shit together.'"

Before the show, Tré told the television crew for the event: "We're gonna keep it weird. iHeartRadio is gonna be a festival like you've never seen before. All the biggest, craziest acts all put together. I don't know what to expect, and you shouldn't either."

Things got weird early backstage. The band spent the better part of six hours in their dressing rooms, as everyone else's entourages were hanging in the hallway. Entourages are just not Green Day's thing. So they stayed sequestered, waiting for their turn to play. Eventually Mike and Billie Joe started wrestling, trying to distract him from the bar for a few minutes. "I thought 'if I can just get some of this out of him.'" Mike told *Rolling Stone.* "But with the mood depressants and alcohol, it just doesn't end up in a jovial party."

When Green Day hit the stage, they blew through a tight "American Idiot," during which Billie Joe exhorted the crowd to "get up off your fucking asses, Las Vegas!" During "21 Guns," he was all over the stage, once again yelling, "Get your fucking hands in the air." During "Longview," he

Billie Joe in his first show after finishing rehab, bright-eyed and bushy-tailed.
Chuchitogd 13/Wikimedia Commons

went into the audience, handed the mic around, let people take selfies, and got a massive bearhug from a bearded fan before security and the road crew got him back onstage.

The first hint of trouble came during "Oh Love," the first single from *¡Uno!*, which was released that day. The promoters flashed the first of the "time remaining" cards, to which Billie Joe remarked, "Nine minutes? Do you want a fucking rock show?" At the end of "St. Jimmy" the time got flashed again, "We have four fucking minutes. What are we going to do in four fucking minutes?" Then they launched into "Basket Case." The audience was finally beginning to get into it, pogoing, singing along. Then Billie Joe stopped the song, and he melted down after seeing the "one minute" sign. "One minute? I'm not fucking Justin Bieber!" Then, he unleashed a tirade against the promoters and the people flashing the time cards, with every third word being some variation of "fuck." He yelled about how they had been playing for over twenty years. The rant culminated in the destruction of his Les Paul Junior guitar. "One minute? God fucking loves you all. We'll be back," he said, and the band left.

It should be noted that a similar thing happened a month earlier when the band played a surprise set at the Reading Festival in Reading, England. They had to cut short "Boulevard of Broken Dreams," with Billie Joe telling the crowd, "We're having a little fucking problem with time."

After Billie's iHeartRadio meltdown, Tré's ex-wife told *NME*: "The night of the show [Billy Joe] had been drinking. In Las Vegas there's a lot of temptation to drink and it's tough to be around when you're fighting against it." Billie Joe had been sober for a year before that. "He's my son's godfather so it's very hard for kids to see this happen," she added.

He woke up the next morning and asked his wife what kind of a disaster it had been. She told him that it was not good. He got on the phone with the band's manager, Pat Magnarella, who was beside himself. He ordered Billie Joe onto a plane home and into rehab right now.

He Went to Rehab, Yeah, Yeah, Yeah

So, the day after the iHeartRadio debacle, Billie Joe flew back to Oakland and went into rehab. The announcement was fairly vague, not saying what he was rehabbing from. The band did, however, tell the Associated Press that they apologized "to those they offended at the iHeartRadio Festival" and said their set was not cut short by Clear Channel, the host of the two-day event.

Billie Joe spent a bit of time at a clinic and then went home to finish detoxification and rehabilitation under supervision. During that time, he went through withdrawal, which happens with both alcohol and certain drugs with opiates in them, like morphine and OxyContin. Withdrawal is never pretty. While the mental anguish is bad enough, the physical toll that the substances have taken on the body are ugly: sweating, lacking control over many bodily functions, shaking, and constantly craving the poison—the body does not just want it, it *needs* it—are common. "The sick part is," Billie Joe told Fricke, "I wanted to get all of the narcotics out of my system so I could start drinking."

While it is never a good time to go through withdrawal, it could not have happened at a worse time for the band. They had decided to make a bold move: not just putting out one record for their next release but instead doing a staggered release of three albums over the course of six months. Those six months were supposed to be spent on the road promoting those records. When *¡Uno!* came out, all Billie Joe, Mike, and Tré could do was watch.

Aftermath

When Zac Carper, lead vocalist for the band FIDLAR, got out of rehab, after losing his girlfriend and nearly everything else in his life to heroin, Billie Joe called him. "He just told me, 'Dude, fucking don't worry about what people think of you.' That was a turning point. Billie Joe has been through everything," Carper told *Rolling Stone*'s Jon Dolan.

After his private and then very public airing of his demons, Billie Joe seemed resolute that this time he would remain sober. He never wanted to go through anything like that again, but also it was a side of himself that he did not want his fans to see.

As to what people think of *him*, Billie Joe is pretty certain his music will be his legacy, not his substance abuse. "I have so many important things to do," he told Fricke. "I have my family to take care of. I have my band. I'm a crazy-idea person. I always will be. And that will overshadow anything with my addiction problems."

Of course, sobriety has its own challenges. The root causes almost never go away entirely. The things that drive a person to drink are ever present. People with an addictive disease just learn to deal with it, to control it better. One of the reasons twelve-step programs are so effective is that the group of people participating are involved in the same battle, so it is a lot like the bond that soldiers develop. However, even with this support network, many of the neuroses and compulsions behind one's addiction—while getting some air and diminishing with recognition—do not go away quietly. They take new directions, and one of the twelve steps involves changing behaviors. One of the things that fueled Billie Joe's addictions was his long-standing social anxieties. One of the reasons Mike is, and likely has been, so simpatico for so long is that these are demons he knows as well. The difference is, he *hated* to medicate it. It took the onset of a massive attack to get him to take his medication.

One of the things Billie Joe had to deal with in the waning days of his rehab was how he was going to cope with those aspects of his life that he rarely dealt with sober. It had been so long since he had played sober that he wondered if he actually could.

Late in the winter of 2013, Billie Joe came out of isolation and the band got ready to get back on the road, to make up for the lost fall and winter. Armstrong told fans in a statement: "I just want to thank you all for the love and support you've shown for the past few months. Believe me, it hasn't gone unnoticed and I'm eternally grateful to have such an amazing set of friends and family. I'm getting better every day. So now, without further ado, the show must go on."

The band, as an entity, added in a statement to the Associated Press: "We want to thank everyone for hanging in with us for the last few months. We are very excited to hit the road and see all of you again."

Lawrence Livermore saw that sobriety agreed with Billie Joe. He was at the concert at Chicago's Hard Rock Café during the weekend of their induction into the Rock and Roll Hall of Fame, where first Green Day did a set, and then John "Al Sobrante" Kiffmeyer took over the drums and they did a set as Sweet Children. "Billie and Mike must have put in almost three and a half hours onstage," Livermore wrote on his blog. "The band was in top form, showing no signs of the world-weariness and disarray that seemed to be overtaking them on their last tour. Billie Joe especially was a revelation, looking younger, healthier, and more energetic than he had in years.

Part of this was Mike and Tré's doing. They did what was right, what was best for their friend and bandmate. The biggest change was backstage. "The backstage doesn't need to be a bar," Mike told *Rolling Stone*. "And that's okay with me. That's just killing time, coping mechanisms."

But playing live posed, and continues to pose, some quandaries for Billie Joe. The questions of whether he could still do what he did sober was answered as soon as he hit the stage. "If you look at what I do onstage every night," he told *Bang*, "it's like those songs are every form of depression and anxiety, and I'm putting it all into a crowded room. So for me it was always, 'drink a six-pack of beer before I go onstage.' But I can't do that anymore so it was definitely all about facing that in one good go . . . [But,] as soon as you get up there it's just intoxicating to feed off the energy and adrenaline that's going on in the crowd and to be able to remember it afterwards."

However, that energy and adrenaline has a flip side. Like so many post-rehab artists, his backstage habits have had to change. However, the audience at his shows remains pretty constant in their behavior. He realizes that he's "hosting a giant party for people" and told Fricke: "At least 70–75 percent of the people in the audience have been getting a drink on. I've got to watch my step."

13

Mother Adrienne

Portrait of the Punks as Family Men

All told, Green Day has had seven marriages (three for Mike, three for Tré, and one for Billie Joe and Adrienne, who have stuck it out for over twenty years) and seven children (three for Mike, two for Tré, and two for Billie Joe). They have all been family men since just slightly after *Dookie* hit, easily the biggest lifestyle change success wrought on the band.

Billie Joe ❤ Adrienne

"I love the way [Adrienne] still watches our shows," Billie Joe told Matt Hendrickson in *Rolling Stone*. "The thing that's great is that the music still gets under her skin in the same way that it affects me."

Billie Joe and Adrienne have been together pretty nearly since they were in swaddling clothes. They met in Adrienne's home town of Minneapolis, Minnesota, on Green Day's first US tour, on the fourth of July, 1990, and they would be married a couple of days shy of that date four years later. When they met, Billie Joe was eighteen years old. After their first kiss, he wrote the song "2,000 Light Years Away," and Adrienne Nesser got a shout-out in the notes to *Kerplunk*, the album that the song appears on. She has a degree in sociology from University of Minnesota, Mankato. "There are conversations she has—I don't have a fucking clue what they're talking about," Billie Joe told *Rolling Stone*'s David Fricke. "College—I could have learned a lot from that."

They got married on July 2, 1994, in a five-minute civil ceremony. Then, on the very next day, they discovered that they were going to become parents. Talk about Fourth of July fireworks. They honeymooned at the Claremont Hotel in Berkeley, not too far from where they lived.

Rock may not have a more devoted couple than Billie Joe and Adrienne Armstrong. Here Billie Joe sneaks in a smooch. *Michael Tran/FilmMagic/Getty Images*

The Armstrongs have two sons. Joseph Marciano Armstrong, better known as Joey, was born on February 28, 1995. Jakob Danger Armstrong was born September 12, 1998.

Billie Joe and Adrienne have had their down cycles. Part of the reason for the break between *Nimrod* and *Warning* was due to Billie Joe and Adrienne hitting a rough patch. But for the most part, Adrienne is supportive, and she also keeps him honest. "I happen to have a really patient wife," Billie Joe told Aaron Burgess of the *Alternative Press*, "and she's really cool, and she's really a politically conscious person, especially with environmental issues and I think she has this sort of fear of the end of the world. Hopefully between the two of us we can raise a family together and lean on each other."

The political awareness has rubbed off on Billie Joe and, to an extent, on their boys. Some of SWMRS songs have interesting political undertones. But entering the age of Trump, they, and their entire generation, were among Billie Joe's main concerns. "They're kids that were raised on Obama and Harry Potter, and now Voldemort's been elected and Harry Potter's been killed," he told Patrick Clarke of the *The Quietus* a few days after the election. "That's my kid's generation, and I do feel a lot of anxiety for them."

There is a fierceness to Adrienne that is an undercurrent of almost every time Billie Joe talks about her. However, the primary emotion that surfaces when he speaks of his wife is overwhelming affection.

"She's very territorial when it comes to me," he told the *San Francisco Chronicle*'s Jann Uhezski. "I'm the same way about her." He added for Fricke in *Rolling Stone*: "I remember walking out of a show in Chicago. There were these punks, real ones, sitting outside our tour bus. One girl had a forty-ouncer, and she goes 'Billie Joe, come have a drink with us.' I said, 'I can't, I've got my family on the bus.' She goes, 'Well, fuck you then.' I get on the bus and my wife says, 'Did that bitch just tell you to fuck off? I'm gonna kick her ass right now.' I'm holding her back, while my child is naked, jumping on the couch: 'Hi, daddy!'"

Hi, Daddy

One thing Billie Joe knew he did not want was for his sons to grow up like he did, in a frequently parentless household on the one hand, and with five wannabe parents (his siblings) on the other. After his father died, his mother worked as many hours as she could, waitressing at Rod's Hickory Pit. Two years after his father died, his mother remarried, and none of the Armstrong kids were overly fond of their stepfather. As the youngest, he experienced the chaos the most, as he had the least control over it. He wanted more equanimity in his household and preferred to give guidance rather than lay down the law. "My kids and I are able to talk about things without me putting the fear of God into them," he told *Details*' Matt Hendrickson.

As with Adrienne, when he talks about Joey and Jakob, it is with the same kind of fierce affection. He takes pride in the fact that when he was at home, the first thing he did every morning was see them off to school. *Rolling Stone*'s John Colapinto recalled meeting Billie Joe for the first time, saying, "We talked about our kids, and he was like any other dad, waxing proud about his son's performance in a soccer game." Billie Joe has also coached the boys' little league teams.

When Joey was an infant, he kept his parents awake. Never a great sleeper anyway, sometimes when he was awakened by Joey, Billie Joe could not get back to dreamland. It is a common complaint among young fathers. Rather than lying awake in bed or watching late-night TV, Billie Joe put this wakefulness to work, going to his songwriting studio in the basement and writing songs.

Billie Joe didn't merely come to grips with fatherhood; he was changed by it. It turned him from a pot-smoking punk kid living in a book mobile with his two buddies and never staying in one place too long into a relatively responsible adult with family and roots. He grew up largely without a father, and he did not want to screw things up in that regard with his kids. "Having my children, that was the first time I had to fight for and protect something," he told Paul Westerberg and Steve Kandell in *Spin*.

Rock and roll has taken its toll on many families. Somehow Billie Joe manages to keep it together. Green Day spend a lot of time on the road, so they all recognize the need to have quality family time when they are at home. Even when they work on recording now, it is not all-night binges of coffee, other substances, and music. Instead, they work the kind of hours that their neighbors might work, eight- to ten-hour shifts in the studio when they record, several hours of rehearsals, and writing on weekdays when they aren't recording.

Having children has affected the band's writing. It is one of the things that changed the trajectory of the band early in the new millennium, as a social conscience started to supersede snottiness. While the songs may not directly deal with the trials, tribulations, and triumphs of parenthood, many of them are informed by these parental realities. Billie Joe does directly deal with his relationship with his wife. She has been the subject of such ferocious love songs as "Last of the American Girls" and "She's a Rebel." He has said that writing about domestic bliss can be boring, however. He conceded that sometimes he contemplated shaking up his domestic bliss for the very purpose of adding some conflict to his songs.

One of the ironies of Green Day the band versus Tré, Mike, and Billie Joe the dads is having hundreds of thousands of teenaged fans while simultaneously having their own teenagers reject them out of hand, as is the well and proper thing for a teenager to do. Neala Johnson brought up this juxtaposition in an interview, and "Tré pull[ed] out an imaginary megaphone, [saying] 'Clean your room!'" Armstrong, whose sons were fourteen and ten at the time, could only smile in rueful agreement, saying, "My family's been not listening to me for years now.'"

Still, they recognize the behavior as something every teen must go through. "I was a tearaway but my sons are not like that," Billie Joe told England's *Sunday Mail*. "They are brighter and more hard-boiled than I was at their age . . . Their world is significantly larger than my world was back then."

Another reason that references to family in Green Day songs are fleeting and well masked is that the band members don't want the family blowback. It is hard enough having a rock star father and trying to not be known as "Billie Joe Armstrong's kid." It creates even more difficulty when the kids become the subject of dad's art. Raising independent children is hard enough without the spotlight and paparazzi that fame shines indirectly on a celebrity's family. "I don't want it to come back and haunt me," Billie Joe told the *Alternative Press*'s Burgess. "Like, 'Oh, your dad told some story in a magazine about you!' and you're like, 'Oh, fuck.'"

Part of the political consciousness that Adrienne brings to the relationship is a streak of liberalism that borders on radical. The reactionary conservatism of American politics ties the parental Armstrongs' guts in knots. Yet, despite some of the sexual innuendo that went on about the band and that surrounded Billie Joe in particular early on in their career, being a family man has brought out a streak of old school traditionalism in at least one respect.

"I consider myself a conservative parent, believe it or not, in a lot of ways," he told Tracy Smith on *CBS Sunday Morning*. "I think I worry like every other parent does. You worry about education; you worry about where they're getting their information from. You hear things you never thought you'd hear coming out of your baby's mouth."

After Hurricane Katrina, the entire Armstrong family went to New Orleans to build and rebuild homes for the survivors of that natural disaster. Billie Joe is into wholesome family stuff like surfing. When the band was inducted in the Rock and Roll Hall of Fame, he took the whole family, including his mom, out bowling. "It's hard," he told *Details'* Matt Hendrickson. "I've been playing rock and roll since I was 16, and now I have a 16-year-old. There's no better meter for knowing your age than seeing a real 16-year-old. People always think they're so young at heart. I see my son, and I'm like, 'Aw, fuck, I feel old.'"

There is a dichotomy between Green Day as family men who have regular lives in Oakland and Green Day as the band that comes around every few years and rocks the local arena. Mike sees it, especially in Billie Joe, and to *Rolling Stone*'s David Fricke he said: "Billie is music. If you took the music away from Billie, you would still have a good husband and father who takes care of business and is there for his kids. But the rest would be a shell."

Musical Kids

When Mike's daughter Stella was eighteen-months old, her father thought she might have a future as a musician. "She'll bang on my bass and hit two real cool chords," he told Portland, Maine's *Press Herald* reporter Ray Routhier. "I'll listen and I'll say, 'I'm gonna make something out of that.'"

Billie Joe dropped out of high school, and yet there he sits, a very successful man. Sometimes it is hard to explain to his children why he made certain choices, and why they don't have to make the same mistakes. "You know, my oldest son, I talked with him about it recently. I never brought it up before," he told Smith. And what I told him was I'm the luckiest bastard on the planet for doing what I've been able to do . . . it's something I never take for granted, and it doesn't happen to everybody and, you know, my kids like music too."

Indeed, both of Billie Joe's sons are fledgling professional musicians following in their father's footsteps but not that closely. Both Joey and Jakob Armstrong are recording artists in their own right. Joey plays the drums in a band called SWMRS (formerly known as Emily's Army). Billie Joe produced the two Emily's Army albums, but he insisted on working as a producer, not the "rock star dad in the studio." "He wants us to do our own thing," Joey told the *Baltimore Sun*'s Wesley Case. "He doesn't want to change our sound."

Jakob, working under his first and middle name as Jakob Danger, records for Burger Records. The deal came after he played a couple of songs

Proud dad Mike Dirnt. The sticker saying Stella is not a tribute to "Street Car Named Desire." It honors his daughter. *Frank White Photography*

he wrote for his parents. "My dad told me to try and record them," he told *Rolling Stone*'s Brittany Spanos, "so I tried it out, and it sounded really great . . . I'd play instruments on some of the tracks, and I asked my brother if he wanted to play as well. That's how this got going."

He put the music up on SoundCloud, where the folks at Burger Records heard it, and suddenly there were three recording artists in the house (four if you include the EP the entire family recorded together as the Boo). Jakob's live band features Chris Malaspina, a schoolmate he has known "forever." Shades of his father and Mike?

The two brothers collaborate often in the creative process. Joey has given his brother more advice about the process and the business than his dad has. When it comes to music, his parents take a position of benign laissez faire.

However, falling into the family business gets even more difficult when a member of that family is famous. Both Joey and Jakob would rather fly under the radar. Joey played his first gig when he was twelve. He walked off the stage without anyone mentioning his heritage. He though his "secret" was safe, and it wasn't until the next band came onstage and the singer picked up a microphone that Joey's anonymity was blown. "He said, 'Give a round of applause for Li'l Green Day,'" Joey recalled to Case. "I was really bummed out."

But after they recorded their first album, *Don't Be a Dick*, Emily's Army started to get their own accolades, including one that even Joey's father had never earned. The band was named one of MTVU's Fall Freshmen 5, an honor that had helped propel the careers of Bruno Mars, Amy Winehouse, Silversun Pickups, Passion Pit, and Best Coast.

The band changed their name to SWMRS when they added bass player Seb Mueller to the existing lineup of Armstrong and brothers Cole and Max Becker (lead vocals and guitar, respectively). They had something of an underground hit with the song "Miley," a tribute to former Disney star Miley Cyrus. She impressed Cole with her attitude, her work with homeless LGBT youth, and her duet with Against Me's Laura Jane Grace.

As SWMRS, the band has a bit more of its own cachet. "We definitely get taken more seriously," Max Becker told *DIY*'s Ewan Atkinson. "We don't get compared to Green Day nearly as much . . . It will probably never go away as it's Joey's dad, but we are a more distinct band now—we don't play pop punk anymore. We very much have our own unique sound."

That sound takes punk and fuses it with an old-school hip hop bottom. However, even as a SWMR, Cole Becker echoed the drummer's dad, Billie Joe. "This is what we love to do. We want to be able to do this until we die."

Still, to Cole and Max, Billie Joe is "basically just another dad."

Dealing with Parents

When Billie Joe's father died, his mother was in her late fifties. She had six children, and she suddenly had to support them as a single mother. This left her little time to be a hands-on parent, which made being the youngest child that much more difficult. For one thing, it left Billie Joe with a lifelong disaffection for authority. Before his father's death, things were different. "I was just a typical kid, just a little bit shorter than everybody else," he told the *San Francisco Chronicle*'s Jaan Uhelszki. "I had friends, and got dirty all the time."

One of the ways Billie Joe got through school with a minimum amount of trouble was by keeping a low profile for most of it. He tried very hard to be invisible. Mike, on the other hand, was a social animal—yin to Billie Joe's yang. He told *Rolling Stone*'s Alec Foege: "I was one of those kids who'd walk around the neighborhood and talk to the adults and learn a lot. I'm good with people."

Tré's childhood was strange also. (Wait, whose isn't?) He grew up in a remote shack with his father, mother, and sister. His father's military experience in the Vietnam War could sometimes make him a bit intimidating. On the other hand, Frank II would also party with his family. He avoided using his stature to scare his kids into cooperation as best as he could. "Me and my dad got a lot closer when I moved out at 17," Tré told *NME*.

When children get wealthy, one of the first things they are apt to do is offer to do something for their parents. Which is what the members of Green Day did. Ollie Armstrong told her son that she was perfectly happy, but as a gift he still sent her and her boyfriend to Hawaii.

However, as he progressed in his career, his mom never stopped worrying about him. (She's a mom, after all.) The personal nature of being a songwriter frightened her, as did the amount of effort he put into performing and his whole onstage demeanor.

Mike told *USA Today*'s Elysa Gardner that his parents are "very supportive of what we do—but they have their own lives, too. I'll ask them to come out and see something, and it'll be, 'I'm not getting on a plane.'"

Fame, Fortune, Family

Because of their roots, Green Day had modest ambitions and goals. They just wanted to play music for the rest of their lives and manage to support their families. It had also been the ambition of Billie Joe's father, though he fell a bit short of it, having to work a day job to support his music habit and his family. These aims were a guiding principle when Billie Joe was growing up in the Rodeo area. Green Day's fame made the Bay Area punk zine *Maximumrocknroll* (whose writers were never big fans in the first place) burst a blood vessel in their brains out of pure rage. The whole millions of albums, fame, and fortune thing just confused Green Day, as they never really even saw it as a possibility until it happened. "Someone said to me before a show," Mike recalled to Ian Fortnam, "'Fifteen thousand people at this arena—this is everything you ever dreamed of.' I turned to him and said, 'Correction. It's everything I never dreamed of.'"

They never visualized arenas. They were happy playing clubs, selling 20,000 copies of their records, and getting by a little better each year. "I just set up my life so I could be happy regardless of what my income was," Mike told *Rolling Stone*'s Alec Foege. "If you can set up a lifestyle where you're always going to be happy—mine was around musicians and friends—and have no other expectations, then anything else that happens is icing on the cake."

"I always hear people who are rock stars say things like, 'My kids keep me grounded,' or 'My family keeps me grounded,'" Billie Joe said to Aaron

Burgess of *Alternative Press.* "And it's like, well, isn't it supposed to be the other way around? Aren't you supposed to be grounded for your family?"

One of the ways Green Day's members stay grounded is by sticking close to their roots. While they couldn't wait to get out of their hick hometowns, they didn't wander too far afield. All three of them live about twenty miles away from Rodeo, where Billie Joe and Mike grew up. For Tré, the distance to the old homestead in Willets is closer to 140 miles.

Domesticity is another one of the many things that keep the group grounded. When Billie Joe went into rehab, no one knew what to say to Mike and Tré (or Adrienne, for that matter), so no one said anything about anything. When *¡Uno!* came out, no one called to congratulate the band. The tenuous status of the band at that point scared people. Mike found the circumstances depressing. "Thank God, my wife was there for me and able to help me process my emotions," he told *Rolling Stone*'s David Fricke.

The members of Green Day generally follow the rule of KISS—Keep It Simple, Stupid. They have enough money that they can have everything they want, but that doesn't mean that they need to get things that they don't want. When Jonathan Gold interviewed Billie Joe shortly after the release of *Insomniac,* he was genuinely surprised to find little of the effects of their recently acquired wealth. "If the proceeds from 14 million Green Day albums have manifested themselves in a Bono-sized closet full of Tag Heuers . . . you will find no sign of it here."

14

Standing on My Beat-Up Car

Ridin' Around in My Automobile

Being in a band is like having a classic car," Mike told *Rock Sound*'s Ryan Bird. "You have to constantly tune it up and care for it, because if you don't it's going to rust and fall apart."

This is an apt metaphor coming from a member of Green Day. For a considerable amount of time in the post-*Dookie* era, accumulating an extensive collection of classic cars and motorcycles was a serious avocation. Much of the parking lot at their Jingletown Studios was taken up with the collection. However, even before they achieved fame and prosperity, Billie Joe's main ride was a 1967 Ford Fairlane, a car older than he was.

Late in 1995, *Rolling Stone*'s Alec Foege took a ride with Billie Joe around the East Bay in Billie Joe's Fairlane. The car was black with leopard print upholstery. Foege noted that it was a '62, but it was likely Billie Joe's beloved '67. When Billie Joe spoke with the *San Francisco Chronicle*'s Jaan Uhelszki shortly after the meteoric rise of *Dookie* and the band, she wondered about how the sudden windfall had affected the group. Billie Joe's response was: "I got my car primered. I have the same car. I drive a Ford Fairlane and I got it primered. That was about it."

Mike drives a BMW, and Billie owned at least a couple of the Bavarian vehicles, as that is the car he was in when he got busted for a DUI. Tré favors SUVs, possibly a throwback to his growing up in Willets.

In 2011, *Street Muscle* magazine did a feature on Billie Joe's beat up 1968 Mercury Monterey convertible, renowned as the car that breaks down in the beginning of the "Boulevard of Broken Dreams" video. Truly a collectable car, despite its somewhat disreputable condition, it is one of only 1,000 of the model that Mercury made. Billie Joe replaced the logo on the hood with "Green Day" in a similar typeface, and he added a small heart-like-a-hand-grenade sculpture as a hood ornament. He traded out the original steering

The band loves Billie Joe's old Fairlane, which forced them to "walk alone" in the "Boulevard of Broken Dreams" video. *Kevin Winter/Getty Images*

wheel for one decorated with chain links. The upholstery is leopard skin and the knob on the gearshift is a skull with glowing red eyes.

By the summer of 2014, Green Day started to liquidate some of their collectables. Billie Joe's 1972 BMW 2002tii was featured on eBay. This might have had to do with Jingletown being up for sale and the band wanting to clear out their collection from the parking lot. The car showed up in David Fricke's post-rehab interview with Billie Joe. It is a much earlier model than the black convertible he got arrested in for his 2003 DUI. Special in the world of BMWs, this is the car that helped the company keep solvent in the inflationary 1970s. As a collectable, it has a reputation for being a lot of fun to drive and reasonably priced.

A year later, one of Mike's vehicles, a 1963 VW Microbus pickup truck with a double crew cab, went up for auction. It was accompanied by a tiny camper trailer that had been fully refurbished with cabinets and a kitchen. In 2016, a 1965 Karmann Ghia—Volkswagen's answer to a roadster that

Mike had owned—went under the cyber-gavel. It was in mint condition. One of Billie Joe's vehicles, a red 1974 Honda CB400 Super Sport Motorcycle with a 408 cc engine and less than 33,000 miles on it, was available by auction, as was one of Mike's bikes, a black 1976 Honda CB750 Café Racer customized by motorcycle legend Steve Carpenter.

Each of the cars up for auction came with a letter of authenticity and an instrument (musical) signed by the vehicle's former owner. Later in the summer, one of Billie Joe's older Fords, a 1949 "Shoebox" with less than 80,000 miles on it, appeared on eBay. It had also previously appeared in one of the band's videos.

15

When I Come Around

The Band of Buddies

"This is my high school band," Billie Joe shouted from the stage of KROQ's Almost Acoustic Christmas in 2016.

Billie Joe met Mike when they were ten years old. They have been virtually joined at the hip ever since. They both met Tré when all of them were seventeen. They have been playing together for over twenty-five years, and they still hang out together. "We've grown up together," Billie Joe told *Guitar World*. "Literally."

"We were passionate about our songs and band," Tré told *Rolling Stone*'s David Fricke. "Since then, we've put the same love and energy into it. We do it compassionately. We do it together."

Vexing Years

There are times that try even the best of friendships. Between *Warning* and *American Idiot*, there was a time that the band nearly called it a day. It used to be fun; it used to be the three of them getting high, playing gigs, and having a good time. Then, slowly, it became a business, and the worst part was that their creativity was the product the business sold. And to make matters even more unpleasant, business was bad; after blowing the doors off the business with *Dookie*, the next couple of albums didn't— couldn't—sell as well. The band members were not communicating with each other. No one wanted to destroy the equilibrium, but no one was very happy with it either. Mike and Tré were beginning to see Billie Joe as a tyrant. Billie Joe was afraid to show them new songs because they would vent their anger on the music. It was one of the few times Billie Joe gave any thought to quitting.

"It was a time where we had to evaluate our situation and our relationship as a band, and truly get into making the records of our dreams," Billie Joe told *Billboard*'s Mitchell Peters. "But quitting? Nah. Nobody leaves this band unless it's in a coffin."

Do the math. They started playing together when they were seventeen years old. To get into the Rock and Roll Hall of Fame, you have to have released your first record twenty-five years earlier. So, at some point during the *American Idiot* Tour or the making of *21st Century Breakdown*, they had been together for half of their lives.

"I've been in this band longer than I haven't been in this band," Mike added to Peters. "I tend to refer to periods of time as the record we were doing. I'll look through old pictures and say, 'Oh, that was *Nimrod*,' like someone in college would say, 'Oh, that was my freshman year.' The album cycles become that chapter of your life."

What they finally decided was that they had to sweat the small stuff. Despite how Dr. Phil-like it sounded, they had to work on their relationship to keep it functioning. The first step was having once-a-week band meetings where they would just talk. "We bared our souls to one another," Mike told *Rolling Stone*'s Matt Hendrickson.

"Admitting that we cared for each other was a big thing," Tré added. "We didn't hold anything back."

Reopening the lines of communication allowed them to accomplish several things: they could work out the problems that they were bottling up; they could rebuild the bonds and revisit what their long-time friendship had been built on; and they could go on to make some of the best recordings of their career. Think about this: How many bands in the Rock and Roll Hall of Fame are still making records that matter? Not a whole lot of them.

Building Bonds

An earmark of the indie-band-on-a-club-tour situation is that the musicians either like each other or go home. Back in the Ford Econoline and bookmobile days, Billie Joe, Mike, and Tré lived in each other's pockets, a situation best illustrated by Jane's Addiction leader Perry Farrell, who once described the close quarters of the tour van, saying, "We got to the point where we knew the smell of each other's farts."

As anyone gets older, situations change. There are families and individual interests. People abrade each other when they are too close for too long. While the touring situation has become more comfortable, with many luxury tour buses and truckloads of equipment versus everyone and everything in the van, being on the road still means sharing dressing rooms and spending lots of time together. Any relationship needs room to breathe. "We do give each other space," Billie Joe told the *Alternative Press*'s

Rob Ortenzi. "We give ourselves time to go hang out outside of the studio, too, ride motorcycles together or something like that . . . I've always had an image of bands where I thought there should be a gang mentality or a family mentality, and I want to keep our band together the same way."

One thing they had to work out was the creative process. One of the things that caused the problems that got resolved in order to make *American Idiot* was Mike and Tré started to feel like Billie Joe's backing band as opposed to an integral part of the creative process. Certainly Billie Joe was the band's primary songwriter, but they had to define their roles. "They stay out of my way until I complete my idea," Billie Joe told *Guitar World*. "Then they come in with their opinion after that. And they're always there for me, all the time. That's what's great about them. Mike, Tré and I were hanging out with Lars from Metallica last night, and he was like, 'I can't believe you guys are such good friends!' And I was like, 'Well, that goes without saying. Isn't it supposed to be like that?'"

Band members support each other—Green Day circa *Warning*.

Green Day is a rarity, a rock band with staying power. One of the ways to maintain that creative tenacity is knowing that during every minute of every day your partners are also your best friends, people you can trust absolutely. Some bands last but wear out, wear on each other (think the Who, the Kinks, Pink Floyd, or the Rolling Stones), and have their best creative days as a band behind them. Other bands—like the Beatles or Creedence Clearwater Revival—burn hot and fast and leave their legacy to reverberate forever on. And with some bands, you never hear about rows or fistfights, never see them do anything but laugh together in public (think Rush . . . and Green Day).

"I always wanted to be in a band that lasts," Billie Joe told Ryan Bird of *Rock Sound*. "I've always wanted to go the distance and evolve, and I think in the back of our minds we've all felt that way since day one. We still dream about music the way we did when we were 16 years old, and that's something that I personally think we'll never lose."

Sam Bayer, who directed all of the videos for *American Idiot*, noted to Marc Spitz: "They were famous. They had done big stuff, but it's transcended that. But . . . they haven't changed. They're three friends who love one another."

"I can't imagine not being in Green Day," Mike told *NME*. "Everything in my life is based around this music and this band."

Work Ethic

Billie Joe is the closest thing to a perpetual motion machine that there is. He is Rock and Roll's Energizer Bunny—he keeps going and going. That was one of the things that led him to rehab; he just could not shut down the music in his head that needed to get out. "Billie has a work ethic that I've never seen in any field of work," Tré told *NME*. "There's no construction worker or veterinarian you could show me who works as hard as he does. He'll have four things going at once but then a song will hit him, and he'll go straight to that and try to squeeze everything out of his brain that he can at that moment."

Sometimes that drive can get daunting, even for Mike and Tré. They recognize how fortunate they are to play with a best friend who is also a creative dynamo, and they do their best to help shape and realize the vision of what Green Day is at any given moment. However, as Mike told David Fricke, sometimes he has wondered, "Do we really need to climb another mountain, right in the middle of climbing this mountain?"

Green Day is one of the tightest bands on the planet. Billie Joe, Mike, and Tré might seem to be all over the place, but they hardly ever miss a note. One reason is because they rehearse constantly. It is like going to a job every weekday, albeit a job they love. As noted in the chapter on their family, they get off the road and still have band practices and meetings on a regular, almost daily, basis. In the early days, before they actually saw the money from *Dookie* (although everyone assumed they already had), they used the garage of one of their old high school teachers as an anchor. Now they all have their own garages. "We still get into the garage and blast out catchy songs," Billie Joe told *Time* magazine's Ericka Souter. "We just flip a coin to see which one we'll be in for the month."

In Sickness and in Health

After Billie Joe got done with rehab in 2013, he ran into Mike in Oakland. "Billie apologized to me from the bottom of his heart," Mike told Fricke. "It was just two old friends on a park bench. I hope to be on that park bench with him when I'm old, feeding fucking birds and having conversations."

The years after the trilogy were harrowing at best. First there was Billie Joe's detox and rehab. Then Mike's wife Brittany discovered a lump in her breast, and she and Mike had to deal with that. Jason White was then diagnosed with tonsil cancer. It is events like that, matters of life and death, that allow people to find out who their real friends are.

"We had to take a collective deep breath and look out for each other," Billie Joe told *USA Today*'s Patrick Ryan. "It got pretty scary for a while, but we just had to be there for each other as friends. We're in a really good place now because of all the stuff that everyone's had to overcome."

Sometimes at parties or events or even when they were out shopping for groceries, someone would recognize them and seek advice, asking, "My son wants to play in a band. What should he do?" And to that, Mike would answer, "Play with your friends."

16

The Saints Are Coming

Green Day's Humanitarian Work

After performing live at the post-Katrina reopening of New Orleans' Superdome, U2 and Green Day got together at Abbey Road Studio with producers Rick Rubin and Jacknife Lee to mix the live recording and record a studio version. The proceeds from the single went to raise money for Music Rising, the fund that U2 guitarist The Edge started to buy instruments and support music programs in the devastated city. The single was nominated for a Grammy Award in the category of Best Rock Performance by a Duo or Group with Vocal. They also recorded a performance for ReAct Now, a telethon for Katrina relief.

Green Day and the members thereof do lots of good works and things for charity, and they do it like it's no big deal. More often than not, they don't make a lot of noise about it; they just do it.

Charity Gigs

The Bridge School in Hillsborough, California, works with people with severe speech or physical impediments (or both), helping them with assistive technology and lifelong education. Neil Young has been a proponent of the school since it was in the planning stages and has run an annual, mostly acoustic all-star concert to raise funds for the school since 1988. Green Day did a couple of sets at the 1999 shows.

Billie Joe joined Bono, Stevie Wonder, Norah Jones, Alicia Keys, Velvet Revolver, Tim McGraw, and Brian Wilson in a performance of the Beatles' "Across the Universe" at the 2005 Grammy Awards. The song was made available on iTunes, and all the proceeds went to help Japan recover from the tsunami that demolished parts of the country. In addition to this, Green

Day pledged all download profits from "Boulevard of Broken Dreams" to the relief effort.

They also played at Acoustic-4-A-Cure, James Hetfield, and Sammy Hagar's annual event to support the Pediatric Cancer Program at University of California, San Francisco. In addition to the charitable aspect of the shows, the music can often be fascinating. Where else would you get to see Joe Satriani, James Hetfield, and Billie Joe playing "Turn the Page" together on acoustic guitars?

Even before Green Day became stars, when they were on the cusp of "making it," they would do things like play a couple of shows at the Oakland Convention Center and donate all the proceeds, including merchandise profits, to Food Not Bombs, an organization that feeds homeless people; the Berkeley Free Clinic; the Haight-Ashbury Free Clinic; and the San Francisco Coalition on Homelessness. Charity begins at home, and Green Day support a lot of local Bay Area causes and even help out their peers. They were allowed to play Gilman Street for the first time in over a decade when they did a benefit for DIY publishing house AK Press, which had lost its warehouse and inventory in a fire.

To raise awareness and money for the tragedy of the war in Darfur, the group recorded a version of John Lennon's "Working Class Hero" for the album *Instant Karma: The Amnesty International Campaign to Save Darfur.* Billie Joe played "Wake Me Up When September Ends" on the 2010 Stand Up to Cancer telethon. It was a fitting tribute to his father, who died of esophageal cancer. He also helped honor Joan Jett and raise money for Little Kids Rock, an organization that offers free music education and instruments to over 100,000 low-income school children. He played "Don't Abuse Me" with Jett, sharing a mic with "Little" Steven Van Zandt, one of the charity's main supporters. The show raised $1.5 million.

Live 8

In advance of the July 2005 meeting of the Group of Eight (G8), eight of the wealthiest, most highly industrialized nations—Canada, France, Germany, Italy, Japan, Russia, the United Kingdom, and the United States—Bob Geldof organized a major event in support of Make Poverty History and the Global Call for Action Against Poverty. The events also coincided with and celebrated the tenth anniversary of the Live Aid concerts. Far more ambitious than the previous event, the 2005 concerts were called Live 8. On July 2, there were concerts in all eight of the participating countries (including two in the United Kingdom), along with shows in South Africa. They ran, for the most part, simultaneously, with all ten streams webcast on AOL and sections of each show broadcast on nearly 200 television networks and ten times that many radio networks worldwide. Over 1,000 musicians participated, including Green Day.

Green Day played the Berlin show, which attracted close to half a million people. (Over a million crowded the area in front of Philadelphia's Museum of Art.) "Playing in front of half a million people in Berlin and millions more on TV around the world was an amazing experience," Billie Joe recalled for Gibson.com's Courtney Grimes. "It was great to be part of the effort. Hopefully people around the world understood the point was to convince the world's leaders to end third-world debt and help end poverty in the poorest nations." For Neala Johnson of the Melbourne *Herald Sun*, he added: "It's always neat when you can get together with a ton of other bands and show solidarity, where it's not just this gig or festival. Everybody leaves their ego at the door . . . You're there to kick ass for a cause, and it's always better to have a good reason to get out there and kill it."

To that, the effort was successful. While it did not end debt and poverty in developing nations, it did get the G8 to double the amount of money they had dedicated to working on the problem. Half of that money would go to the effort to alleviate poverty in Africa.

Other Causes

Mike has collaborated with Macbeth—a shoe, clothing, and accessory company—to create lines of vegan footwear. He commits all his royalties to charities like the National Military Family Association's Operation Purple, an organization that helps military families stay connected with their deployed family members. It also provides camps for the children of deployed military parents, offering an outlet for the youngsters and a respite for the parent at home.

Tré is also a fan of sartorial eloquence, and one of the charities he supports is Out of the Closet, a chain of thrift stores that supports people struggling with HIV and AIDS, even offering free HIV testing services at several locations. The *Bay Area Reporter*'s Cornelius Washington caught Tré donating dozens of luxury brand prêt-à-porter clothing items to a branch of the stores. "I love what they do," he told Washington. "The help is direct; it goes right to the people who need it."

Gay rights, gay pride, and gay charities are also near and dear to Green Day's collective heart. (See the chapter on sexuality.) They call their shows safe zones for the disenfranchised. In a *Guardian* webchat, Billie Joe said: "We accept anyone who feels marginalized at any Green Day event. Period. Especially if you're gay or trans, black, white, brown, or any nationality. Period. Green Day is a safe place for you to be." Not too far from the creed at Gilman Street.

They heard about a lesbian couple who went to their high school prom in Tupelo, Mississippi, only to find themselves among only eight other people. They hadn't been invited to the private prom that had been planned after a judge ruled that the couple could attend the public event. This incensed Green Day, as well as singer Lance Bass, celebrity chef Cat Cora, and the American Humanist Association. Together, they sponsored an all-inclusive statewide prom. The prom was organized by the Mississippi Safe Schools Coalition and anyone was invited to attend. Lance Bass appeared at the event.

Mike helped raise over fourteen million dollars to support community health and children's education needs at the Napa Valley Vintners annual event, a gala auction. Tré hosts an annual golf tournament to support Music in Schools Today (MuST). The event raises funds for the music programs at schools in the Bay Area. Mike usually competes.

Avid environmentalists, Mike, Tré, and Billie Joe teamed up with the Natural Resource Defense Council to spread the word about replacing oil with alternative energy sources. Billie Joe and Mike's Oakland Coffee Company goes out of their way to make sure that their product is as environmentally friendly as possible. They even searched out revolutionary biodegradable packaging, including biodegradable K-cups, that keeps the coffee fresh. Oakland Coffee also supports the people who grow the coffee beans, both in sustainability for their crops and in the health and welfare of the people themselves.

Green Day joined Queen's Brian May, Radiohead's Ed O'Brien, and dozens of others in support of the Standing Rock Sioux tribe's efforts to prevent the Dakota Access Pipeline from going through their land. They also joined such artists as Shakira, Justin Bieber, Eminem, Kiss, and Lady Gaga in raising funds for City of Hope by selling limited edition T-shirts on the artists' websites and the charity's. City of Hope researches and treats cancer, diabetes, HIV, and AIDS, and provides education about these conditions as well.

Even Billie Joe's kids get into the act. The Cystic Fibrosis Foundation honored Emily's Army, the band in which Joey Armstrong plays alongside Cole and Max Becker. The band was named in honor of the Becker brother's close family friend, who suffers from the disease. The Becker boys and their parents have been working toward a cure for the disease for over a decade. The band and Mr. and Mrs. Becker all were honored for "the positive impact they have on CF families."

But charity goes beyond giving money or raising funds. After Katrina, Billie Joe and his family did more than join U2 to raise funds for musicians who lost their instruments. They volunteered with Habitat for Humanity to help build and rebuild homes for those left homeless by the flood. Billie Joe also signed a hard hat for an online fundraising auction benefitting the organization.

Billie Joe told *Out* magazine: "It seems to be one thing after the next. I don't want to be a burden on this country. I want to figure out how to be helpful."

17

American Idiots

Politics

A fellow Bay Area musician, John Fogerty (who grew up in El Cerrito just down the road from where Green Day grew up in Rodeo), explained on his website how he came to write "Fortunate Son," the Creedence Clearwater Revival hit: "It's a confrontation between me and Richard Nixon. The haves, the people who have it all . . . People I don't respect." "Fortunate Son" is a song any punk could learn from. It gave CCR's musical passion a purpose.

Billie Joe and Mike came from that East Bay area over a generation after Fogerty, and they seem to have a similar sentiment toward the Republican administrations they have lived through, only it didn't show up in their music right away. They learned about political rhetoric (and political theater) at Gilman Street. Perhaps it was the politically conscious Adrienne who helped this develop, or perhaps it was just mounting outrage at the kind of country their children were growing up in.

So, a decade out from singing about marijuana and masturbation, Green Day started exhibiting a political consciousness. Billie Joe noted the change to Neala Johnson of Australia's *Courier Mail*, admitting that ten years earlier "those kids may have been in a bit of denial."

Early on, Green Day's songs were about ennui and apathy. "Longview" became sort of a slacker national anthem. Despite the lessons they had learned at 924 Gilman in the early days, politics was something they studiously avoided, at least in their music. Then came a confluence of events that changed Billie Joe's mind and the group's orientation. In a hotly contested presidential election in 2000, George W. Bush took the electoral vote while his opponent, Al Gore, took the popular vote. Then, on September 11, 2001, al-Qaeda terrorists hijacked four passenger jets, flying two into the twin towers of New York's World Trade Center and one into the Pentagon. The plane headed for the White House was brought down by its passengers and crashed in a field in Pennsylvania. It was a major act of foreign terrorism that took place on American soil, and it shut the country down for a week. Taking advice from his cabinet, Bush declared war on the Taliban government of Afghanistan, launching America into the longest foreign conflict in the country's history.

Then, in 2003, the Bush administration became convinced that Iraq had weapons of mass destruction and, with a coalition of allied forces, declared war on Iraq. When his father, George H. W. Bush, was POTUS, he had invaded Iraq with a coalition of United Nations forces and drove the Iraqi invaders out of Kuwait, but the armed forces had to leave before they could topple Iraqi despot Saddam Hussein. Citing the weapons of mass destruction (which turned out to not exist), Bush Jr. put the US military at war on two separate fronts, probably with hopes of finishing his father's efforts.

As Vietnam was the first "TV War," the invasions of Afghanistan and Iraq ran on TV like reality programs, fueled by and fueling the 24/7 news cycle that was already a mainstay of cable TV. "Embedded" journalists rode in tanks and went on sorties with the troops in between commercials for erectile dysfunction cures and financial products. Like so many people during that period, Billie Joe was overwhelmed with input. He told NPR's Terry Gross: "I felt this moment of rage and patriotism, I guess. If you'd want to call it that." That moment expressed itself in the song "American Idiot," which just poured out of him one day.

And George W. Bush became to Billie Joe in 2003 what Richard Nixon was to John Fogerty thirty-five years earlier.

Politics and Music

People have been singing political songs for centuries. Music has been a major element of political debate and propaganda in songs like "The Rising of the Moon," a song of Irish rebellion; Woodie Guthrie's songs of unionizing; songs of the Vietnam War era, like Country Joe and the Fish's "I Feel Like I'm Fixin' to Die Rag" and Crosby, Stills, Nash, and Young's "Ohio;" and songs on the Clash's *Sandinista*. At Gilman Street, Green Day saw latter-day political firebrands like the Dead Kennedys.

Billie Joe had several reasons for avoiding politics in his music. At Gilman, many of the bands he learned politics from did it in a polemic way that he did not care to emulate. Billie Joe's songs have always been extremely personal in the sense that they were about where he fits in the scheme of things, as he saw it. "You start trying to make bolder statements, as long as it comes across as natural or not preachy," he told Paul Westerberg and Steve Kandell in *Spin*. "Dead Kennedys were always good at it—Jello [Biafra—the Dead Kennedys' lead singer] could always recite things about [former California Governor] Jerry Brown or whatever. It was like getting a political lesson. I can't do that. I would rather sing about what my place in the world is. It's more about singing about what you don't want to become."

Billie Joe knew what he didn't want to become. He didn't want to become like Bush. He didn't want to become like the people who advised Bush. He didn't want to become like the people who blindly, without comment, followed Bush. He thought they were stupid and possibly evil.

But he also didn't want to deal with it as a songwriter initially. Green Day were already working on an album that was not too different from *Warning*. After several trial runs, running away and running back home (see the chapter on *American Idiot* songs), anger, nationalism, rage, and love just started happening because he realized what he didn't want to become the most. "American Idiot" and "Holiday" poured out of him as naturally as any song he had ever written before he realized that he had written something political. For Billie Joe, it has always been about the song. He has frequently said that any good political song has to come from the same place you'd write a love song. These did.

What surprised him the most was that *no one else that he heard was doing it*! The punk community was doing what it accused him of doing back in his teens: writing music about girls and sex and drugs, and being a punk. In the face of all the danger, in the face of terrorist attacks and then the government's domestic attacks on people's civil liberties, no one else was trying to bite back. "Every single era has had escapist music: In the 1950s, there was the pop music that came after Little Richard," Billie Joe told the *Los Angeles Times*' Lorraine Ali. "After the turbulent '60s, you got '70s schlock—quiet and boring, lots of earth tones—then punk came around. Music goes through these cycles, but this happens to be the longest cycle I remember without someone breaking through on a meaningful level; someone who really has something to say."

He decided that he needed to say it. Certainly the people this affected the most, those in their late teens and early twenties, had no idea what to do about the situation, had trouble processing it, and felt disaffected by it. Their reaction was to ignore it as a way of expressing their rage and confusion. "That's their anger," he added for Ali. "'You're making me angry, so I'm turning my back on you.' They're done dealing with it all. They're like, 'I'm going to binge-watch zombies eating each other.'"

He recalled the anti-Thatcher ravings of the Sex Pistols and the politically astute attacks of the Clash. "I've gotten most of my education through music," Billie Joe told the *Edmonton Journal*'s Angela Pacienza. "Music can make a difference in people's lives. It's not just there for entertainment."

American Idiots in the Global Village

As the US incursions in the Middle East continued, the rest of the world began to react to all the military action. In Russia, over the course of a couple of years, an entire audience was held hostage as terrorists seized a theater and later blew up a government building, killing around sixty people. Trains blew up in Spain. Even the United States sustained another attack when terrorists shot up Los Angeles International Airport. People saw this as pushback from Bush's Middle Eastern adventurism. While Americans, faced with the Bush administration's false ultimatum that "you are with me or you are with them," kept largely silent, there were protests all across Europe. "There's never been so many anti-American demonstrations in the world for any president until George Bush, and that to me is very poor foreign policy," Billie Joe told Neala Johnson. "People didn't necessarily like [America] with Clinton, but they tolerated us because at least it wasn't like he was trying to police the entire world. Whereas [with] George Bush, now we're back in that Reagan era where it's all about the military."

To which Mike added, "Proclaiming ourselves as being this ultimate superpower, fucking the greatest nation in the world."

"And that's not what I represent," Billie Joe concluded.

And so *American Idiot* came spilling out. Artists walk a tightrope when they sing about political issues. Go too far and the song sounds preachy. Don't go far enough and the song sounds wishy-washy. Some of the most effective protest songs were for unions (in the twenties, thirties, and forties), for civil rights (in the fifties and sixties, although there are some great ones today as well), and against the war in Vietnam. Where World Wars I and II had songs *in favor* of them ("Over There," "Boogie Woogie Bugle Boy"), Vietnam created contentious controversy because the people chosen to fight the battles—young men who were drafted to do it—had no clear reason for getting involved. Vietnam did not blow up a naval base or blast a passenger ship out of the water. So there were songs about not wanting to go to war, including "Where Have All the Flowers Gone" and "Draft Dodger Rag," and about the surrounding tumult caused by the war, including "For What It's Worth" and "Alice's Restaurant." Part of the reason there were fewer songs about American adventurism in Afghanistan and Iraq was the all-volunteer military that fought those wars. But the waste affected all Americans and people all over the world.

"The only people who should sing about social issues or politics are the ones who aren't full of shit," Billie Joe told *Time* magazine (although they expurgated it). "It can't just be some empty rhetoric and a bunch of finger-pointing." For *Detail*'s Matt Hendrickson, Billie Joe added: "I don't want to become Rage Against the Machine. Bono is having dinner with George Bush to get money from him [for debt relief in developing countries]. I don't operate that way. I stick to my opinions."

Sometimes we accrue knowledge from the mistakes of previous generations. Whereas many in Fogerty's generation abhorred returning Vietnam vets, Green Day dedicated their Video of the Year Moonman for "American Idiot" at the 2005 MTV Video Music Awards to the US soldiers then fighting in Iraq, saying: "Here's to our soldiers, let's bring 'em home safe."

Eight Years On

By the time of *21st Century Breakdown*, things had not improved. In addition to still having American soldiers on the ground in both Iraq and Afghanistan (we had not yet brought 'em home safe), the country's economy had collapsed when several financial institutions, like Salomon Brothers and Morgan Stanley —whose ads ran alongside the Viagra commercials on CNN during the days of embedded journalists—threatened bankruptcy in the wake of a rash of failed mortgages allowing people to buy more homes than they could afford. "We're in a financial crisis," Billie Joe told the *New York Times*' Jon Pareles. "People are losing their homes. Everybody was waiting, week by week, wondering what the next worst thing that's going to happen. But at the same time, it is the most hopeful moment . . . What a strange time."

One aspect of the situation was the continued growth of the twenty-four-hours-a-day news cycle. There were over half a dozen all-news channels that never went dark, and they had to have something to feed that beast. It fell to journalists who were trained in the "famine, fire, and freaks" school of television news to fill this time. As Billie Joe told *Guitar World*: "It's a different crisis every week, you know? Especially since 2005. Natural disasters, the environment is fucked up, the automotive industry is taking a dive, there's a financial crisis, economic bailouts, there's two wars we're still fighting . . .

There are people who think Barack Obama is the Antichrist and we are entering end times. And it's almost like they want to fulfill a prophecy."

Billie Joe was a big fan of Barack Obama. While his approval for Obama did not turn up in his music—no one wants to hear music about political contentment—he was a big supporter. Obama gave him hope after eight years of George Bush. "After his acceptance speech, I have to admit, it took me an hour to get the lump out of my throat," Billie Joe told *Rolling Stone*'s Brian Hyatt shortly after the 2008 Democratic convention. "Obama inspires people, and this country needs inspiration. People are jaded, pissed off and embarrassed." However, he proceeded with caution. "I don't want it to turn into a cult of personality. He's not Magic Man. The great thing would be if he could lead by example and inspire people to get their own shit together."

Heading into the 2012 elections, *Rolling Stone*'s David Browne asked about the rock stars the Republicans trotted out during their convention, like Journey and Kid Rock, and all the shout-outs speakers like Paul Ryan gave to AC/DC and Led Zeppelin. Billie Joe said that it was to counter the rock star appeal and aura of the POTUS himself.

Even when Green Day set out to have some fun, as they tried to do on the trilogy, they wound up with at least a touch of politics. The song "99 Revolutions" celebrated the Occupy Movement, which had started when people took over a park near Wall Street to protest the fact that 1 percent of people controlled most of the wealth on the planet.

Fighting Censorship, One Store at a Time

It wasn't the politics but the language that offended Walmart when *21st Century Breakdown* was released. However, the band's victory was political, a matter of the Constitution's guarantee of freedom of speech.

Walmart sells more records than any music retailer by a long shot. This is largely because Walmart is the most widely available record retailer, in addition to everything else it sells. Even people who don't own computers or don't have web access have a Walmart relatively close by.

While the record section in Walmart has shrunk in the past few years, you can still find it toward the back of the stores, hawking the latest music, catalogue favorites (about 60 percent of all music sold are catalogue items, not new music), and all sorts of loss leaders offered in the hopes that on the way through the entire store to the record section (which is also right next to the video games), the music consumer might buy something else as well.

During the eighties, there was controversy about "obscene" lyrics. While they couldn't be banned, a group called the Parent's Music Resource Center exerted some political muscle (one of the founders was the now ex-wife of the then vice president of the United States, Al Gore) to get record companies to voluntarily put a parental warning sticker or notice on albums with naughty language, lots of sex, or both. Walmart made it policy never to carry records with a warning label. However, they were not above asking record companies to ask their artists to make "clean" versions of their records—the record companies had been making "clean" edits of records for radio play for years. Some recording artists would, and some wouldn't. Green Day wouldn't.

"They want artists to censor their records in order to be carried there . . . We just said no," Billie Joe said in *The Progressive*. "As the biggest record store in America," Mike added for the *Philadelphia Daily News*' Howard Gensler, "they should probably have an obligation to sell people the correct art."

Take a Bow for the New *Revolution Radio*

Revolution Radio, despite its title and tracks like "Bang Bang," was not supposed to be an overtly political album like *American Idiot*. "I think after Trump got elected, everything changed," Billie Joe told *The Quietus*'s Patrick Clarke. "There was a part of the record that's very personal and uplifting, but there's the [political] part, now that's on steroids. It feels very real right now."

At an early show promoting *Revolution Radio* down the Jersey Shore, just across the Raritan Bay from Staten Island and sometimes within visual range of Manhattan, Billie Joe slowed things down while playing "Holiday" and started talking to the audience. "What do you think of our candidates for the presidency of the United States?" *NME*'s Jonny Ensall reported. The crowd booed. "What do you think of New York's finest, Mr. Donald Trump?" The booing increased. "No racism! No racism in this fucking room right now!"

Later he told Ensall: "I tried to find the ties between what we call terrorism, whether it's ISIS or whatever, and the militia mentality that Americans have and their entitlement to arms. For me, I look at it and it confuses the shit out of me, because I'm like: What's the difference?"

Green Day were in Paris the night Trump won the election. "I went to bed that night," he told Clarke. "I was like 'Yes, Hillary's gonna get it.' But then I woke up and I had a fascist president."

Like so many people after the 2016 election, Billie Joe had a lot of trouble processing the whole idea of a Trump presidency. But slowly, he, Mike, and Tré started to figure it out. One of the lessons learned from *American Idiot* was that they were punks and punks make noise. When they played the American Music Awards, Billie Joe let the president elect have it. This was a president who had been endorsed by the Ku Klux Klan and had selected an unabashed white supremacist for his cabinet. While performing "Bang Bang," they started chanting "No Trump, no KKK, no fascist USA." "He's not my president," Billie Joe told a press gathering. He added for Clarke: "The faction of Trump voters celebrating by painting swastikas on walls and saying 'make America white again.' It's a monster waking up that's been dormant for a long time. It scares the living shit out of me." Mike urged America to "keep our voices loud and keep them heard. Don't give up who we are. Fight for our civil liberties."

The whole process has put Green Day in an uncomfortable, if not untenable, place. They were among the most vocal of the people protesting the Trump presidency, but they did not necessarily want to be the voice of a generation in that regard. "I don't want to be a politician," Billy Joe told the *San Francisco Chronicle*'s Jaan Uhelszki. "I'm a musician and I even have a hard time believing that sometimes."

On the other hand, he noted to Johnson, "If people feel like storming the streets while listening to 'Holiday,' go for it!"

18

Tattoos of Memories

Green Day Ink

Tattoo artist Kat Von D has put ink on a lot of rock royalty. The first tattoos she ever did are worn by members of the Misfits. Other clients have included members of Judas Priest and Lady Gaga. She did a lot of work on the late, great Lemmy Kilmister. Von D also put ink on Billie Joe and Tré. "I love Billie," she told *NME*'s Leonie Cooper. "I met him through tattooing, so we did almost like half a sleeve on him, and I tattooed Tré as well."

The "Horseshoes and Hand Grenades" tattoo she did for Tré is featured in her book, *The Tattoo Chronicles.* "I really love that song, and I got the tattoo before we recorded it," Tré said. "I'm glad it made the album." She also did the photo strip of Adrienne on Billie Joe's arm.

Among the things Billie Joe has tattooed on his body are:

- A soccer ball
- Several skulls, including one playing cards, and the Adeline Logo
- A crouching tiger
- Several references to his wife, Adrienne, including her name above praying angels, a portrait of her that looks like a strip from a photo machine, and the number 80, which is one of her pet names
- Lots of colored stars
- A smoking baby
- The words "All Ages," no doubt a tribute to Gilman Street
- The names of both his sons, Joey and Jakob
- The logo from *Jesus Christ Superstar*
- The word "punx" just west of his navel and just above his left knuckles
- A vintage car
- The words "St. Jimmy"

Mike's tattoos include:

- The skull and crossbones logo of the Frustrators, his side band

- A dagger with the word "brother" on it and encircled by a snake, which is a copy of a tattoo worn by late band friend and former Sweet Children member Jason Relva (who is memorialized musically in the song "J.A.R.")
- His daughter's name—Estella—surrounded by stars
- A large dented can inscribed with the words "Product of East Bay"
- The face from the *1,039/Smoothed Out Slappy Hours* CD booklet
- The Japanese character for "pot."

Tré's tats include:

- A little girl watching a red balloon shaped like a heart that looks like it escaped her hand
- A massive snake
- A broken window with a TV falling out of it
- The name of former girlfriend Dena Roberson on his chest

Check out those sleeves. Mike Dirnt has some serious ink. *Sven-Sebastian Sajak/Wikimedia Commons*

He is also rumored to have a tattoo on his butt: Mike's name in a heart with an arrow through it. All three of them have EBPM tattoos. This acronym allegedly stands for East Bay Pop Mafia.

While Green Day were being courted by record companies after *Kerplunk*, they told one A&R rep they would sign with his label if he got a Green Day tattoo on his ass. A few days later at a meeting in his office with the band, he dropped trou to show them his new tattoo. It was fake. Needless to say, the guy was not Rob Cavallo. Green Day went elsewhere.

There are pages on the internet of fans' Green Day–inspired tats. Tré recalled one incident where a fan showed him his tats. "A guy asked me to sign his arm. [He had a tattoo that] said Rage and Love and it had the *21st Century Breakdown* [logo]. He said he was going to tattoo my name on him. I signed it: Hit Me."

19

Dominated Love Slave

Green Day and Sexuality

The *Bay Area Reporter*'s Cornelius Washington once asked Tré if Green Day would ever write a song that was obviously gay-specific. Tré responded, "Well, we're all pretty gay, so I don't think that's necessary!"

When Green Day burst into the broader swath of pop cultural prominence in 1994, one of the most divisive aspects of the band was their androgynous look. They were covered with tats, but they also wore makeup. The makeup wasn't glam. It was aggressive and a bit messy, but very obvious. It practically coined the portmanteau "guyliner." When homophobes in the crowd saw the look, they tended to abandon ship.

Billie Joe Armstrong—Bisexual?

If the audience questioned the group's sexuality, group members questioned it as well. Billie Joe claims that he has always had bisexual inclinations, more theoretical than actual by most accounts. Part of the claim might be challenging the "taboo." Peter Townshend also said similar things around the release of his solo album, *Empty Glass.* No one was more gobsmacked by it than his bandmate Roger Daltry.

For public consumption at least, all of the members are devoted husbands in straight relationships. That doesn't stop the haters from hating, though. If you Google "Billie Joe Armstrong bisexual," you will find quite a few images of Billie Joe kissing different guys. He told *Out*: "There's one side of me that thinks of it like the old Bugs Bunny cartoons, where he plants one on Elmer J. Fudd. But there's that other side of it, like, 'Wow, you're doing that in an arena somewhere like Hartford, Connecticut.' It resonates in different ways."

Mostly, it is a challenge to homophobia. He thinks sexuality in general should really be a nonissue. Why should people be defined by their sexuality, and why should other people make it their business to worry about the sexual choices another person makes? Gay rights have come a long way in the past half-century since the police raid on the Stonewall Inn in New York's Greenwich Village, and the riots that followed it, helped bring the cause of gay rights out of the closet.

Billie Joe Armstrong gets ready to take a bite out of one of the fans he brought onstage.
Gary Miller/FilmMagic

Billie Joe's uncle Stonewall Jackson was gay. Jackson was part of the family for as long as he could remember, so Billie Joe had no idea about the "taboo" nature of his uncle's sex life. "It never occurred to me that it was something that was supposed to be offensive," he told *Out* magazine. "He was my mother's brother, and the women of my family were always more sensitive to the issue . . . a lot more so than my redneck uncles."

Songs of Sexual Orientation

Even *Dookie* had its elements of bisexuality. There was, for example, the song "Coming Clean," in which Billie Joe publicly explored his sexually questioning nature, his feelings for women, and his feelings about men. Growing up in the Bay Area, gay life was always evident, and the cosmopolitan people of the area didn't view it as being wrong. This attitude was part of the Gilman gestalt. Unfortunately, it was not part of his high school's gestalt, and he was taunted by some of the yahoos who thought it made a difference.

Elsewhere, the horn-flavored "King for a Day" takes on cross-dressing, with lines like "Who put the drag in drag queen?" But Armstrong hopes the subject matter will be lost on a segment of the band's audience. It has overtones of the sound of British football hooliganism "Oi!" and he is often amused by the macho frat rats who sing along with the title but don't follow the verses that talk about dressing up as women.

Billie Joe recalls that the first time he saw Tré, Tré was wearing a tutu and what Billie Joe described as an old woman's swimming cap. When they play "King for a Day" live, it is the centerpiece of the show, a medley with all sorts of songs crammed into it, the band wearing crowns and regal robes . . . and dresses.

When asked who looks best in a dress, Billie Joe answered, "Tré:" Tré answered, "Billie Joe;" and Mike just said, "Well, we know it's not me. I'm ruggedly handsome so I look like a Monty Python girl."

On their first major label tour, they took as their supporting act their former Lookout! Records labelmates—queercore heroes Pansy Division—who played such tunes as "Rock 'n' Roll Queer Bar" and "James Bondage."

Billie Joe calls singer Kathleen Hanna of seminal (if you'll pardon the patriarchal adjective) riot grrrl band Bikini Kill and the lesbian-feminist group Le Tigre one of his favorite vocalists and people. He even got her to sing a bit on *21st Century Breakdown.* "If they made a car called Kathleen Hanna, I would drive it," he told *Out.*

Faggot America

If anyone missed it, the song "King for a Day" is about cross-dressing. *Naomi Lir/Wikimedia Commons*

As a songwriter and the band's primary lyricist, Billie Joe knows the power of words and chooses them very carefully. The power of what some people consider sexually offensive language came to play when radio first started playing "American Idiot." Radio stations in some markets started editing the line, "Maybe I am the faggot America/I'm not part of the redneck agenda." When he heard they were bleeping the song, he thought it would be the phrase "redneck agenda." "There was a fear of people thinking I was using ['faggot'] in a derogatory way, but I thought it was empowering," he said. "Hell, nobody ever called me 'redneck' in high school."

The epithet crops up elsewhere on *American Idiot*, in the song "Holiday": "Kill all the fags that don't agree." Both songs poke fun at the homophobia that still runs rampant in America, and the especially post-Bush-era idea that people who oppose blind patriotism must be either commies or "fags."

When Masturbation's Lost Its Fun

Some of the earliest attention Green Day got had to do with songs about masturbation. On "Longview" Billie Joe sings about "when masturbation's lost its fun." He was asked if he had ever reached that point. "I don't know exactly," he answered a fan in *Q*. "I masturbated three times yesterday. Was it fun? About as much fun as I'm going to get when my wife's not around."

Another sexual issue Green Day brings to the fore, beyond self-pleasuring, homosexuality, and cross-dressing is . . . not dressing. Billie Joe has had bouts with nakedness onstage, from going the full monty at Madison Square Garden during the "Jingle Ball" in 1994 to mooning dozens of audiences at the end of a mediocre show (that is, mediocre by either the band's or the audience's standards). The "Jingle Ball" (kind of gives a whole new meaning to the phrase) was heavily photographed and wound up in, among other media, *Playgirl* magazine.

Tré has written some of the more deviant sex songs in the Green Day repertoire, like "All by Myself," in which he pleasures himself on his absent girlfriend's bed, or the country flavored "Dominated Love Slave." He also knows that "In London you can get a good flogging for £400," as reported by *Kerrang!*'s Ian Winwood. "It's a private school type of thing."

When, in *Q* magazine, an English fan asked Tré which cartoon character he'd like to have sex with, Tré said "Boo-Boo Bear." This actually even upset his bandmates. Billie Joe just said, "Don't say that." Mike added, "That's sick on two levels." Tré shrugged his shoulders and said, "Scrappy Do, then." He has also said that he has sexual fantasies about Scrappy's friends Velma and Daphne. He told *Kerrang!*, "If I was going to do Daphne, I'd want Scooby getting his tongue in there, too."

In Australia for the *21st Century Breakdown* Tour, they had a few days in Perth before the actual start of the shows down under. In typical Green Day fashion, they stumbled upon one of the city's wilder events: lesbian mud wrestling at one of the local nightclubs.

Interestingly, straight sex is something not often dealt with in Green Day music, although all three main members seem more interested in women than men. Mike and Tré have each been married three times, trying to get that right. Billie Joe has been married to his wife Adrienne since 1994. When they gave a verbal preview of songs from the trilogy, Billie Joe noted: "I think it's so personal and it is so voyeuristic. And . . . this is the first time we've ever really sung about fucking." Which is, of course the original meaning of "rock and roll."

Part 2

Kill the DJ

The Green Day Discography—The Records and the Recording and Songwriting Process

20

Song Panic

The Process of Writing Green Day Songs

Billie Joe Armstrong wrote "Why Do You Want Him?" when he was twelve years old. Green Day eventually went on to record it for the *Slappy* EP. He has been writing ever since and has created an impressive body of work. (See chapter 43 on charts and awards to find out just how impressive.)

Writing hit songs is hard. If it weren't, everyone would be doing it. And a lot of people try. So what makes Green Day such successful songwriters? Is it a formula? Can I have some? What makes Green Day's songs so loved, and how have they kept it up for nearly three decades?

One of the factors is that Green Day is down-to-earth, fully entrenched. They have lived in the East Bay all their lives. They all have families. They live relatively simply—not poorly, but they don't own mansions (although they could). They do have some semi-extravagant hobbies, like collecting classic cars, but like so much that they do, they are pretty unpretentious about it. "No matter what anyone says," Mike insisted to *Rolling Stone*'s Alec Foege, "I'm too deeply rooted to just turn asshole overnight."

This is exceedingly important to Billie Joe as well. His deep connection to Oakland and the East Bay in general gives him a sense of place and community, as does his working-class background. How can he offer singing observations on society if he isn't part of it, after all? Billie Joe Armstrong's main rule for successful songs: the songwriter has to be in touch with the audience, has to be a member of it. They must relate for the songs to be relatable. Billie Joe extrapolated on this in *Alternative Press*: "I hope we never become rock royalty . . . I just have a desire to make great albums." To Jaan Uhelszki, he added: "The last thing I want to do is be just another rock star complaining about being famous."

Green Day sing about what's on their mind, and by staying rooted, they sing about what's on a lot of people's minds. They also have a sense of humor. They don't take themselves too seriously, but they take their music dead seriously.

"I'd rather write a song about committing suicide than about a girl," Billie Joe told *Spin*'s Jonathan Gold. "My wife always calls me Eeyore after the Winnie the Pooh character. And the songs that come the most naturally, the best songs, seem to have a pathetic quality to them . . . There are things that I can't talk about that I can only communicate through a song."

Juxtapose this with the fact that every song Billie Joe writes is initially written for himself. Early on, fans telling him they were touched by his songs confused him. "I definitely don't try to write songs that someone's definitely going to relate to," he told Foege.

In fact, he got into a small flame war over defending his music after the release of *Insomniac*. An angry mother wrote a letter to the band because she was "very disturbed" by what she heard when her eight-year-old son listened to the album, which his grandmother bought him for his birthday. She called the album "horrifying" and asked Billie Joe how he could take pride in anything like that. "All the thoughts you are helping to put in the minds of our youth is [sic] scary."

Billie Joe responded in a handwritten letter on notebook paper, claiming: "I don't write music for parents, grandparents, or eight year olds. I write for myself and I'll say anything I damn well please."

They have had to defend themselves against other things as well, like people claiming that they stole musical ideas. As related in the "I Fought The Law" chapter, one of the dumbest of these claims was by a relatively obscure English band called Other Garden, who said that their song "Never Got the Chance" was a whole lot like the title track to the album *Warning*. While the writer of the Other Garden song, Colin Merry, wanted was $100,000, both groups came to the conclusion that they had borrowed liberally from the Kinks' "Picture Book."

Influences

But this brings up an important issue: creators are only as good as their influences. As the saying goes, "Hacks borrow. Artists steal." Certainly, as the youngest in a family of six, Billie Joe (and by extension, Mike) had access to a lot of music. Billie Joe has publicly thanked his older brother Alan for turning him on to the Kinks. When asked, he said he considers "Afternoon Tea" and "Waterloo Sunset" their best and that they were among the most perfectly put together songs of the British Invasion.

He remembers his older sister Anna taking him to Berkeley's venerable (and as of this writing, still active) recorded music heaven and haven,

Rasputin Records, for his fourteenth birthday. She told him to get whatever he wanted but drew the line at buying a mainstream heavy metal record. He wound up walking out with *Let It Be*, by the Beatles, of course, and *Sorry Ma, I Forgot to Take Out the Trash*, by the Replacements. A couple of years after that, she took him to see the Replacements at the Fillmore.

Billie Joe revered the Replacements. One of the ways they influenced him was giving him a clue on inserting snark into song (think "Waitress in the Sky"). So getting to sit down with the group's Paul Westerberg was somewhere in between pleasure and an orgasm for him. In one of these meetings, *Spin* magazine's Steve Kandell got to be a fly on the wall and mediator. Billie Joe confessed: "The first time I met Paul—I don't know what the equivalent would be for Paul, maybe Keith Richards or Johnny Thunders—but for me, I was meeting my hero . . . Being in a band, you have to be a fan first. So when you meet people who have something to say about how some song affected them, those are people I want to connect with. I am still that person myself."

Billie Joe became heavily influenced by other Twin Cities artists, some of his older contemporaries who had been playing a while when Green Day started touring the country in their late teens. Beyond the Replacements, he often speaks of bands like Hüsker Dü, whom he says got him into punk in the first place. Some even say that Green Day accomplished what Bob Mould and his band tried to: bringing a more accessible pop sound in a punk package.

The band was even influenced by artists who predated their birth, like the Kinks and the Beatles, as mentioned, but also by the Zombies and other British invasion bands. The Who were obviously influential as the band moved into the 2000s. Green Day very aptly covered "My Generation" back in the Sweet Children days, and, just as appropriately, they covered "A Quick One (While He's Away)"—the mini-opera that tested the waters for *Tommy*—as an iTunes bonus track for *21st Century Breakdown*. They performed the former many times over the years, and played the latter at shows at Madison Square Garden in New York and as the Foxboro Hot Tubs in London. "I look at *Tommy* by the Who and think it should be played like someone interpreting Beethoven," Billie Joe told *Rolling Stone*.

Green Day had the honor of inducting Iggy Pop and the Stooges into the Rock and Roll Hall of Fame in 2010, and it was easy to tell that Billie Joe, Mike and Tré all loved the band. To many, the Stooges were *the* proto-punk band. "Their songs are like weapons," Armstrong said to the audience during his induction speech. "It's the sound of blood and guts, sex and drugs, heart and soul, love and hate, poetry and peanut butter."

Another influence from the early childhood years of Green Day is Cheap Trick. Green Day has covered "Surrender" in concert, and Soundsjustlike.com found two of the songs in the *¡Uno! ¡Dos! ¡Tré!* trilogy to be notably similar (in their opinion) to the Cheap Trick hit. While "Carpe Diem" from *¡Uno!* does have a few riffs in common, there are also commonalities with "I Fought The Law" (Bobby Fuller 4, probably via the Clash). By the same token, the other song they mention, "99 Revolutions" from *¡Tré!*, also features flavors from Billy Idol's "Dancing With Myself."

Of course, they cite bands from the mid- to late seventies heyday of punk. They cannot say enough about the Ramones, with whom they are often compared. In honor of the band, Tré named his daughter Ramona, and Billie Joe named his son Joseph (and calls him Joey). As far as Billie Joe is concerned, the Ramones invented punk rock. Another influential band that Green Day often gets compared to is England's Buzzcocks. This started when *Dookie* came out, and people could not help but notice the thematic similarities between Green Day's "Longview" and the Buzzcocks' "Orgasm Addict."

A lot of songs in the Green Day catalog have bits and pieces that might or might not have been cribbed from other sources. That has more to do with the musical vocabulary of rock and roll than any malicious or felonious intent. As John Fogerty, another influential East Bay rocker, noted when he was accused of copying his *own* song, "What do you want me to do, get an inoculation?" As Billie Joe is fond of saying, this music is in his DNA. The common element in the music that influences him and the band is genuineness. "[It's] all really good songs written by authentic people," he told *Guitar World*. "You take your influences and try to sing your own song to them."

Process

So, how do Green Day actually go about writing songs? What is their method? There are a lot of bits and pieces that go into the making of the band's original music.

One of the hallmarks of Green Day's music is the aforementioned authenticity. They feel that every song that they record has that nugget of reality in it that makes it accessible to their audience, or any audience. Every song has to have a ring of truth.

Some songwriters start with lyrics. Others build from a chord pattern or a riff. Some begin with the melody. At times Green Day has written songs all these ways, but Billie Joe maintains that his favorite way to write songs—the way he comes up with his best songs—is starting with the melody. "I just love melody," he told *Guitar World.* "You just look for a melody to hit you over the head."

Sometimes he works on the piano (which was actually his first instrument, or at least the first one he had some lessons on during the Fiatrones days), and sometimes he starts with a riff on the guitar. If there is an overarching element to the Green Day sound, it is the members of the band itself. For example, Billie Joe told *Guitar World* that if *American Idiot* and *21st Century Breakdown* had anything in common, it was "the source they're coming from, which is me, Mike and Tré. So there are bound to be similarities."

Most of Green Day's songs are listed as being at least cowritten by the entire band. This has developed into one of the few consistent elements in the songwriting process. Tré and Mike generally try to keep clear of Billie while he is writing an initial draft of a song. They then bring in their ideas to complete the piece. "I'm always writing songs," Mike told E. E. Bradman in *Bass Player.* "I could write melodic riffs and tracks all day long. Obviously, Billy [sic] is the main songwriter in this band, but there are lots of great collaborations all over our records. I was talking . . . on the phone one day and playing bass at the same time, and I wrote something, recorded it on my iPhone, and brought it up to Billy's [sic] house that night. It ended up being the main chord structure for a new song, 'Missing You' [from *¡Tré!*]."

One of the things that make Green Day songs so popular is their lyrics. The words to Green Day songs can be funny, profane, and pointed. They have a poetry that goes beyond rhyming. The lyrics are often as catchy as their melodies—sometimes they are even catchier —and Green Day take considerable pride in the words to their songs.

Billie Joe considers his songs to be audio photographs of a particular idea or time. "Half the shit I write," he told *Guitar World,* "I don't even know what I'm writing while I'm writing it. It just starts to come together . . . I'll get a melody in my head. Then I have to wait for a lyric to hit me." Billie Joe often uses harsh imagery and language in his songs. He does this to drive home his ideas and release his anger at things that he has been saving up in a small compartment of his brain to spit out at the right moment.

There are also elements of classic song forms. Green Day are rock's reigning masters of the three-minute long verse-chorus-verse-chorus-bridge-verse-chorus radio-ready song. They also like to alter it, which is how the rock operettas within rock operas in *American Idiot* and *21st Century Breakdown* happened.

But, when all is said and done, there is one element that really defines Green Day songs. As Billie Joe told Jaan Uhelszki "It's nice when people can sing along."

21

1,000 Hours

Who Are These Guys Green Day, and What Have They Done with My Sweet Children?

Other than a cassette demo that Sweet Children reportedly sold at shows, *1,000 Hours*, Green Day's first EP for Lookout! Records, was their first commercial recording. It was supposed to be the first commercial recording for Sweet Children. However, about two weeks before the EP was due to come out, they changed their name to Green Day, mostly because they felt that Sweet Children was too similar to another band called Sweet Baby (and whatever happened to them?).

"I was just about to put out their first record (*1,000 Hours*) and I went ballistic," said former Lookout! Records owner Larry Livermore about hearing this bit of news. "I was like, 'Everybody knows you as Sweet Children. How am I supposed to sell a record by a band called Green Day? Nobody knows who the hell Green Day is. And besides, Green Day is a dumb name. It doesn't mean anything.' Stuff like that. Well, I was wrong. I guess I'm better at picking bands than picking names. Green Day turned out to be a very good name indeed."

Billie Joe explained it to *Time* magazine, saying: "I wrote a song called 'Green Day' because I was smoking a lot of dope. Our drummer [John "Al Sobrante" Kiffmeyer] put *Green Day* on his jacket and said, 'Maybe we should call the band that.' And I said, 'That's a good idea.'"

The EP was recorded in December 1988, when Mike and Billie Joe were seventeen years old. It was produced by Andy Ernst and the band at the Art of Ears Studio, across the bay in San Francisco. Ernst had played in bands ranging for a neo-soul group called Sass (that opened for R&B heavyweights like the Commodores and Tower of Power) and New Wave band the Stats. Green Day was the first band he produced that he did not belong to. He

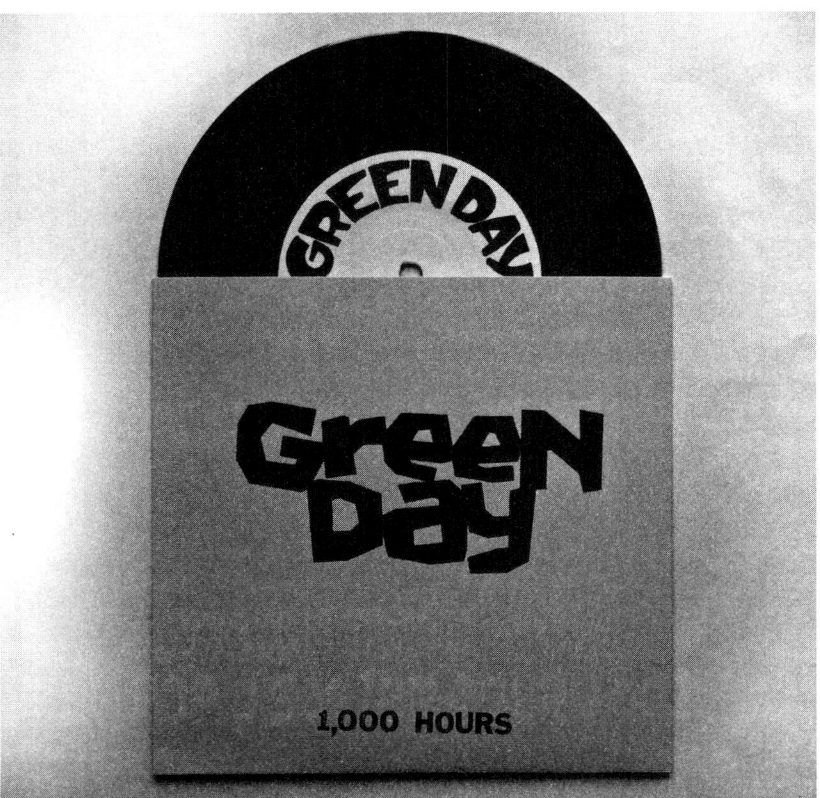

They changed their name to Green Day just in time for the EP not to be called "Sweet Children."

would also work on the *39/Smooth* album, the *Slappy* EP, and *Kerplunk*, as well as albums by other Lookout! bands like Screeching Weasel and Rancid.

1,000 Hours was released in April of 1989. It was pressed on vinyl in varying colors and had two alternate covers, a green one and a pink one. Billie Joe's name was misspelled on the package. The four tracks on the album were the title song, "Dry Ice," "Only of You," and "The One I Want." They were all written by Green Day with lyrics by Billie Joe, except for the last song, which featured lyrics by Billie Joe and Mike.

39/Smooth

Alan's Almost 40? Smooth!

Over their winter break from school in 1989, the group went back into San Francisco's Art of Ears Studio with Andy Ernst to record their first full album, *39/Smooth*. Tracked on December 29, 1989, and mixed on January 2, 1990, it amounted to just two days in the studio. Lookout! Records chief Larry Livermore noted that it probably took them longer "to tune up the snare drum on *Dookie*."

"We didn't have much money at Lookout! in those days to pay for recording costs," he added on Greenday.net, "but even still, they could have taken a couple more days than they did and I would have been happy to pay for it. But their drummer at the time, John Kiffmeyer, AKA Al Sobrante, was very big on spending as little money as possible and doing it as fast as possible. I think that was largely an outgrowth of his punk roots . . . but I was still pretty happy with how the album came out."

In fact, to save money, Billie Joe and Mike tracked the vocals together. It was the only album Kiffmeyer recorded for the band, though he probably makes decent royalties on the one song he wrote the lyrics to, "I Was There," and the other songs that are credited to the entire band. Recorded for $675, the album has sold almost a million copies all told.

The title is alleged to have two sources. "Smooth" was sort of a watchword in the Green Day camp, a group reaction to many things. Then, when Billie Joe's older brother turned thirty-nine, he joked that Green Day should put that into the title of the new album they were recording. He was joking, but the band did it anyway. Released April 13, 1990, *39/Smooth* came out on black and green vinyl and cassette. There were only 800 of the green vinyl editions pressed. Some of the album art was by Jesse Michaels of Operation Ivy, another Lookout! group. The inner sleeve featured Billie Joe's handwritten lyrics and letters from Kiffmeyer and Livermore rejecting an offer to sign with IRS Records (a subsidiary of A&M), pledging allegiance to Lookout!. That would last for one more album.

Green Day's first full album, recorded over Winter Break from high school. This is a later edition including the *1,000 Hours* EP and the *Slappy* EP.

The album featured the song "Green Day." The ten-track album clocks in at a bit over half an hour. It introduced Green Day's combination of Bay Area punk ethos with classic snot pop, a sort of rough draft of what Green Day would become, while establishing their youthful who-gives-a-fuck attitude with the beginnings of their solid songcraft. It sold 3,000 copies in its first year and enjoyed a coattail effect when Dookie caught fire. That year *39/Smooth* sold 55,000 copies. As noted, it has sold, in its various versions, close to a million copies.

The 1991 CD release combined the album with the two Lookout! EPs and a track cut for the Flipside Records compilation *The Big One.* The CD made a sort of portmanteau of the names—*1039/Smoothed Out Slappy* Hours. Reprise re-released it on March 24, 2009, on 140-gram vinyl, packaged with 7-inch versions of the EPs.

Slappy

A Few Hours Work

On April 20, 1990, Green Day spent a few hours with Andy Ernst at Art of Ears Studio in San Francisco tracking four songs for a new EP. They mixed it in a few more hours three days later. In retrospect, Billie Joe says that this is the recording where the Green Day sound started to solidify.

That EP, *Slappy*, was released during the summer of 1990 as Green Day were on the road making their first tour of North America. It features the first song Billie Joe ever wrote (at the age of twelve), "Why Do You Want

Slappy because they slapped it together in about four hours?

Him?" While it was believed that the song was about his loathed stepfather, Billie Joe denies this. Another song on the EP, "409 in the Coffee Maker" was based on a prank Billie Joe pulled on one of his teachers. A re-recording of the song was the B-side to the UK version of the single "Basket Case." They also covered Operation Ivy's "Knowledge," the song that they often use for the fan rock band section of their concerts.

As with their previous Lookout! records, *Slappy* was initially available, in limited amounts, on various colored vinyl, though the majority were pressed on plain black. One of the little Easter eggs on the record is the quote "Might Bleed Today" on the outer rim of the label artwork on side A. Another is a message that says "To raise money for the tour, Mike shucked clams, Billie Joe tossed pizzas, and John drove a diaper truck." The cover photo of Mickey the dog was taken by John Kiffmeyer. Billie Joe and Mike's friend (and former Sweet Child) Jason Relva had nicknamed the dog Slappy.

Billie Joe told Aaron Burgess in *Alternative Press* in 2009, "If [I] was to look back at like the songs that were on the *Slappy* EP, I probably would've wanted for those songs to be on *Kerplunk*." Instead, when Lookout! issued the CD *1039/Smoothed Out Slappy Hours*, it wound up on that album.

Sweet Children EP

Forward into the Past

The day Mike graduated from high school, Green Day went on the road for their first tour of North America. While in Minneapolis, Minnesota, they went into 6 Ft. Under studio for a couple of hours and recorded four songs from the Sweet Children repertoire for Skeen Records. It was their first time in the studio without Andy Ernst.

The cover stars Mike's legs in the role of . . . Mike's legs.

Skene Records founder Jeff Spiegel had started the label a couple of years earlier, and the second compilation on the label, Caution, featured Crimpshine, a Gilman Street standby. He also was friendly with Jesse Michaels of Operation Ivy and acquainted with David Hayes, Larry Livermore's partner at Lookout! Records. Another thing he had in common with Green Day was that he credited the Ramones with turning him on to punk, having seen them live while he was in high school. So it wasn't that outrageous for Green Day to have met him.

The EP included a cover of the Who's "My Generation" that also pays homage to David Lynch's contemporary noir film *Blue Velvet*, when Billie Joe quotes the film's antagonist Frank Booth, saying, "Heineken? Fuck that shit!" It has the songs "Sweet Children," "Strangeland," and a song that had Billie Joe and Mike collaborating on the lyrics, "Best Thing in Town."

The first front cover features Mike's legs onstage by a mic stand. Subsequent covers included a lightly mangled VW. The EP sold almost 500 copies the day it was released, a third of the initial pressing of 1500. The first pressing was on black vinyl with a limited number on pink vinyl. It went into four subsequent pressings, each with different artwork. The fourth pressing came out after the material on the EP was included on the band's next album, *Kerplunk*, which explains that circumstance on the back of the cover.

This would be the last Green Day recording to include John "Al Sobrante" Kiffmeyer.

25

Kerplunk

Welcome to Paradise

The band went through a lot of changes before they went into the studio to record the follow-up to *39/Smooth.* John Kiffmeyer decided to attend Humboldt State University. He was already attending Contra Costa College during the years he was with Green Day, but that was a mere fifteen-minute drive north to Rodeo and south to 924 Gilman St. Humboldt was about five hours north, not far from the Oregon border, certainly too far to travel for band rehearsals.

So, the band lost their propulsion. They needed a drummer. In the months that followed they went through a slew of drummers, trying different things. They were nearly to the point of such frustration that they considered dissolving the band.

Here's where things get a little confusing. In a bio for the Lookouts, Larry Livermore said that on July 10, 1990, Billie Joe played on the sessions for the Lookouts EP *IV.* However, Green Day were on tour through early August. On July 10, 1990, they were in Bloomington, Indiana, doing a gig at Rocket's Famous Pizza. Now, they had a day off the previous day, so it is possible that he flew home, did the session, and then flew back, but neither the band nor the record company had that kind of budget.

Either way, Billie Joe and Mike had met Lookouts drummer Tré Cool before. The Lookouts had played at the gig that introduced Sweet Children to Livermore in the first place. They had also seen the Lookouts at 924 Gilman Street.

At some point during the summer of 1990, the Lookouts broke up, or at least drifted apart. This left Tré available to play with anyone he chose, and after jamming with Billie Joe and Mike a few times in late September, he decided that he could hang with them. Despite their relative youth (all three of them were seventeen years old), these were veteran musicians, all of them playing live gigs since they were twelve. By late October, they debuted the new lineup of Green Day.

"When Tré first started playing with me and Billie," Mike told *Bass Player*'s E. E. Bradman, "he was a sick drummer, and I had to get better, quick, to keep up with him."

Late in the spring of 1991, they started the process of recording their second album for Lookout!. Back in Art of Ears Studio with Andy Ernst, they cut six tracks with their new drummer. These were the only six tracks they had. Mike recalls there being a great deal of pot smoked during the sessions. (Go figure.)

The band spent most of the summer touring around North America, and when they got back to Berkeley in September, they went in and cut six more tracks. In all, they spent four days in the studio, and it cost all of $2,000.

Livermore first heard the album on an airplane as he was heading back to Berkeley from Los Angeles, where the album was mastered. In Gillian Gaar's *Green Day: Rebels with a Cause*, Livermore recounts how he put a dub of the master into his cassette player and thought the record was "so good it was almost scary," adding, "I knew instantly that life was never going to be the same for Lookout! Records or Green Day."

The band toured relentlessly. After a handful of local gigs, they took off for Europe. Most of the pre-release work on *Kerplunk* was done while Green Day were making their first turn through England, Ireland, Wales, Scotland, Spain, Germany, Poland, Denmark, Czechoslovakia, Austria, Belgium, the Netherlands, and Lithuania, playing largely on equipment borrowed at each venue. They got their first copies of the album when they were in Southampton, England, and turned the gig at the Joiner's Arms into a record release party. The album actually came out commercially a month later, on January 17, 1992. It allegedly sold 10,000 copies in the first week of release.

Initially, several stores and chains refused to stock the album because of the cover art. The front cover is a drawing of a young woman holding a smoking gun. On the back cover is a young man with a bullet hole in his back.

The album featured a bit of fiction on the inner sleeve (and later on the CD booklet) called "My Adventure with Green Day." Attributed to "Laurie L.," it is generally acknowledged to be the work of Larry Livermore. The album booklet also features a thank you to Adrienne Nesser. The song "2,000 Light Years Away" that opens the album is about Billie Joe's frustration with their long-distance romance. The album would ultimately set things in motion that would allow Billie Joe to marry her. It also thanks their friend Jason Relva and Brain Stew, a.k.a. James Washburn, another friend of the band, as well as separately thanking both John Kiffmeyer and Al Sobrante. The liner material also informs listeners that the album is dedicated to the memory of Gravy, Mike's recently deceased pet cat.

Kerplunk featured an early version of "Welcome to Paradise," a song they would re-record for their next album. "Dominated Love Slave," a country tune in the vein of the Beatles cover of Buck Owens' "Act Naturally," was written by Tré, who also sings and plays the guitar on it. "Christie Road," another one of the *Kerplunk* songs, is an actual thoroughfare in Martinez, California. It runs along the railroad tracks, which is mentioned on the record.

Gotta watch out for those Riot Grrrrls! The cover of *Kerplunk* became one of the first controversies that Green Day enjoyed on a national (if limited) scale.

A later version of the back cover. The album now includes the recordings from the *Sweet Children* EP (last four tracks). Note also the poor guy with the hole in his back.

The December 2007 issue of *Blender* put the album at No. 47 on their list of the "100 Greatest Rock Albums Ever." It was certified Platinum—signifying sales of a million copies—in America by the RIAA on August 8, 2003. It has sold over four million copies worldwide.

Intermezzo

A Band in Transition

As Larry Livermore observed, after *Kerplunk* nothing would be the same for him or Green Day. As *Kerplunk* became a quiet, underground phenomenon, a lot was happening in the Green Day camp. When a band is playing clubs for short money and American Legion Hall shows produced by fifteen-year olds, they can generally handle most of their business affairs. Suddenly, Green Day was playing bigger venues, and for "slimier promoters."

The basic idea was that the business of being Green Day was getting in the way of being Green Day. There are very few bands that actually enjoy balancing the books and the other business aspects of being a band. They like a buffer between the art and the commerce of making music for money. This is why most bands are willing to pay 15 percent to a manager to keep the art and the commerce separate. Green Day would prefer being on tour to dealing with answering letters about deals and making sure their checking account was not overdrawn.

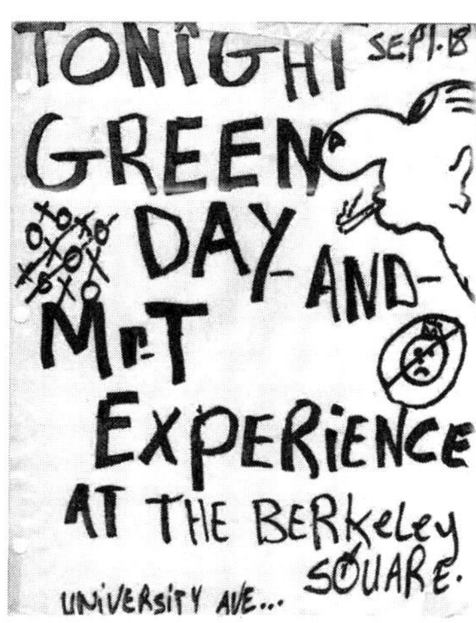

Indie bands could still get away with this: a last minute, hand-drawn poster for a September 18, 1992, gig in Berkeley. Green Day were beginning to outgrow this kind of gig.

In April of 1993, the band got involved with Bay Area attorneys Eliot Cahn and Jeffery Saltzman. They were turned on to the rock and roll lawyers by a friend of the band, and they wound up contracted to the pair's Cahn-Man Management. The legal duo had already done business with alternative heavyweights like Mudhoney and Primus.

Green Day was still on Lookout! based on a handshake deal consummat-

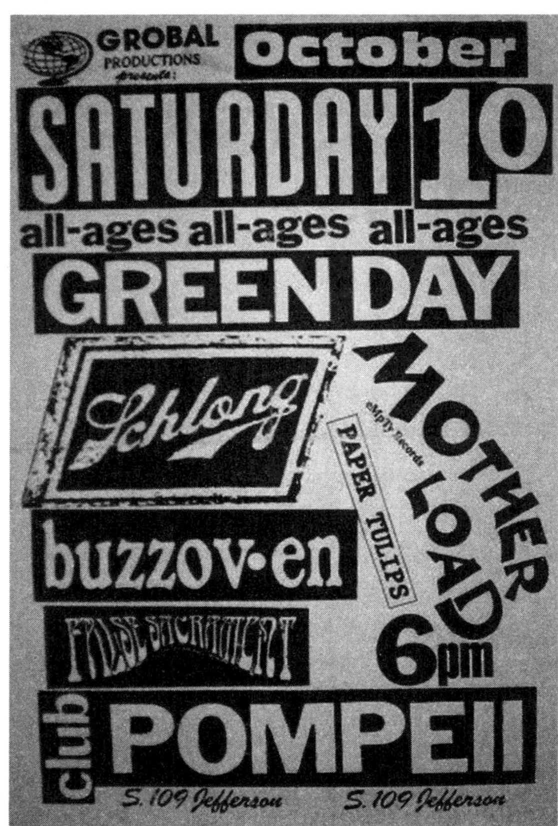

Being on an indie without any real backup meant driving from Victoria, British Columbia, to Spokane, Washington, only to discover the gig had been cancelled!

ed in Livermore's cabin, and for a while that was enough. "I thought [Lookout!] was the ultimate independent label," Billie Joe told the *Ultimate Green Day Authority* website.

Now, conventional wisdom at this time for A&R departments at record companies (those are the folks who sign artists to labels) was that when an independent record sold more than 20,000 copies, they would hit the companies' radar. Green Day did half that amount of business the week *Kerplunk* was released. When the album hit 50,000, Saltzman and Cahn started fielding offers.

The band's general attitude toward this was twofold: On the one hand, they felt that whatever was going to happen would happen. On the other hand, they knew exactly what they wanted from a major label record contract: complete artistic freedom. They had gotten this far doing what they wanted, and they didn't see why they should compromise going forward. Their frequently stated opinion on the subject of "selling out" was that it only happened when you compromised your ideas and ideals.

27

Dookie

Do You Have the Time to Listen to Me Whine?

The courtship rituals of labels and bands during the nineties—the height of record industry decadence—were as colorful as any mating ritual on Animal Planet. A&R departments had unlimited Gold Cards and weren't afraid to use them. This suited Green Day. They ate, drank, flew, and stayed at hotels they could only dream about two years earlier, decimating minibars and milking room service.

"We wanted to be the bosses and not let somebody else tell us what to do . . . we thought, 'Fuck this, it's our lives.' It's like getting married or something." Tré told *Green Day Vault.*

Columbia flew the band to New York City and gave them the three-hour tour. David Geffen had a meeting with them and tried to play the Nirvana card, telling them that he thought of Kurt Cobain as a son. On one of the trips to LA that the pursuit required, they convinced a Geffen A&R exec to send them to Disneyland. They had a ball. However, they decided even before the day of recreation with The Mouse that they didn't want to be the redheaded stepchild to Nirvana. Besides, they had already decided to go with another company.

The winner of the Green Day prize was a junior A&R guy from Reprise Records, Rob Cavallo. There were several pretty compelling reasons, despite the band's deadpan explanation that they must have been stoned. He produced an album by the Muffs that Billie Joe really liked, and he was a musician. They invited him to their rehearsal space, toked up, handed him a guitar, and jammed on Beatles songs and others for over an hour. And Reprise offered "mutual creative control" of their recordings.

They signed with Reprise for a relatively small advance of $215,000. Half of that went into making their major label debut, the rest (after management took their share) got them new equipment, a van, and went (along with the royalties from Lookout! and tour income) to keeping them housed and fed.

Making *Dookie*

In fact, they didn't even have to drive to get *Dookie* made. The album was recorded at Fantasy Studios, and they rode down Ellsworth Street where Billie Joe and Tré lived and then Parker Street on their bicycles. Coincidentally, this is where Billie Joe had recorded "Look for Love" when he was five years old.

Mike had to rent a bass because after six months on the road, his own instruments were trashed. For three weeks, they were in the studio from noon to midnight. Much of the material was road tested and audience approved, so they were sharp and tight. It was the rare song that took more than three takes. Billie Joe recorded all the vocals in two days. He just got on the mic and nailed one song after another. In part because they liked the Muffs' album so much, and in part because they liked him, Cavallo produced the record. It was largely done in five weeks.

"They knew they were hot shit," engineer Neill King told *Sound on Sound* magazine. "They knew the material was terrific, and it was just a case of us getting it right."

"We knew we were entering an arena of bands that we didn't like," Armstrong told *Rolling Stone* with a laugh. "It was important for us to be ourselves, no matter what."

Many inside of Reprise were dubious of Cavallo's new signing. As far as they were concerned, punk had pretty much vanished with the Clash and their ilk. Beyond that, the genre was never a big seller. But Cavallo had faith that they could make it, even in some minor way, figuring even if only "1,000 cool kids" bought it, the record wouldn't have cost Reprise anything.

Making their major label debut was serious business, as none of them wanted to go back to shucking clams, tossing pizzas, and bussing tables. They even exchanged their vice of choice (pot) with something a little more stimulating: coffee, lots and lots of coffee. They wanted to drink in the major label recording experience.

After cutting the album, the band went on tour as opening act for Bad Religion. On the tour, they tightened up "Longview" and "Chump." One of the advantages of being in the music business big leagues was the ability to go back into the studio and recut songs. One of the advantages of their recording history and having tightened the songs up on the road was that they were able to cut, dub, and mix the two songs in a day and a half. The entire album was revved up and stripped down. Billie Joe played very few guitar solos along with being extremely quick on the vocals. The key thing was that it was an album that people would want to listen to, end to end, and

A Child's Garden of Scatology: There's more shit on the *Dookie* cover than you can shake a stick at . . . or use the stick to wipe off the bottom of your shoe!

over and over again. For that, it first had to be an album that they could (and would) listen to that way.

The working title of the project, *Liquid Dookie*, was a commentary on what happens when you eat crappy food while on tour. It was what they called a "van joke." They shortened it to the slightly less disgusting *Dookie*. This was more flexible. In addition to being slang for excrement, it was also slang for money and pot. The cover played to the scatology of the title and depicted a bunch of dogs throwing huge turds at college professors, a Jesus-like figure, and dozens of others, as the name Green Day rose in a mushroom cloud.

Songs

"Our songs have a split personality. They're pretty happy. You can put an exclamation point on the brattiness," Mike told Fricke, adding, "[but the lyrics] are also very dark and serious,"

They were also personal and included what was running around in the band members' minds when they started putting the songs together. Billie Joe's frustration about his long distance relationship with Adrienne fueled "When I Come Around." On the other hand, "Longview" and the "hidden track" "All by Myself" were about spanking the monkey. Tré wrote and sang "All by Myself" into a four-track recorder at a party at somebody's house. "Longview" was largely based on a bass part that Mike came up with while tripping, and the title came from the town in Washington where they first performed the song in 1992.

"A lot of the themes—about self-esteem, boredom, whatever—are similar to what . . . grunge bands were writing about, but it . . . isn't as heavy handed." Cavallo told the *Chicago Tribune*'s Greg Kot. He added for *USA Today*'s Edna Gunderson: "It has a fun, expressive, high-energy power. It's very youthful and exuberant, but angry at the same time."

There were songs like "Basket Case" about anxiety and panic attacks, which Billie Joe and Mike were both subject to. "The lyrics kept changing," Billie Joe told NPR's Terry Gross. "It started out as a relationship song, and I got the idea for it to be more neurotic."

Boredom was a frequent topic, as in "Longview" and "Burnout"; so were ex-girlfriends, as in "Chump," "Sassafras Roots," and "She" (which are all allegedly about the same girlfriend, who eventually joined the Peace Corps and went to Ecuador). The album also dealt with less spoken about teen anxieties, such as breaking from home (Mike's "Emenius Sleepus," "In The End," and a remake of *Kerplunk*'s "Welcome to Paradise") and sexual orientation ("Coming Clean"). While Billie Joe said he never actually had relations with another man, he did frequently have struggles with his sexuality.

One of the things that "made" *Dookie* the monster hit that it became were the videos. These chaotic bits of film were right in MTV's wheelhouse at a time when they really were "Music Television." The video for the first single, "Longview," started out with the afternoon routine of the MTV teen audience of the time—sitting on a couch watching television. The audience could identify with this, and it hit them where they lived. It was an actual basement with low hanging pipes in a one-bedroom home where several people lived. The video ends with the feathers from the couch cushions covering everything. What teenager hasn't at least wanted to trash the sofa at one time or another? Just before the shoot for the video, Armstrong was sitting on that very sofa watching TV when he heard the news of the death of Nirvana's Kurt Cobain. While there was no "official" video for "Welcome to Paradise," the second single from *Dookie*, the live video gave fans a chance to see the manic energy of the band in concert. "Basket Case" was actually filmed in a retired mental facility. "When I Come Around" had the three-man gang wandering through the Bay Area one evening. One scene featured future Green Day member Jason White.

These songs became modern rock staples from 1994 through today. "Longview," "When I Come Around," and "Basket Case" topped *Billboard*'s Modern Rock Chart, while "Welcome to Paradise" rose to No. 7 and "She" hit No. 5. In England, "Basket Case" rose only to No. 55 on its initial release. Six months later, as it became a major international hit, it was re-released and hit a more-like-it No. 7, while "Longview," "Welcome to Paradise," and "She" all hit the top 30.

Reaction

The public liked *Dookie* too, moving it on beyond punk. Although it first appeared on the *Billboard* 200 at No. 141, it grew into a Top 10-selling album of 1994, running through its first pressing in February and shifting 65,000 copies by early April 1994. The album topped the *Billboard* "Heatseekers" chart three weeks after it was released. By April 2, it was in the *Billboard* 200 chart's top half at No. 99. It peaked nearly a year after it was released at No. 2.

While *Maximumrocknroll* had nothing good to say about the band, and more often had nothing to say about a band that chose the possibility of growing success over the insularity of the punk scene that spawned them, music critics from around the country liked the album. It ranked No. 12 in the annual *Village Voice* "Pazz and Jop" poll for 1994, a survey of thousands of people who write about rock and roll. In the *New York Times*, it was noted that *Dookie* was the only Top 10-selling album that was also in the Top 10 of its critics poll. *Time* magazine called it the best rock record of 1994. *NME* gave it seven of ten stars while *Spin* gave it eight of ten. *Billboard* gave the album four of five stars, and *Alternative Press* gave it five out of five. "Disillusion and malaise never sounded so sprightly," Jacob Trowbridge wrote on Whatculture.com.

Even Green Day's inspirations liked it. Joey Ramone gave them his seal of approval, calling the band "cool." Joe Strummer from the Clash was a little more verbose in his assessment of the band, when he told *Melody Maker*, "When Green Day come out of my radio, let me tell you, it sounds a lot better than the rest of the shit coming out of it."

However, none of this sat well with the arbiters of punk cred. Just by signing with Reprise, Green Day ruined their relationship with 924 Gilman. They were banned from playing there (not that the club could have held the kind of crowd they would draw). The ban lasted over twenty years, but they did play there again in 2015 at a fundraiser, and they also sponsored a fundraiser to help to save the club from the vagaries of rising rents as Berkeley gentrified. Fourteen local bands played one track each from the album. It had to be held at Berkeley's Fox Theater because, again, Gilman was too small.

Cavallo maintains that *Dookie* made his career. He told Gibson.com, "I didn't turn out to be the evil record producer who killed Green Day's sound."

Billie Joe is ever conscious of how lucky he is and ever grateful for the album. Hit songs and a hit album are gifts that keep on giving, and if Green Day never wanted to work again, the members would still likely be wealthy men. To date, the album has sold over twenty million copies worldwide, with at least ten million of those in America.

28

Insomniac

My Wallet's Fat and So Is My Head

So, suddenly, after a decade in the clubs, half a dozen years after your first album, you become the biggest deal in music. What's a band to do? After selling millions of copies of an album, what do you do for an encore? "Life got more complicated," Billie Joe told the *San Francisco Chronicle*'s Jaan Uhelszki, "once we got successful." Indeed, there was a period when Armstrong, so tortured by the thought of following up *Dookie*, considered disbanding.

Perhaps the band should have covered the Brains' "Money Changes Everything" because Green Day went through some major changes after the success of *Dookie*. For one thing, all of them became family men. This led to lots of sleepless nights with making babies and changing babies and other night-blooming projects. This kept Billie Joe awake, and when he couldn't get back to sleep he took to his home studio and started writing songs.

Beyond that, Mike was having some health problems. He was born with a heart defect, and it had started getting worse. "I'll be standing there and all of a sudden I'll feel like somebody's jammed a needle into my chest," he told *Guitar World*. "I'd basically drop to the ground, gasping. And then my heart's always sore. It's a scary problem to have with the one part of your body that they don't know how to fix."

In July of 1995, the band went into Hyde Street Studios in San Francisco, once again with producer Rob Cavallo. Over the next six weeks, they recorded and delivered fourteen tracks to Reprise (which wasn't difficult, as Cavallo was also their A&R person). "It's a lot harder, a lot faster, and a lot angrier than *Dookie*," Cavallo told *Spin*'s Craig Marks.

Indeed, it became a mission to make something exceedingly loud yet exceptionally lean and impeccably crafted. Tré changed his cymbals on nearly every track. Billie Joe worked at getting just the right guitar and amp combination for each song.

And then there was all the coffee. "Every time we went to roll tape," Tré told *Rolling Stone*'s Alec Foege, "we said, 'OK, this is it. We're going to squeeze every last drop of energy that we have, and we're going to put it into two minutes.' And if it wasn't all together, then we'd just . . . drink some coffee, then go back and go, 'Yeah, let's do this.'"

Anger seemed to be a prevalent element in the recording. It is reflected in the almost brittle sound of it, in the slash of Billie Joe's guitars, in the whack of Tré's snare. It was easily the hardest sounding album they had ever recorded, and maybe the hardest sound that they will ever record. "We're hoping to scare a few people off with this," Mike told Ian Fortnam. "I swear to God I wouldn't mind cutting it down to one quarter of the audience we have."

"We didn't want to piss people off, but we were pissed off ourselves, so the record came out harder," Billie Joe added in *Kerrang!*. "We weren't going to cry about *Dookie* and go 'That sucks, millions of people are buying our record and people like us.' We just keep going." However they adamantly would not record anything that sounded like *Son of Dookie.*

They also didn't put a whole lot of effort into setting up and promoting the record. Part of the reason was apathy, but another part—and maybe one of many causes of the anger that permeates the music—was they had just fired their management and appointed one of their roadies as their "business liaison." The record company avoided asking too much of the band for the same reason they want bands to have management to begin with: they don't want dreadlocked amateurs (as the liaison was) running amok in their hallways. So *Insomniac* came out with very little of the fanfare that might have preceded the follow-up to a monster like *Dookie.*

Green Day were clearly of two minds about the recording: On the one hand, they liked it a lot. It was vicious and furious with great songs and a truly punk attitude in the oldest sense of the word. They were feeling punk about everything. "It was very aggressive through the whole thing," Billie Joe told *Billboard*'s Craig Rosen. "It was relentless." On the other hand, they wanted as little to do with promoting it as possible.

Songs

Their new songs also reflected another dichotomy: they were a band that reveled in its working class roots yet were suddenly very wealthy. They started dealing with some political ideas, singing about "class structure" and not being a "part of your elite" in "Stuck with Me." Other songs dealt with money in other ways. "Brat" is about kids waiting for wealthy parents to die so they can inherit their estates.

"Stuck with Me" is one of the stranger stories of Green Day in the studio. They couldn't think of a name for the song. Around the same time they recorded this unnamable song, they recorded a track called "Stuck with Me." Just for the sake of having something to call it, they started to refer to the unnamed song as "Do Da Da." However, someone mislabeled the two tracks. So, "Stuck with Me" became "Do Da Da," which was relegated to B-side status, and the unnamed song found its way onto *Insomniac* as "Stuck with Me." Did you follow that?

There were other psychic wounds that *Insomniac* bled from. "86" dealt with the fallout between 924 Gilman Street and the band. Not only were they *persona non grata* as a band, people did not even want them to show up as longtime members of the collective. "I ran into this old friend when I went back to Gilman last December," Billie Joe told Marks, "and all he could say was, 'Wow, what the fuck are you doing here?'"

Some of the songs dealt with other elements of what was going on with the band. "Panic Song" dealt with a problem that both Billie Joe and Mike still suffer from: panic attacks. These attacks became more urgent when Mike's health took a turn. Later on, they became a very large issue for Billie Joe, although the attacks themselves were less of an issue than the meds he took to alleviate them.

"Tight Wad Hill" had a different sort of drug connection. It is an actual place, though that is only its nickname. It is about a road behind Pinole High where people who didn't want to pay to see the football team play could watch the game. It also was a place where people who wanted to tweak or toke could do so in company. In the song, Billie Joe imagines it as a place where the druggies make their headquarters. A lot of meth users did hang out there apparently. The meth connection also carried over into probably the first pop single ever to deal directly with tweaking, "Geek Stink Breath."

These were clearly darker subjects than the inspired goofiness of *Dookie*. This was certainly not *Dookie II*.

Cover Art

Even the cover was more serious. Created by collage artists Winston Smith, who had done many of the Dead Kennedys' covers, it was based on a work called *God Told Me to Skin You Alive*, and the image was as much the stuff of insomnia-causing nightmares as the image's title. It features a

Mephistophelian figure playing the violin before a wall of fire; a smiling woman holding Billie Joe's guitar, Blue, in one hand and a pistol to the head of a sleeping man on a hammock in the other; a couple of chimpanzees; and a dentist at work (an image borrowed from one of Smith's Dead Kennedys collages). The gallery copy is nearly the same, except that the woman holds a classical guitar.

The back cover collage, *All the Girls Play Mental Games*, while less frightening, is even more insidious. It features an army sergeant taking an automatic weapon out of a refrigerator into which a woman with angel wings and wearing an apron is about to put a bottle of milk. Meanwhile, a woman in a robe does her makeup as a man in a vest holds a giant lemur on his lap and a baby in a highchair feeds an organ grinder monkey. Outside this cozy domestic scene, the window displays a holocaust. Nowhere in the album art does a picture of the band appear. "Everyone already knows what we look like," Billie Joe told Marks.

Smith had met Tré during the Lookout! Records days, and Smith told him if he ever needed a record cover, to give him a call. Apparently, Tré did. While radically different from the cover of *Dookie*, it does have the common element of being full of "Easter eggs," like three skulls that only appear when the cover is held at the correct angle. Amazed by the intricacy of the piece, Billie Joe asked Smith how he was able to create them so quickly. Smith replied, "It's easy, I'm an insomniac." Whether this (possibly apocryphal) story accounts for the record's title, or it refers to Billie Joe's own sleepless nights, or perhaps both, the album was originally going to be called *Tight Wad Hill.*

Reprise released *Insomniac* on October 10, 1995. The Japanese edition had an extra song, "I Wanna Be on TV," a cover of a track by an earlier Bay Area hardcore band, Fang. The Australian release came with a live, six-song EP. There was very little critical backlash, as often happens after a big hit, but many noticed the bleaker and more bitter lyrics and the harder edge to the music. In true punk tradition, to paraphrase the Clash, Green Day turned anger into power. Uhelszki described the album as "three minute blasts of rage."

These "blasts of rage" were very upsetting to one mother. She caught wind of the tape of *Insomniac* her son was listening to, a gift his grandmother had given to him for his eighth birthday. She felt she had to write the band and tell them how appalling she found the music: "That tape is not something that any singer/songwriter should take any pride in at all. It is horrifying . . . I know it is possible for the group to make 'good music,'

God Told Me to Skin You Alive: The Cover of *Insomniac.*

because I heard . . . the song entitled 'When I Come Around' [which is] one of my son's favorites. It's a song that he and his dad sang together . . . in the car . . . Why don't you do something positive and clean up your act?"

Now, what did she think when she heard her eight-year-old (and her husband!) start singing "I'm just roaming for the moment, sleazin' my backyard, so don't get so uptight?" Billie Joe responded, "I find people like you offensive . . . Next time, I suggest you do a little research before you purchase such 'rubbish' for your little boy."

Of course, *Insomniac* did not sell as well as *Dookie.* Very few albums ever sell as well as *Dookie. Insomniac* did sell four million copies worldwide, but it didn't have the hit power of their major label debut. The album hit No. 4

during its second week on the *Billboard* 200, and while the album lacked the pop appeal of its predecessor, the single "Geek Stink Breath" got as high as No. 3 on the alternative charts, as did the single "Brain Stew/Jaded." The final single from the album, "Walking Contradiction," only reached No. 21 on the alternative charts.

"People keep asking us if we're bummed that *Insomniac* was a failure," Mike told Uhelszki. "Failure? It sold 4 million copies. So, of course, I tell 'em we feel fine."

Nimrod

Blood, Sweat, and Booze

Green Day hit the road shortly after *Insomniac* came out, as they did with every record. They had been doing this since even before they recorded, playing coast to coast when Mike got out of high school in 1990 and doing it again in 1991, with the addition of spending most of the fall in Europe. Now, some six years on, it had become a drag in several ways: burn out; missing their young families; and the nature of the venues they were playing, from places that had broken glass on the mosh pit floor to the lack of intimacy owing to the size of the places their fame had forced them to now play. Probably a combination of them, with the key factor being that touring had ceased to be fun, and about midway through the European leg of the *Insomniac* tour, they cancelled the rest of the remaining shows, citing sheer exhaustion. It came close to breaking up the band. On the road, Billie Joe would say stuff like "Not a day has gone in the last year and a half that I don't thing about quitting."

They took a year off. This gave them time to recover from the stresses of the road, spend some time with their growing families, and generally chill out. This also allowed them more time to write, and by the time they were ready to record their next project, they went into the studio with about three dozen songs. But throughout this process, they decided they wanted this album to be different. To begin with, Billie Joe wrote almost all of it on acoustic guitar, letting the songs take on their own life when the band got together.

For some reason, they decided to record in Los Angeles, occupying Conway Studios, with Rob Cavallo once again in the producer's seat, from March through July of 1997. The band camped out at the Sunset Marquis in LA for the four months that it took to record, about the time it took to make all of their previous releases put together. They were in the studio from noon to two o'clock in the morning, but they concede that a lot of that time was spent in the lounge playing pool and foosball.

As *Kerplunk* was fueled by pot and *Dookie* was fueled by caffeine, the new project was fueled by alcohol. This led to mayhem at the Marquis, with one of the group members (they won't reveal which one) walking the halls of the hotel naked and knocking on the other guests' doors. Cavallo decided to bring in a couple of "babysitters"—his own father and manager Pat Magnarella—to stem the chaos a bit. A television still managed to fly from Tré's window. "There was glass everywhere," Billie Joe marveled.

The stated goal of the album was to loosen the bonds of punk and start to expand their sound. This might have been a reaction to some of the reviews of *Insomniac* that commented on the band's lack of "growth": The songs from *Insomniac*, the running theme of some of the reviews went, could have just as well been on *39/Smooth*. At the very least, Green Day wanted to break out of the constrictions of three chords. They had been toying with the idea, they claimed, for six years; that is, from the time of *Kerplunk*. "We've always screwed around with different types of music during our jams," Mike told the *New York Times Syndicate*'s Scott McLennan, "but we'd say, 'OK let's stop and get back to the album.'"

"[We] really bled over this record," Billie Joe told *Billboard*'s Craig Rosen about the four months in the studio, "to the point of straight-up delirium."

Songs

Using the Clash's *London Calling* and Bikini Kill's *Reject All American* as touchstones, the songs went from flat out punk to the acoustic song "Good Riddance (Time of Your Life)." That song was actually seven years old, written about the same old girlfriend who inspired the *Dookie* trifecta of "Chump," "Sassafras Root," and "She" (and would inspire several other songs that turned up later). Billie Joe introduced it to the band and Cavallo while they were recording *Dookie*, but they all decided it didn't fit, and it certainly didn't fit onto *Insomniac*, even though it debuted as the B-side of "Brain Stew/Jaded."

"I remember having a meeting with Mike and Tré about that song," Billie Joe recalled to *The Sydney Telegraph*'s Kathy McCabe, "because it was obvious they couldn't play on it . . . We talked about it for a while and decided it was the right thing to do at the time because we wanted to extend our audience, and we knew that song would help."

Even though Mike and Tré were not really featured, it seemed wrong just to have an acoustic guitar and vocal on the album. Cavallo thought that the song would sound great with violins (played by Conan McCallum).

He sent the band down to the foosball table. It took about half an hour to record (apparently he already had the parts done by Beck's dad, arranger David Campbell, before the session), and they fit right in with the chorus: "Something unpredictable but in the end it's right." It was the band's biggest seller in the United Kingdom, though it only topped out on the British charts at No. 11. It topped out at No. 11 on the *Billboard* Hot 100 as well, but it stayed on the chart for forty-three weeks, the band's longest running single as of this writing. It also saw a lot of other use:

- It was featured at the end of the final episode of *Seinfeld*.
- Two episodes of *ER* used it. This was extra appropriate, as Noah Wyle, one of the stars of *ER*, was featured in the "Good Riddance (Time of Your Life)" video.
- It was featured on the *Glee Graduation* soundtrack.
- It became the official theme song for the Professional Golfers Tour for a while.
- It was used in proms and graduations the world over.

"Could you ever imagine a song like that would get used as much as it did?" he asked McCabe.

It brought Green Day into an entirely different market—middle-of-the-road radio. Many of the people who heard it there thought that Green Day was a new band and went out and bought the album. Many quickly exchanged it for the single version of the song after hearing the other things on the album.

Another *Dookie* refugee, "Haushinka," didn't make sonic sense for the earlier album either, but it worked in the context of the new one, especially as it segued nicely from "Jinx." And it wasn't as if Green Day had not used strings elsewhere on the album. The first single from the album, "Hitchin' a Ride," opened with a very brief violin solo by Petra Haden of LA power poppers that dog. (She is also one of the triplet daughters of late jazz stalwart Charlie Haden.) They also "borrowed" Gabriel McNair and Stephen Bradley from No Doubt's horn section for their ode to cross-dressing, "King for a Day," which became one of the band's favorite live workouts.

"Hitchin' a Ride" and "Walking Alone" dealt with the band's struggles with sobriety. This had become a big issue at the time, especially for Billie Joe. "Redundant" dealt with the marital strife Billie Joe was having with Adrienne. He was still passionately in love with her, but their relationship seemed to have hit a rut. "Uptight" dealt with their ongoing trials with other emotional problems and sounded a bit like Blondie's "Dreaming."

People returned the album, complaining that the rest of it sounded nothing like the hit.

"Prosthetic Head" has overtones of Richard Hell's underground classic "The Kid with the Replaceable Head." The instrumental "Last Ride In" could have come off the flipside of a Santos and Johnny ("Sleepwalk") or Tornados (of "Telstar" fame) 45. "Nice Guys Finish Last" was a memo to the band's managers and attorneys.

The most punk songs on the album, "Platypus (I Hate You)"—which was directed at *Maximumrocknroll* publisher and 924 Gilman Street honcho Tim Yohannon—and "Take Back" would not have sounded out of place on a Dead Kennedys album. "Reject" was inspired by the letter about *Insomniac*'s NSF8-year-olds content. "I still love punk," Billie Joe told *Billboard*'s Craig Rosen. "I'm only 25 years old, and I still love it."

As they had cut three dozen songs for the album, rewarmed a couple of leftovers, and only used half of the available recordings for the American release, some of the foreign editions made use of these songs from their doggie bag. The Japanese version had one extra song, "Desensitized." The Australian version had that and three others: "Suffocate," "Do Da Da," and "You Lied."

The Album

The name of the album was based on a common use of the word "nimrod," which came about from a Bugs Bunny cartoon. In the Bible, Nimrod was one of Noah's relatives, a warrior king, and a mighty hunter. In a 1930s Looney Toon, Bugs sarcastically refers to Elmer Fudd as a little Nimrod, in the Biblical context. Most people didn't get it and thought that he was calling Elmer a buffoon. And so, as the cartoon played on movie screens across the country and later became a staple of television cartoon shows (among the band's favorites), the word took on that meaning. "It's some guy from the Old Testament," Billie Joe acknowledged to *NY Rock*'s Gabriella. "For some strange reason, it turned into a curse; it's another word for dork."

Nimrod hit the record stores on October 14, 1997. While some had come to doubt the band's relevance after *Insomniac* and then a yearlong disappearing act, they still were invited onto *Top of the Pops* on the BBC, the *Late Show with David Letterman*, and the *Howard Stern Show* on K-rock radio. *Nimrod* debuted and peaked at No. 10 on the *Billboard* 200 chart, selling over 81,000 copies that week, and stayed on the *Billboard* 200 for seventy weeks. By March of 2000, *Nimrod* had sold two million units in the US alone.

In November, Green Day did an in-store promotion for the album, playing a set at Tower Records' East Village location in New York City. The band trashed the place (you can read more about it in chapter 41), causing $50,000 worth of damages, which required the store to close the next day so it could affect repairs.

Videos

Reprise put out the single "Hitchin' a Ride" in August 1997, and by the second week of September, it hit No. 12 on the *Billboard* Modern Rock chart. MTV debuted the video, a kind of live action Betty Boop cartoon. It wound up reaching No. 5 on the Modern Rock chart, No. 9 on the Mainstream Rock chart, and even No. 39 on the Hot 100.

"Good Riddance (Time of Your Life)" was the second single. The video captured the song's wistfulness and won an MTV Video Music Award for Best Alternative Video.

If anything, however, the video for the next single, "Redundant," was cooler. A tribute to the short film *Tango*—a piece of visual fugal exposition by Polish filmmaker Zbigniew Rybczyński—it features the band playing as a group of people repeat a series of movements around the band and themselves. Despite this inventive video, and the strength of the previous single, "Redundant" only got to No. 16 on the *Billboard* Modern Rock chart, although it hit No. 2 on the singles chart in Australia.

The final single, "Nice Guys Finish Last," showed the album running out of commercial steam, only getting into the low 30s on the *Billboard* Modern Rock chart. The video for it was a football parody, with the Green Day Packers playing in a football stadium replete with cheerleaders, tailgating fans, and a victory celebration. Completing the sports metaphor, the song was featured in the 1999 film *Varsity Blues* and was nominated for an MTV Movie Award for best song from a movie.

Reviews

Critics tend to love *Nimrod*, though often in retrospect. In 2016, *Kerrang!*'s Nick Ruskell wrote about it being Green Day's best: "The songs—'Scattered,' 'Haushinka,' 'The Grouch'—are all hormone-pumping, lip-curling, ear-hijacking pearls of perfection. And those aren't even the hits . . . *Nimrod* finds Green Day comfortable and confident . . . the biggest punk band in the world and one of the best live bands on it."

After the borderline grim *Insomniac*, writers appreciated, and even seemed relieved by, the return of the band's sense of humor. Nearly everyone noticed just how diverse the record was. "This record goes out on . . . a limb," Jaan Uhelszki wrote in the *San Francisco Chronicle*, "showcasing the kind of music the band grew up on and often plays during off hours. Although the musicians have expanded their boundaries, they still see Green Day as a punk band."

In a 3.5 out of 5 star review in *Rolling Stone*, Greg Kot wrote: "This music is a long way from Green Day's apprenticeship at the Gilman Street punk clubs [sic], in Berkeley, Calif. But now that the band has seen the world, it's only fitting that Green Day should finally make an album that sounds as if it has."

In an odd occurrence, the band's thoughts were in sync with the critics. "I think we had something to prove with this album," Billie Joe told *Kerrang!*. "[We were] putting pressure on ourselves to write a different kinda album."

Tré was somewhat more effusive. "This fucking album is the best fucking album you're gonna fucking get this fucking decade" is how Ian Fortnam reported his response.

30

Warning

Victim of Authority?

The *Nimrod* Tour played to theaters and auditoriums rather than the larger stadiums, sheds, and arenas they had been playing since *Dookie.* In a way, it brought them back to the *Kerplunk* period, where they could, in certain markets, attract 1,500 people to a show. The period after *Nimrod* was about double that, but still the shows were far more intimate than the previous post-*Dookie* tours. Green Day were no longer in the mainstream, having had their fifteen minutes. The turn of the millennium saw the ascendency of rap metal as the popular rock noise. Punk was passé.

When Green Day came off the road from the extensive *Nimrod* Tour, they took a yearlong break from touring. Billie Joe *needed* to spend some time at home. He had just gotten off the road from Europe in time to accept an MTV Moonman for "Good Riddance (Time of Your Life)" at the 1998 Video Music Awards. Two days later, Adrienne gave birth to their second child, Jakob Danger Armstrong. Then, a month and a half later, he was off to South America. Things had been rocky with Adrienne for a few years, and her time as a married single mother probably left her less than happy about the relationship.

If their personal relationships were complicated, so was this patch of the band's career. Coming off of a monster record like *Dookie* has destroyed lesser bands than Green Day, but Billie Joe, Mike, and Tré recognized that, while it was not a make it or break it time, it was a pass through a sort of music business limbo. As the *New York Times* critic John Pareles put it, they were "at an awkward point in their career, torn between settling down and acting up."

While the band got together five days a week to rehearse and write—displaying a determination not unlike that required of running a business—they played only five gigs in 1999, all of them local, three of them for charity: two nights in October for Neil Young's Bridge School benefit, which kept them busy on Cabbage Night and Halloween, and a rent party for 924

Gilman Street, which had waived its Green Day moratorium enough to let Mike's side project, the Frustrators (see Chapter 44 on "Stray Art" for more), play earlier in the year.

In the Studio

By spring, they had an embarrassment of riches in terms of songs they had written over the previous year and a half. Rather than risk the mayhem that attended the *Nimrod* sessions in LA, they decided to record close to home at Oakland's Studio 880 to further keep the home fires burning. They went in

Self-produced, *Warning* foreshadowed the band becoming more political.

on April Fool's Day, 2000, as auspicious a time as any to begin a Green Day album. By May 25, it was in the can.

They had started working with R.E.M. producer Scott Litt, but it didn't work out. So, for the first time since the *Sweet Children* EP, the band produced themselves, with Rob Cavallo taking on the role of executive producer. It was a title many A&R people were assuming on their bands' projects.

Billie Joe's favorite album during this period was Bob Dylan's *Bringing It All Back Home*, certainly one of the best singer/songwriter albums ever recorded. It encouraged the band to keep experimenting beyond "punk," and it also turned up the volume on the political elements of Billie Joe's lyrics.

The group dynamic seemed to change a little. The guitars were mixed a bit lower, the lock groove of Mike and Tré getting more emphasis. There were also a lot more acoustic guitars in the mix. While "Macy's Day Parade" tipped its musical cap to "Good Riddance (Time of Your Life)," most of the songs were more akin to the kind of acoustic strumming Pete Townshend injected into *Tommy* (think "Pinball Wizard"). What came out of the studio is easily Green Day's most restrained album.

Warning featured a slew of "guest artists." They once again called on No Doubt's Stephen Bradley to play horn and David Campbell to arrange the strings. West Coast Jazz stalwart Gary Meek played sax. Benmont Tench, one of Tom Petty's Heartbreakers, added vocals to the song "Fashion Victim."

All Those Good Songs, Part One

Warning came out on October 3, 2000. On MTV's *First Listen*, Green Day debuted the record nearly a month before its release. They played the BBC's *Top of the Pops* and, the day before the album came out, appeared on Howard Stern's radio program and the *Late Show with David Letterman*. A couple of days later, they were in the studio of WBCN in Boston.

In retrospect, many of the songs on the album presaged the rest of Green Day's output in the new millennium. "Macy's Day Parade" deals with consumerism while "Warning" questions who is more dangerous, the police or the people. The five-minute-plus, multi-themed track "Misery" was the closest thing to a rock operetta that Green Day had ever created, even echoing *Three Penny Opera* (which brought the world "Mack the Knife" and was by the team that wrote "Whisky Bar," covered by David Bowie and the Doors). The album also featured Tré on accordion and Billie Joe on mandolin in the service of the very *noir* song "Fashion Victim," which deals with the fascism of clothing. "Hold On," which bears a melodic similarity to Elvis Costello's "Veronica" with a "Love Me Do" harmonica lick, deals with maintaining your own identity. The title track also encourages individuality and urges people to question the powers that be. "Minority" was expressly written out of fear that Al Gore was too boring to become president and that would lead to a younger, dumber, more conservative, and less tractable Bush White House.

Waiting for the shooting to start: Mike Dirnt on the set for the "Minority" video.
Sandra Castillo

But there were also the songs that thumbed their noses at propriety. "Blood, Sex and Booze" dealt with S&M in a slightly more serious way than *Kerplunk*'s "Dominated Love Slave." At one point during the album, Billie Joe said, the band brought in a dominatrix (the joys of self-production). They hired her to whip the second engineer. They were subsequently surprised to see her running the catering company on one of their video shoots.

"Church on Sunday" brings a load of irony to a relationship song that is ultimately about trust. "Deadbeat Holiday," veiled as it is, might be one of the few commentaries Green Day wrote about the vagaries of fame. In a lot of ways, *Warning* offered a more content, less neurotic Green Day, even as it finds them trying to find a balance between the teenage angst of their past and their current status as responsible adults.

The Declining Charts and Sales

The first single from *Warning*, "Minority" topped the *Billboard* Modern Rock chart and reached No. 15 on the Mainstream Rock chart. It barely broke the top 20 on the UK Top 40. While MTV had pretty much stopped playing music by *Warning*'s release, the band made a video of them playing the song on a parade float, with baton twirlers marching in front, and three huge Thanksgiving Day Parade-style balloons of Tré, Mike, and Billie Joe.

The title track hit No. 3 on the Modern Rock chart and didn't even manage to crack the top 20 on the Mainstream Rock chart, topping out at No. 24. It hit No. 27 in the UK Top 40. The video clip showed the band playing in a studio apartment of a guy who likes to do "dangerous" stuff like ripping the tag off his mattress, staring at the sun, running with scissors, and eating before swimming.

The third single, "Waiting," barely made an impact, hitting No. 26 on the Modern Rock chart and No. 34 in the UK Top 40. The video looks like one of the house parties the band was playing just a decade earlier. "Macy's Day Parade" made even less of an impact, not even charting. The black and white video had Billie Joe, barely recognizable, dressed in a suit and tie with his hair slicked back, walking through mounds of junk, fitting for a song about consumerism.

Warning sold a bit over 150,000 copies in its first week of its release. The album would hit No. 4 on the *Billboard* 200 Album chart, and it stayed on the chart for twenty-five weeks. By December, it had sold half a million copies and earned a Gold record. It topped the album charts in Australia, Italy, and the United Kingdom.

All Those Good Songs, Part Two

While in the studio, Green Day were forced to pass on an invitation to open for the Rolling Stones. Then, right after they finished recording, Mike had surgery to repair a repetitive stress injury. However, between recording the album and releasing it, the group finally accepted a long-standing invitation to join the Vans Warped Tour, appearing alongside Good Charlotte, NOFX, and dozens of other bands, all playing highly compressed half hour sets of their hits. (For a more personal angle on this, see the foreword by Kevin Lyman, founder of the Warped Tour.) People kept asking them about the album that they had finished but hadn't released. "Hey, we feel stupid trying to sit here and describe the record and sell it," Mike told the *Boston Globe*'s Steve Morse. "We're happy with it. It's a Green Day record. It's bound to have good songs on it. More than one, at least. You'll have a hell of a time downloading all these good songs."

Nearly every critic commented on all those good songs, the pop craft at work on *Warning*. The nature of the reviews depended on how much that particular writer appreciated pop craft from the standard bearers of punk. All three of the band members were twenty-eight years old, and some critics decided that the group had earned the right to grow up. Others felt betrayed by it. Jaan Uhelszki, in *Rolling Stone,* said it was their least punk and most serious recording as both musicians and songwriters. *Entertainment Weekly* gave the album a B+, slightly less than the A- it received in the *Village Voice*'s "Christgau's Consumer Guide." Japan's *Daily Yomiuri* noted that it rocked "with the same bouncy intensity as *Dookie.*" Another critic commented that the album was fun, just not as "childish." On the other hand, one critic likened the album to Bon Jovi singing karaoke at a wedding. Brett Anderson of the *Washington Post* noted, "They seem stogy compared with their foulmouthed younger days . . . *Warning* is the product of three men trying to capitalize on the success of their youth." However, even he noted the "sure-handed" melodies.

In a long-form review in the *Voice,* "Metal" Mike Saunders somewhat presciently found *Warning* akin to the Beatles' *Rubber Soul.* Like *Rubber Soul,* it proved to be that kind of a transitional album for Green Day. As Yahoo!'s Neal Weiss observed, *Warning* could be "a starting point to take the band seriously."

31

International Superhits! and *Shenanigans*

Green Day's Midlife Crisis

Even though they had just released arguably their least "punk" album in *Warning*, Green Day felt the need to reach out to a younger audience and spent much of the next year doing that. They had already done the Vans Warped Tour to demonstrate their continued relevance. To an extent, it worked. Rather than being viewed as rock and roll irrelevancies and has-beens, they began to change the perception of them to that of pop punk progenitors. Many of the bands they inspired started giving them their props.

There were hopes that a greatest hits record might be informative, that these new younger fans could use it as a starting place to get into Green Day. To that end, they compiled *International Superhits!* and its companion piece, *International Supervideos!*. Reprise released the pair on November 13, 2001, a little more than a year after *Warning*. Four of the twenty-one songs on the hour-long album came from *Warning*, as did three of the videos. The video for "Macy's Day Parade" was actually made to promote *International Superhits!* rather than *Warning*. There is one previously unreleased track on the album, the acoustic "Pop Rocks and Coke," and a re-recording of the B-side for "Waiting," "Maria."

The *International Superhits!* cover appeared in a lot of movies and television shows:

- In the Billie Crystal and Robert DeNiro comedy *Analyze That*, it appears as a poster on the wall of a teenager's room.
- In the *George Lopez Show*, the same poster appears in the room of a teenaged girl.

- In the *Brothers Garcia*, one of the characters works in a record shop that has an *International Superhits!* poster on the wall. There is also an ad for the record posted on the shop's storage room door.
- In *Sabrina the Teenage Witch*, there is an *International Superhits!* poster over the water cooler at Sabrina's place of business.

"It's interesting doing a greatest hits album," Billie Joe told the *Sydney Sunday Telegraph*'s Kathy McCabe, "because when I was young I got into a lot of bands like the Stones and the Beatles and the Ramones through their greatest hits records."

What went unsaid (at least to McCabe) was that greatest hits collections were often the provenance of bands on the wane or bands that had

Five albums and a passel of hits into their career, the time was ripe for a "best of" collection.

imploded. Green Day sales had certainly hit a precipitous downward curve, and the greatest hits album really had not helped matters. It was met with more commercial indifference than any album since they had signed to Reprise, topping out on the *Billboard* 200 at No. 40; it rose as high as No. 4 in Japan and as low as No. 67 on the German charts. While it went Gold two months after it was released, it would take another three years and another hit album before it went Platinum.

"[It] really put the lid on a lot of our accomplishments, put a lock on it, though we can open the lid any time we want," Mike added for Johnson. "It's the definitive starting ground for moving forward. We're not trying to bury the past, but bookmark it."

As with *Warning*, the record failed (relatively) despite some glowing reviews. On *All Music*, Stephen Thomas Erlewine noted that a collection of their hits made them sound better than ever. Others commented on just how long the band had been out there playing and how remarkable the singles were.

Green Day took *International Superhits!* on the road, playing the opening slot with Blink-182 on the Pop Disaster Tour. "Everybody likes a big match," Mike told Kevin C. Johnson of the *St. Louis Post-Dispatch*. "This is a match made in heaven, or a match made in hell for those who didn't want it to happen."

Although Green Day always went on first, each band got equal playing time. By all accounts, Green Day blew Blink-182 off the stage every night. Despite the terrific shows, things were not happy in the Green Day camp. There was a great deal of tension between Billie Joe and his bandmates. Billie Joe's drinking had gotten bad, and he was behaving irresponsibly.

Amidst this turmoil, Reprise put out *Shenanigans*. The fourteen-track album compiled some of the band's stray art—non-album B-sides, extra tracks, songs from soundtracks, and the like. It came out with just a month left of the Pop Disaster Tour, but none of the songs got played during those shows.

The album actually did better in the short run than *International Superhits!*, rising to No. 27 on the *Billboard* 200. However, the album didn't even achieve Gold status, and it was the only Reprise album to that date that hadn't. So, Green Day's sales continued to decline.

When they finished the Pop Disaster tour and played a week of dates in the United Kingdom, they came off the road and started thinking about doing a new album, or perhaps not doing an album. They sat on the precipice of breaking up. Billie Joe's drinking caused much chagrin amongst the

A band with the number of fans Green Day still had could afford to make an album of rarities, B-sides, and other odds and sods for the die-hard completists.

people closest to him: Adrienne, Mike and Tré. His two bandmates felt marginalized by Billie Joe—that he had become Green Day and they were his sidemen. Sensing their resentment, Billie Joe hesitated to bring songs to the band. As the tension got thicker, Billie Joe went so far as to call his oldest friend, Mike, and ask if he wanted to go on with the band.

"Breaking up was an option," Mike told *Rolling Stone*'s Matt Hendrickson. "We were arguing a lot and we were miserable."

They had spent the time since *Warning*, and possibly since *Nimrod*, in a state of stasis. Even with waning record sales, they were still a powerful and popular live act, and beyond that, they were still a money-making entity. No one wanted to do too much to challenge that. Billie Joe would write a song and then hear Tré and Mike in his head telling him it wasn't worth the time to pursue. If they wanted to go on, they could not go on like that.

They decided they did want to go on, but they had to clear the air. So, in 2002, they began work on an album with the working title of *Cigarettes and Valentines.* As they did that, they also entered into a process that was part group therapy and part mediation, meeting once a week just to work on that process. They hashed out a settlement that basically required Billie Joe to show his friends more professional respect and not treat Mike and Tré "like staff" but more like his closest advisors and, more importantly, his closest friends. In turn, they agreed to criticize fairly, constructively, and respectfully. And pretty soon, they were back to what they did best: making music.

32

American Idiot

The Needle in the Vein of the Establishment

Green Day got home from Europe at the very end of August 2001. Two weeks later, the unthinkable happened. As much of America woke up and turned on their TVs, they were greeted by the site of a jet plane impaled through the upper stories of one of the towers of New York City's World Trade Center. As many watched, a second plane flew into the other tower. Not long afterwards, the towers collapsed. Another plane flew into the Pentagon, and a plane aimed at the White House was brought down by a group of passengers and crashed in a field in Pennsylvania. The terrorist group al-Qaeda claimed responsibility for the dramatic attacks. What followed was a call to arms that entered the US into the quagmire of Middle Eastern religion and politics. "Right after 9/11," Billie Joe told NPR's *Fresh Air* host Terry Gross, "watching the . . . tanks going into Iraq and these embedded journalists going in live, it felt like a cross between war and reality television."

There were a lot of personal problems during this period. Tré and his second wife, Claudia, were in the throes of a divorce and dealing with issues regarding their child, Frankito, and their property. "There were a lot of waterworks making this record," Tré told *Rolling Stone*'s Matt Hendrickson. "I went through the worst time of my life."

Tré wasn't the only one going through emotional trauma. Mike's second marriage was also in trouble. The day they finished recording the album, Sarah finally left him. He described the divorce to Hendrickson as "a blessing but just an emotional drain," adding: "It was horrible and great. When we mastered the record, I cried through the entire thing."

There were also a lot of band problems over the next couple of years. However, the thought of post-9/11 America stayed in the back of Billie Joe's mind.

Cigarettes and Valentines

In the meantime, the band spent a good chunk of the summer of 2002 working on their relationships with each other and on *Cigarettes and Valentines.* They were recording punk polkas. They were doing incredibly nasty versions of Christmas carols. They were dabbling in non-Western sounds. They spent about four months doing this, getting the album to the point where the twenty songs were ready to be mastered. And then the album vanished into thin air, disappearing entirely from the recording studio. If the songs were stolen, as the band initially maintained, none of the material ever showed up on bootlegs or on the Web. If they were "mislaid," as Billie Joe

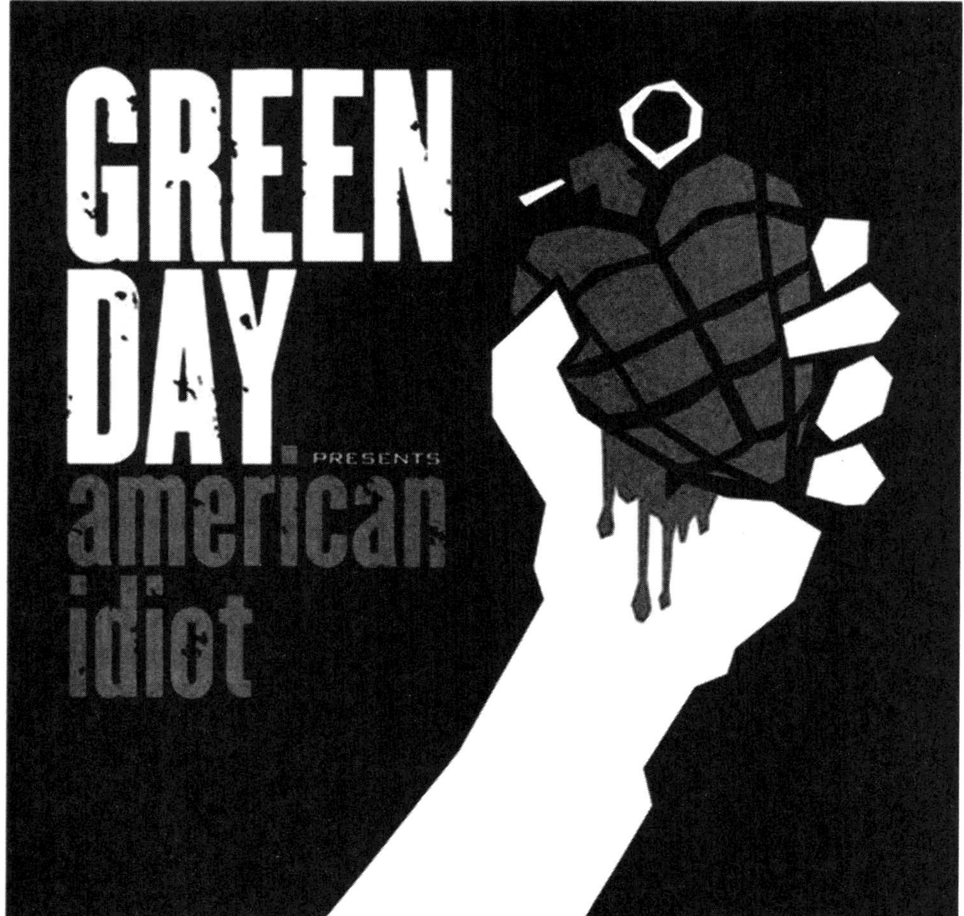

The heart-shaped hand grenade, launched at the Bush administration.

told *Q* magazine, no one ever found them. While Mike's assertion of them getting accidently deleted rings truer to the circumstances, it sounds more viable that they had problems with what they had recorded in the light of the band's decline. The key question was whether they wanted to do the same material over again. The answer was supplied in another question by producer Rob Cavallo: "Do you think that stuff was the best you can do?"

When this happened, Billie Joe bolted for New York City. "He was really questioning what he was doing," Adrienne told Hendrickson. "It was scary because where he had to go to get this record wasn't a place I'm sure I wanted him to be."

The way Mike described the situation to Jim Harrington of the relatively local paper the *San Jose Mercury News* probably rings truest. The stuff they had already recorded would have had them making another *Nimrod*, another *Warning*. When Cavallo asked his question, it was not over missing tapes but over the batch of completed songs. Then Billie Joe came back from New York with the song "American Idiot."

During the early part of the 2000s, there were a lot of things to reflect on: America's ongoing adventurism in Iraq and Afghanistan, the beginnings of the financial rumblings that would shake the country to its core, and just how the rest of the world was seeing Bush's America. One day, it all just tumbled out of Billie Joe. "I just felt this great sort of confusion," he told NPR's Terry Gross, adding that "[the song 'American Idiot'] wrote itself in probably 30 seconds."

Fun

"American Idiot" was so much better than what they had recently done that they shelved the previous project and started over. It took this blast to make Green Day realize that they wanted to do what their best music did, what *all* the best music does: they wanted to reflect their times in a heartfelt way and challenge perceptions. To *Goldmine*, John Lucasey—owner of 880 studios, where they did the *Cigarettes and Valentines* recordings and *Warning*—said: "They just looked at each other and said, 'Fuck it, we've got to do the album we want, and we've got to do it on our time. We're not in Hollywood, and people aren't gonna prod us anymore.' So all of a sudden they started having fun."

The first order of fun and therapy was to stop being Green Day for a little while. They invited some friends into the studio and cut a record of synth-heavy noo-wave as the Network, taking pseudonyms like the Snoo, Captain

Underpants, and Van Gough. They put out the record *Money Money 20/20* on Billie Joe's indie label, Adeline records, and set up a mock-acrimonious flame war between the Network and Green Day, though they did play a couple of shows together. They even went so far as to take video of a concert and put it out as a DVD.

Green Day also took a few days to cut a couple of tracks for one of their idols, Iggy Pop. He was recording *Skull Ring*, his version of a duets album with several different bands supplying the instrumental work, including the Stooges, the Trolls, Peaches, Sum 41, and Green Day. Billie Joe brought the song "Private Hell" to the session and cowrote the track "Supermarket" with Iggy.

"No Rules"

Once they purged their system, cleaning the bad taste of *Cigarettes and Valentines* out of their brains, they went back to just jamming and bouncing ideas off of each other. One day while they were hanging around in the studio, drum tech Kenny Butler challenged Mike to write a song. Mike brought the idea for a thirty-second-long song called "Nobody Likes You" into the studio when the band reconvened. This inspired Billie Joe and Tré to writer their own thirty-second-long songs.

During their therapy/mediation sessions, a lot of uncomfortable truths were told. One of them was Billie Joe's desire to write an epic like "Bohemian Rhapsody." He had once told the *Washington Post*'s Mark Jenkins, "I think we have a *Sandinista* in our future . . . or more likely a *Sgt. Pepper's* or a *Zen Arcade*." They stitched their thirty-second opuses together and came up with a piece that very nearly filled that description (though it was probably closer to the Who's pre-*Tommy* warm-up "A Quick One (While He's Away)" than the Queen song), which they called "Homecoming." This gave them the kernel of an idea. They continued working with the mantra "No Rules. Just have fun. Just write music."

"If I wanted to go in and write a rap song," Mike told Harrington, "if Tré wanted to write a polka melody, or I wanted to do an acoustic guitar thing, it didn't matter whether it was going on the record or not. It was just a matter of being creative and doing it."

Tré confirmed this, putting a message on the band's website saying, "We're practicing every day and we sound pretty good. We officially put up the list of songs for the new record now on the wall of our band space. It's sort of a tradition. We put up a list and we adds songs when we get them written."

"American Idiot" gave the band impetus. "Homecoming" gave the band a new way to put that impetus to work. Within a few months they had written close to three dozen songs. Then they noticed a thread between a lot of them. They put together thirteen of them that told a sort of story about alienation, a theme that they dealt with thoroughly on *Dookie*, but this was from a new viewpoint that had been shaped by more than a decade of personal experience. They were not the same people and not the same band.

Around the time of *Dookie*, Billie Joe told Peter Howell of the *Toronto Star*, "Kids don't have the patience to sit through a two-hour album of concept shit, big rock dinosaur cock rock stuff." Now they were making one, but it was still on their own terms, as he added: "Me, and Mike and Tré, we play music the way we like it, and that's what really matters. There's [sic] been a lot of good people that have grasped onto it." They could only hope that this would renew that grasp.

The process was similar for the even more epic "Jesus of Suburbia" (which was actually a lot closer to "Bohemian Rhapsody"). They once again generated a bunch of short songs that added to the developing concept of the album they were making. Then they worked on ways to make the songs cohesive. What didn't work was discarded. And the process pushed on.

Once they realized that they were working on a full-fledged rock opera, they started to check out predecessors. They listened to *The Rise and Fall of Ziggy Stardust and the Spiders from Mars*. They listened to *Tommy*. They were especially enthralled with *Quadrophenia*, which is perhaps why the only *American Idiot* character with an actual name—Jimmy—shares that name with the protagonist of the Who rock opera. They listened to *The Rocky Horror Picture Show* soundtrack. Even *West Side Story*. This would serve them well down the road.

In the Studio

They recorded between April 18, 2003, and March 26, 2004. They first demoed all the songs at Studio 880 in Oakland. To record the actual masters for the album, they went to Ocean Way Recording in Hollywood. Having set up the track order during the demo process, they recorded every song in the order in which it appears on the album, the better to tell the story.

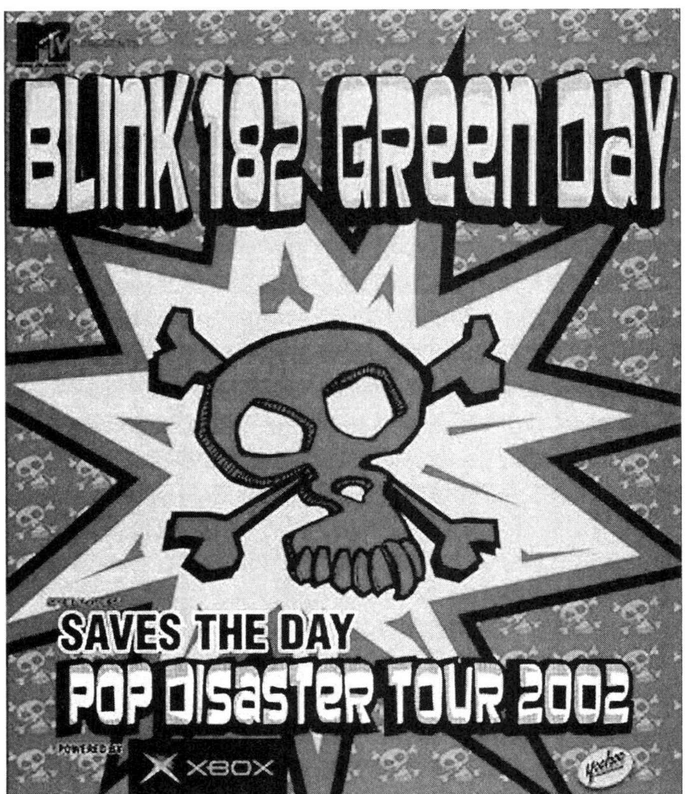

A greatest hits album under their belts, Green Day went on tour with their red-headed step-children, Blink-182, to win the next generation of fans.

"[We] made a record that had to be accepted as an album, not a bunch of singles," Tré told *Billboard*'s Melinda Newman.

Early on in Green Day's career, they would knock off a track in a day and an album in a couple of weeks, but the recording process for *American Idiot* was meticulous. Tré brought several different drum kits to the sessions and seventy-five different snare drums. They recorded the drum tracks to two-inch tape to make them consistently pop. Then they dubbed the parts over to the digital recording software to mix it. They recorded each song all the way through, adding all the overdub tracks and vocals before they moved on to the next.

Some of the experimentation from the jams and demoing carried through to the album. Tré played a tabla solo introduction to "Extraordinary Girl" (which was originally called "Radio Baghdad").

He had cut a sponsorship deal with Ludwig drums and brought in some of the more esoteric instruments that the company had given him access to, like a glockenspiel, a tympani, and tubular bells. For "Wake Me Up When September Ends," he rigged up a hi-hat stand with a shekere. Mike went after the kind of bass sound that John Entwistle got with the Who.

They opened up the band even more as well. Le Tigre lead singer and mastermind Kathleen Hanna, long one of Billie Joe's musical heroes, added vocals to "Letterbomb." Jason Freese added sax parts, and Rob Cavallo, a guitarist by trade, contributed some keyboards. Where *39/Smooth* had cost around $600 in the studio, *American Idiot* cost a thousand times as much.

Songs

American Idiot contains an hour's worth of music, more if you have one of the special editions. That alone was a new thing for Green Day. While *International Superhits!* clocked in at about an hour, every other record they made came in between thirty and forty-five minutes. "It still has the quality of a record like *Dookie* or *Nimrod*, where it's short-attention-span theater," Billie Joe told Glasgow's *Evening Times*' Vicky Davidson, "but we brought it up to a new level for us."

Toward the end of June, they gave the press a taste of what they were working on, sharing the nine-minute-long "Jesus of Suburbia." They also said that the project would be a punk rock opera. Many media outlets preceded the announcement with the words "no joke."

There was an edge Green Day had been honing for years; they were trying to transcend the adolescent goofiness of *Dookie* and be relevant to themselves if to no one else. Yet the previous couple of albums were pretty tame. The song "American Idiot" gave them a new direction and a new and pertinent way to explore their own current angst, which had little to do with getting high, masturbating, and boredom. "In every song I write," Billie Joe told NPR's Terry Gross, "the one thing I find is feeling lost and trying to find your way. I think 'American Idiot' is a series of questions. I think 'Holiday' is a series of questions. It's like you're trying to battle your way out of your own ignorance."

Some songs are flat-out calls for revolution, but it's never clear what kind of revolution they call for. "She's a Rebel" talks about the revolution as the dawning of our lives. It deals with alienation but in a far different way than *Dookie*. At that time, alienation meant getting stoned and numbing out (part of what "Give Me Novocain" deals with). "Boulevard of Broken Dreams" says a person can draw strength from alienation and loneliness.

But the political overtones of much of the album were unmistakable, and they drew people in. Enough people were tired of the wars, tired of the rich getting richer, and they responded to the messages of "Holiday" and "American Idiot." Green Day humanized these ideas, personalized them. "The political aspect of the album just sets the climate of the story," Tré told Mark Brown of the *Denver Rocky Mountain News*. "There are three voices on the record—the political voice and the interpersonal struggles and the choices the characters have to make. Even though people relate it to George Bush, it's just about the establishment."

With *American Idiot*, Green Day had alienated the other side of the spectrum. Even some fellow neo-punks complained that the album was un-American and capitalized on the basest feelings that Americans were having. But more people appreciated it. "They came out with this album that, in some people's eyes, could be anti-American with some of the lyrics, just because it's so political," a fan told Jay Cridlin of the *St. Petersburg Times*. "That's going back to their punk-rock roots."

People got so caught up in the lyrics that the major pop craft that went into the writing and recording of the album slipped their minds. And the skill that went into making the album was truly remarkable, creating a seamless amalgam of politics, polemics, and personal concerns. Yet the melodies and the band's playing propel the album, and these were so tight and so good that they set the lyrics off like bombs.

Then there was the elegiac ballad "Wake Me Up When September Ends." Where some people, given the context of so much of the material on the album, thought it was about post-9/11 America (and it is easy to read that into the song), it was far more personal than that. It took Billie Joe, the artist and songwriter, nearly two decades to process the death of his father so that he could finally have a cathartic creative moment. No one was more stunned by this than Billie Joe. It was the first time he put some of his feelings about his father's passing into art.

In his review of the album, the *Contra Costa Times*' Tony Hicks probably caught the core of the album best: "We hear a suburban kid becoming self-aware and going through the accompanying emotions. The storyline isn't so rare, but the broad context in modern terms is powerful . . . Green Day has gone from being ultimate goofball punkers to really caring about their world, and they've made their most important record to show it."

The Album

Ironically, for all the anti-establishment leanings of the band, the winter before *American Idiot* came out, Green Day caught considerable flak by recording a version of "I Fought the Law" by the Bobby Fuller Four (via the Clash) for a Super Bowl advertisement that promoted Apple's iTunes service. Many (often the same people who saw their signing to Reprise as abandoning their principals) called them out for being corporate sellouts.

Reprise released *American Idiot* on September 20, 2004. The band did four live shows surrounding the album's release, playing it through from end to end at Hollywood's Henry Fonda Music Box Theater, New York's Irving Plaza, Chicago's Vic Theater, and Toronto's Phoenix Concert Theater. The *Hollywood Reporter*'s Darryl Morden caught the show at the Fonda. He wrote: "It was everything great rock and roll can be: heroic and wary, surging with unabashedly grand melodies, piledriving beats and softer reflection. They charged with bravado and sang of regrets and second chances with that ultimate joy in giving the world a guitar-driven crash-and-bash raspberry and middle finger."

In addition to these dates, they played the *Late Show with David Letterman* and *Sessions at AOL* on the day of the album's release. Then they went to Europe and promoted the album on Germany's *Fritz Radio* and England's *Later with Jools Holland.* They flew from the Jools Holland show directly to New Orleans, where they opened a three-month-long tour of North America, segueing a week later into close to a month in Europe, coming back to the United States to attend the Grammy Awards and to film an episode of *VH1 Storytellers.* They then headed off to the Australian MTV Video Music Awards, which kicked off a tour of Australia and Japan.

In America, the album sold over a quarter of a million copies in its first week, despite being banned by Walmart. It entered the *Billboard* 200 as the band's first No. 1 album, which included being the biggest seller on the iTunes digital store that week. It would stay in the top 10 on the chart for over a year and remain in the top 200 for close to two years. It also opened at No. 1 in the United Kingdom, Ireland, Australia, Japan, and Canada. Reprise shipped 1.5 million copies of the album worldwide. It charted in twenty-seven countries, topping the charts in nineteen of them. It came in a variety of editions, including one in the form of a diary with pictures and bus tickets along with handwritten lyrics entered under various dates on which the "entry" happened.

The single "American Idiot" topped the Alternative charts, reached No. 5 on the Hot Single sales chart, Digital Track sales chart (topping the Canadian Digital songs chart), and Mainstream Rock charts. The song also entered at No. 61 on the *Billboard* Hot 100. The single sold a million copies and went Gold. "Boulevard of Broken Dreams" reached No. 2 on the Hot 100, and went to No. 1 on six radio charts, including the Mainstream Top 40, the Adult Top 40, Alternative, and Mainstream Rock. It eventually also went Gold. "Holiday" rose to No. 19 on the Hot 100, No. 13 on the Mainstream Top 40, and No. 5 on the Adult Top 40, and it sold over two million copies to go Platinum. "Wake Me Up When September Ends" charted as the No. 1 Rock Digital song, No. 2 on the Adult Top 40 and Alternative charts, No. 6 on the Hot 100, No. 4 on the Mainstream Top 40, and No. 12 on Mainstream Rock, and it also went Platinum. "Jesus of Suburbia" went to No. 27 on the Alternative chart.

All told, *American Idiot* sold over fifteen million copies worldwide.

There were several versions of *American Idiot*. The digital edition had four bonus tracks: "Too Much Too Soon," "Shoplifter," "Governator," and a music video of "Jesus of Suburbia." The Japanese release had one extra track called "Favorite Son" and also featured a bonus disk of a live concert.

The Critics

Salon.com's Charles Taylor got caught up in the album's political insurgency and muscular sound, writing, "Green Day played as if their music had the power to pick up Bush and Cheney by the throat and shake them lifeless." In *Rolling Stone*, John Colapinto wrote that the album "gives voice to the disenfranchised suburban underclass of Americans who feel wholly unrepresented by the current leadership of oilmen and Ivy Leaguers." The *Toronto Star*'s Ben Raynor called *American Idiot* "an instant apology to every nation perturbed by the actions of the Bush administration."

Kerrang! said: "[*American Idiot* is] thoroughly inventive and brilliantly articulate. The awful truth about troubled times from a band who know just *why* they did this and just what it's worth." *Pitchfork* stated, "Green Day's dissent and frustration has inspired a new strength of craft in them as well."

Newsweek's Lorraine Ali called it "one of the best rock albums and biggest surprises of the year—a punk-rock opera and one of the only mainstream offerings to really address the emotional, moral and political confusion of our times." She added that "the clowns got serious and no one could look away . . . somebody finally said something, and of all people, it was Green Day."

IGN.com's "JR" practically gushed: "You will emerge from your experience with *American Idiot* physically tired, emotionally drained and, quite possibly, changed forever . . . Nothing else comes close. *American Idiot* is flawless."

The *Village Voice*'s Robert Christgau, long an advocate of the band, only gave the album a C+ in his Consumer Guide column, noting that the lyrics were not polemic enough for him. He wrote they lacked "sociopolitical context . . . there's no economics, no race, hardly any compassion."

"We Are the Waiting" even wound up as a subject of a sermonette about the nature of faith in the *Presbyterian Record*, and surprisingly enough, writer Jean Morris found the track inspiring. She noted how appropriate it was that the album's liner notes indicate that the song takes place on Easter. "The song," she wrote, "holds the tension of question and proclamation."

Videos

The band made videos for nearly every song on the album, all directed by Sam Beyer. "American Idiot" was a live video shoot of the band playing in front of an extended American flag with green stripes that eventually run off and inundate the band. There is an air of discomfort, not just because of the green slime that covers the band, but also the changes of speed, sometimes centering on only one member as the other two play at regular speed.

"Boulevard of Broken Dreams" begins with the band's convertible breaking down. Over effects that make the video look like old film, the three members of the band walk with each other (as opposed to alone). The vultures, however, are a nice touch.

The video for "Wake Me Up When September Ends" proves that context is everything. *American Idiot* took Billie Joe's elegiac song about his father's death from cancer, the dynamics moving from sadness to anger. In the video, the song transforms into the main character's disappointment with the way his year has gone, cranking up the angst about what this might say about the rest of his life. Then director Sam Beyer turns it into a statement on military courage and domestic cowardice. After an impassioned, bucolic opening scene, Billie Joe sings as a guy (played by Jamie Bell) and his girlfriend (played by Evan Rachel Wood) go through the motions of a relationship. The guy sees—in true punk rock fashion—no future at home, deceives his girlfriend, joins the Marines, gets shipped off to Iraq, and never comes home. In a way, the video was prophetic as it marked the beginning of Bell and Wood's on-again/off-again relationship, which ended in several colorful breakups, a wedding, a son, and a divorce.

"Holiday" begins with planes flying in formation, and a bomb illustrated with the words "Green Day" gets dropped. (Perhaps it's the one that caused the mushroom cloud on the *Dookie* cover?) Then, it cuts to the band cruising in another convertible, going to a bar, dancing, and fighting. Tré puts on a dress, Billie Joe goes car surfing, and a lovely time is had by all.

The *Kerrang!* Award–winning video for "Jesus of Suburbia" starts with a scene similar to the opening scene of "Wake Me Up When September Ends," but it's urban instead of rural. As the band starts, it shows a guy (ostensibly the title character) having a debauched time in the dystopian area where he lives: having sex in the aisle of a 7-Eleven, writing graffiti, being with about half a dozen girls, fighting, drinking, trashing a bathroom, shoplifting, and many other pursuits. Eventually the bathroom gets painted and repaired. Jesus of Suburbia cuts his hand with a razor blade, leaves a handprint on the newly painted wall, and leaves his home.

"Saint Jimmy" was shot in stark, high-contrast, very stylized black and white. As the video is part concert video and part montage of backstage stuff, not a whole lot happens. The pyro looks cool in black and white, and there are shots of Billie Joe shooting a water rifle, inciting the audience, and flashing a moon. Good song, though.

While not shot in black and white, the desaturated color of the "She's a Rebel" video sometimes looks black and white. Shot mostly with a fish-eye lens, it follows a young woman on a train trip. When she is not on the train, she spends a lot of time on the street lighting cigarettes and other items, generating piles of spent matches. She's a rebel and she's got a thing for lighting matches. "Give Me Novocain" features the live band playing the song onstage (and features Jason White on electric guitar). Aside from some fooling around with the color saturation, it's pretty simple. "Whatsername" features—often in split screen—a woman with either pink or blue hair drinking, smacking some corrugated steel, and lip-synching (and playing air guitar) to the song. "Letter Bomb" is interesting in that it seems to cop clips from a dozen or so Green Day videos from their entire career, from "Longview" to "St. Jimmy" at random. There does not seem to be a video for either "Extraordinary Girl" or "We Are the Waiting." At least none I've ever seen.

"I think the reason why we've taken the steps we have is not just because you want to write music and make great records for the rest of your life," Billie Joe told *Alternative Press*, "but you want to be one of the best rock bands of all time." He defied the notion that Green Day had moved from punks to genre hoppers. The way he saw it, anything they did reflected taking Green Day to the max.

American Idiot brought Green Day back to the game in a big way. Unlike *Dookie*, which the band has still not outsold, *American Idiot* both defined and redefined the band's career. By extension, it helped to redefine modern-day rock.

Bullet in a Bible

Green Day Comes Alive

Right smack in the middle of the European leg of the *American Idiot* Tour, on June 18 and 19, 2005, Green Day played to the largest crowd they'd ever faced. Over the course of two days, they played to over 130,000 people at the National Bowl in Milton Keynes, England. The National Bowl is a huge venue, described as being the size of three football fields (not sure if that is American football or English football [a.k.a. soccer]). It has been called the biggest show in punk rock history.

Both shows were recorded for a live Green Day album (their first) and film. Producer Rob Cavallo and engineer Doug McKean oversaw the audio recording. Sam Beyer, who did all the other videos for *American Idiot*, directed the multi-camera video shoot.

The crowd was whipped into a frenzy by opening acts Hard-Fi, Jimmy Eat World, New Found Glory, and Taking Back Sunday. (The event started during the afternoon.) For most of those bands, it was by far the largest crowd they ever played to. But the crowd was obviously psyched for Green Day, from the first chord of "American Idiot" through the last moment of "Wake Me Up When September Ends." Beyer described the scene to MTV News, saying: "65,000 kids and the kids all know the words and are crying and got their lighters in the air. That was pretty amazing. When I watch it I still get goose bumps."

The audio recording of the album *Bullet in a Bible* runs a bit over an hour, with fourteen tracks. The album was packaged with a DVD copy of the film. Half of the songs come from *American Idiot*:

- "American Idiot"
- "Jesus of Suburbia"
- "Holiday"
- "We Are the Waiting"
- "St. Jimmy"

The first official live Green Day album (and film), recorded over two days to audiences of 65,000 at the Milton Keynes National Bowl.

- "Wake Me Up When September Ends"
- "Boulevard of Broken Dreams"

The rest are the hits they can't *not* play:

- "Longview"
- "Hitchin' a Ride"
- "Brain Stew"
- "Basket Case"
- "King for a Day" (with "Shout" and "Always Look on the Bright Side of Life")
- "Minority"
- "Good Riddance (Time of Your Life)"

Songs that they played that didn't make it onto the album:

- "Jaded"
- "Knowledge" (played by audience members)
- "Maria"
- "Homecoming"
- "We Are the Champions"

Bullet in a Bible was Green Day's first sanctioned live album for Reprise. It was released on November 15, 2005, a little more than a year after *American Idiot*, which was still on the charts. It peaked on the *Billboard* 200 at No. 8, and spent fourteen weeks on the chart. In the United Kingdom, it hit No. 6, a favorite of the home crowd. It was also in the top 10 in Australia, Austria, Germany, Italy, New Zealand, Portugal, and Sweden. Reprise released the audio portion of the *Bullet in a Bible* as a double album a bit less than four years later as part of a program to reissue (or put out first versions of) every Green Day album on vinyl.

Stephen Thomas Erlewine wrote on Allmusic.com, "[This] is Green Day, the arena punk pros, who know how to fill a stadium while sounding as if they're playing in a packed little club . . . a testimonial to the band at its peak."

Clashmusic.com referred to the live performance as "possibly the band's defining moment."

One of the dissenting voices on the album was the Killers' Brandon Flowers. He had previously called *American Idiot* opportunistic, and called the band out for the title track's "calculated anti-Americanism." He once again took issue with the version of "American Idiot" on the live album being sung by 65,000 British people. "I saw it as a very negative thing towards Americans," he said to *NME*. "I was really offended." Of course he went on to say that the forthcoming Killers album was far superior in its portrayal of America, hoping it came "from a more positive place."

21st Century Breakdown

Panic and Promise and Prosperity

As they did with *Dookie* in 1995, Green Day faced the daunting task of following up a monster hit album, an album that more than one person suggested was one of the most important rock records ever made. "When we started working on *21st Century Breakdown*, we knew that there was pressure, but to me that was something we embraced and used to our advantage," Billie Joe told Ryan Bird of England's *Rock Sound* magazine. "[It] was like, 'okay, let's make an even bigger and better album and let's take it as far as we can.'"

"We were arrogant enough to think we were going to outdo *American Idiot*," he added in *Guitar World*, "and we were completely humbled by the process of trying."

There was an interesting trend in how Green Day released their major label original albums (as opposed to compilations and live albums): There was a year between *Dookie* and *Insomniac*. Two years separated *Insomniac* from *Nimrod*. Three years passed between *Nimrod* and *Warning*. And four years separated *Warning* and *American Idiot*. A little less than five years passed between *American Idiot* and *21st Century Breakdown*.

Not that they waited that long to get started. They began writing in 2006 after taking time off in the wake of the grueling *American Idiot* tour. That year Billie Joe played a couple of shows by himself, and the band only played one show that year, all of which were interesting in their own right:

- In May, Billie Joe played a tribute to Elvis Costello, videoed for VH1's *Decades of Rock* at the Taj Mahal Casino in Atlantic City, New Jersey. Like the other acts involved—Death Cab for Cutie and Fiona Apple—he played several of Elvis's songs and several of his own songs, some with Elvis and the Imposters, and he performed on nine tunes all told.

- On September 25, the group teamed up with U2 to play "The Saints Are Coming," a 1978 UK hit for the Scottish punk band the Skids, before the New Orleans' Saints home opener at the recently refurbished Superdome. The stadium, like most of the city, had sustained severe damage due to the ravages of Hurricane Katrina when it passed through a year earlier. In a pre-game show, they also played "Wake Me Up When September Ends," "House of the Rising Sun," and U2's "It's a Beautiful Day," joined by a couple of social and pleasure club brass bands on the latter. Bono and Billie Joe modified the lyrics of all the songs to fit the event.
- Finally, on December 9, Billie Joe went to Hawaii and performed with U2 on the final show of their *Vertigo* Tour.

Green Day also contributed to another recording geared to charity—*Instant Karma: The Amnesty International Campaign to Save Darfur*, an album of John Lennon covers. The Lennon Estate (read: Yoko Ono) agreed to donate all publishing proceeds to Amnesty International. Green Day recorded a version of "Working Class Hero" that made it about halfway up the *Billboard* Hot 100 chart. It reflected their longtime self-image while being quite true to the original. The musical part of the video begins with Billie Joe on solo acoustic guitar before adding Tré, Mike, and finally Jason White, who had become a fixture in their live band and in the studio.

Yet another distraction was the stage musical being made from *American Idiot*. It had started percolating in 2008 when Broadway director Michael Mayer told *Variety* how much he loved the album, and he had a yen to put it onstage, but he was sure someone else was doing it. Broadway producer Tom Hulce (who played the title character in the film *Amadeus*) knew better and set up a meeting with Mayer and Green Day's people. From that time on, it was yet another thing for the band to be dealing with while making this incredibly hard record. Several *21st Century Breakdown* songs were added to the *American Idiot* mix for the show.

Making the Music

With the alternating current of making a follow-up to *American Idiot* and all the distractions that they dealt with in the process, it was fortunate, as Mike pointed out to KITS Radio's Madden, that the band "had the luxury of taking more time with the record." They took a number of roads to get there. One was trying an experiment in random genres. They tacked some drumheads on the wall of their rehearsal space, divided them into sections with a Sharpie and turned them into wheels of musical fortune with different genres in each section. "We would spin it," Tré told MTV News, "and it would say like, 'Death Metal, 60s Garage Psychedelic,' or whatever, and then we'd be forced to go in and write something with that."

They played with a lot of ideas. One was shooting an animated movie starring . . . Green Day. The album would be what they came up with as a soundtrack. This idea went by the boards. For one thing, it would be very expensive. Billie Joe told MTV News, "It was like, 'Let's keep moving forward and see where the music takes us.'"

"I think the first song I wrote was 'Mass Hysteria,'" he told *Guitar World*. That song would become part of the climactic track of the album's concept, "American Eulogy." He added: "Then 'Know Your Enemy' came up a couple of songs later. So by that point you think, 'Okay, now I know where this is going,' and you start to follow the narrative, musically and lyrically."

By the time they began to workshop their next album in the fall of 2007, Billie Joe said he had written forty-five songs, many of them on piano. As he had since *39/Smooth*, he wrote from the place he was at the time. He turned thirty-five during the process and was feeling his age. He commented on this several times over the course of the album, mentioning "the class of 2013," which would be graduating class for Joey, who was just starting high school when the album was being made. "Some days you feel younger than other days, and some days you feel older," he told Aaron Burgess of *Alternative Press*. "When I'm in a really creative mode, I feel ageless."

The process was intense, and the band was getting exasperated with it. They needed to blow off some steam. One way they did this was broadcasting their rehearsals on WCUF, their own pirate radio station. This entertained the odd commuter who stumbled onto it. When they cranked up the power, however, they blacked out their entire block. At that point they got a *billet-doux* from the FCC suggesting they terminate operations.

They also took a few months to let the music that they were working on age and, as they did with the Network during the creation of *American Idiot*, became another band. A website appeared for a group called the Foxboro Hot Tubs, a garage band with a singer that sounded suspiciously like Billie Joe. They recorded the album *Stop Drop and Roll!!!* on the Tascam eight-track unit they were using for their demos. "We took a sidestep," Billie Joe told Jaqui Swift of London's the *Sun*. "When you're being creative you take things so seriously. Going out as the Hot Tubs allowed us some fun."

On Billie Joe's songwriting demos, the vocals were mixed low, so while Mike and Tré could discern melody, they couldn't quite make out the words.

It was over a year into the process, during a working vacation in Costa Mesa, before he read the lyrics to them in the order that he thought they should be played. Mike told *Billboard*'s Mitchell Peters, "We started looking at what was making sense, and seeing the correlations from song to song, and what songs were naturally making different chapters of this record."

In the Studios

Of course, all of this was behind the scenes, and aside from the aforementioned forays into the public eye, very few outside their circle had any idea what was going on the with band. *American Idiot* was already four years old when the band posted a video of them working with producer Butch Vig. Vig had produced Nirvana's breakthrough album *Nevermind* and the Smashing Pumpkins albums *Gish* and *Siamese Dream*, among dozens of others. He cut his teeth as a recording studio owner and drummer in local bands in and around Madison, Wisconsin. He was also an active musician, working with the band Garbage, though they were on hiatus at the time.

"When we began working together," Vig told *EQ*'s Ken Micallef, "the songs we were equally attracted to were called 'the beasts.' They were untamable—overly long or complicated with lots of ideas that weren't focused." Vig

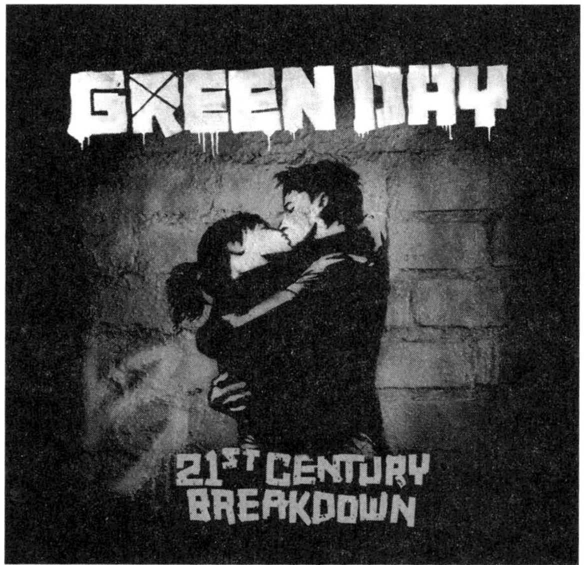

How do you follow up a second megahit? Shake things up a bit, like changing producers—enter Bruce Vig.

spent four months in pre-production with the band getting that material focused. They all took the disparate ideas that Billie Joe and the band had put together and rehearsed them until they were Green Day tight.

Vig pushed the band into places that were way out of their comfort zone, yet they still sounded like no one but Green Day. They recorded songs, and Vig would go through ways the songs could be better. The band would go away, implement the suggestions, and record them again. They did this for weeks on end.

"I am . . . allowing the process to happen naturally, without having to force it, and that is a *painstaking* process, let me tell you," Billie Joe told Burgess. "It's miserable. For a bunch of guys with ADHD, it's hard to have patience."

When they had put together a satisfactory set of demos, the band went to Ocean Way Studio in Los Angeles, the place where much of *American Idiot* was recorded, to make the actual album version of the songs and make it "sound gigantic." In addition to trying to up their game creatively, they goaded themselves musically. Billie added nearly an octave to his upper range. Mike told *Billboard*'s Mitchell Peters that *21st Century Breakdown* was "probably the most physical record we've ever done. It's physically hard to play." To which Tré added that playing the record buffed him up, saying: "[I have] new muscles on my arms that I don't know where the hell they came from."

As most bands do, Green Day prefer fans not knowing where they are at any given time, especially when they are recording. However, Antimusic.com wanted to know *whether* they were recording, so someone went to Ocean Way Studio. They found parking spaces reserved for Green Day, indicating that the band was, indeed, in. While they did not post this information in deference to the band, they did mention in January 2009 that the spots were no longer reserved, leading the site to announce that the recording was more than likely completed.

"I came into the studio at one point," Mike told the *New York Times*' Jon Parales, "and I went: 'It's been over three years.'" It had taken the band that long to make the album, including spending four months with Vig at Ocean Way, second- and third-guessing their decisions, and tinkering with the material. Eventually Vig convinced them that enough was enough. They had to let it go out into the world. Billie Joe equated the process to giving birth, and the separation with this musical child he and the band had spent three years gestating as postpartum depression.

"This album could have killed us," Billie Joe told Swift. "We all became sick as dogs," Tré added. "I was close to being hospitalized, but they caught me in time . . . When we started this I was walking pneumonia."

In February, Reprise brought in some higher echelon media outlets—like *Entertainment Weekly*, *Billboard*, and *Rolling Stone*—to hear a half dozen rough mixes and get people excited about the project. At this point "East Jesus Nowhere" was still called "March of the Dogs." By March 4, the title track had leaked on the Internet.

What they finally came up with was eighteen songs (including an *American Idiot*-like suite), arranged in three acts. While not so much a "rock opera"—like *American Idiot*, which told a story—*21st Century Breakdown* is more along the lines of a "concept album." "There isn't a linear story," Billie Joe told *Guitar World*. "I think the characters of Christian and Gloria reflect something about the songs—the symbolism of two people trying to live in this era. So it isn't all political; there are love songs in there, too."

In April 2009, Green Day did a set of half a dozen shows at venues in Oakland and across the bay in San Francisco, what Tré described to *Billboard*'s Mitchell Peters as a "guerrilla Bay Area Green Day assault." They spaced them out, doing a night at San Francisco's Independent, a night at the DNA Lounge, then a week later playing three shows at Oakland's Fox Theater, and finishing off at the Uptown, also in Oakland. Everyone in attendance got a program with the album's complete lyrics.

Since coming off the road from the *American Idiot* Tour, they had played a grand total of four shows, two of them involving little more than a few minutes of live performance: the show with U2 and the season-ending show of *American Idol*. "We've been deprived of playing live for so long . . . we were playing as if our lives depended on it," Billie Joe added to Peters. "It was kind of like playing your first show all over again."

Topping the Charts

21st Century Breakdown was finally released on May 15, 2009. It topped the *Billboard* 200 album chart in its first week in the United States and fifteen other countries. This was the best global chart showing of Green Day's career to that point. It was awarded a Platinum record on February 17, 2011, and worldwide the record sold 3.5 million copies. And this happened despite being banned by Walmart in the United States because of the "Parental Warning" Tippa Stickas. The massive retailer and Reprise asked the band to create a censored version, but the band refused. "There's

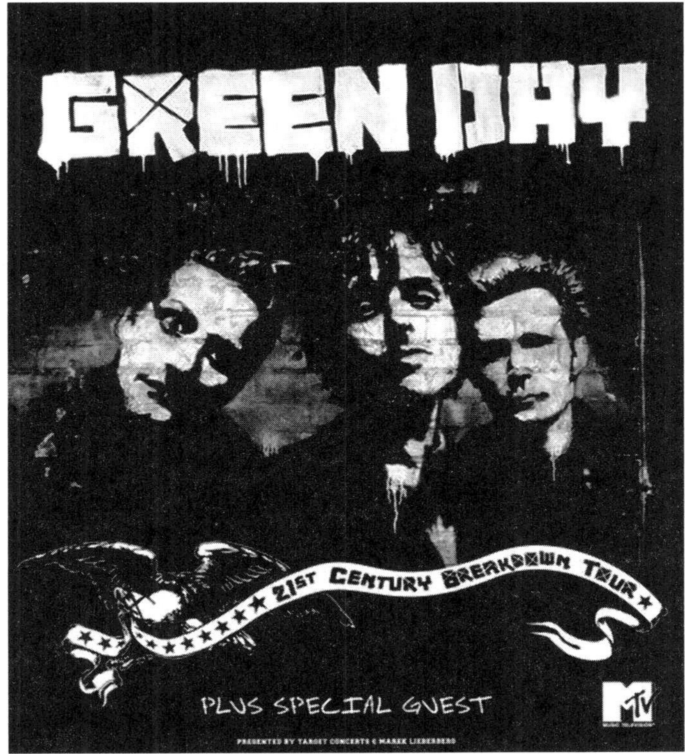

The band hit the road with a vengeance. Eighteen months, on and off, in a tour bus.

nothing dirty about our records," Billie Joe told the *Philadelphia Daily News'* Howard Gensler. "They want artists to censor their records in order to be carried there. We just said no. We've never done it before. You feel like you're in 1953 or something."

"If they think it's dangerous," he told photographer Bob Gruen, "why don't they just move it out of the record department and sell it over by the guns and knives and the other dangerous things they sell?"

A Canadian, however, could walk into any Walmart north of the border, from Vancouver to Prince Edward Island, and walk out with a copy of Green Day's album. "They're not governed by the religious right," Mike told the *National Post*'s Sandra Sperounes. "I don't think Canadians are so afraid of bad words and reality."

While Walmart found the disc too hot for its version of Middle America, the competition—in this case Target—put out a special "chain only" version with two discs, one containing a live concert from Japan. A CD/DVD edition had videos of "Know Your Enemy," "21 Guns," and the title track. A very special edition came with a hardback book containing the disc and handwritten lyrics, though it was not quite as elaborate as *American Idiot*'s diary.

There were lots of extra tracks and non-album B-sides, depending on where you bought the album or single. Some had a version of the Who's proto-rock opera "A Quick One (While He's Away)." Others included extra tracks like Bob Dylan's "Like a Rolling Stone," or Elvis's (through Arthur "Big Boy" Crudup) "That's All Right." There was also the original track "Lights Out." Even without the extras, the album ran almost seventy minutes long.

Set in Detroit, the story (such as it is) follows Christian and Gloria as they deal with the refuse left behind by George W. Bush's presidency. Billie Joe described it to Neala Johnson of Australia's *Courier Mail* as "the aftermath, the end of an era, and a portrait, snapshot, of the rubble around us." Christian and Gloria represent many of the dualities of Billie Joe's nature. Gloria fights for her beliefs; Christian wants to tear everything down.

Singles

The first *21st Century Breakdown* single, "Know Your Enemy," came out a month before the release date of the album, which was April 16, 2009. Billie Joe said the song is about liberation, particularly freeing your mind from the media, and warns against being "blinded by the lies in your eyes." It was initially recorded during the 2008 Republican National Convention, where the McCain/Palin ticket was given Frankensteinish life. The video for the song is largely a concert shoot, though it ends with an amazing image of the band on fire, perhaps a reference to the "girl on fire" in the second book of *The Hunger Games*, which was released the same year as the album. "Know Your Enemy" was used as the music leading into the 2009 NCAA Men's Basketball Championship.

"21 Guns" came out as a single on May 25, 2009, ten days after the album's release. The second single, this became one of Green Day's most popular songs, an acoustic verse with strings that transforms into an anti-war power ballad. The video features the band playing in a living room that gets slowly trashed by gunfire. Bullets demolish the room's couch (as opposed to the couch in "Longview" being demolished with a knife), sending feathers flying everywhere. It ends with the two non-band members in the video striking the pose of the lovers on the album's cover. The song features a shout-out to Paul McCartney in the lyric "When it's time to live and let die." "21 Guns" reached No. 22 on *Billboard*'s Hot 100 singles, topped out at No. 3 on the Alternative charts, and was nominated for two Grammy Awards.

The next single, "East Jesus Nowhere," came out on October 19, 2009. The song represents Billie Joe's agnostic, anti-organized-religion stance. The song was inspired by Bill Maher's film *Religulous* and the service for the baptism of a friend's baby. After hearing the song, the friend asked, "Was it really that bad?"

The theme of what the band sees as the hypocrisy of organized religion and its role in controlling the poor resonates throughout *21st Century Breakdown*. It starts with the names of the main characters, Christian and Gloria. Billie Joe says that he feels like he is a spiritual person and acknowledges a "higher power," but he sees organized religion as manipulative, citing holy wars that have raged over the last century, from Ireland to Iraq. "The hard part of it is when someone has blind faith," he added for Swift. "You can't reason with them and they don't even respect your opinion."

Needless to say, many church groups were less than thrilled and made that known on no uncertain terms. Tré shrugged it off to *Spin*: "We haven't been struck by lightning. No one has put any burning crosses on our lawns."

The title track came out as a single on December 21, 2009. It is a song about where Billie Joe came from and the fiscal challenges facing most Americans in the wake of the financial crisis that brought us the phrase "too big to fail." In true punk fashion, it glorifies the underdog. The video was shot in the stark, high-contrast black and white of "St. Jimmy." It features images of men kissing and businessmen giving a "Sieg Heil" salute, along with concert footage.

The final single from *21st Century Breakdown*, "Last of the American Girls," came out on March 22, 2010. It connects Hurricane Katrina with Adrienne—a "hurricane in the heart of devastation, she's a natural disaster." It captures her liberal politics, and Gloria's as well. The video has a furnished home in an open field, with three women going through the motions of the song. Again it ends with a trio framed in flames, in this case the three women.

The Other Songs

The minute-long a cappella opening track "Song of the Century" sounds like it might have come from one of the pirate radio broadcasts. "Before the

Lobotomy" bounces between being an acoustic ballad and a stadium rocker before making a brief return to the acoustic. The idea for this dynamic bit of rock came from a *San Francisco Chronicle* headline to an article about a guy who wrote a book about his lobotomy. His parents thought he was too hyperactive. It also has over tones of liquid idiocy: "Dumbing yourself down with drugs and alcohol." It captures a self-destructive streak that is Christian's tragic flaw, and by extension Billie Joe's. He described it to *Q* magazine as "a self-destruct button . . . this shiny red button that you just want to push."

If Green Day ever performed a love song, that song is "Last Night on Earth." Written for Adrienne, the track that might have been a John Lennon outtake from *Double Fantasy*. It was songs like this that made *21st Century Breakdown* Billie Joe's most personal album.

"The Static Age" is about the overload of input during the information age. "Murder City," a modern nickname for Detroit, played on its traditional role as the Motor City. The provisionally optimistic refrain of "desperate but not hopeless" reflects that; whereas "Know Your Enemy" was written during the Republican National Convention, this song was written after Obama took office.

"Peacemaker" would not sound out of place in a spaghetti western or Quentin Tarantino film, especially with its reprise of "Vendetta, Sweet Vendetta." Similarly, the drug-addled "*¿Viva La Gloria? (Little Girl)*" has Brecht and Weil overtones reminiscent of *Warning*'s "Misery." This is followed by another song about drugs, the piano-driven "Restless Heart Syndrome." If "Last Night on Earth" sounds like a Lennon outtake, "Restless Heart Syndrome" is evocative of George Harrison's work on the *White Album*. It relates to "Know Your Enemy," asserting that "You are your own worst enemy, know your enemy." We have seen the enemy, and it is us.

Billie Joe called "Christian's Inferno" diabolical, a song full of hate, and the most vicious song he had ever written. The song exposes an angry despair that Billie Joe acknowledges, and he feels a lot of people can relate to it.

The group listened to a lot of Bruce Springsteen while making *21st Century Breakdown*, and Mike remarked that the album was a rock opera or concept album in the same way *Born to Run* was. That, along with the fact that Billie Joe wrote a lot of it on the piano, is evident in "*¡Viva La Gloria!*" as the introduction recalls "Thunder Road" in so many ways. "American Eulogy," a medley of "Mass Hysteria" and "Modern World," ties up the loose ends of the concept; it reprises "Song of the Century," makes reference to "the class of 13" (Joey Armstrong's high school class), and gives Christian and Gloria a final shout out.

The last song on the album (unless you play it on shuffle), "See the Light," hopes that by getting through the record, the listener might try to find his or her own deeper meaning. Perhaps the simplest song in structure on the album, it doesn't even have a bridge, just a verse and chorus.

Promotion

Even before *21st Century Breakdown* hit the street, Green Day had hit the road. They shot promotional pieces through Germany, France, and England during the first weeks of May, playing the occasional concert because they knew they'd be there. They came back midway through the month to be in New York City on May 15, when the album hit. They played three songs on *Saturday Night Live*: "East Jesus Nowhere," "Know Your Enemy," and "21 Guns." That Monday night, they played "East Jesus Nowhere" on the *Late Show with David Letterman*, and then in the evening they did an intimate "secret" show at the Bowery Ballroom, where they played a dozen songs from the album pretty much in order. Then they did another eleven songs, including rarities like "Who Wrote Holden Caulfield?" and "Dominated Love Slave."

The next day they played a similar set at another "secret" show about a mile north at Webster Hall as part of Myspace (remember that?) Music's The List concerts. The night after, they played a shorter set a mile or so northeast of there at the P. C. Richard & Son Theater in Times Square. It may have

The tour took them all over the world, including their old pre-*Dookie* stomping grounds in Madrid.

seemed like they were biding their time for their appearances the night after on *The Colbert Report*, where they performed "Know Your Enemy." On May 22, they played for the *Good Morning America* Summer Concert Series at Central Park's Rumsey Playfield (home of Summerstage). They did an eight-song set, mostly of favorites like "Longview," "American Idiot," and "She," with only a trio of songs from the new album.

Next on the agenda were three days of promotion in Japan, where they played "Know Your Enemy" on both the MTV Video Music Awards Japan show and on *Music Station*.

They did a final flurry of American promotion, playing "Know Your Enemy" on *The Tonight Show with Conan O'Brien* on June 2 and doing an eight-song set (including two Foxboro Hot Tubs tunes) on *Last Call with Carson Daly* the next night. They took over the Fonda Theater again for a full show the night after that, and then on the next day they did a six-song set on the *Kevin and Bean Show* on KROQ. With some of the most extensive promotion of their career done, they took a month off and started touring in earnest that summer and through the winter.

The Critics

Of the new album, Whatculture.com's Jacob Trowbridge said: "[*21st Century Breakdown* is] the peculiar sound of a band simultaneously aiming for the sky and settling for a retread . . . It was like watching *Anchorman 2* . . . or pretty much any sequel to a cult comedy . . . you knew they were trying to give fans more of what they loved before, but in doing so, the final product felt hollow. *21st Century Breakdown* was simply too big for its britches." In *Rolling Stone*, David Fricke called the album "a compound bomb of classic-rock ecstasy, no-mercy punk assault and pop song wiles," adding, "It's like the Clash's *London Calling*, the Who's *Quadrophenia* and Hüsker Dü's *Zen Arcade* all compressed into 18 songs."

In England, the *Guardian* gave it 4 out of 5 stars, calling it an "apocalyptic protest album" that picked up where *American Idiot* left off and saying that it evoked the work of Bruce Springsteen and *Fight Club* author Chuck Palahniuk. The *Quietus's* Toby Cook wrote: "It's fair to say that Green Day have pushed themselves with *21st Century Breakdown*. If you'd been plagued by visions of some Warner exec waving a wad of dollar bills in their direction, shouting: 'Look, look, just re-hash *American Idiot* and all this can be yours!' thankfully, for the most part, you can rest reassured that Green Day ignored this temptation."

Jon Parales of the *New York Times* wrote: "At a time when younger punk-pop bands are singing about girl trouble and professional envy, Green Day has dared to offer something far denser and more demanding: a whirlwind of thoughts about activism, redemption and destruction . . . in songs where idealism and the urge to annihilate are constantly grappling, never far apart."

Billie Joe was more philosophical about the album. "[We're] perpetually dissatisfied whether it's with the world or home life or whatever," he told Johnson. "It doesn't mean we're negative, it's just we like to attack those things. If there's a challenge, we have a weapon called Green Day we can pull out."

American Idiot: The Original Broadway Cast Recording

Macy's Day Parade

Almost immediately after *21st Century Breakdown* came out, Green Day started working on a project that had sort of been in the back of their minds since the creation of *American Idiot*. They would often speak of the Original Cast Albums that they listened to as they contemplated their rock opera. They thought it would make an excellent movie.

It still might. Tom Hank's production company bought the rights, and at the time of this writing, it is in production at HBO. However, award-winning Broadway director Michael Mayer heard the promise of a visual presentation of the album onstage. The play *Green Day's American Idiot* opened initially on the band's home turf at the Berkeley Repertory Theater (a little less than three miles from 924 Gilman Street) on September 15, 2009. It was held over twice and then moved to Broadway, going into previews on March 24, 2010, and opening on April 20, 2010, at the St. James Theater, an appropriate place for St. Jimmy to take the stage.

> "*American Idiot* was always supposed to be a rock opera with different parts to it, and this takes it into a different dimension," Billie Joe told *Q*. "The characters I've always wanted to lay out are there, played by different people and sung in different voices. If you look at *American Idiot* as an opera, then that's what you're going to get."

Between the closing in Berkeley and the opening in New York, Green Day and the cast spent parts of November 2009 through January of 2010 in Electric Lady Studios on Eighth Street in Manhattan. This made the album

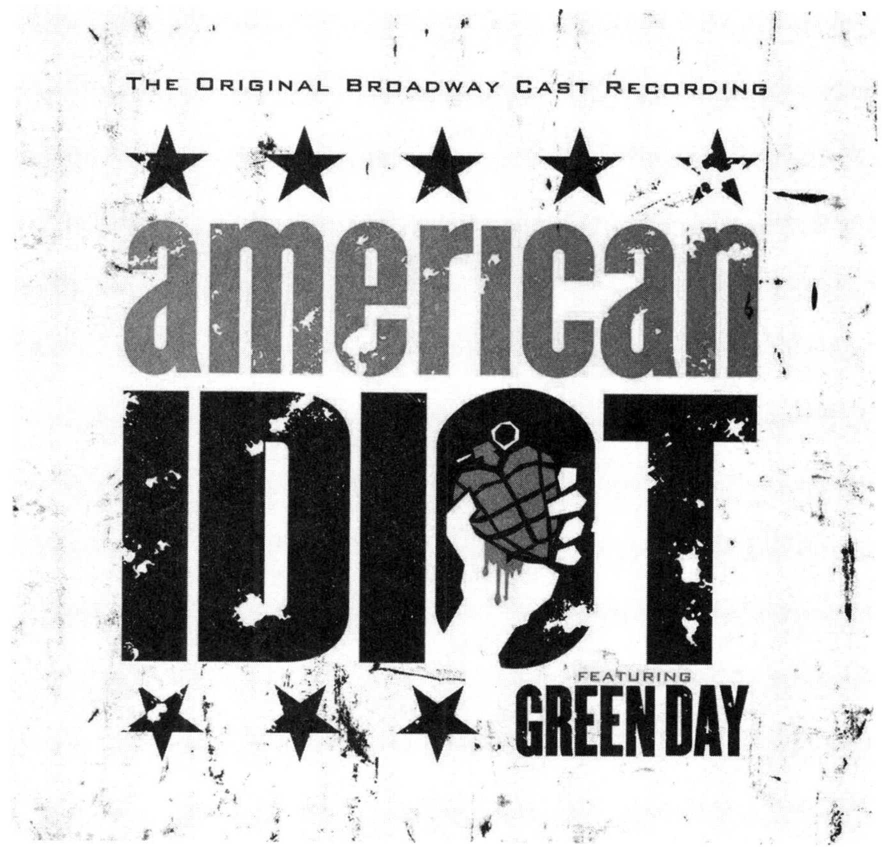

It is rare that you have a Grammy-winning rock band on an original Broadway show soundtrack, which helped this one win a Grammy of its own.

pretty unique, with the band responsible for the music supplying the backing tracks for the cast. Before the album's release, Reprise put out a single of the show's version of "21 Guns." The album came out the day the show opened at the St. James, though it had already been available digitally for a week via the MTV website.

It was a double album. With a running time of 82:10, this is effectively the audio portion of the entire play, as there was virtually no dialogue that was not sung. Later a single-CD version of the album, *American Idiot: Selections from the Original Broadway Cast Recording*, came out, featuring about half of the material from the show.

The full album rose to No. 43 on the *Billboard* 200, a respectable number for a modern Broadway cast album. It was the No. 1 cast album in America and a top 20 popular album in Austria.

The cast album was considerably different from the album on which it was based. For one thing, it had nearly twice as much music. The album included two versions of the previously unreleased song "When It's Time," one with the cast and one just featuring the band. It is compelling to hear other voices sing this music even as the band plays these familiar songs that they recorded, toured, and knew so well. The band played with the cast (then from the Berkeley version of the show) to open the 2010 Grammy Awards. Green Day even played a short set a couple of days after the show opened for a surprised audience. The original cast did not include Billie Joe playing St. Jimmy, though he did play the role on and off over the course of the Broadway show's official one-year-and-a-few-days run.

Critics

Stephen Thomas Erlewine rated the album 8 out of 10 on Allmusic.com, saying, "The original cast recording actually feels like rock and roll, no doubt because Green Day functioned as the house band . . . lending muscle so heavy it's disarming, particularly when it's paired with the cast's ready-for-stage vocals . . . there's never been a Broadway cast album that sounds as nasty as this."

Consequence of Sound reviewed the record, saying, "This recording of the cast from *American Idiot: The Musical* serves a dual purpose now, as both brilliant proof of the intensity and creativity behind Green Day's universally palatable subject matter on *Idiot* and *Breakdown*, and proof of a soundtrack that might as well be a tribute to Green Day on its own . . . To its credit however, at least it was done spectacularly well."

At the 2011 Grammy Awards, the musical beat such Broadway standard musicals as *Sondheim on Sondheim*, *A Little Night Music,* and *Promises, Promises*—as well as *Fela!*, the upstart Jay Z-produced tribute to Nigerian star Fela Anikulapo Kuti—for the Best Musical Show Album award.

36

Awesome as Fuck

Let's Go, Tokyo!

The *21st Century Breakdown* Tour took Green Day around the world, starting with forty dates through North America that culminated in an appearance playing "East Jesus Nowhere" at the North American edition of the MTV Music Awards. About a week later, they started twenty-eight dates over two months in Europe, including the MTV European Music Awards. They came back to America just in time to play "21 Guns" on the American Music Awards, took a week off, and spent a fortnight in the Antipodes. After spending the Winter Solstice holidays at home, they spent the last three weeks of January 2010 wending their way through Asia. On two nights, they played the Saitama Super Arena, filming both shows, not unlike what they did at Milton Keynes five years before.

They would spend considerably more time on the road that year, but they took the latter end of the winter and much of the spring off. A lot of that time was spent dealing with the Broadway version of *American Idiot*, including opening night, a short post-show set in April, and the Tony Awards in June (interrupting a jaunt through Europe).

Reprise suspected that there would be a lot of distractions like that before Green Day could pump out another studio opus, and so they put out an album of songs recorded throughout the tour called *Awesome as Fuck* (though the cover art read *Awesome as F**k*). Before the holiday season of 2005, there were no sanctioned live records by Green Day in their fifteen-year career; now, however, twenty-one years in, there would be a second. In a review in *Pop Matters*, Chris Conaton noted that the album had "a bit of the odor of a record company stop-gap about it." He was not too far off the mark.

The Music

The band started talking about it on the road during the summer of 2010. They announced it from the stage in the greater Denver area late in August. They tweeted a trailer for the film component of the two-disc set, saying: "We've been recording our live shows since the beginning of the tour. Live album coming. A ton of songs!"

And, indeed, the music on the sound recording came from all over the tour: seventeen songs from sixteen separate shows on four continents compiled onto one disc and the entire show from the Saitama show on the

Recorded live during sixteen separate concerts, culled from recordings of the entire *21st Century Breakdown* Tour.

other. While it featured five songs from *21st Century Breakdown* and three from *American Idiot, Awesome as Fuck* also marked the first appearance of the song "Cigarettes and Valentines," the title track from the mysterious disappearing record that led to *American Idiot.* It also featured some relatively deep cuts, like "Burnout," the *39/Smooth* tune "Going to Pasalacqua," and "Who Wrote Holden Caulfield."

On the other hand, only half a dozen songs on the video did not duplicate the audio disc. These included a Sweet Children tune, a cover of the Who's "My Generation," a couple of tunes from *21st Century Breakdown,* a couple from *American Idiot,* and "Welcome to Paradise." With a wild sax solo and huge rave up modulation, they turn "The Static Age" into something that sounds more like "Born to Run." The audience takes entire verses on "American Idiot" and "Good Riddance (Time of Your Life)."

The album came out on March 21, 2011. It was available to stream earlier exclusively on the *NME* website (do you know your *NME*?). The album topped the charts in Australia and Argentina, and it also topped the United Kingdom's Rock Albums chart (and was No. 14 on the Mainstream Albums chart). In the United States, *Awesome as Fuck* reached No. 14 on the *Billboard* 200 and No. 4 on both the *Billboard* Rock Albums chart and Alternative Albums chart.

Reviews

Allmusic.com's Stephen Thomas Erlewine gave the record three stars, writing that the album "satisfies without surprising . . . they hit their marks with enthusiasm, which is enough to make *Awesome as Fuck* fun, if not quite a live album for the ages." In a three-and-a-half star review in *Rolling Stone,* David Fricke called it "a contagious account of the power-fun streak that still runs through the band, even after two punk operas."

In a "C" appraisal in *Entertainment Weekly,* Greg Kot called the album "both a high-octane greatest hits collection and a not always flattering portrait of the band's evolution from bratty Northern California punks to stadium rock juggernaut."

¡Uno!, ¡Dos!, ¡Tré!

"No Direction"

When they were in the studio working on the *American Idiot Original Broadway Cast Recording*, Billie Joe told *Q* magazine that they were at work on a new project, only saying that the release date was "definitely not this year, probably not next." He called it unquestionably "Green Day, but with a touch of Foxboro Hot Tubs, too."

"We're always writing songs," he told MTV News, "But we don't know what, when or where a record's gonna come out. But a couple of years down the line, it's gonna get real serious."

Unlike many of their projects, which started after they took a break from touring, the trilogy started its life while they were on the road. They booked time in studios in Berlin, Stockholm, Scotland, and Amsterdam so they could get the songs down, however raw they might be. For one thing, it was therapeutic. They spent time in the recording studio rather than getting their drink on.

These were not whole songs; they were more like ideas for songs, with the band using the studio as a notepad. When Billie Joe took the role of St. Jimmy on Broadway for two months, he continued to do this. After spending his work time with all the creative people involved in putting on the musical, he took the inspiration back to his apartment and Portastudio, recording bits and pieces of songs before going off to the theater for another jolt of inspiration.

When he came back west, he presented nearly sixty songs to Mike, Tré, and Jason, who became a full-fledged member of the band. They started jamming every weekday. They really enjoyed it and it felt natural, while the hours made it also feel working class.

They continued to write and jam. Their intention was to create a single album of really great songs, but the ideas came at them like a stampede. "We'd be in New York and a song would happen," Billie Joe told *Rock Sound*'s

What is this madness? Green Day release three albums in four months. A record company's nightmare!

Ryan Bird. "We'd be at the beach and a song would happen. We'd be home in Oakland and a song would happen. It just didn't stop." "The quality of the songs was strong," Mike added, "and it kept getting stronger to the point where it seemed illogical not to do more than one record."

One thing they were bound and determined to avoid was polemic. It had been over a decade since they had released a non-political record, a record without an exterior plan and ulterior motive. Both of those records had taken a lot out of the band, and they wanted to get back to what they did when they wanted to have fun: play punk.

In the Studio

They started recording in earnest on Valentine's Day, 2012. They announced the occasion with a tweet: "Happy Valentine's day! Officially started recording the new record today. It's FUCK TIME!!!" Note the singular "new record." At this point they were still shooting for one album.

Longtime producer (and by this time Warner Bros. Records CEO) Rob Cavallo took some time off from his corner office to work with them at the band's Jingletown Studios in Oakland. Tom Kitt, who orchestrated *American Idiot* for Broadway, wrote several string arrangements. On June 26, they emerged from Jingletown with three albums worth of music.

It had started out as a single-album project, but it grew like kudzu. They shaved the seventy or so songs that they had arranged down to around thirty but still had others they wanted to work on. Mike told *Bass Player*'s E. E. Bradman: "Making one super-long record sounded stupid, and everyone's done double records. Billie came up with the idea of doing a trilogy, and I loved it."

Thus the recordings began in earnest. Working to get everything down in one take for the freshness and energy, one of the rooms of Jingletown (which they had renamed from Studio 808 when they bought it for their own private clubhouse/playpen) became Green Day's Jamatorium. There they rehearsed while engineer Chris Dugan recorded with just a couple of live, ambient mics.

A major change in the Green Day dynamic was Jason's presence in the studio. Whereas in the past every song with more than one guitar part was all Billie Joe, on the trilogy Jason became something of a musical wild card. "Each guy tracked a pass," Dugan told *EQ*'s Ken Micallef, "so we had two guitar parts by two different guys on every song. They each had different amps." Therefore, they each had a different sound.

Twenty songs into the project, they noticed that the albums had three separate paths: power pop songs about grabbing life by the balls; the soundtrack to that blowout party that is more fun than should be allowed by law while it's going on, but a terrible mistake in retrospect; and more reflective songs. When they had actually been programmed as three albums, Billie Joe broke them down as a record about getting the party started, a record of the party happening and the depths of hell in the party, and finally a record about cleaning up after the party, self-reflection, and the hangover.

All that woodshedding left them—in typical Green Day fashion—very well rehearsed. Ultimately, they wound up cutting three full albums' worth of songs in three months—not exactly the two days that *39/Smooth* took, but the stakes were far higher.

When they got out of the studio, they announced that they were releasing three albums of new music over the course of five months, between September and January. There was considerable incredulity over the idea. "People ask me all the time why we're putting out three records," he told *Rock Sound*'s Ryan Bird. "And the honest answer is I don't have a fucking clue! That's something I'm really enjoying. Right now we're embracing the chaos of being a rock and roll band."

However, he noted to Reprise that this all would count as one release. "There was no getting around that. That was fine." For the purposes of this book, that is how we will deal with them, as well.

The three albums were dubbed *¡Uno!*, *¡Dos!*, and *¡Tré!* (a long way to go for a pun). "I was in my kitchen," Billie Joe told Gallo, "and thought 'What if we called them "*Uno*," "*Dos*," and "*Tré*," just as a joke?' And I told my wife about it and she said, 'Actually, that's kind of a brilliant idea.'"

On June 21, 2012, the band gave the artwork its first exposure through a video on their YouTube channel. The covers featured a black and white graphic of each member over a swirling psychedelic background: Billie Joe was *¡Uno!*, Mike was *¡Dos!*, and, of course, Tré was *¡Tré!*. Putting each of their faces on the separate covers was Mike's inspiration, a riff on the KISS solo albums of the mid-seventies.

There was skepticism at the record company, but since the boss was producing and backing the project, they got behind it and figured out ways to promote it. Before releasing the trilogy, they did what had become a prerelease ritual with the band: they performed a series of intimate shows to see how the music played before a crowd, albeit a small friendly crowd. (Many of the tickets sold through their fan club.) "That was terrifying," Billie Joe told Gallo. "It reminded me of the times we played in front of crowds that had never heard us before—nothing was familiar . . . We were treating ourselves like we were a new band."

It's Fuck Time

The initial single from *¡Uno!*, "Oh Love," came out on July 16, 2012, topping the *Billboard* Rock Songs chart in the United States and becoming only the third song to debut at No. 1 on that chart. (The other two were Linkin Park's "The Catalyst" and the Foo Fighters' "Rope.") "Kill the DJ" came out as a single only in Europe and Oceania on August 14, 2012. The third single,

"Let Yourself Go," came out on September 5, reaching No. 2 on the UK Rock charts, but only rising to No. 17 on the *Billboard* Alternative chart and No. 29 on the Rock Songs chart. They played the song live on *Good Morning America* and the MTV Video Awards. "Nuclear Family," the album's final single, came out as a "stream it then buy it" deal on Spotify, while a video of the song, which featured the band playing in Jingletown, was available through Yahoo! and the Green Day Authority website.

All of this happened before Reprise released *¡Uno!* on September 21, 2012. It entered the *Billboard* Top 200 Albums and the UK Top Albums charts at No. 2 and made its Canadian debut at No. 3. In the United States and Canada, that was as high as it went. But it topped the UK Rock Album chart and the charts in Austria, Ecuador, Hungary, Italy, and Peru. In its first week out in the United States, it sold 139,000 copies, a little less than half of what *21st Century Breakdown* sold in its first week. The sales faded quickly after that. By 2016, it still had not sold the 500,000 copies it would take for a Gold record.

Even the band thought of "*¡Dos!* as the spawn of the Foxboro Hot Tubs, and they included the Green Day versions of the FBHT non-album songs "Fuck Time" and the album's only single, "Stray Heart," which played on the BBC and was initially released for streaming on the band's website on October 6, 2012. The Idiot Club announced a general call for fans to go to downtown LA if they wanted to be in the video for the song on October 19. It came out on November 7.

Reprise made the album available for streaming on *Rolling Stone*'s website on November 6, ahead of a general release date of November 12, 2012. "Stray Heart" came out as a single the same day, but only in Europe and Australia. The vinyl version of the album did not even have the single on it. The song was switched with "Drama Queen," which would appear on *¡Tré!*, as they realigned the digital versions of the release after LPs were mastered. *¡Dos!* topped the UK Rock Album chart but only hit No. 10 on the general UK Album chart. It peaked at No. 2 on the *Billboard* Rock Album and Alternative Album chart, while it climbed to No. 9 on the *Billboard* Top 200. This time, the unthinkable happened. For the first time since *Dookie*, the album sold less than 100,000 copies in the first week, clocking in at 69,000 copies. It, too, has failed to reach Gold status. (*Dookie* sold around 9,000 copies in the first week.) As opposed to *Dookie*, sales of the trilogy album decreased on a weekly basis.

The trilogy became part of a piece of daring TV on October 19, 2012. The soundtrack to the first half hour of the episode "Unspoken" from the

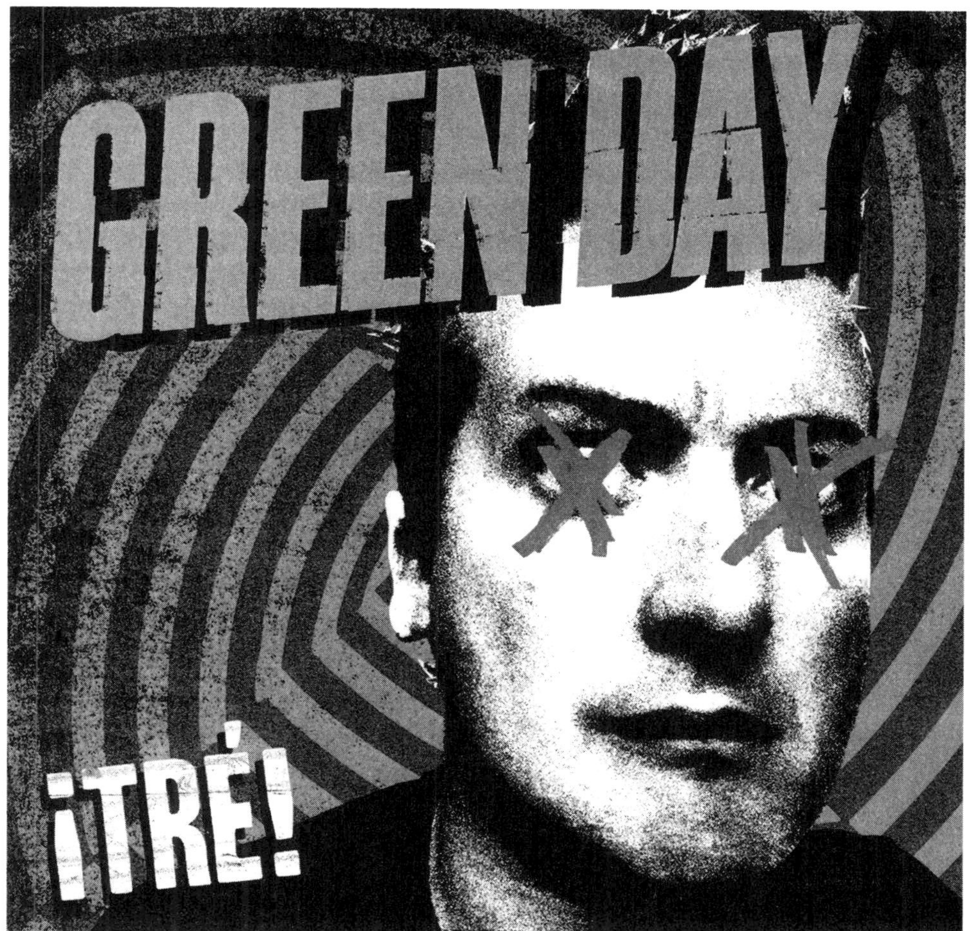

¡Tré! was released over the course of four days worldwide, during which Tré celebrated his fortieth birthday. "Do you have any idea how long I've waited for this? A whole album named after me! It's even got my face on it. How sweet is that?"

popular TV show *CSI: NY* consisted of songs from the trilogy: the *¡Uno!* track "Kill the DJ"; The *¡Dos!* songs "Stop When the Red Lights Flash," "Amy," and "Nightlife"; and the *¡Tré!* track "The Forgotten." The show was watched by almost ten million people that night and countless others in reruns. "Stop When the Red Lights Flash" also appeared on the video game *Need for Speed: Most Wanted* and its soundtrack album.

While the initial announcement about the trilogy said that *¡Tré!* would come out on January 15, 2013, the band's inability to tour and promote the recording due to Billie Joe's time in rehab led Reprise to reschedule the record so it could be available to holiday shoppers. They moved up the release date to December 7, 2012, (a day that will live in infamy?) in Australia, December 10 in the United Kingdom, and December 11 in the United States, two days after the eponymous Tré turned forty years old. "Do you have any idea how long I've waited for this?" Tré asked Bird. "A whole album named after me! It's even got my face on it. How sweet is that?"

The first single from *¡Tré!*, "The Forgotten" was initially released as a video on October 23, 2012. As the song was also part of the soundtrack to *The Twilight Saga: Breaking Dawn—Part 2*, which came out a couple of weeks later, that video featured images from the forthcoming film. The band said that they licensed the song to the movie enthusiastically, liking the idea of being a part of the *Twilight* pop culture phenomenon. "The Forgotten," another ballad, was driven by piano and strings. It did not chart in the United States, and neither did the second single, "X Kid." The band teased the song with a video of a cassette playing the song. The single was released on February 12, 2013, just about a year after the band began recording the project.

¡Tré! got as high as No. 3 on the *Billboard* Rock Albums chart and No. 2 on the Alternative Albums chart, hitting No. 13 on the Top 200 Albums chart. In the United Kingdom, it reached No. 2 on the Rock Albums chart and No. 31 on the Mainstream Albums chart. It's first week of sales were even lower than *¡Dos!*; it shifted only 58,000 copies.

There were contingencies at play other than Billie Joe's withdrawal from public life for rehab. *All* album sales had plummeted. However, that started around the time of *Nimrod*. Between 1997 and 2012, the total number of sales of sound recordings was down by 50 percent. Also, the trilogy was a tremendous amount of music for most people to digest. Then there was the format. True, Guns N' Roses were able to release two volumes of *Use Your Illusion*, both multi-Platinum albums, but they were released on the same day, giving listeners the choice of buying one of the albums, both, or neither. This was also at the early height of their fame. Triple albums were uncommon but not unheard of. The Clash had done it with *Sandinista*, though most people thought that triple album would have made a better double album. Bands like Magnetic Fields and artists like Joanna Newsome made relatively well-received triple albums, but they were marketed as three albums for the price of one. Making all that music available within a seventy-eight-day window was a sales disaster.

From a promotional point of view, seventy-eight days was little enough time to break music from one album onto the radio. By the time *¡Tré!* came around, there was only one out of the 1,200 surveyed alternate rock stations that was playing the single "The Forgotten," even with the *Twilight Saga* tie-in.

Songs

With all of that music, one of the things the trilogy mostly managed to avoid was the polemics of the last two studio albums. This was intentional. After the previous two studio albums, the band had become the musical equivalent of Bill Maher. They did not want to be cast that way. However, a couple of songs fell into that category, particularly "99 Revolutions," a tribute to the Occupy Movement. The song was featured in the 2012 Will Ferrell/Zach Galifianakis political spoof *The Candidate.*

The *¡Dos!* track "Nightlife" features female MC Lady Cobra over something resembling a hip-hop beat. Whereas Mike called the general studio vibe the band's *Exile on Main Street,* this song was more their take on "Miss You."

The last track of *¡Dos!,* "Amy," celebrated the life and death of singer Amy Winehouse. Billie Joe says it took him less than twenty minutes to write the song. "What she did," he added for Gallo, "her knowledge of old music and old Motown, it's something in the chain of music that is gone forever." Older soul music informed several pieces in the trilogy. With the piano and string section on *¡Tré!*'s "Brutal Love," Billie Joe was going for a sweeping feel inspired by Stax recordings of the sixties.

"A Little Boy Named Train" was based on Armstrong's life and also the story of one of his son's classmates, an intersex individual whose parents removed his penis at birth and who lived wanting to be acknowledged as a man. The parents were not sure how to raise the child and did not even give the child a name. It would change frequently. One of the names the person went by was Train. The song deals with not being one thing or another, being perpetually lost.

Billie Joe wrote *¡Tré!*'s second single, "X Kid," about the suicide of a friend of his two years earlier. The unnamed buddy had a severe case of the Peter Pan blues and refused to grow up, but that was an insight Billie Joe had after the tragedy. He reflected on how that was actually a part of his makeup that he had to come to grips with. Billie Joe had turned forty while making the record, and like so many Boomers and Xers, he had trouble with the idea of being a grown-up. He decided, however, that he could cop to not being a child any more either. X-Kid was the way he preferred to express his identity.

"Dirty Rotten Bastards" had its own agenda. Billie Joe envisioned it as "an arena song, then a sing along" in a similar vein to "Jesus of Suburbia."

Critical Reactions

Of the trilogy, *Rock Sound* claimed, "[It's] an eclectic blend of songs that are sometimes vast, often ambitious and at times startlingly urgent—it's an experience that quickly becomes intense in a very different, very exciting way."

Whatculture.com, in describing *¡Uno!*, said: "A hook heavy, uncomplicated collection of comfort rock with nothing to prove . . . That's not to suggest that there's any major regression in their musicianship. No, they sound tighter and more skillful than ever, displaying an attention to detail that eluded them in the early 90s . . . *¡Uno!* could be the most underrated Green Day album of all." The *New York Times*' Jon Caramanica wrote: " *¡Uno!* is Green Day at its most basic, yet somehow simpler. The snarling guitars of Mr. Armstrong are there, and the assured drumming of Tré Cool, too . . . Apart from vocal processing, many of these songs would have sounded fine on *Dookie*." In a four-star review of *¡Uno!*, *Rolling Stone*'s David Fricke wrote: "Every track is written like a single—the glam-jam jolt of 'Nuclear Family,' the Cheap Trick–style zoom and vocal sunshine of 'Fell for You'—then thrown at you like a grenade . . . After the *Quadrophenia*-like weight and worry of 2004's *American Idiot* and 2009's *21st Century Breakdown*, *¡Uno!* feels like plain relief."

Whatculture.com's take on *¡Dos!* was: "If you enjoyed Green Day's ultra-brief, 'secret' side project, Foxboro Hot Tubs, then this is the album for you. It's old-school, 50s inspired party rock. It's dirty in a way Green Day's never been before . . . *¡Dos!* sounds like the most fun these guys have had recording in a long time . . . [It] triumphantly unveils Green Day's covert garage rock tendencies and allows them to soar majestically."

Whatculture.com noted of *¡Tré!*: "By the time this third album rolls around, all the excitement has left, you're a little hung over from all the fun . . . *¡Tré!* is the sonic equivalent of a leftover, warm beer that someone at the party barely touched, and while you normally wouldn't let it go to waste . . . you've already drank 25 beers, and they were much more refreshing." The Associated Press's John Carucci called *¡Tré!* "a bit more diverse than the other [albums in the trilogy], with a slightly mellower and more mature

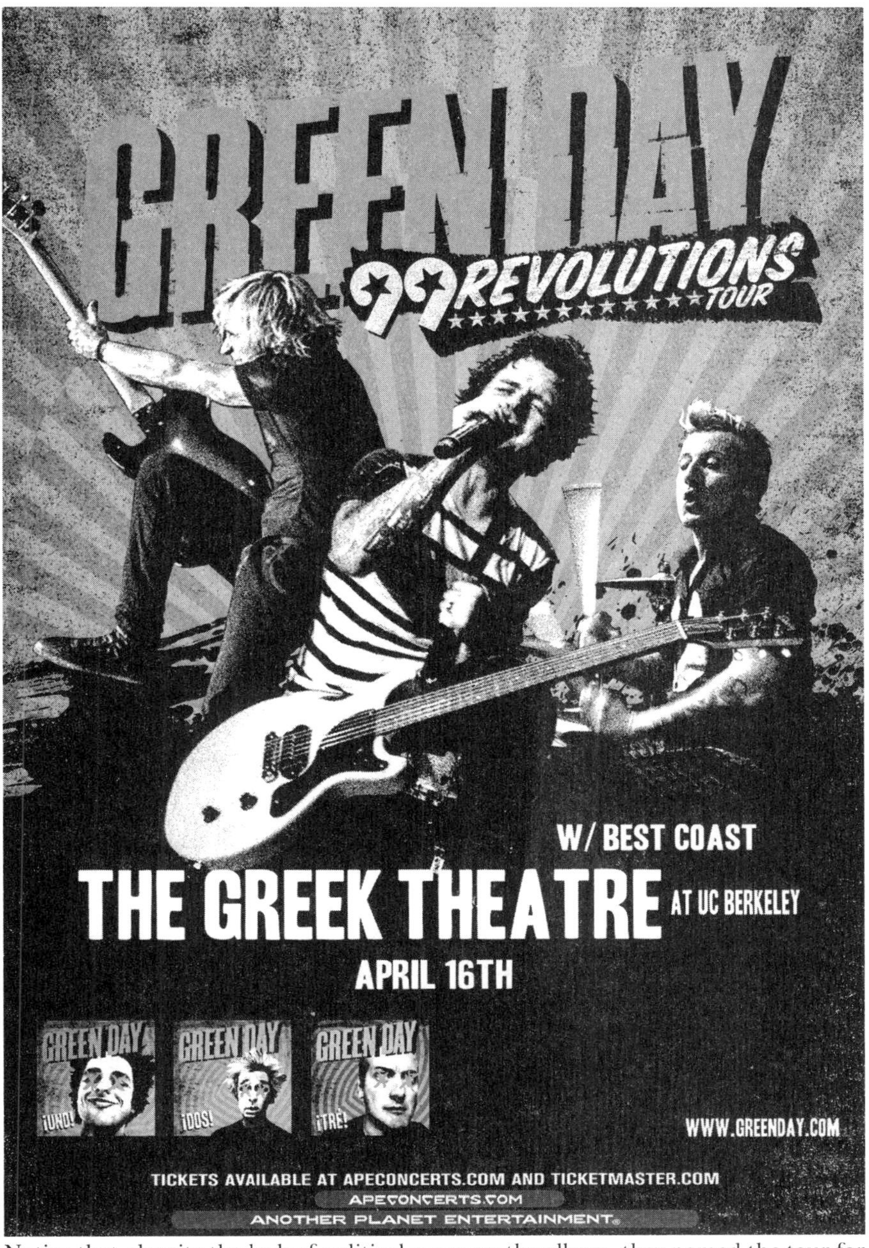

Notice that, despite the lack of political songs on the album, they named the tour for the one partisan song, which was inspired by Occupy Wall Street.

sound," adding, "Imagine 1997's *Nimrod*, but with more songs like 'Good Riddance (Time of Your Life).'"

In a three-and-a-half star review of ¡Dos!, *Rolling Stone's* Jon Dolan wrote: "Like *¡Uno!*, *¡Dos!* is full of . . . moments where the band follows lineal threads from *Dookie*-era punk into all manner of overheated angst—nervy-jam mod soul on 'Stray Heart,' Who-mad maximum R&B on 'Wow! That's Loud,' and even mascara-streaked soul balladry on the album-closing 'Amy,' where Billie Joe Armstrong makes like the skate-park Sam Cooke. Armstrong, Mike Dirnt and Tré Cool harness the sound of immolating, teenage-wasteland lust for an album with a distinct sense of life coming off the rails."

This of course was in reconsideration after Billie Joe's tirade at the iHeartRadio concert and subsequent journey into rehab. *Billboard*'s Gary Graff looked at *¡Dos!* that way as well, writing: "'Amy' closes the album as a stark guitar-and-voice piece . . . Given recent circumstances it's a sobering reminder of where Armstrong might have headed, giving *¡Dos!* some unintended gravitas . . . mostly a good time album with a few dark tinges."

In retrospect, *Billboard* said: "On their 2009 album, Green Day told their fans that 'Silence is the enemy against your urgency/So rally up the demons of your soul.' On *¡Dos!* Armstrong declares, 'It's fuck time!' on a song called 'Fuck Time.' That's a reductive juxtaposition, but it does demonstrate how committed the band is to reverting to the lusty nihilism of 1995's *Insomniac* on these full-lengths . . . eight years after harnessing their kinetic energy toward the highly entertaining melodrama of *American Idiot*, Green Day on *¡Uno!*, *¡Dos!* and *¡Tré!* sounds like a band that doesn't want to reenter the political realm but is unsure of what new realm to enter."

Aftermath

"Those records have absolutely no direction to them," Billie Joe admitted in retrospect to *Q* magazine. "It was about being prolific for the sake of it."

After a sobering year, Billie Joe decided that in hindsight "embracing the chaos of being a rock and roll band" might not have been the best way to go forward. He admitted that some of the music was forced and that it got to the point where they were a writing juggernaut, creating songs for the sake of creating songs. He liked a lot of it, and if he had it to do over again, he still probably would. "The intention was to make it more raw and off the cuff and the opposite happened, but I do like the songs," he added for Brian Hiatt in *Rolling Stone*. "I think it was a fun album to make."

To date, the trilogy albums are the only Green Day non-compilation albums not to go at least Gold in the United States—all the rest are Platinum. This means none of them have sold more than 500,000 copies yet. There was some arrogance (perhaps a lot of arrogance) and not a little hubris involved in the decision to release the music as a trilogy. "I'm not going to conform to some consumer speed," Billie Joe had told Gallo. "I believe people want to hear this kind of music, that people want to hear records that have a story . . . Or maybe they don't. I have no idea."

It turned out that, in that format at least, they didn't.

Demolicious

If We Were Still on Lookout! Records

Green Day have supported Record Store Day pretty much since it became a thing. Their special treats for the day had included the first copies of the vinyl reissue of *Dookie*, a cover of Hüsker Dü's "Don't Want to Know If You Are Lonely," and test pressings of *¡Uno!*. But for the event in 2014 they planned something special: a two-record set of the demos the band cut before making the actual *¡Uno!*, *¡Dos!*, and *¡Tré!* albums. The Record Store Day releases were available as two LPs on colored vinyl, a CD, and a cassette.

Called *Demolicious*, the album contained an acoustic version of the *¡Uno!* tune "Stay the Night," as well as the previously unreleased track "State of Shock." On its release, Mike posted on Instagram, "This is how *¡Uno!* *¡Dos!* and *¡Tré!* would have sounded if We Were Still On Lookout! Records I love it!!!!"

The cover art was done by Tom Neely, who is notable for his indie comic *Henry & Glenn Forever* and Image's *The Humans*, and illustrator Kristina Collantes.

The album hit No. 119 on the UK Albums chart and No. 112 on the *Billboard* 200.

Reviews

Fred Thomas of *All Music* wrote: "The recording quality of many of these 'demos' rivals the production on proper albums for many indie acts, and even sounds fuller at times than the low-budget early records of Green Day themselves . . . the tunes on *Demolicious* end up feeling more direct and more fun." In a three-star review, Yeow Kai Chai of Singapore's the *Straits Times* noted, "This butt-tight combo of frenetic drum-work, springy guitar riffs and that nasal whine . . . proves this is still what he and his band excel at."

The raw material for the trilogy. Perhaps they just should have released this.

Of course, arbiters of cred Punknews.org said: "Even for a demo album these tracks are over polished and over produced . . . do not expect this album to have the edge Green Day had back in the Lookout! Records days . . . *Demolicious* reinforces the notion that they are incredibly far away from being the great 924 Gilman band they once were and that they are a bloated, major label, power pop band, and have been for quite a while."

Revolution Radio

"Cherry Bombs and Gasoline"

The time after the trilogy's release was rife with all sorts of issues in the Green Day camp. Most obviously, there was Billie Joe's rehab, which had helped subvert anything like promotion for the trilogy. In 2014, breast cancer struck Mike's wife Brittney. Then Jason White—who had become a full band member for the *¡Uno!*, *¡Dos!*, and *¡Tré!* albums—came down with tonsil cancer. It took a full year for both of them to go into remission.

In the meantime, a recovered Billie Joe threw himself into projects to help fill his time off and to explore other areas of creativity. With Norah Jones, a woman with more Grammy Awards than even he had, he cut an album that was a track-for-track version of one of the Everly Brothers' less famous albums. Then he got called on to write the music for a play called *These Paper Bullets*. He had a major supporting role in one film, and finally, he had his first starring role in a feature film.

Back to Work

By the time everyone gathered for Green Day's April 15 induction into the Rock and Roll Hall of Fame, it seemed like high time to get back to work as Green Day. While in New York acting in the film that would become *Ordinary World*, Billie Joe found himself driving into Manhattan and ran smack into a Black Lives Matter demonstration that was protesting a Missouri grand jury not indicting police officer Darren Wilson for the slaying of teenager Michael Brown in Ferguson, Missouri. The demonstrators blocked the streets and backed up traffic for miles. Armstrong parked his car and joined the protest. "It was a trip to see people rebel against the old order," he told *Rolling Stone*. While he had kept the politics-to-other-stuff ratio down on *¡Uno!*, *¡Dos!*, and *¡Tré!*, there was still the song "99 Revolutions," inspired by the Occupy Movement. This feet-on-the-ground experience with Black

Lives Matter inspired him even more. It became the fodder for the title track of the group's next album, *Revolution Radio.* "[Suddenly] I had a couple of songs out of nowhere so that's just kind of the way it starts."

Billie Joe had recently built a new studio, which he called Otis, in Oakland. He went in and started playing (and recording) the guitar. The first thing that satisfied him was an early version of "Bang Bang." Then he came up with the song "Somewhere Now." He had already written a song for the movie he starred in. The film was originally called *Geezer,* but when it was released commercially, it was renamed after that song, "Ordinary World."

As opposed to the forced creation of *¡Uno!*, *¡Dos!* and *¡Tré!*, this time the approach in the studio was "the exact opposite and just sort of let life roll out and then see what happens," he told *Rolling Stone*'s Andy Greene.

After Green Day's induction into the Rock and Roll Hall of Fame in April of 2015, Billie Joe spoke with Greene about the event and the aftermath. Toward the end of the conversation, Greene reminded Billie Joe that it had been more than three years since the band had released new music (not counting the previously unreleased tracks, *Demolicious,* for Record Store Day). Billie Joe told Greene that he was actively writing for Green Day after working on a few side projects and had four or five songs that the band was excited about. "I'm gonna take it really slow," he said. "I'm gonna make sure every moment is inspired and that we have something that's really special to us."

After the problematic trilogy, that seemed prudent. Instead of drug-fueled writing for the sake of writing—a process that hurt some of the material, he admitted—they were reaching for quality content. "Fuck Time" was over.

"Let me tell you, they were just fantastic," Warner CEO and longtime frequent Green Day producer Rob Cavallo told *Rolling Stone.* "He is absolutely at the top of his game. Fans can be sure when they do return, the music will be amazing."

While they would claim that they worked on the album mostly in secret, in January 2016 they started to post pictures from the studio on Instagram. In one, Billie Joe was standing behind a microphone in the studio. Another was a Billie Joe selfie with producer and Black Eyed Peas leader will.i.am (both sporting impressive stubble). This led Fuse's Jason Lipschitz to wonder if it was the end of pop punk and the beginning of Elepunk.

So, it was not a secret that a new album would be coming; just when it would come and what it would be were a mystery. In April, a fan ran into

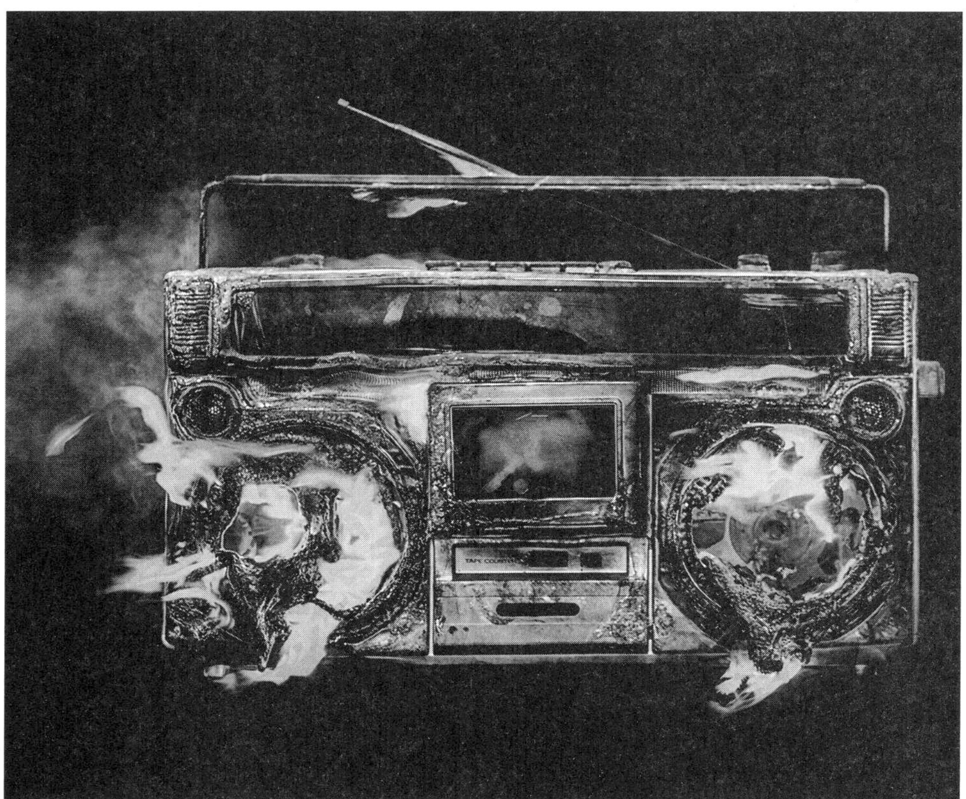

The idea started with a Black Lives Matter march that shut down the Brooklyn Bridge when Billie Joe was trying to cross it. "It was a trip to see people rebel against the old order."

Billie Joe in Oakland and asked whether Green Day were recording. Billie Joe said yes (as if the Instragram posts weren't evidence enough) and that he hoped it would come out in the fall. This was duly reported to the Green Day Community forum. *Newsweek* got wind of this and put in a call to the group's publicist, Brian Bumbery of BB Gun PR. He confirmed that they were in the studio but would not give a date. The whole process took about six months, with the band going into the studio from noon to 5:00 p.m. each day.

The band produced the album themselves, which was the first time they did that since *Warning*. "Let's get in there, the three of us with our engineer Chris Dugan and just do this ourselves," Billie Joe told Greene about deciding to self-produce. "This time I just wanted to feel the freedom of just depending on ourselves and getting in a room. There's no in-between person and we're forced to sort of be in there with each other."

One of the things the layoff allowed for was some woodshedding. Mike did something he had never done in a quarter century as a musician—he took some lessons. "Tré's drumming on this record is I think the best he's ever done," Billie Joe told *Rolling Stone*. "I could say the same for Mike's bass playing . . . it was really great to see how he sort of flourished on those bass lines." Tré remarked that it was the first time since *Dookie* that he tuned his own drums, a job that he tended to leave to his drum techs in the studio and onstage. "It was cool," he told *Kerrang!*. "It was hands on."

Songs

"We were trying to make the music and voices in Billie's head come to life," Tré added for *Entertainment Weekly*. "We didn't tell anybody that we were recording, except our wives. We gave ourselves time and we weren't watching the clock. That took the pressure off."

The first song they worked on was "Somewhere Now." As Mike recalled it to *Kerrang!*'s Ian Woodward, "When Billie Joe wrote it, from that point on it started to feel like the beginning of a record."

Billie Joe took this as his cue to be adventurous as well. Ripping a page out of the Jimmy Page guitar style guide, he started playing with a bow. It comes up on the songs "Outlaws" and "Forever Now."

In early August, the buzz got louder. Buffalo on-air personality Nik Rivers heard the first single release from the new Green Day album, "Bang Bang," at Lollapalooza in Chicago and reported back, "So, if you are a fan of the early, punky Green Day, you will love the new song . . . think *Dookie*, but not 'When I Come Around' *Dookie*, but more 'Welcome to Paradise,' 'Burnout' & 'Chump' *Dookie*."

By the time *Revolution Radio* hit the racks, download sites, and streaming services on October 7, 2016, Green Day had made three songs public: "Bang Bang" came out on August 11, the title track on September 6, and "Still Breathing" came out on September 23. Among other things, those songs coming out before the late-September deadline made them eligible for the 2017 Grammy Awards. Even if the releases did not garner the group nominations, it might lead to an appearance on the televised show. "Still Breathing" came out just a day before the September 24 cutoff date, exactly two weeks before the album hit. The song seemed to reflect all the trials and tribulations the band and their families had been through since the trilogy tanked. "We had to take a collective deep breath and look out for each other," Billie Joe told *USA Today*'s Patrick Ryan.

Before the release, the group announced a series of small shows in big cities, including a performance at the Hockey World Cup in Toronto, which they ultimately had to cancel due to a virulent flu that seemed to affect everyone in the Green Day camp. On the ticket resale market, tickets for the group's concert at New York's Webster Hall *averaged* $775 for a ducat with a face value of $20.

The title track, "Revolution Radio"—as previously mentioned—germinated in a New York City Black Lives Matter demonstration. In an A-review of the song, Eric Renner Brown wrote that the song was loaded with "high-octane riffs and deceptively catchy melodies," commenting also on the refrain of "legalize the truth," a running theme of *21st Century Breakdown*. Mike called it "the perfect title track" when talking to *Kerrang!*'s Ian Winwood. *Entertainment Weekly*'s Eric Renner Brown agreed, saying the song secured their reputation as "one of the most incendiary bands in the game."

In 2001, a mugger held Billie Joe up at gunpoint. Since then, he has developed a visceral fear of guns. This certainly is reflected in "Bang Bang," a song that captures the cultural madness of the mass shootings that seem to happen every week in the United States in the era of Facebook and Twitter. "There's a lot of rage happening," he told *Rolling Stone*. "To get into the brain of someone like that was freaky . . . After I wrote it, all I wanted to do was get that out of my brain because it just freaked me out."

"The song is dangerous," Tré told *Entertainment Weekly*, "and it captures the spirit of the new record." BCheights.com observed, "'Bang Bang' exists as the bastard child of 90s Green Day sound and the 2000s Green Day lyrics, a combination of the thing that originally gave it success and the thing that made it famous once again."

Billie Joe wrote the song shortly after Roger Elliot went on a shooting spree in Isla Vista, California, about 300 miles south of Oakland, close enough for Billie Joe to find the whole thing especially troubling yet also intriguing, especially the shooter's use of social media to publish his memoir/manifesto.

Another song on the album, "Troubled Times," deals with the Paris attack on November 13, 2015, when terrorists bombed restaurants and a stadium, and shot up a concert hall where Eagles of Death Metal were playing a show. All told, 130 died during the night of terror, and hundreds more were wounded. "A friend of ours, Eden Galindo, is the guitarist of Eagles of Death Metal," Billie Joe told *Q* magazine. "I don't think terrorism hit home right in our backyard the way it did that night." Initially he didn't want to put the song on the new album, as it was so personal, but the subsequent gunning down of forty-nine people at an Orlando, Florida, gay nightclub in June of 2016 spurred him to release it.

One of the most personal songs on the album, "Still Breathing," is informed by all the health predicaments among Green Day's members, friends, and family. It takes on the universal aspects of well-being, or the lack of it. Billie Joe told himself all he needed to do was be honest, be himself, and keep it simple. "In doing that," he said on a Rollingstone.com podcast, "I sort of uncovered a lot about myself, and I think what other people go through with losing something but feeling like you gained something."

Again, he was reticent about the song. He felt that capitalizing on a friend's tribulations would be shallow and even a bit tawdry. In the end, the band decided that it was too good a song not to go with. "I hope it makes people happy and creates a difference in some way," he told *Rolling Stone*, "just by people recognizing themselves in the song." Tré added for *Entertainment Weekly*, "All those health issues are behind us. We're going into this record cycle with a lot of gratitude, a lot of humility."

Billie Joe is apt to introduce the song live and say, "The great thing about survival mode is that you survived. This song is for you." It may be one of the best, most touching songs Green Day has ever done. As MTV News remarked, "Just surviving whatever life throws at you is pretty punk rock."

Similarly, the album opener "Somewhere Now" has overtones of the aftermath of rehab. "How did life on the wild side get so dull," the song asks. What happens when the wild side is out to kill you? How do you reprogram yourself to deal with that wild side? "How do you deal with dealing with yourself," Armstrong told *Rolling Stone*. "Before it was, I'll have a beer. Now, you have to sort of learn how to breathe a little bit more. I have never been good at boredom. I never know what to do when it's, like, you and you're alone with yourself."

Billie Joe was keen to point out that most of the album was written before the presidential races heated up. Some of the songs might sound prescient, but unlike *American Idiot*, which wanted to oust a sitting president, the expanded and exploded rhetoric of *Revolution Radio* had no such lofty ideals. "Bang Bang" and "Say Goodbye" were not intended so much as songs that spoke truth to power as songs that spoke to the upsetting events at the time. As time went on, however, these songs began to seem almost prescient of the events that would happen a year after they were written. "This is the first time that an election has preyed on fear and anger," Billie Joe said to *Rolling Stone*. "Everybody's freaked out."

Tré agreed in *Entertainment Weekly*, saying, "I wish we could take credit for being supergeniuses and having crystal balls, but our balls are normal, like everyone else's."

The band's blue-collar roots are dealt with in the song "Too Dumb to Die," about living a totally working-class life, from womb to tomb, being constantly scared of the future, and numbing that fear by drinking or smoking pot or any of a thousand other chemical vices. However, it also was another song informed by memories of his father, a union truck driver whom he recalled spending a lot of time on picket lines with the Teamsters. They were memories that made Billie Joe proud.

The song "Youngblood" was about his relationship with Adrienne. "I've written songs about her before, but they kind of always come out by accident," he told Winwood. "It's weird, because when I try to write something about her, or for her, it never works out." However, he added for *Rolling Stone*, "She's easy to write about because she's so awesome."

In all, he noted, as he had when they released *American Idiot*, that this album was also about feeling lost amid the chaos of everyday life. It is the major running thread through the entire Green Day discography.

The Media

Very shortly after the release, the band appeared on Howard Stern's show. They had a good time, and Stern allowed them to play four songs. The lead single, "Bang Bang," was the most added song at Alternative and Active rock radio stations across America the week it came out. It became the group's fourth song to top the *Billboard* Mainstream Rock Songs chart, going from No. 5 to No. 1 in its third week on the chart, a feat previously achieved by only two other bands: the Foo Fighters and Metallica. Interestingly, there were no Mainstream Rock No. 1s on *Dookie*. In fact, Green Day did not top the chart prior to the release of "Boulevard of Broken Dreams," which spent fourteen weeks at No. 1. "Bang Bang" also topped the *Mediabase* active rock airplay chart, getting played on the radio nearly 2,000 times in some weeks. By October 6, 2016, the album was No. 1 on iTunes.

On *Billboard*, the album topped the mainstream 200 Albums charts, the Top Rock Albums chart, the Top Alternative Album chart, the Top Album Sales chart, the Top Current Album chart, the Digital Album chart, and the Vinyl Album chart. It was also the No. 1 album in the United Kingdom, Canada, and Italy; No. 2 in Germany and Australia; and No. 3 in Greece. "Bang Bang" was No. 1 on the Rock Airplay, Alternative, Mainstream Rock,

And hitting the road once more, playing to huge crowds at festivals, stadiums, and arenas, denouncing Donald Trump at every turn.

and Canada Rock charts, and "Still Breathing" made it to the top 10 on the Mainstream Rock, Rock Airplay, and Alternative charts concurrently, with "Bang Bang" still charting.

Their No. 1 on Alternative for "Bang Bang" set a couple of milestones: it was their tenth No. 1 in the genre, and it made them one of five bands to have Alternative chart-toppers over the course of three decades. The others were Red Hot Chili Peppers, the Foo Fighters, their fellow pop disasters Blink-182, and their old football buddies U2.

Videos

The video to "Bang Bang" shows a trio wearing Green Day masks (which should have been a promotional item, although they did eventually go on sale) to rob a bank while the band plays yet another house concert. Eventually the unmasked bank robbers show up at the house party and start throwing the purloined bills up in the air. While it doesn't seem to have much to do with the song (except that the masked robbers are armed in the bank), the video does have a few amusing twists, not the least of which are the masks themselves and the idiocy of the media in the video not *recognizing them as masks.* The clip was directed by Rancid front man, former Operation Ivy leader, and friend of the band Tim Armstrong (no relation to Billie Joe).

In the world of lyric videos, Green Day's tend to be among the most creative, with clever quick 'n' nasty animations and interesting type treatments. Some of the images, like a bullet penetrating the palm of a hand about to join another hand prayerfully in "Say Goodbye," are outright outstanding. While the songs "Youngblood," "Say Goodbye," "Ordinary World," and

"Revolution Radio" did not get "official" videos, they did get lyric videos. So did "Still Breathing," but it also received the full clip treatment. And as wonderful as the song is, the video only augments its where-there-is-life-there-is-hope message. Billie Joe's and Mike's recent forays into cinema have had a salubrious effect on their video presence. While they can pull off angsty-miserable-soulful here, Tré only seems to be able to manage wistful.

Critics

In a peer review, Fall Out Boy's Pete Wentz noted to *NME*: "I've only heard two songs off the new album, and I thought they were great. It was like a return to form, the Green Day that I grew up with."

The reviews for *Revolution Radio* were generally strong. Saeed Saeed of Abu Dhabi's the *National* wrote: "Three decades after the band . . . formed, *Revolution Radio* is about survival and taking the next step. It is Green Day sending out the message that they are still alive and kicking. Welcome back." The Associated Press's Pablo Gorondi noted: "Singer and guitarist Billie Joe Armstrong's most recent New Year's resolution was 'to destroy the phrase "pop punk" forever.' On *Revolution Radio*, he and the rest of the band fail splendidly."

In a B review in the *AV Club*, Alex McCown-Levy remarked: "The best tracks cry with the frustration of someone who simply can't resign themselves to their world, their place in it, and most of all, themselves . . . But that's one of Green Day's strengths: Billie Joe spouts platitudes regularly, but he never seems to believe them." *Entertainment Weekly*'s Kevin O'Donnell wrote, "On their 12th studio LP they're dialing down the excess, and the result is a focused set that rocks as fearlessly as their Gilman Street glory days." And according to the *Guardian*'s Phil Mongredien: "The choruses are punchier, the lyrics more focused . . . Even the chugging 'Outlaws' transcends its similarity to Bon Jovi's mawkish 'Never Say Goodbye' to ultimately charm."

In a B+ review of the record, Cleveland.com noted: "[*Revolution Radio* is] a thrilling execution of everything Green Day has attempted over the past seven years . . . The tracks also feature some of Green Day's best guitar and drumming work in years. But the real standout is Armstrong's songwriting. Having emerged from a 2012 stint in rehab for substance abuse, Armstrong seems as focused and self-aware as ever." The *New York Times*' Jon Pareles observed: "Tumult and desperation ignite the music on *Revolution Radio* . . . Green Day's new [songs] aren't so easily summed up, but they can roar through their contradictions." Alec Kuehlnele of the Arizona *Daily Wildcat* said: "*Revolution Radio* still feels fresh and mature. Its thematic nature allows the members of Green Day to reflect on their discontent with time catching up with them, while it is also a major step for their future artistic endeavors." *Paste* magazine's review agreed: "Now here's a rock record that's content to be a rock record. *Revolution Radio* is a loud, energized power-pop album in moody punk clothing. It sounds pretty goddamn radiant when it's playing and leaves little impression when it isn't . . . after all these decades, Green Day still sounds like Green Day: palm-muted power chords, sneering vocals, and 4/4 drum breaks."

In a *Rolling Stone* podcast, writer Andy Greene commented: "I think what's very clever about it is it's not super ambitious. It's not over thought . . . It's a strong rock record that I think fans are going to just love. It's not a big epic thing, which is a nice change of pace." To which Executive Editor Nathan Brackett added, "[It's] kind of a mix of everything they do well.'"

The Song That Strangles Me

The Unusual Musical Complexity of Green Day's Punk

Writing about the decline of classical music, a somewhat embittered Luke Rix-Standing of Nouse.co.uk claimed, "Any cretin with fingers can now pick up a guitar and whack out some Green Day in a month or two, but a fledgling violinist is a dozen years hard practice and a 50-man orchestra away from their first concerto."

But how true is that, really? While it might not take twelve years to master, the simplicity Rix-Standing sees in Green Day is deceptive. Fall Out Boy's Patrick Stump's father was a folk singer and jazz-fusion player. This left Stump, admittedly, out of step with his friends who listened to punk. Then he heard Green Day. "So, the thing that struck me right off the bat was how musical it was," he said while inducting Green Day into the Rock and Roll Hall of Fame. He commented on the possibly intuitive grasp of music theory and the awareness of music history that informed everything they played. Pointing to Billie Joe, Stump complimented the shimmering open chords. He veritably gushed about Mike's bass work, comparing him to the incomparable Motown session bassist James Jamerson (one of the inventors of the "Sound of Young America" in the sixties) and the unequaled jazz bassist Jaco Pastorius from Weather Report, one of the most distinctive bass players of his generation. He added: "And there's not a drummer under the age of thirty who didn't spend their entire summer trying to learn . . . to play that rapid-fire fill in the beginning of 'Basket Case' just like Tré. And guess what? No one can."

U2 will tell you that punk rock is about three chords and the truth. That ethos is evident in much of the Class-of-76 punk, from the Sex Pistols to the Ramones. Even in Green Day's earlier work, more musical ideas and dexterity are evident. "Basket Case" has sharp minor chords, and "Longview" has that loopy (and allegedly acid-inspired) bass line underneath the basic three chords. This was not simple music.

Green Day pretty much re-created pop punk in the image of the Ramones and the Buzzcocks, and then, when they had nothing to lose really (after *Dookie*, they were pretty much set for life), they set about expanding what punk could be and could do. This allowed Billie Joe to flourish as a songwriter, building fearlessly onto the simplicity of punk with all the intricacies of great rock and roll throughout the last seven decades, from the Beatles to girl groups to Phil Spector-like walls of sound, and even venturing ever so subtly into indigenous music, show tunes, and progressive rock. Mike Dirnt has been seen at Rush concerts showing admiration from one trio to another.

If *Dookie* was powerfully influential—inspiring nearly as many bands to pick up instruments as Elvis, the Beatles, and the Ramones had before them—the music on the albums that followed it became progressively more complex and more subtly influential. Check out *Warning*'s "Macy's Day Parade" and then listen to Dashboard Confessional. Hear the similarities? As Billie Joe explained it to MTV, "It's like trying to take that power-pop or pop punk or whatever you want to call it, and stretching it into places that are further than we've ever gone."

Billie Joe told *Alternative Press*'s Aaron Burgess that he made an effort to "try and expand on the idea of what is supposed to be three-chord mayhem." He went on to say: "How do you do it in a way where the arrangements are just unpredictable? So, I'm pushing myself to be progressive in songwriting and being a songwriter."

Emerging fully blown with *American Idiot*, the structures got far more intricate, sophisticated, and ambitious. There were the suites: two epic nine-minute collections consisting of short, thirty-second (or so) songs "Homecoming" and "Jesus of Suburbia." Both are mini-rock operas within a rock opera. It was one of the oddest, most unexpected social media posts from a musician when Billie Joe tweeted from the studio, "We're writing nine-minute epics, which is scary to think about."

The songs on *American Idiot* had pianos, bells, handclaps, and vocal harmonies. In the midst of the suites, songs change time signatures. They work in waltz time. The music is intricate and ambitious. The two suites "Jesus of Suburbia" and "Homecoming" seamlessly pull together five disparate songs into cohesive wholes. The group had to really challenge themselves to play them live. It was the kind of challenge they live for, and they had to be in their best form to get it done. As Tré told Simon Collins of Perth's *West Australian* in advance of their Down Under Tour for the album, "You're getting tip-top Green Day."

For the title track of *21st Century Breakdown,* Billie Joe used a similar method to the epic suites on *American Idiot* to similar effect. He took a four-track demo of the anthemic "21st Century Breakdown" and mashed it up with a totally different song, the Celtic-influenced "Class of 13." "Those were two completely different songs," he told *Guitar Player,* "and I thought, 'You know, if I drop the key of "21st Century Breakdown," and I put it together with "Class of 13," that could work.'"

There is a lot of recombinant do-re-mi in Billie Joe's DNA. It helps him think through the expansion of the way Green Day sounds and consequently the way popular music sounds. Rock and roll began as something simple, but like so many other things, when it matured it started to develop complexities and nuances. As with so much of life, these things help keep it from getting too boring. He told *EQ*'s Ken Micallef: "A line could be inspired by a musical or something Randy Newman would write . . . My DNA is finding melody."

As mentioned earlier, when they were working on *21st Century Breakdown,* Butch Vig and the band called some of the songs "The Beasts." They were out of control—"overly long or complicated songs with lots of interesting ideas that weren't focused." One of the major triumphs of the album is how well they tamed these "beasts."

Technique

While the music sounds easy, it is actually pretty difficult to sound like Green Day. Billie Joe's technique of palm muting his guitar—using his picking hand to dampen the strings while he is playing them—can be challenging to get right. Try playing "Murder City" from *21st Century Breakdown* the ways Billie Joe plays it if you don't believe that. Mike's bass lines are often deceptively complex, going to unexpected places. Beyond that, groups that want to duplicate Green Day's sound often have to have more than the power trio making the music (but then these days, especially in concert, so does Green Day).

Guitar World marveled at his guitar work, claiming: "He can switch from punk's agitprop, barre-chord chop to classic rock's chiming power chords clangor at the turn of an eight note rest, piling on richly melodic leads in all the right places." They added: "Dirnt and Cool remain one of the most formidable rhythm sections in current rock. The bass lines are unassailably solid, yet admirably fleet footed, while the drumming is a dizzying amalgam of manic energy and tight control."

Tré countered this to *NME*, saying: "[It] was never about showing off how fast I could play or how many notes I could play—although I can play very fast and I can play a lot of notes if I want to. But it's more about choosing your moments and doing what's right for the music."

An autodidactic bass player, with lines like the rambling, jazz-infected walking part of "Longview" to the nine yards of staccato sixteenth notes on "Panic Song," Mike still wonders how he would play if he had actually taken lessons in his younger days. But he learned a thing or two (or three) in three decades of growing up in public as a musician. Early on, in the Sweet Children days, he tackled one of the great bass breaks in rock, John Entwistle's short solo in "My Generation." The bass work on "Basket Case" is highly underrated, one of the elements that propels the song and adds a layer of counter melody over the clipped chords. His bass work on *¡Tré!*'s "Dirty Rotten Bastards" is lightning quick, thanks largely to the encouragement of Billie Joe and Tré.

Unlike so many players in contemporary rock's virtuosity-equals-speed atmosphere, songs like this are anomalies rather than the rule. Like so much about Green Day, his playing is in service of the songs. He told E. E. Bradman that he doesn't want to be the shreddingest bass player in music; rather, he said: "I want to be the catchiest. If we're all out there writing our parts, I want to be the guy everyone ends up playing along with, because I wrote the hook."

In addition to being a musician, Tré is a music advocate. He works hard for an organization called Music in Our Schools Today (MuST). In a (rare) serious moment, when asked during a *Guardian* webchat how they would change the music business if they could, Tré said he would have the industry help students to build a more musically literate society. "Teach music in schools," he said. "Give kids free instruments when they're young and encourage them to play them."

Part 3

Wow! That's Loud

Green Day *off* the Record (CD, Download, Cassette, 8-Track, or Gently Down the Stream)

Last Night Onstage

The Live Adventures and Misadventures of Green Day, from the Van and the Hardcore Circuit to Jets and Stadiums Worldwide

On the Road

If you ever wonder whether rock is dead, you just need to go to a Green Day show. "We played a show in Berlin," Billie Joe told *Entertainment Weekly*'s David Browne, "and there were 20,000 people going completely insane. To me, that traditional style of playing rock and roll is still alive and well." This was a lot better than in their club days, when Billie Joe left Berlin with a serious case of body crabs.

Beyond being great songwriters and musicians, Green Day have become master entertainers. Even jaded critics like the *Hollywood Reporter*'s Eric Petersen, who must see over 200 shows a year, called Green Day (circa *21st Century Breakdown*) "one of the most flat-out enjoyable arena shows this town has seen in years." He added, "[Billie Joe Armstrong] pulled no punches in his zeal to obliterate the wall between performer and patron simply insisting that the crowd have a good time."

While most concerts are a communal experience by nature, Green Day go out of their way to create a community at their live shows. Their gigs are rife with all the trappings of the big rock and roll live extravaganza: Huge video screens, a vast array of pyro, and monster water pistols to drench their fans—especially welcome during the summer festival season.

No Hotel Room Is Safe

The on-the-road antics of many rock bands are legendary and often mythological. Ask Robert Plant of Led Zeppelin about some of the more depraved behavior his band is "credited" with, and he's likely to say something like, "Oh, that was the crew. I was sitting in my room reading Nietzsche."

During the early years, Green Day's "after show adventures" mostly happened in the van. For example, during the Sweet Children days, they played a show in the northern California town of Garberville, about 237 miles from Rodeo if you were avoiding tolls. On the other hand, it was only fifty miles from the home Larry Livermore of the Lookouts, who were also on the bill. So Larry invited them to his place, which was up in the mountains by Willets. (His nearest neighbors were the family of Lookouts drummer Frank Wright, who Livermore dubbed Tré Cool.) Billie Joe, Mike, and John/Al slept in the van. Livermore recalls hearing his dogs barking all night—not an unusual thing. However, when he went to check on the boys (Billie Joe and Mike were seventeen at the time, and John/Al was a couple of years older), they were very relieved to see him. Livermore recalls, "Mike said, 'Man, we had to piss so bad, but we were afraid to get out of the van because we thought those dogs would kill and eat us.'"

They graduated from the beat-up van to a tricked out bookmobile that Tré's father put together for them. It had sleeping spaces and even a Sega Genesis system built into it. On the bookmobile's debut tour, Tré's dad decided he wanted to be their driver. "It was fine," Tré told CBS News, "until he started crossing the line—of like being a father and being a bus driver. Like he would complain about dirty socks and stuff. It's like 'Dude, we're a punk band. We *are* dirty socks!'"

As they started to get more popular, play bigger venues, and actually sleep in hotels rather than the van, they indulged in the grand rock and roll tradition of fighting boredom by destroying things. When they check into hotels, they like to use the names of dead presidents of the United States—Billie Joe might be Abraham Lincoln, Mike might be Franklin Roosevelt, and Tré might be Ulysses Grant. While it happens less frequently (or is less reported), they have an impressive history of adding a lot of Lincolns and Grants to their lodging bills. They could wreak havoc on a hotel room with the best of them.

But hotel rooms were not the only things they trashed. Their appearance at the New York branch of the late, lamented record chain Tower Records is the stuff of legends. As Dakota Smith of MTV News chronicled the event, Billie incited the crowd from the moment they got onstage, saying: "Do whatever you want. This is not Tower Records. This is a Green Day concert!" He spray-painted "Nimrod" on the back wall, crowd surfed to the store's front window with the can of spray paint and wrote "Fuck You" on the window, and then mooned the East Village. When he got back onstage, he attempted to throw a monitor off and was thwarted by one of the store employees. Tré, however, did manage to throw his bass drum off the stage.

While doing the *Recovery* TV show in Australia a couple of years later, they spent about eight minutes chatting with the show's host, Dylan Lewis, with Billie Joe occasionally playing his harmonica and the band being their usual insouciant selves. While not scheduled to perform, they got up and convinced the house band (conveniently a trio) to surrender their instruments, while the nonplussed Lewis kept saying, "You can't do that. This is live TV." As if to answer that, the band launched into "Grouch," with the chorus of "The world owes me so fuck you" broadcast throughout the Antipodes. When they finished, the group returned the instruments and were escorted off the premises by studio security.

While Green Day have their share of van, backstage, and hotel stories, most of their best and weirdest tales actually happened while they were playing.

"They Played as If They Were the Beatles at Shea Stadium"

Part of the punk ethos has always been bringing it live. As Billie Joe is fond of saying, it has been a part of Green Day's DNA from day one. As Lookout! Records owner Larry Livermore recalled of the event when he decided to sign them, they were on the bill of a 1988 house party with his band, the Lookouts:

> It was a party for a bunch of kids that went to high school with Tré. . . there was snow on the roads up in the mountains where the party was supposed to be. Almost none of the kids showed up, even the kid whose house it was . . . so the other kids ended up breaking into the house and setting up a generator . . . So Sweet Children/Green Day ended up playing for literally five kids, and yet they played as if they were the Beatles at Shea Stadium. I mean they played their hearts out.

He also recalled a show a year later, at which someone had bought the seventeen-year-old members of Green Day a lot of beer. According to Livermore, "The amazing thing was that even though they were having a hard time figuring out where they were or remembering all the words to

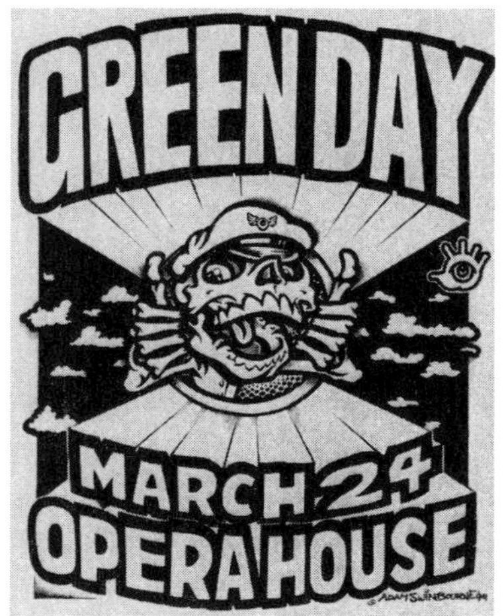

Playing Toronto in 1994, at the very edge of *Dookie* fever.

their songs, they still played better than any of the other bands [on the bill] who'd been at it way longer."

At a concert in Toronto on October 25, 1995, the audience began throwing sneakers at the band. Billie Joe unleashed a string of obscenities, asking the crowd in the strongest way to stop. Eventually he asked one of the barefoot boys in the mosh pit to come and claim his property. The kid got up onstage, claimed his property, took a bow, and started lacing his kicks with his back to Billie. As he was doing it, Billie put on a boar's head mask, somehow produced a butcher's knife, and approached the unsuspecting shoe-tosser, who jumped back into the mosh pit as the crowd roared. The sneakers, however, continued to sail. Mike got hit in the head with a flying high top. When the song finally ended, Billie decided to moon the crowd. The shoe tossing went on well beyond the 2001 *Warning* Tour, during which they were bombarded during a show at the Bren Center at UC Irvine.

During the *American Idiot* Tour, Billie took to performing in a George W. Bush mask during shows leading up to the elections. He would yell at the crowds, "I'm George W. Bush—but my friends call me asshole." He behaved similarly during a small-club tour for *Revolution Radio* just before the 2016 elections, when the band played in New York City and New Jersey and got loud about the forthcoming election, particularly about Donald Trump. "We are coming together tonight in New Jersey to call bullshit on all the fucking politicians tonight!" Billie Joe roared, and as the crowd roared back, the band exploded into "Holiday," during which they changed the lyrics "pulverize the Eiffel Tower" to "pulverize the Trump Tower." He later introduced the song "Know Your Enemy" by identifying New Jersey Governor Chris Christie as "the enemy."

Throughout the *American Idiot* Tour, despite playing in huge venues, the band continued to give up their instruments to members of the audience, as Billie taught them how to play "Knowledge," by one of Green Day's mentor bands, Operation Ivy. Playing Lollapalooza in Chicago in 2010, they had no fewer than five fans onstage: a French exchange student who waved a

French flag throughout "Know Your Enemy"; a ten-year-old girl who Billie Joe asked, "Do you want to start a fucking war?"; an older fan who sang "We Are the Waiting"; a small choir of older fans who also joined in; and a guy who sang all of "Longview."

Mosh pits are essential to Green Day shows, and even during stadium shows, there is a place set off for those who want to slamdance. However, an unsafe mosh pit is a problem. As anyone who has been in a pit knows, dancers rarely get hurt by the other moshers, hardly ever to the extent that they need to take an ambulance out of the show. More dangerous, the group discovered, were the hired venue security. On their second major tour, they did something about it. The band's production manager Mitch Cramer began to work with the security people, explaining the idea of the mosh pit, as it had rarely been an issue in larger venues before Green Day started playing them. This involved extensive briefings before the shows, including a two-page set of security guidelines. The guards were not permitted to "strong arm" the fans or push kids through or out of the pit barricade. They were allowed to pat down the audience to forbid certain items from getting into the arena.

Cramer himself would stand by the mosh pit barrier. "It's not unusual for me to jump into the pit if things are getting crazy," he told *Amusement Business*'s Athena Schaffer. "If you let the kids control where they go, you are going to have less injuries and problems than if you try to control them. Stopping kids coming over the walls, you're going to have confrontations. That's when kids and/or security are going to get hurt. You've got to let them just come over because the ones that want to be on the floor

An invitation to several tens of thousands of English fans to gather in London and see Green Day and a passel of other bands play.

will get on the floor. If you let them just do it, chances of risking injury are so much slighter."

Already worn out by the *Insomniac* tour, the band was becoming more disaffected with every show as they worked their way across Europe. The last straw came when they were going to play the Haus Auensee in Leipzig, Germany. Billie Joe claims that there was inadequate electricity, lax security, and worst of all, the area where the mosh pit was going to be set up was littered with broken glass. "It was criminal," Billie Joe told Gabriella of *NY Rocks.* "We'd rather have a disappointed audience than an audience that got seriously hurt or even killed. Moshing and broken glass don't go together and a punk concert isn't fun without a pit."

By the Time They Got to Woodstock

A bunch of their most legendary stage antics took place at Woodstock '94. It started with a mud fight that erupted when a combination of the rain and the crowd made mud plentiful. Many people gleefully covered themselves in it. The melee started when Billie Joe said he didn't want to be like the "mud hippies" out in the crowd. One person in the audience slung some of the mud onto the stage, and Billie promptly picked some up and put it into his mouth. The audience then started throwing mud in earnest. Billie tried to give as good as he got, but he was clearly outnumbered and only had access to secondhand mud. Then fans started coming up onstage, which led the security crews to try to clear the stage. Despite the fact that he was wearing an instrument, one of the guards mistook Mike for one of the wayward audience members and tackled him. Mike lost three teeth in the incident. "It turned into something completely unexpected," Billie reported on the Green Day Authority website. "It was the closest thing to total chaos I've ever seen in my whole life." It was only part of the chaos that highlighted the twenty-fifth anniversary of the renowned "Three Days of Peace and Music" in 1969. By Billie Joe's reckoning, there had been several deaths, about a hundred people an hour reporting to the emergency tents, and 750 people had broken their legs. He added for *Spin*'s Jonathan Gold, "At any moment, that place could have fully self-destructed."

The band's manager (at the time), Elliot Cahn—who had played the original Woodstock as a member of Sha Na Na—was upset. He told *Entertainment Weekly*, "I've got a hurt guy in my band, so I gotta say I'm pretty bummed about it."

Billie's mother, who watched the whole thing on Pay Per View, was embarrassed and let her son know it. She wrote her son a letter chiding him for fighting and pulling his pants down onstage.

Less than a month later, chaos greeted Green Day again about 200 miles due east. Boston radio station WFNX promoted a free Green Day concert at the Hatch Shell, right on the banks of the Charles River, downtown. They expected perhaps 10,000 people and got six or seven times that many. Therefore, despite the presence of police, about forty state troopers, and even a fifteen-member work release team from a local prison, there was not enough crowd control to manage the audience.

Mere minutes after the band started, the barriers between the crowd and the stage were down. The audience turned into a mob and started to rock the lighting towers. Others started pulling up the park's flowers, an activity that Billie Joe jumped down from the stage to join them in. The promoter, afraid that the entire stage might collapse, pulled the band off the stage, ending the show about twenty minutes after it started, in the middle of a song. This incensed the crowd even more, turning them into a mob of about 5,000 (of the 65,000 who attended), and the mayhem spread onto the streets of downtown Boston. The police went into full riot control mode, complete with tear gas. By the time the smoke cleared, fifty fans had been arrested, and another fifty were treated for injuries ranging from sprains to drug-related problems. The group watched this from underneath the shell, guarded by the prison crew, who asked for autographs. "Not one of them fucked off," Tré marveled on the Green Day Authority website. "They all went back to jail the next day."

Billie Joe is notorious for mooning audiences, especially after a show he considers mediocre or worse. Apparently, that is what the show at the Mecca Auditorium in Milwaukee, Wisconsin, was like because that was what he did. What made that show different was the police were waiting for him after the show ended, whereupon they cited him for indecent exposure as he made his way to the limo, put him into their own police limo with the disco lights, and took him into the police station. The police had apparently learned from the experience in Boston and waited until the show had ended before taking action (smart move). Billie Joe was taken into custody for a few hours; then he paid a fine and was set free.

Billie Joe did more than drop trou at an AIDS benefit at New York's Madison Square Garden. Moving into the seventh hour of the Z-100 Jingle Ball Christmas show, Green Day took the stage. When called back for an encore, at around two o'clock in the morning, Billie Joe came back onstage wearing nothing but his guitar. The *New York Post* remarked the next morning that the move "turned a musical endurance test into what will be one of the most talked about concerts of the year."

This was relatively early in the band's career. He told NPR.com, "I didn't know if I was ever going to play Madison Square Garden again, so I said, 'Well, there's one way to remember this occasion—to be the guy who was naked [there].'"

Then of course there is the audience wanting to get out of their clothes and into the act. During a *Dookie* show at the Nassau Coliseum in New York, a topless woman got on her friend's shoulders. "[Billie Joe] first said, 'Mom, put your clothes back on,'" Jon Pareles reported in the *New York Times*, "then admonished the nearby boys not to grope her."

While it is all good, clean fun until someone gets hurt, Mike seems to bear the brunt of the injuries. He is the one, after all, who lost teeth at Woodstock. At the 1998 KROQ Weenie Roast, a very inebriated Arion Salazar, bassist for Third Eye Blind, stormed onto the stage during Green Day's set to hug his counterpart Mike Dirnt. This surprised Mike, who thought it was someone from the audience. He hit and kicked Salazar and they scuffled onstage until security led Salazar off. The scuffle continued backstage after the show, until someone (no one was quite clear as to who) hit Mike over the head with a beer bottle. The attack fractured Mike's skull, and he was hospitalized overnight.

The Blink-182 Tour and Other Pop Disasters

By the time they went on their second tour as a major label recording artist, and first as headliners, they had evolved from using a beat-up van and then a refurbished bookmobile to headlining a show that took four hours to set up and employed a dozen people, four trucks, and two busses. They brought their own barricades, caterers, stage, sound, and lights with them.

Even when they were sharing a bill with (and opening for) their own misbegotten musical stepchildren Blink-182 on the Pop Disaster Tour, they toured large, travelling with thirteen buses to carry personnel and nine semis to carry equipment. At that time, they also travelled with a trailer (behind one of the buses) carrying an assortment of dirt bikes, motorbikes, and bicycles, allowing the members of the band to get around a bit easier. For example, when the tour pulled into New York, Tré took a trip to Ground Zero.

They would often invite local bands to play outside a venue on a stage that Billie, Joe, Mike and Tré carried on one of their trucks. Frequently, one or all of the members of the band, along with the entourage, would watch the show from behind the stage. Sometimes (like on the Pop Disaster Tour) they would take a band like that on tour for the outside gig.

The Pop Disaster Tour was the tour that no one thought would happen. Too much ego, too much competition. "Both bands wanted to send out the finger to those who thought it wouldn't happen," Mike told Kevin C. Johnson of the *St. Louis Post-Dispatch*. The media, particularly music journalists, had tried to make the public believe that there was bad blood between the bands, but the actual fact was that they barely knew each other before the tour, and as the tour went on, they discovered that they liked each other.

One of the things they accomplished on the Pop Disaster Tour was blowing Blink-182 off the stage nearly every night. Green Day were reaching out to the Blink-182 audience, and in that they were largely successful. "We set out to reclaim our throne as the most incredible live punk band there is," Billie Joe told *Kerrang!*'s Ian Winwood. "All the young kids coming to see Blink, it was nice to have the chance to wreck their whole perception of how things are."

And how were things? Well, as Peterson put it, "Green Day devoured the place." For bands that were notorious for their partying, and especially their consumption of alcoholic beverages at the time, it seems ironic that one of the tour sponsors was Yoo-Hoo chocolate drink.

About fifteen years later, the sound of history (sort of) repeating itself could be heard in Berkeley when Green Day and Blink-182 headlined the Live 105 Not So Silent Night Christmas show. However, it wasn't quite the same, as the show ran two nights and Green Day headlined the first night, Blink-182 the second. They both also headlined the bill at Austria's Nova Festival late that spring, along with Simple Plan, Rancid, Linkin Park, System of a Down, and a host of others.

Green Day did a surprise appearance at the 2012 Reading Festival, announcing it on Twitter less than an hour before their set: "Green day [sic]—READING FESTIVAL CONFIRMED!! Onstage in 45 minutes! In the NME/RADIO 1 tent. 11 am!! Be There!" Despite the short notice and early hour, the promoters had to seal off access to the stage, though those who could not actually get into the tent were able to watch the video on the main stage. They played thirteen songs before they had to get off of the stage, ending "Boulevard of Broken Dreams" abruptly and telling the crowd, according to *NME*, "We're having a little fucking problem with time."

Bring the *21st Century Breakdown* home. The record takes place in Detroit; this is the last show to Clarkstown.

This could have been a portent of what would happen about a week later, when the band played the iHeartRadio concert in Las Vegas, where Billie Joe famously had a meltdown over the promoters calling time on the show (more on that in Chapter 12 on chemical matters and rehab, as that's where Billie Joe wound up after the show).

Economy

Early on, when they started to move to the bigger venues, tickets to a Green Day show cost $7.50. That was the price of a movie in some markets. It was their way of being accessible, even in a theater or an arena, and making sure that the fans that wanted to come could come. By the second major label tour, they had had to double the cost of the ticket, but even $15 was uniquely low. "They never change the ticket price and they bring a full production on the road," Reprise's Jim Baltutis told Schaffer. "I can't speak directly for the band, but they don't really make any money when they are on the road. I know they actually lost plenty last time they were out because the ticket prices were so low."

When *Dookie* hit, they went from playing clubs to playing arenas and even stadiums. They had some trouble with the transition. Initially, they liked it. "We'll sell out places we never thought we'd play," Tré told the *St. Louis Post-Dispatch*. "So that's pretty cool." By the time they were ready to hit the road again for *Insomniac*, Billie Joe had other ideas.

"I don't like playing arenas," he told *RIP*'s Tom Lanham. "I went into it being positive and getting excited about it. But I didn't realize that I was the kind of person to whom it's too much of an event and not really a personal thing anymore . . . we were playing for a lot of fuckin' people . . . We played every day, 50 gigs this last leg, and it just wears on ya."

In some ways, he claimed that *Insomniac* was *designed* to allow the band to play to smaller audiences. This became a self-fulfilling prophecy. During the *Insomniac* tour, the change from clubs to bigger venues basically burned the band out. They were playing an arena tour of Europe, and abruptly cancelled the remainder of their shows. As Billie Joe told Gabriella, "At the time, we had been on tour for over two years and slowly our fuses blew . . . We were finished, fucked up. We didn't know anymore who we were, where we were. We just wanted to go home."

Around the time of *Nimrod*, though, they began to figure it out. They realized that what the people who came to see them were not concerned with was how punk they were; they never had been. That was the band's concern. The people wanted to hear the songs they love by these musicians they loved enough to take a night out of their lives and $27 out of their wallets to see them. "I think of myself as a performer," Billie Joe told *Spin*'s Jonathan Gold. "I love Hüsker Dü, but I think David Lee Roth is great, too. Mick Jagger is really able to seduce an audience. I don't think we seduce anybody . . . if you're playing in front of 20,000 people, you need to give them something to look at. I think that's why I get naked so often."

"If you're going to go up there, just own it and kill it and be aggressive," Mike echoed to *Newtimes*' David Friedman.

As their live fortunes vacillated with the ebb and flow of their popularity and as the audiences tapered off, they would move back to smaller venues. They told CMJ's Tom Lanham that they decided that they would rather "go to a place like the Fillmore and the Warfield and know it's actually going to sell out." It beat playing half-empty arenas.

Then came the rebound and *American Idiot*. Green Day became firmly entrenched in the large stadiums as the only way to accommodate the number of fans in any given place that wanted to see them. In a sense, this is why they went the major label route in the first place: they had to play bigger venues to accommodate their audience. While it took them some getting used to, when they toured *American Idiot* they realized that for the immediate future at least they had to play to these large crowds. What they did, though, was telling. They discovered how to play to 30,000 people and make the show feel as close to the intimacy of a club as something that size could.

While far different from clubs or even arenas, they have continued to use what worked for them live from day one. There is still a mosh pit in front of the stage, though the setup of a stadium stage, especially if the venue will not accommodate a runway, makes stage-diving a bit of a problem. They still bring audience members up onstage to perform. "When you come to a Green Day show you're there to let loose," Tré told the *Sydney Morning Herald*'s Craig Mathieson. "You're not at school, you're not at home, you're not at your job—there's no one to answer to . . . You don't go to a concert to change the world, you go to a concert to have a good time."

They continue to be an international phenomenon. As an indie act, they toured Europe on their own dime, building up a following. When *Dookie* hit, Reprise set up a forty-date European tour, opening and ending in London, with dates in Holland, Germany, Belgium, Italy, Sweden, Denmark, and Spain, many of which they had hit during those previous tours. In Germany, they opened for seminal Teutonic punk band Die Toten Hosen (literally, the dead trousers). That leg of the tour ran nine shows and played to 80,000 people. In Spain, they played a show that was taped for broadcast on the national radio service. They started setting attendance records by selling out London's 60,000-seat Emirates Stadium in 2013. They have gone from playing to a dozen kids in a club to playing live for half a million people, while millions more watched on TV during the Live 8 concert. When they announced a set of South American shows, the concert at Peru's San Marcos University Stadium in Lima sold 12,000 tickets in one day.

Touring, even when they play to tens of thousands of people, keeps the band honest. To Neala Johnson of Melbourne's *Herald Sun*, Mike said: "That helps keep you from being too self-absorbed in [the record sales] side of things. We're just out playing shows." He added for the Queensland *Courier Mail*: "Our motto was 'play anywhere and everywhere' as we were growing up. We played so many shows, I didn't realize how hard we were actually working toward our ultimate goal: To keep doing what we were doing forever."

Toward that end, they also know when to get off the road—probably a lesson learned from the *Insomniac* Tour. Mike told *Billboard*'s Melinda Newman that one of the ways to stay great on record and on the road is knowing "when to call it quits for a while and go home and rejuvenate and detox."

The Green Day Show

So what is a Green Day show actually like? It generally starts with a guy dressed in a pink bunny suit, holding a beer onstage. Often he cracks a few jokes and then he brings on the band to something grandiose like the "Imperial March" from *Star Wars*, Queen's "Bohemian Rhapsody," or "Also Sprach Zarathustra." They get set up with their instruments, and from there it's off to the races.

The band works from a set list, but often they stray. "[You] come up with this structure of how the songs are going to go from one to the next," Billie Joe told *Time* magazine, "but at the same time you have to be spontaneous and take requests and change the set list at the drop of a hat."

Green Day do not just play a set. They rip through it with as much energy today as they had as young punks playing clubs and retiring to the bookmobile. They will play a thirty-song set of their most high-energy songs, kicking them up a couple of notches for the live experience. There are songs from *Kerplunk* and even earlier. *Dookie* represents often. During the tours for *American Idiot* and *21st Century Breakdown*, they would sometimes dedicate the middle of the show to playing the albums end to end. "I think we deserve to show off a little bit," Tré told Simon Collins of Perth's *The West Australian*. "If we want to play the whole album, goddam, we're gonna play the whole album!"

They turn their anthem to cross-dressing "King for a Day" into a twenty-minute-long extravaganza with horns and costumes. Into the song, they insert parts of AC/DC songs, Guns N' Roses' "Sweet Child o' Mine," the Rolling Stones' "(I Can't Get No) Satisfaction," the Isley Brother's "Shout," and whatever else might come to mind. At Milton Keynes, for example, it was Monty Python's "Always Look on the Bright Side of Life." Billie Joe reaches out to the audience, getting them to holler back lyrics, oooohs, and songs like "Hey Jude."

Almost every song in Green Day's set features some sort of call and response. Billie Joe seems to take personal offense if everyone is not on their feet through the show, and he especially loves the action in the pit. In 2005, he got the audiences chanting "Fuck Bush" (which could be taken any number of ways). In 2016, he got the audience yelling "Fuck Donald Trump" (which should only be taken one way).

The band defines onstage spontaneity. As Billie Joe has often said, he feels a great deal of freedom while he is performing. That spontaneous nature has a way with the crowd. There is stuff that Green Day "always does," and then there are things that might happen for just one night. They have enough songs that you'll never hear all of them during a show, but they liberally add deep cuts, even though they probably have thirty songs that everyone in the audience knows. And they play them with what Universal News Syndicate writer Tom Bergan described as a "passion and veracity that is hard to emulate."

Taking a page from the Who playbook, early on Green Day would trash their instruments at the end of the show. This would climax with Tré setting his drum set on fire when he could. Often the fire marshals would not let him.

There is one thing that will get up Billie Joe's nose when he performs: he cannot fathom people who attend a live event—one they paid good money to see and have anticipated in the months since the tickets were bought—and then spend the two hours or so looking at their cell phones. "You can look at a screen at home," he told *Dailystar*. "You can look at your computer or your phone anywhere . . . take your picture but let's have eye contact, let's have a human experience right now you can't capture on a cell phone."

That human experience makes a Green Day show special. "I think some people walk away from a Green Day concert with the same emotions you would get from some kind of theater performance where the crowd feels involved," Billie Joe told NPR's Maria Chavez. The whole band, but Billie Joe in particular, reach out to the crowd, musically and literally.

A Green Day show will feature fans of all ages and ethnicities. Every show features half a dozen audience members being brought onstage, be it someone to play one of Billie Joe's guitars and sing (and sometimes go home with an instrument) or small groups of people—their "original fans circa *Dookie*"—to sing along with "Longview." They will bring up musicians who they have never met before, turn over their instruments, and teach them how to play Operation Ivy's "Knowledge." During a soundcheck for an appearance on *Good Morning America* at Central Park's Summerstage, they brought a young African American woman onstage to sing, and she knew every word. At a 2016 show at the Aragon Ballroom in Chicago, they played for an audience that *Loyola Phoenix* writer Nick Coulson described as "a testament to Green Day's longevity; millennials, parents, young children, grandparents and grandchildren were in attendance."

"Honestly," Mike told Johnson, "of all the big shows I've seen in my life, this is custom-tailored to Green Day and their fan's liking. When I walk up from the crowd's perspective, I go, 'Wow, this is a really, really cool looking show.'"

"We pride ourselves on trying to put on the best show we can," Billie Joe told *Q* on the occasion of winning their Best Live Band Award, "and we're not afraid to say we happen to be the best live band in the world."

42

Drama Kings

A Gay Romp with Saint Jimmy and Whatsername in Jingletown

Broadway has its ups and downs, but at the turn of the decade in 2010, there was little doubt about one thing: the mean age of people who attended Broadway plays was rising. One of the reasons for this was the Gen Xers and Millennials had little interest in plays with music from the forties or earlier, as many of the revivals had, or music that *sounded* like it was from the forties, as even contemporary musicals often chose to emulate the "Great American Songbook" era of Broadway. That was their grandparent's era, and it held little relevance to them. This generation had been weaned on rock and pop, and these shows did not speak to their generation. "If Broadway is going to continue to be a vital cultural force," *New York Times'* theater critic Charles Isherwood told *Q*'s Rod Wilba, "it needs to start renewing its audience."

It seemed, though, that as 2009 started inevitably slipping into 2010, the penny dropped for theater producers. The Who's *Tommy* had already rocked the great white way. So had Abba's musical *Mamma Mia!* and Billy Joel's *Movin' Out*. The rock opera *Rent* had won a Pulitzer Prize. Shows being workshopped included a stage version of Neil Gaiman's *Coraline* with music by Stephin Merritt of Magnetic Fields. One of the most eagerly awaited and problematic shows being put together was *Spiderman: Turn Off the Dark*, with music by Bono and the Edge of U2. Elton John's *Billy Elliot*, which split the difference between a more traditional Broadway score and popular music—John trying to create a score that he thought would be stage palatable—became a major hit, one of the highest grossing musicals of all time. Other shows, like Paul Simon's *The Capeman*, tanked.

Then Duncan Sheik composed a musical called *Spring Awakening*, a show by a rocker with a cult following couched in a rock idiom and featuring younger performers in a story about coming of age. For older rockers there were shows like *Jersey Boys*, *Memphis*, *Motown*, and *Million Dollar Quartet*. There was a musical about Nigerian political gadfly and musical superstar Fela Anikulapo Kuti. Run D.M.C. were working on a show. Lin Manuel Miranda's *In the Heights* incorporated rap and won the author his first of many Tonys and a MacArthur Foundation "Genius Grant," which he used to complete *Hamilton*. Popular music even permeated the "straight" theater, with Sean "Puff Daddy" Combs starring in a revival of *A Raisin in the Sun*. Broadway was seeking some credibility with the young people that it had so long ignored at its peril. It was a gamble, but not as big of one as it seemed. This generation was willing to pay a couple of hundred dollars for a concert ticket. Why wouldn't they do it for a more stirring theatrical experience? The key was: it had to be stirring.

Billie Joe's Show Tunes

"I started learning standards and stuff at a young age," Billie Joe told CBS News. When he was working with the Fiatrones, he would perform songs like "New York, New York" at veterans hospitals and similar venues. "That's where I get my sense of melody," Billie Joe told the *New York Post*'s Kyle Smith. "I was singing 'Satin Doll.' I did an Al Jolson medley, I did '42nd Street,' and I did 'Kids' from *Bye Bye Birdie*." In San Francisco, he saw shows like *Guys and Dolls*, *Bye Bye Birdie*, and *The Phantom of the Opera*. When he came to Broadway, the ultra-long-running Broadway version of the latter was still playing across the street from the St. James Theater at the Majestic.

When the band was working on the album *American Idiot*, they listened to things like *Tommy* and even *The Rocky Horror Picture Show*, musicals that told a story (and both landed on Broadway). He told the *Village Voice*'s Michael Musto, "I even downloaded some things Ethel Merman sang."

Green Day Meets Mozart

"When we were recording *American Idiot*, we thought it was very theatrical and that it had a story line. We always thought it should be staged somehow," Billie Joe told *Time* magazine. Initially they thought that a movie was the way to go, but a few visits to Los Angeles made them less certain. If the record business was treacherous, TV and movies were a minefield.

One person they did not meet in Los Angeles was director Michael Mayer. Working on finding locations for the film *Flicka*, that would star country music chart-topper Tim McGraw at the time, he was a Broadway veteran who was concurrently working on the aforementioned new musical *Spring Awakening*. When the *American Idiot* album came out, he spent a lot of time finding places to film *Flicka*, driving all over California and the vicinity. As he drove looking for scenery that matched the screenplay, he had the CD of *American Idiot* in the car's player. "I sort of couldn't get enough of it," he told *Playbill*'s Kenneth Jones. "It certainly was dawning on me, day by day, that my god, this really is a rock opera just waiting for someone to stage it."

Since he was also putting together the pieces of *Spring Awakening*, he was in contact with Tom Hulce. The actor who had once torn up Broadway and the movies as Mozart in *Amadeus* was now producing plays on Broadway, and *Spring Awakening* was one of them. As *Spring Awakening* began to happen, Mayer was interviewed for *Variety* magazine and mentioned that he would love to do a musical based on *American Idiot*, but he was sure it was such an obvious project that someone else was already doing it. Hulce read this and called Mayer. He described the conversation for Jones.

"What makes you so sure someone is doing this?" Hulce asked.

"Well," Mayer replied, "I can't imagine that someone isn't."

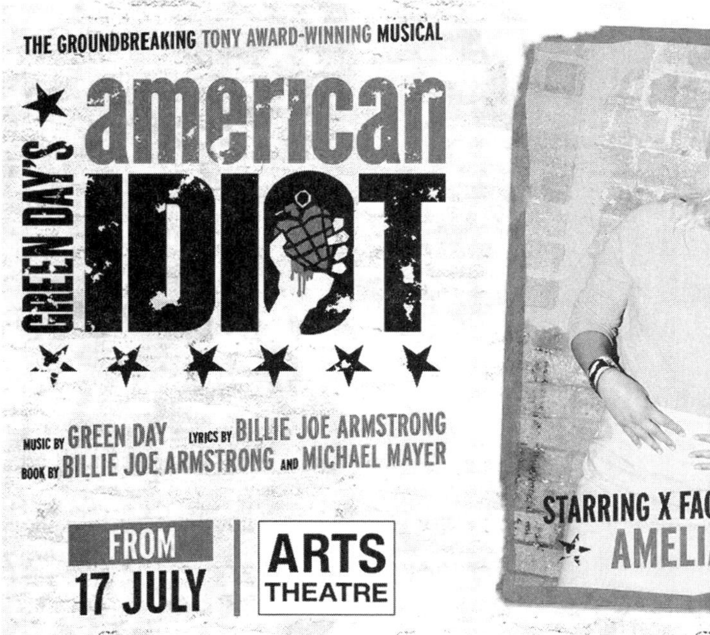

Taking the show on the road. One of several international touring companies of *American Idiot*.

"Is this interesting to you?" Hulce asked.

Mayer told Hulce that he would commit heinous crimes to do the show; Hulce assured him that it probably would not come to that. Hulce called Magnarella Management and set up a meeting between management, himself, and Mayer. They flew out to LA where Mayer pitched his vision of an *American Idiot* musical. He asked for time to put together the bones of such a show and told Magnarella that if he and the band liked that, they would move together and workshop the idea. If that passed muster, they would take the play into production. To show the band what could be accomplished in a rock musical, he took them to see *Spring Awakening*, which was on its way to winning Tonys for Best Musical, Best Book, and Best Score, and a slew of other theatrical awards.

"We were so impressed with that production, as well as his vision for *American Idiot*," Billie Joe told *Undercover*'s Paul Cashmere, "that we knew we'd found the perfect collaborator."

Mayer worked on the project obsessively, even while putting on another (award-winning) musical, *Every Day Rapture*. He brought the music director for that project, Tom Kitt, on as music director for this new project. Another Tony (and Pulitzer Prize) winner, Kitt got busy doing the orchestration.

Mayer's initial scenario had the character 'the Jesus of Suburbia' ensnared inside his own head. Speaking of the music, Kitt told the *Journal News*: "[My] goal from the start is that anything I write still feels like Green Day, not like me. If people suddenly felt that they weren't hearing Green Day anymore, then it would have been a failure."

His early efforts for the workshop involved changing keys for vocalists and amping up the harmonies. In terms of taking any liberties with the music, the first one they tried was on "Whatsername," changing Billie Joe's muted guitars for a piano and a cello. When the band heard it, they were literally in tears. "You don't get to see Green Day play live if you're actually *in* Green Day," Mike told James Montgomery of MTV News. "But to see these voices and the way the cast were singing, you just abandon hope of a tissue and let 'em stream."

As the show developed, Mayer kept Billie Joe completely in the loop. They would email back and forth over every version of every scene. The show stretched the concept of the album without breaking it. Where the album was predominantly in the voice of Jesus of Suburbia, through that of Billie Joe, it had already proven to make for a swell concert, but it was not much of a theater piece. With the addition of several songs—including the two European B-sides from *American Idiot*, four songs that turned up on Green Day's next project, *21st Century Breakdown*, and one previously unreleased song, "When It's Time"—they were able to expand the action. Several more characters were added. The show featured the songs sung by the company, sung between the actors as dialogue, as well as showcase pieces.

At one point, Mayer was stuck on how to deal with the song "Letterbomb." Mayer saw it as one of those showcase pieces for a powerful male voice, but he could not make it work in context. Billie Joe suggested that they have a woman sing it. It played perfectly. "I thought, 'Oh my god. This guy is so meant to make musicals,'" Mayer told the *Wall Street Journal*'s Ellen Gamerman.

"I didn't know women would sound that good singing my songs," Billie Joe marveled to *Time* magazine. "They're even better than the way I sing them."

In order to put the play into production, there was an intensive two-week workshop during the summer of 2009. In the late summer, they then moved the show into the Berkeley Repertory Theater, where they set up the stage and technology, rehearsed and did previews, and constantly worked to refine and hone the show. What they came up with was an hour and a half of nonstop singing, very little spoken dialogue, and the kind of energy that having Green Day music driving the show demands. The show opened at the Berkeley Repertory Theater on September 15, 2009, after eleven preview performances. It was supposed to run for a month. It wound up being held over through November 15.

The Berkeley Repertory Theater has a large subscriber base. These theatrical season tickets are held by families and by older patrons of the arts, among others. However, they were not strangers to theatrical experiments in rock, having also hosted an early version of *Passing Strange*, the award-winning play (and later Spike Lee Joint) by Stew of the band The Negro Problem. "Doing it in our home town at Berkeley Rep was an obvious bonus," Billie Joe told Cashmere. "They're an amazing theater group, and their willingness to take chances is in keeping with the spirit of the album."

To their surprise and gratification, even the gray-haired crowd, captivated by the energy of the show, gave the performers standing ovations. However, the producers were realistic about the nature of the Berkeley Rep audience: there was a bucket of earplugs at the door. Even at this point, though, no one was even thinking (out loud at least) about a move to Broadway.

Give My Regards to Broadway

The play broke all kinds of records at the Berkeley Rep, becoming the highest grossing production in the venerable theater's history, so even though no one said it, the show landing on Broadway was inevitable. Six days into the new year of 2010, the announcement came. The show would open on April 20 at the St. James Theater, with previews starting on March 24. Once again, most of the cast moved.

Just after the first of the year, the tech team started tricking out the St. James Theater with more sound equipment than had ever been used for any previous Broadway show. "And it's all turned up to 11," Hulce said to the *New York Post*'s Kyle Smith. The guitar tech put together a replica of Billie Joe's own rig. Billie Joe also donated a couple of his guitars, and Tré offered up one of his drum kits. "They just opened the closet for us and said, 'Here, play with this,'" the show's sound designer, Brian Ronan, marveled to *Pro Sound News*' Clive Young. "It was great; they're really generous."

At the time, Ronan was a Broadway sound design veteran of fifteen years. (He would win a Tony for his sound design on the Carole King musical *Beautiful*.) Many others in charge of various aspects of the show were equally notable, like Mayer and Kitts. Choreographer Steven Hogget was already the winner of an Olivier Award, a Drama Desk Award, and three Tonys. Kevin Adams won a Tony and an Outer Critics Circle Award for the show's scenic design. Christine Jones won a Tony for the lighting design.

The cast and the band opened the 2010 Grammy Awards with a version of "21 Guns." They had just been in Electric Lady Studio with Billie Joe, Mike, Tré, and some of the musicians from the show backing them. (Billie Joe, Mike, and Tré had to learn the new arrangements.)

About a month before the opening, the cast was invited to perform at an exclusive cocktail reception for the winners of USA Network's Character Approved Awards, at which Green Day was honored. Other winners included Alex Rigopulos and Eran Egozy, the creators of *Guitar Hero* and *Rock Band*.

There was some confusion about whether the band would be part of the show as it went into previews. It was called *Green Day's American Idiot*. They did, after all, accompany the cast at the Grammys. The show used the album's iconic "Heart Like a Hand Grenade" image in its marketing and graphics. The band also appeared in a video of the cast singing "21 Guns," with Billie Joe onstage singing with the cast. The confusion necessitated a disclaimer during the Berkeley run: "This is not a Green Day concert—this is the stage version of *American Idiot* developed by Green Day and Michael Mayer. Although the band will not appear onstage, the show will definitely rock."

From the very beginning, Billie Joe insisted that there be a rock band involved and that it be onstage with the actors. He did not want a "Broadway version of rock songs" (like *Rent*). That was a primary concern, and something Hulce, Mayer, and Kitt got from the get-go. Billie Joe even spent time coaching the show's guitarists and teaching them his techniques.

For Billie Joe, this was a peak experience. When asked by CBS News to rank it among his experiences, he said, "Top. It's the absolute biggest thing that's ever happened to us." To which Mike commented, "To have flesh and blood people performing our songs back at us and take it to a whole 'nother level, it's indescribable." Billie Joe added for *Out* magazine's Danity, "I feel like it legitimizes us as songwriters and as a band in a whole new way that I never really imagined."

As the musical got ready to open on Broadway, Green Day teamed up with their old friends at MTV to help promote the show. The band and the cast did a performance for MTV2, they had a Green Day Rocks Broadway contest, and the band appeared in the *Green Day Rocks Broadway* special a week before the show opened. "Obviously, it's not just the catchy songs, it goes deeper than that," Billie Joe told Montgomery. "And I think that's the heart of *American Idiot*. It goes deeper than just politics, there's a story line behind it. There's an emotion behind it."

The Actors

"It's a story about kids in a world where the TV is always on and they are struggling to find their own voice," actor John Gallagher—who played Johnny, the Jesus of Suburbia—told Harding. "In the end, Johnny goes through something a lot of people struggle with and comes out still standing." Long before he joined the cast, he knew how to play the whole *American Idiot* album on guitar. Musically it was not much of a stretch.

Some members of the cast—like Gallagher, who won a Tony Award for his role in *Spring Awakening*—were already recognizable presences on Broadway. Stark Sands, who played Tunny, was nominated for a Tony for his role in *Journey's End*. Other cast members had performed in such notable shows as *Avenue Q*, *Passing Strange*, and *Jesus Christ Superstar*, all groundbreaking musicals in their own rights. More members of the cast became the rising stars of theater in both the United States and England because of their appearance in the show.

Rebecca Naomi Jones, the original Whatsername, found playing the part liberating. There's nothing better for dealing with body image issues than being onstage in your underwear for upwards of an hour and a half. "I know the character I'm playing is not sitting around apologizing for how she looks. It's been kind of freeing, actually," she told the *Wall Street Journal*. "There's something to be said for seeing a character there who looks like a human being."

"This isn't a rated PG sort of affair," Billie Joe added for James Montgomery of MTV News about people's misconceptions dealing with the theater. "I saw this play, *Next to Normal*, or, like, *Spring Awakening*—both of these deal with really heavy, current themes." He added for *Q* magazine, "There are no Disney moments in the show."

"We're kind of overwhelmed a little bit about it being on Broadway to be honest," Billie Joe told Montgomery. "This is where you want to be."

Opening Night

The show opened on April 20, 2010, the date (4/20) being a sly reference to the history and name of the band that wrote it. The reviews were generally positive, but even the ones with good things to say were sometimes mixed. The *New York Daily News*, for example, noted that the direction packed a visceral punch, the actors were top-notch, the songs sound great, but asked: "Could you have spared a story? And a couple of characters who aren't clichéd stick figures?" Reuters concurred, noting "the youthful ensemble goes through their nonstop paces with breathtaking energy," but the show's book didn't flesh out the album's premise sufficiently. Similarly, *Newsweek* said: "It has raucous energy and frequently spectacular stagecraft. It doesn't hold together as well as it should, but there's something entirely welcome going on here."

Charles Isherwood of the *New York Times*, one of America's toughest theater critics, wrote one of the most positive reviews of the show, saying: "Rage and love, those consuming emotions felt with a particularly acute pang in youth, all but burn up the stage in *American Idiot*, the thrillingly raucous and gorgeously wrought Broadway musical adapted from the blockbuster pop punk album by Green Day . . . [the show] detonates a fierce aesthetic charge in this ho-hum Broadway season . . . ultimately as moving as anything I've seen on Broadway this season. Or maybe a few seasons past."

The original Broadway cast album came out on opening night (and was available at the theater—it had been a long time since Green Day sold records at a gig). On the night of the third official performance on Broadway, Green Day came onstage as an encore. They played the show's title track and "Basket Case." One of the cast members tried to crowd surf, more than likely puzzling the audience. He made it about three rows. Such performances were not unprecedented on Broadway. When *Movin' Out* was on Broadway, Billy Joel would occasionally sit in with the band after the show. In the first week, *Green Day's American Idiot* took in a respectable $777,680. It was still a long way from making back its development money, which had run to about $6 million.

At one of the New York City Foxboro Hot Tubs shows that took place early in the play's run, cast members came up onstage amid the chaos, mugging and messing with the band until Billie Joe told them, "I love you guys, but you have to get the fuck off the stage," according to *Rolling Stone*'s J. Edward Keyes.

When Tony Vincent, the original St. Jimmy, took a break from the show, and with slightly flagging box office, Billie Joe spent a week in the role in September of 2010. Mayer observed to Wilba that he brought a "seductive

Its name in lights on the marquee of the St. James Theater on Broadway.

Fryede/Wikimedia Commons

trickster" element to the role. He also goosed the box office, doubling the show's take from the previous week. During Billie Joe's run as Saint Jimmy, he and Mayer had an after-show program they called "Idiot University," a discussion between the two writers of the show that featured cast members and other people on the creative team. They brought him back for a good portion of the winter of 2011. In February of 2011, Melissa Etheridge took her shot at the role when Billie Joe needed to take a week off. Whereas Tony Vincent played the role as a scary David Bowie and Billie Joe played it almost demonically, Etheridge played the role seductively.

While he was playing St. Jimmy on Broadway, the original Broadway soundtrack won the Grammy Award for Best Musical Show Album. It beat out the Afrobeat extravaganza *Fela!*, the revival of the Burt Bacharach and Hal David chestnut *Promises, Promises*, and the albums from two Stephen Sondheim shows, *A Little Night Music* and *Sondheim on Sondheim*. Of those titles, *American Idiot* was the only show that was still running when the Grammys were passed out.

Taking the Show on the Road

After closing on Broadway a year and a day after it opened, *American Idiot* hit the road in a big way. Companies were formed in America and in England. Similar to Jones's reaction to playing Whatsername, Amelia Lily, who played Whatsername in a UK touring company of the musical, told Jim Palmer of the *Richmond and Twickenham Times*: "I had some really intense scenes—a bed scene and lots of intense moments in the show. After doing it I feel so much more confident as an actress."

Another member of the London cast—Newton Faulkner, who played Johnny—had been in a Green Day cover band with the actor who was playing St. Jimmy. In the United Kingdom, Faulkner is a double-Platinum recording artist in his own right, having knocked Amy Winehouse out of the No. 1 slot in the UK charts with his first album, *Hand Built by Robots*.

The musical has also become a staple among amateur and high school theatrical companies. In 2016, it opened at the Contra Costa Civic Theater in El Cerrito, one of the East Bay towns in the neighborhood where the band members grew up. In Enfield, Connecticut, the Enfield High School Drama Club decided to do the show. The "no Disney moments" assertion came back to haunt the musical. As soon as auditions were announced, the school's principal started receiving calls from parents objecting to the play's "swearing, drug use, and sex." Billie Joe was incensed. He wrote an open letter to the school's principal:

> I realize the content of the Broadway production of *AI* is not quite "suitable" for a younger audience. However there is a high school rendition of the production and I believe that's the one Enfield was planning to perform which is suitable for most people. It would be a shame if these high schoolers were shut down over some of the content that may be challenging for some of the audience, but the bigger issue is censorship, [sic] this production tackles issues in a post 9/11 world and I believe the kids should be heard, and most of all be creative in telling a story about our history. I hope you reconsider and allow them to create an amazing night of theater!

The club wound up putting on *Little Shop of Horrors.*

Other Stages

In 2013, several years after *American Idiot's* original theatrical run (it still is frequently put on by amateur companies), Billie Joe wrote original music for a show called *These Paper Bullets,* Rolin Jones's reworking of Shakespeare's *Much Ado About Nothing,* originally for the Yale Repertory Theater. The show takes the basic premise of the Shakespeare play and puts it into the hands of a Beatles-like band performing four of Billie Joe's songs, which Kitts arranged. Billie Joe sang one of them for a promotional video. It played in New Haven, Connecticut; Los Angeles; and very briefly Off-Broadway.

In 2011, it was announced that Tom Hanks's Playtone Productions would produce a movie version of *American Idiot.* The idea hung in the air for a while, and eventually HBO got the rights to do it as a movie project.

I Wanna Be on TV (and in the Movies)

Green Day on the Small Screen and Large

When the band was initially toying with the idea of a visual representation of *American Idiot*, theater was not their first choice. The band first sought to go Hollywood with the piece. "Then," Billie Joe noted to *Billboard*, "we took some meetings and realized the movie industry makes the music industry look like a mom-and-pop store."

Despite this, Billie Joe knows a thing or two about being on TV and in the movies. He got his finger tattooed with his wife's name on *Inked*. He played the character Irv Kratzer, a ghostly gambler, on the UPN show *Haunted*. Nurse Jackie picked him up in a 2012 episode of that show. That same year he was a mentor as part of "Team Christina" for five episodes of *The Voice*. The whole band was featured in an episode of MTV's *Reverb*. They also played the *American Idol* finale in 2007. This is beyond all the appearances on MTV (and elsewhere) in their music videos.

The entire band was the main focus (or at least most of the focus) of films like the Pop Disaster Tour movie *Riding in Vans with Boys*; the *American Idiot* Tour chronicle *Bullet in a Bible*; the Network's *Disease Is Punishment*; John Roeker's "making of *American Idiot* (the album)" film *Heart Like a Hand Grenade*; the film journal of the *21st Century Breakdown* Tour, *Awesome as Fuck*; the trilogy documentary ¡Cuatro!; and Doug Hamilton's telling of how the musical *American Idiot* got put together, *Broadway Idiot*. The entire band also speak for themselves in Corbet Redford's film on Gilman Street, *Turn It Around: The Story of East Bay Punk*. They gave voice to a gang of paintball-playing teens, with Tré playing the leader of the group, on *King of the Hill*.

Billie Joe has been in several documentaries, including 2003's Rodney "On the ROQ" Bingenheimer biopic, *The Mayor of Sunset Strip*, and Jai

Al-Attus's film about the reblooming and rebooming of punk rock in northern California, *One Nine Nine Four.*

They don't even have to be present or have their music on a show to turn up on TV. In an episode of *Rescue Me,* two of the firefighters are talking about a quote. One of them asks, "Is that from the Bible?" The other responds, "It's Green Day, asshole!" On the first season of *24,* the children of the character who will be president come home from a Green Day concert. In the film *High Fidelity,* a woman walks into Championship Records looking for a Green Day album, sparking a conversation that ranges from the Clash to Stiff Little Fingers to *Blonde on Blonde.* In the movie *10 Things I Hate about You,* one of the characters is shown buying a copy of *Insomniac.* The film *Angus* includes the song "J.A.R." and Green Day is also referenced several times in the film's dialogue. They are mentioned in an ongoing riff about a radio contest where the first caller gets concert tickets.

As popular as they are with garage bands around the world, so they are with fictitious bands on television. On *Sabrina the Teenage Witch,* one of Sabrina's friends is in a band that gets to open for a Green Day show. On the cartoon *Jimmy Neutron,* Jimmy and his friends form a band and play "Warning."

The whole band lent voices to the animated black comedy about the Manson Family, *Live Freaky! Die Freaky!* Billie Joe provided the voice of one of the main characters, Charles Hanson. He plays himself (as do nearly a dozen other musicians) in the Judd Apatow movie *This Is 40.*

At the Movies

During the break after he finished rehab, while everyone else was getting healthy, Billie Joe took on two movie roles. The first was a supporting role as Leighton Meester's slacker boyfriend in Frank Whalley's *Like Sunday, Like Rain.* While it did very well on the festival circuit, it did not do well at the box office in general release.

In 2014, Billie Joe and his son Joseph took up residence in New York City for the filming of a movie with the working title *Geezer.* It was Billie Joe's first starring role. The film was still called *Geezer* when it opened at the Tribeca Film Festival. The name was later changed to *Ordinary World,* and it featured the *Revolution Radio* song of the same name. In it, Billie Joe basically plays the character of himself if *Dookie* had not sold ten million copies. He's a dad, has two children, lives in Queens (which is not too unlike Oakland), works at a hardware store, and is totally frustrated by the whole situation. When his wife forgets his birthday, his brother puts up the money for a major hotel blowout that brings his old band together again. Actress Judy Greer agreed to be in the film mostly because Billie Joe was in it. "I wanted to work with Billie Joe Armstrong," she told the Associated Press. "He's amazing. I have been a Green Day fan since forever. I though he was brilliant and it was so

Live Freaky, Die Freaky, an animated film featuring the voices of all the boys in the band.

much fun to watch him work . . . He's a total peach. He is such a normal guy. He loves his sons and his wife and his dogs and just loves to play music. I thought this was such a good role for him."

There are moments that probably spoke to the early days of his Green Day fame, like when he is booking a big suite in a fancy hotel. The concierge is convinced the scruffy Billie Joe cannot afford it, only to have him pull $1,000 cash out of his pocket.

While making *Ordinary World*, they decided to record all the music live. This had a lot to do with the history that Billie Joe and costar Fred Armisen had. "Green Day played [on a bill] with Fred's band in Beloit, Wisconsin, in 1991 at, like, an Elks' Lodge," Billie Joe told the *New Yorker*. He added: "In a lot of other rock and roll movies, you see a lot of lip-synching, people not really playing. With us, we're actually a band, we're actually playing. We got in a room and rehearsed the songs together. In the opening scene in the club, we're actually playing in front of people, so you get a feel from

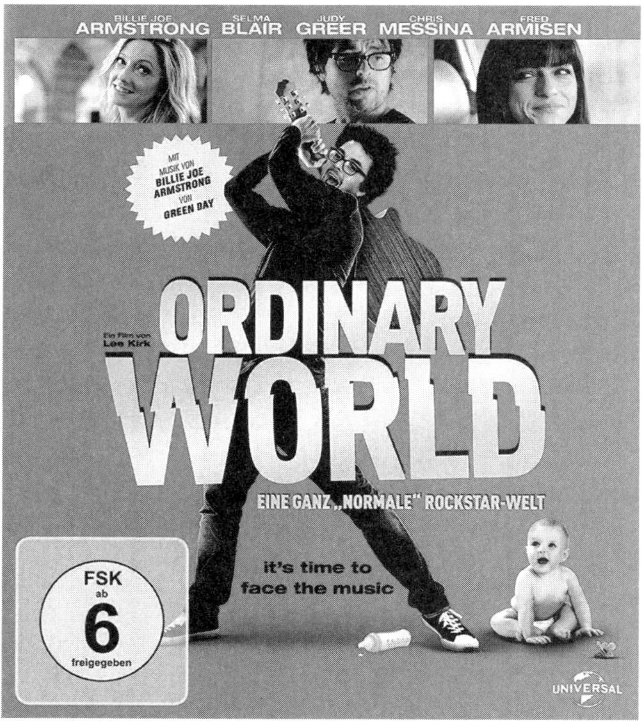

Billie Joe's first starring role as Billie Joe Armstrong if *Dookie* never happened. Because Dookie happens.

the people in the audience . . . Even the hotel room scene is all live. It was really fun."

Billie Joe wrote original songs for the movie: "Devil's Kind" and "Body Bag" were exclusive to the film.

At the after-party for the film's Tribeca Film Festival debut, Tré and Billie Joe played the songs he wrote for the film and a couple of Green Day songs. Then, they welcomed Joan Jett, who makes a cameo appearance in the film, up onstage to join them. They started playing "American Idiot," but somehow (actually, it's pretty easy to hear how) they slipped into Jett's "Bad Reputation." Joan maintained her "bad reputation," rocking a see-through blouse for the evening.

Video Augmented the Radio Star

If Green Day were not necessarily made by MTV, they had an amazing symbiotic relationship with the music TV channel when it actually played music videos. Their Reprise debut video "Longview" must have been technically difficult to shoot—it showed the band in their natural habitat at the time, a beat up basement with old furniture and low-hanging pipes, which had to have wrought hell on the lighting and camera crews. With its freaked-out bass part and wanton destruction of a sofa sending debris everywhere, it became one of the channel's most popular videos. It seemed that the only people at MTV who didn't like it were Beavis and Butt-Head, who noted that Billie Joe's mouth looked like it was "all encrusted with globules of feces."

They followed this with the insane asylum-set "Basket Case" (shot in a defunct mental institution), which eventually found Billie Joe, Mike, and Tré wrapped up in straightjackets. The song got heavy play on MTV and earned nine MTV Video Music Award nominations (winning exactly none).

For the "Walking Contradiction" video, a number of cars (including a police cruiser), a piano, and ultimately a building give their all for the cause. The accident-laden video features some formidable stunts, like a utility worker falling from a cherry picker, a newsie getting buried under his stand, and any number of moving, crashing vehicles just missing Billie Joe, Tré, and Mike. The band did all their own stunts, including the one when Billie Joe—walking through traffic while reading a newspaper—nearly gets run over at the intersection of Centre Street and 7th Street in Los Angeles. Tré pretty much had to coerce Billie Joe to do that scene. "Tré scared me into it," Billie Joe said on the Green Day Authority website. "I was so scared. I thought I was gonna die right there with all the cameras on me. Well, I can think of worse ways to die."

Post Music Television

Long after MTV started to eschew music videos for shows like *Jackass*, Green Day was making good and even great videos. The video for "Wake Me Up When September Ends" changed Billie Joe's heartfelt song about his father's death into a rumination on war. The video introduced Evan Rachel Wood and Jamie Bell to each other. They were together for several years and had a child before calling it quits.

Mark Webb's videos for *21st Century Breakdown* seem to deal with a theme of wanton destruction even more than the album does. The "21 Guns" video touches base with a lot of older images, going back to that first video, "Longview," with a sofa getting trashed and spewing feathers everywhere, only this time the weapon of choice is not a knife but a gun (or perhaps twenty-one of them). The follow-up, "Last of the American Girls," finds the woman from the "21 Guns" video (presumably Gloria) living in the desert. Her space has everything but walls (perhaps they were all shot away during the "21 Guns" barrage?), and in place of the boyfriend (ostensibly Christian), she has acquired two blond-wigged go-go dancing clones who mirror her every move. As anyone living in the desert might, she takes a bath, listens to some records, watches some TV, does her nails, takes target practice, and blows up a car.

One of the most remarkable Green Day videos, and indeed music videos in general, is "Redundant." In the video—on a set that resembles a stylized living room and anteroom with several doors, windows, and arched entranceways—a group of people perform the same fourteen actions over and over again, working the action around the band playing disinterestedly in the foreground. As a window all the way in the rear displays waving palm trees:

- Someone tosses a newspaper into the anteroom.
- A woman enters from stage right, yawns, stretches, picks up the paper, opens it, and walks off stage left.
- One of several people takes a painting off the wall over the rear window and replaces it with another one; then another comes in and replaces that one with the first.
- An elderly woman walks through the room and wanders until she locates an exit.

- A young woman walks in from stage left, puts a box on a table next to the couch, goes to the rear window, and scrambles out.
- A man walks into the room, picks up the box the young woman left, and leaves.
- Another man in a Stetson walks around the room and exits.
- A woman who looks like Bettie Page takes off her bright red dress and walks out in her bra and bloomers.
- An older man walks into the room in his skivvies, puts on a pair of pants, and walks out.
- Another older man enters, puts a plant on a table, and exits.
- A woman with an ice bucket walks in, picks up the plant, and leaves.
- A young couple dance in, make their way to the couch, neck for a while, and then leave to the rear.
- A guy vacuums a bit of the room and walks out.
- Another young woman in a pair of bright red gym shorts climbs in through a side window, looks around, and exits through the anteroom.

These actions are repeated with increasing complexity as more and more people become involved. When the song winds down, everyone leaves the room, including the band. On his way out, Billie Joe grabs the paper. The cycle is broken, and when the woman walks in to collect the paper, she doesn't find it and screams in terror.

Several of the people who made Green Day videos went on to bigger and perhaps better things. Jonathan Sela, the cinematographer for the "21 Guns" video, has moved on to films like *John Wick* and *Transformers.* The song "21 Guns" appeared in the latter film.

Tonight Our Guests Are . . .

Beyond their music videos, Green Day earned a reputation for translating to the small screen and being colorful guests on talk shows. When they first appeared on Conan O'Brien's version of *Late Night* for their first ever network TV performance in March of 1994, their equipment started feeding back, nearly obliterating O'Brien's introduction. "They can hardly wait to begin," O'Brien joked, but the band was serious. They ripped through a version of "Welcome to Paradise" that left people breathless.

Several months later, they were the guests on the *Late Show with David Letterman.* Again they left a high-energy burn on the stage, playing "Basket Case." A few weeks after that, they were on *Saturday Night Live* and tore through "When I Come Around," and gave a glimpse of coming attractions, playing "Geek Stink Breath" about a year before it came out on *Insomniac.* They also made two appearances on the show *Mad TV.* They played "Warning" on one and "Blood, Sex and Booze" on the other. The latter song was also in the film *Freddy Got Fingered.*

When Jimmy Fallon took over the *Tonight Show,* he added some interesting conceptual ideas, like having musical guests do a song with him and (house band) the Roots playing on toy instruments. Another was to have a week of musicians paying tribute to a classic album. When the show spent a week on the Rolling Stones' *Exile on Main Street,* Green Day joined artists like Sheryl Crow, Phish, and Keith Urban in taking on a song. The one they played was "Rip This Joint."

Despite his high-profile rehab in 2013, Billie Joe played Charlie Chaplin in a 2016 episode of Comedy Central's *Drunk History.* He also joined Chris Rock and Alice Waters on an episode of *Real Time with Bill Maher.*

The band or their music has been part of shows from Germany, Japan, Australia, and many other places. They have played on British shows like *Live from Abbey Road* and *Later,* hosted by former Squeeze keyboard player Jules Holland. They appeared on the ITV concert show *Hotel Babylon* in 1996 (not to be confused with the BBC soap opera of a decade later).

Green Day played the MTV New Year's Eve show in 1998 and 1999, and they spent NYE 2009 with Carson Daly on NBC. Their appearance on MTV's *Behind the Music* featured twenty-seven edits for "bad language." This was second only to Oasis. Three years before their own induction into the Rock and Roll Hall of Fame, they blasted the show open with "Letterbomb" in 2012. Billie Joe then went on to install Guns N' Roses into the Hall and later sang background vocals when they performed "Mr. Brownstone," a performance that had been rehearsed moments before the show began in the bathroom of Guns N' Roses' dressing room.

And the Winner Is

Guest appearances were not limited to talk shows and *SNL.* Green Day became fixtures on the Grammy Awards from *Dookie* onwards. While they have been in the Grammy winner's circle five times, they have performed on the show even more frequently, appearing on the 2005 broadcast playing "American Idiot," giving an award (and announcing their next album) in 2009, and showing up once again in 2010.

Similarly, while they did not win an MTV Video Music Awards Moonman trophy until 1998, they had already played on the telecast of the awards show previous to that in 1994 and 1997 as well as later, in 2005, 2009, and 2012. They have played or appeared on award shows ranging from the plethora of other MTV/VH1 presentations in the United States, Europe, and Australia to the Tony Awards for theater to the Video Game Awards.

Music on TV and in the Movies

One of the most watched TV shows of the 1990s was the finale of the program about nothing, *Seinfeld.* One of the last things heard on that last episode of Seinfeld was the Green Day song "Good Riddance (Time of Your Life)." The song also figured prominently in two episodes of *ER* and an episode of *Do Over.* It even turns up in a documentary on the series *High Chaparall.* Everyone seems to love the song. On the MTV *Diary of Avril Lavigne,* Avril sings along to "Good Riddance (Time of Your Life)" in the back of a limousine. Then, in another episode, she is on a boat (Avril sure can travel) and starts singing "Longview."

"Boulevard of Broken Dreams" was used in *Smallville, Third Watch,* and *The Office.* The band played it live on *SNL* and at the 2004 Billboard Music Awards. They played "American Idiot" on the *Late Show with David Letterman* the same night Democratic presidential candidate John Kerry appeared on the program. The short-lived Syfy show *Alphas* used the song "Let Yourself Go." The TV movie *This Is How the World Ends* contains "Welcome to Paradise." The closing credits song on the first episode of HBO's *Silicon Valley* was "Minority." The exit song to the *Andy Milonakis Show* on MTV was "American Idiot."

Disney/Pixar features the song "Westbound Sign" from *Insomniac* in the trailer to the film *Cars.* "Welcome to Paradise" was used in the trailer for the film *Surf's Up.* "Brain Stew" was remixed for the soundtrack to the 1998 version of *Godzilla* and also pops up during a scene in the Disney gymnastics dramedy *Stick It.* The high school football epic *Varsity Blues* very appropriately features "Nice Guys Finish Last." "Outsider" is on *The New Guy* soundtrack; "Scumbag" appears on *American Pie 2*; the MTV film *Joe's Apartment* includes the *Insomniac* song "86"; and *Austin Powers: The Spy Who Shagged Me* featured the Grammy-nominated instrumental "Espionage" in a chase scene. The early song "2,000 Light Years Away" was on the soundtrack to *The Jerky Boys.* In *Accepted,* "Holiday" turns up in a party scene. One of the main musical themes of *The Twilight Saga: Breaking Dawn—Part 2* was the song "The Forgotten." The film *Waiting for "Superman"* made use of the song

"American Idiot," at once ironic and apropos for a documentary on the state of America's schools.

Green Day dominated the 2004 MTV Movie Awards with bits of *American Idiot* being used as walk-up music. *Anchorman: The Legend of Ron Burgundy* won its Best On-Screen Team Award to the tune of "Stuck with Me." "Holiday" played for the announcement of Leonardo DiCaprio's nomination for Best Male Performance. Their music also figured into announcements of people who actually made it into the winner's circle. When Dustin Hoffman won Best Comedic Performance for *Meet the Fockers*, the award was presented to the tune of "American Idiot" (wonder if he was pleased or offended?). When *Napoleon Dynamite* won Best Movie, the losing films were consoled when the winners collected their Moonman statues to the tune of "Boulevard of Broken Dreams."

CSI: NY did a pretty gutsy experiment with Green Day music, having virtually no dialogue for the first half of the episode "Unspoken." Instead, they let the visuals and the Green Day trilogy songs "Stop When the Red Lights Flash," "Amy," "Nightlife," "The Forgotten," and "Kill the DJ" tell the story. Their music had previously been used on the show, on a 2005 episode that sported the song "Holiday."

A 2005 ad for Yahoo! Music features a sprite animation of the band playing "Holiday." A Nokia commercial for the Canadian MuchMusic Video Awards included an "American Idiot" ringtone. The Independent Film Channel cut a deal with Green Day and Reprise, and for much of 2005, "Jesus of Suburbia" became the soundtrack to its promotional videos and programming interstitials.

One of the most unusual uses of a Green Day song was a highlight of an episode in the second season of *Mr. Robot*. During an introspective moment as the main character, Eliot, is wondering whether all the subversive work he is doing is worth it, a music-box version of "Basket Case" plays in the background. It is so subtle, even Green Day fans might miss it.

Everyone's Gone to the Movies

The Fiatarones, who recorded Billie Joe's first single when he was five years old, recognized his star quality almost as soon as they saw him. This trend continued and expanded as he became a rock star. For example, when the film *Empire Records* was casting, they thought Billie Joe would be perfect for the wisecracking Berko. Unfortunately, Billie Joe had to be on the road for much of the next two years, so they had to settle for Coyote Shivers.

Green Day has been a subject and often *the* subject in numerous documentaries. Several were linked to band projects that were chronicled on video. When they played their biggest ever shows for two nights at Milton Keynes England's National Bowl before some 130,000 fans over the course of two nights during the *American Idiot* tour, the event was documented by director Samuel Bayer, who had done all the official music videos for the album. "This is the antithesis of what punk is supposed to be," Bayer told MTV News. "Punk bands aren't supposed to play in front of 65,000 people and punk bands aren't supposed to be huge . . . The kids all know the words and are crying and got their lighters up in the air, I mean . . . when I watch it I still get goose bumps."

"It's the first time I've ever gotten to see myself in a concert situation, so it's pretty cool," Billie Joe noted of his experience watching the documentary, *Bullet in a Bible.* "We tried to capture something that was like our favorite concert films, *Don't Look Back* or *Rattle and Hum* or *Song Remains the Same* or *Rude Boy.* Those are my heroes."

Beyond catching the band at a peak in their performing power, as a group that had come to grips with the fact that they *had* to play to crowds this big or stay in one place for weeks at a time, it also presented some intimate moments backstage. *Bullet in a Bible*'s premiere had a red carpet at the ArcLight Cinema and was attended by the opening acts for the show (not featured in the film), New Found Glory and Taking Back Sunday.

When the band decided to record and release three separate albums in 2011, the process was filmed by director Tim Wheeler. It became the "rockumentary" *¡Cuatro!*. Green Day had long been using social media, especially YouTube, to reach out to their fans with progress reports on projects. The film helped consolidate the experience (minus a lot of the drug use that went into the making of the project). A 45-minute highlight reel of the movie was shown on various MTV affiliates several months before the actual 105-minute cut was release. It was nominated for a Grammy for Best Music Film.

Unlike much of the band's cinematic output, John Roecker's decade-in-the-making documentary on *American Idiot* called *Heart Like a Hand Grenade* saw a theatrical release before becoming home media. There was a Hollywood opening at Grauman's, and it played in cinemas around the world.

Even before the play *American Idiot* finished its run on Broadway, there was talk of a film. One thing Billie Joe was adamant about was that it eschew the kind of excesses that Ken Russell used when he made the film of the

Who's *Tommy*. "I'd like to do something that comes across more as a movie than a musical."

By 2016, the film had become an HBO original project. Billie Joe confirmed he would play St. Jimmy in the film. He also confirmed that this would be an entirely different animal from the musical. He described the project to *NME*, saying: "[It's] more surreal . . . I think there are parts of it that might offend people—which is good. I think it's a good time to offend people . . . there's just going to be a lot of imagery that we couldn't pull off in the musical in the stage version . . . it will be shocking in a way which makes you think."

Among the non-documentary films the band has appeared in, one of the most famous is *The Simpsons Movie*, in which Green Day appear as animated versions of themselves. They played a Green Day version of the Danny Elfman theme song.

Other Screens

While their pre-*Dookie* bookmobile tour vehicle was not the sort of vehicle they tour in now, it did have some of the same amenities, including a Sega Genesis. While they are admittedly not very good at video games, the games are a major part of contemporary popular culture. When contemporary popular culture is your business, it pays to pay attention. Little wonder, then, that Green Day's visages and sounds have made their way on to an assortment of video games.

In the 2001 release *Halo Combat Evolved*, one of the multiplayer menu screens contains a Green Day Easter egg, with the line "Sometimes I give myself the creeps and my mind plays tricks on me" from "Basket Case." A computer simulation of Billie Joe appears in *Tony Hawk's American Wasteland*. "For someone who doesn't know how to skateboard," he told *Sports Illustrated*'s Richard Deitsch, "I'm going to be ripping it up."

Their first major video game was the obvious one. Music-oriented game developers Harmonix had already put together several dance-oriented games and the original *Guitar Hero*. They teamed up with MTV Games and Electronic Arts to create a video game that let players become members of a rock band. The first version of *Rock Band* was issued in November of 2007 and became one of the hot holiday gifts of the year. They got content for the games from many well-known bands, including the Yeah Yeah Yeahs, Blue Oyster Cult, the Hives, and the Red Hot Chili Peppers. They wanted to put out band specific versions of the game. The first group they approached was

Apple Corps, the business entity behind the Beatles. The second group to get its own edition of *Rock Band* was Green Day.

"They were already doing The Beatles game, which was in production at the time and were showing us that one," Billie Joe recalled for *GQ*. "I think that's what really we were excited about. If it's good enough for The Beatles it's good enough for us."

The first time Tré encountered *Rock Band* was in a California pub. They had hooked the game up to a TV in a corner of the bar and people were playing the game and drinking and having a grand old time. "It was an instant party," he told MTV News's James Montgomery. "There were grownups playing video games."

Billie Joe had noticed that a lot of the material on *Rock Band* was by older classic rock bands, so Green Day added some more contemporary music to the mix. He liked the idea that playing the toy plastic instrument controllers might inspire people to actually get real instruments. Tré was not so sure. "These games do for music what Mortal Kombat does for karate studios," he told *GQ*. "I don't think it affects it one way or the other."

In December of 2009, Green Day made a three pack of songs from *21st Century Breakdown* available for *Rock Band* on Wii, Xbox, and PlayStation 3. They sold for $1.99 (160 Microsoft points or 200 Wii points) per song or all three at a cost of $5.49 (440 Microsoft points or 600 Wii points) for "Christian's Inferno," "Last of the American Girls," and "¡Viva La Gloria!"

The band's biggest problem with the whole project was that they were all abysmal at it. "I've played the drums [in *Rock Band*]," Billie Joe told *Time* magazine, "and I'm terrible."

"It's hard," Mike told Montgomery, "but you certainly catch on. . . . Eventually."

Around the time ¡Uno! was released, Green Day teamed up with online game and media company Rovio for a promotional version of the game Angry Birds. This edition featured porcine caricatures of Green Day as the four pigs. (It included a Jason White "pig.") The game was set at a Green Day concert and had twenty levels along with two additional "Golden Grenade" levels. In those "Golden Grenade" levels, the "pigs" picked up instruments and started playing. There were also two "Heart Like a Hand Grenade" grenades.

About a week after it came out initially, another ten levels, plus one more golden "Heart Like a Hand Grenade" grenade, were added. Whereas the old "HLAHG" grenade level played the *¡Uno!* song "Troublemaker," the new level played the *¡Dos!* tune "Lazy Bones." Also during the new level, pigs performed a sort of porcine pyramid that spelled out "Green Day." The level selection screen played the single "Oh, Love."

Verizon was one of the corporate sponsors of the *21st Century Breakdown* Tour. As a special promotion to their customers (at least the ones who liked Green Day), Verizon further contracted with the band to make video of the concert available on its mobile V CAST service as well as video on demand for Fios users. The video was shot using twelve high-definition cameras during an August show in Phoenix, Arizona.

Stray Art

Green Day's Side Projects, from Eats to Gueets

Humanity cannot live by music alone. Even members of Green Day. While they spend great amounts of time practicing, on the road and in the studio, they also have some interesting avocations to vent the creative urges that Green Day doesn't satisfy. Mike, for example, loves stand-up comedy, and he has even performed some in LA where, he told *Rolling Stone*'s Matt Henderson, "I killed for three minutes out of four." They all have had side project bands and worked with other artists, as well as in other areas both musical and not.

"It's about being able to do something without having the constraints of being Green Day," Billie Joe told *Guitar Player*'s Art Thompson. "It's a way to stretch out in a different way, leave the trappings of what people expect of you, and just be able to do what you want. I think it's also cool to be able to play smaller places and go in under the radar."

Here are some of their avocations.

"Our Other Bands"

A lot of the members of popular bands have musical side projects, allowing them to play with people other than their regular cohort. In some cases, like Mike's Frustrators or Billie Joe's Pinhead Gunpowder, they are the sole Green Day member amongst musicians from other bands and projects. One way Green Day is different is they have projects that expand the band to allow them to take different roles in playing music.

The Network

Allegedly there is no connection between the Network and Green Day. Apart from them being largely the same group. It is one of those open secrets that no one will admit to publicly (though the Pinhead Gunpowder website outed Billie Joe as Fink, and the four members from the Green Day camp are listed as the songwriters). So all this is folklore.

When Green Day were working on *American Idiot*, things got intense in several ways. There were the infamous lost tapes, some anger issues that needed working out, and just the tension of making something that they knew could be great as good as it possibly could be. One of the ways they blew off steam was to bring in some other musicians (again, allegedly members of Devo, though some say the keyboards were played by Jason Freese) and record what would have ten years earlier been called a "fizz-pop" album, that branch of noo-wave that relied on synths and regimented guitars.

In September of 2003, a group called the Network released an album called *Money Money 2020* on Adeline Records. They claimed to be aliens sent to "rid us of the mediocre music that has inhabited our planet for too long." They had names like Fink, Van Gough, the Snoo, and Balducci. Onstage they took a page out of fellow Bay Area undergrounders the Residents' and Slipknot's playbooks: they wore masks.

Fink's voice is pretty much unmistakably Billie Joe's. The battery of bassist Van Gough and drummer the Snoo have some of the musical mannerisms of Mike and Tré, as the guitarist Balducci uses some of Jason White's moves. Of course both bands would deny these similarities. In a press conference, members of both bands got into an argument that turned into a minor scuffle, but the Network did open up shows on the *American Idiot* tour along with Jimmy Eat World. But no one is saying who they *really* are. Perhaps they are actually refugees from Daft Punk?

The original version of *Money Money 2020* had both the CD of music and a DVD of music videos. A later release just had the CD. They also released a live DVD, *Disease Is Punishment*, recorded at Los Angeles's Key Club.

Foxboro Hot Tubs

Green Day were in the midst of recording their most grueling album, following up one of their most artistically and commercially successful albums, and putting together the nuts and bolts of a theatrical version of said album. As the tension began to build, they decided they had to kick out the jams before they went crazy. "[It] gave us a platform to put something out and have some fun and get out from underneath the Green Monster," Mike told *Billboard*'s Mitchell Peters.

Thus, after a few bottles of wine, they became the Foxboro Hot Tubs, likely named after the Foxboro Downs area in nearby Hercules, California, in the East Bay. "The Foxboro Hot Tubs was a place we used to sneak booze and chicks into late at night," they said.

In part, forming the Hot Tubs was a reaction to becoming an arena and stadium band *and becoming inured to it.* Where Green Day have always been remarkably tight onstage, playing together like the well-oiled rock machine they are, the Foxboro Hot Tubs were tight in another way: on beer. After an FHT gig, the stage was practically awash in empty Pabst Blue Ribbon cans—during a "secret show" at New York's Bowery Electric, it was estimated that nearly a thousand cans had gone various directions, sprayed into the audience, poured over each other's heads, and of course down their gullets. Billie Joe spent the better part of the show crowd surfing.

"It was just sort of get in a room and have some fun, play whatever you want, and write a song in ten minutes," Hot Tub member Jason White told Thompson. "Fly by the seat of your pants and just go." They just started playing their favorite riffs from their favorite bands, such as the Kinks, the Who, the Zombies, and other British Invasion heroes. The music first appeared on the web on December 11, 2007.

The album *Stop Drop and Roll!!!*, when it was released as such, debuted at No. 21 on the *Billboard* 200. To continue the references to the sixties, the CD had a side one and side two (and a warning not to play side two). The song "Mother Mary" reached No. 16 on *Billboard*'s Alternative Rock charts. The Fox Tubs were, for all intents and purposes, the driving force behind the trilogy album *¡Dos!*

Initially they tried to keep the two bands distinct. They released a few songs for free online, on a website that talked smack about . . . themselves, or more correctly their alter egos, Green Day.

Eventually, though, with typical humor, they outed themselves in an email to the mass media. "We are the same band. That is basically the only similarity. We are Jason White, Jason Freese, Michael Pritchard, Frank Edwin Wright the Third [Tré Cool] – and the Reverend Strychnine Twitch. We are four (wild and crazy?) guys who love to play music and be spontaneous. We were inspired to record some rockin' eight-track recordings." There were others involved with the Tubs as well, including Prima Donna lead singer Kevin Preston.

Two days after the opening night of *American Idiot* on Broadway, Green Day played a short surprise concert, then turned into the Hot Tubs on their way downtown, and played the aforementioned show at New York

City's Bowery Electric. There were a handful of club shows in Little Rock, Arkansas; New Orleans, Louisiana; Austin, Texas; Phoenix, Arizona; and San Diego, West Hollywood, and Long Beach, California.

"I think we needed that escape for a while to refuel us or bring us together a little bit more," Billie Joe told *Guitar World.*

"My Other Bands"

Lots of successful bands members have side projects that allow them to do something other than their main gig. For Billie Joe, his side project Pinhead Gunpowder has been around nearly as long as Green Day. It allows him to play some truly grimy punk. "Pinhead Gunpowder is a totally different band," original Pinhead Jason White told *Guitar World,* "so it's a collaborative effort between Billie, myself and the other two guys (Bill Schneider and Aaron Cometbus). We all share the writing in the band."

Pinhead Gunpowder generally only gets together every few years. As of this writing, their last record was the 2008 EP *West Side Highway* on Recess Records, and the last shows they played were part of a five-gig mini-tour during February 2012 that included performances at 924 Gilman and the Troubadour in LA, where they played "At Your Funeral," "West Side Highway," and a cover of "Theme from Mahogany."

Billie Joe also cut a limited-release EP with a band called the Boo, which featured a bunch of other people named Armstrong: Adrienne, Jakob, and Joey.

Mike has a long running side project as well, called the Frustrators. Despite the ban on Green Day, the Frustrators played a gig at Gilman in 2001. Mike found the gig gave him a sense of closure where the club was concerned.

The Frustrators record for Adeline and as of this writing have an EP, *Bored in the USA*, and an album, *Achtung Jackass.* The band also includes Terry Linehan from Waterdog on guitar as well as singer Jason Chandler and drummer Art Tedeschi, both from Violent Anal Death.

Extra–Green Day Affairs

The Lookouts—Lookout! Records' owner Larry Livermore's band—featured a very young Tré Cool on drums. When Livermore decided to make a final Lookouts record, he asked Tré to play the drums, and he recruited Billie Joe to play lead guitar and do backing vocals.

In 2003, the entire band cut two tracks, "Private Hell" and "Supermarket," for Iggy Pop's record Skull Ring.

Billie Joe has collaborated with a lot of other artists, including:

- Writing with the Go-Gos and Rancid.
- Singing background on Ryan Adams's "Do Miss America" and the Lonely Island's "I Run NY."
- Playing lead guitar and singing on the first EP for Jesse Michaels's Common Rider. He also worked with Goodbye Harry and Blatz.
- Appearing along with Fiona Apple and Death Cab for Cutie in a VH1 Classics "Decades Rock Live" tribute to Elvis Costello, shot at the Mark Estess Theater of the Taj Mahal Casino in Atlantic City, New Jersey. Every young woman in the crowd screamed really loudly when Billie Joe hit the stage to give Costello's "No Action" the punk reading the song deserved. Then Elvis and his band tried to return the favor with a take on "Wake Me Up When September Ends." They also did an acoustic version of Costello's "Lip Service" together. Billie Joe came back on for the end of the show, along with Apple and the members of DC4C to do versions of Smokey Robinson's "You've Really Got a Hold on Me" and Nick Lowe's "(What's So Funny 'Bout) Peace, Love, and Understanding."
- Occasionally playing acoustic shows, either solo or with Jason White, at small clubs on short notice. They sometimes get announced to the Idiot Nation, Green Day's fan club.
- Joining Avicii in the studio (along with Coldplay's Chris Martin, Jon Bon Jovi, Michael Einziger from Incubus, Zac Brown, Wyclef Jean, and Matisyahu) for the *Stories* album, but apparently his track "No Pleasing a Woman" did not make it onto the release.
- Meeting some of the New York underground during a hiatus in New York City, as he hung out at many jam sessions.
- Living a dream when his friend and hero Paul Westerberg of the Replacements messed up his back and could not play his parts live, though the band had committed to play several large shows. Armstrong took the stage at the 2014 Coachella festival, playing and singing while Westerberg lie onstage on a sofa. There was a repeat performance at the Shaky Knees festival.
- Producing records for the Riverdales and Emily's Army, which has since changed their name to SWMRS and features Joey Armstrong on drums.

All this beyond his work in theater, movies, and TV (which is dealt with in depth in the previous chapter).

Mike's extra Green Day excursions, beyond the Frustrators, have found him working with Screeching Weasel and Corrupted Morals.

Jason White (also a member of Pinhead Gunpowder) formed a band with former Jawbreaker drummer Adam Pfahler called California, which opened for Philadelphia's Beach Slang in May of 2016. Jason records his own songs in his garage studio and occasionally works with his old band Big Cats when he goes back to the town he grew up in, Little Rock, Arkansas. "I go back there a couple of times a year and we'll do a holiday show, and we also write songs and record together," Jason told Thompson.

Foreverly

Sometime in 2010 or 2011, Billie Joe discovered the odd-duck Everly Brother's album *Songs Our Daddy Taught Us*, which put a period to three years of smashes for the Everlys on Cadence records. As opposed to songs that made them famous like "Wake Up Little Susie" and "Bye Bye Love," this

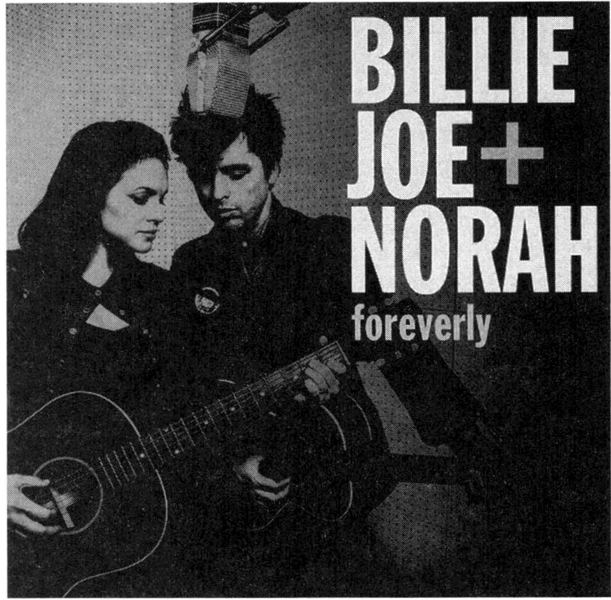

Billie Joe and Nora Jones. With about a dozen Grammy Awards between them, they set out to pay tribute to the Everly Brothers.

record was a paean to the music they played live on the radio in Iowa as a family act when they were teens, and songs they would play at home with their dad, Ike. It included old folk songs like "Barbra Allen," "Who's Gonna Shoe Your Pretty Little Feet," and "Roving Gambler"; classic country like "Long Time Gone" and "Silver Haired Daddy of Mine"; and ballads like "Down in the Willow Garden." A passion project for the brothers, it was their reward for creating so many hit records for Cadence.

Clearly, if these were indeed songs that their father taught them, Ike Everly had a genuine dark streak, as so many of these songs deal with death, unrequited love, bad men, and destruction. Billie Joe listened to the record every morning for a while, and although he did not specify it, this was his first recording project after rehab. Though he said that making the record was not a particularly cathartic experience, perhaps listening to it had been.

One of things Billie Joe marveled at was the idea of this information being passed on from father to son, and he developed a yen to pass it on to a new generation. It also appealed to the side of his musical makeup inspired by his own mother, who was raised in Oklahoma and a big country music fan. "I played it for my mom," he told NPR's Steve Inskeep. "She started to two-step around the house."

When Billie Joe brought the idea up to his wife, Adrienne, she suggested this might be an opportunity for him to work with Norah Jones. Jones's grandparents were also from Oklahoma, so she too was partially raised on country music. She loved the idea, especially after she heard the album. She told Inskeep, "This record is really dark. There's [sic] lots of dead children and dead wives; and a lot of stories, really dark stories."

Jones mostly sang Phil Everly's high harmonies (she also took lead on "I'm Here to Get My Baby out of Jail"). Billie Joe performed Don's parts. The band consisted of Billie Joe on guitar and pump organ; Jones on guitar, six-string banjo, chimes, pump organ, and piano; Tim Luntzel on bass; Dan Rieser on drums; Jonny Lam on pedal steel guitar; and Charlie Burnham on violin, mandolin, and harmonica—especially stunning on "Roving Gambler." Billie Joe even went so far as to use a Gibson J-180 acoustic guitar to make the album, which had been known as the "Everly Brothers model" since the late fifties.

The whole project gained an even darker edge when Phil Everly died about two months after the record was released. Billie Joe paid tribute to Phil Everly at the 2014 Grammy Awards, this time performing a duet with country star Miranda Lambert on "When Will I Be Loved."

Extra-Musical Affairs—Music Business

Many artists have other things going on, especially artists from successful bands like Green Day. Some of them just capitalize on their fame, and for others it is a few steps above a high profile hobby. These side businesses can include their own record company—where they can put out music by their friends—old demo tapes, or pretty much anything that would not be a conflict of interest with their main gig. As a band with diverse interests, Green Day have a batch of these extra-musical affairs.

Adeline Records

Named for Adeline Street, a major thoroughfare through Oakland and into Berkeley, Adeline Records was started by Billie Joe, Jason White, skateboarder Jim Thiebaud, and Screw 32 guitarist Doug Sangalang.

Artists on Adeline included Australian ex-rockabilly, power-pop punks the Living End, Jesse Malin, AFI, Emily's Army, the Network, the Frustrators, Pinhead Gunpowder, Agent 51, and others, and all of Green Day's work on vinyl. The label is distributed by Warner via East West records.

Jingletown Studios

Jingletown is the bohemian enclave of Oakland, a West Coast version of what Soho in New York used to be, with artists living and working in lofts. Like Soho, it was a former industrial area, though in the case of Jingletown it was not the price of real estate but the rezoning to protect the people living there that caused the change. Unlike Soho, Jingletown has managed gentrification while continuing to grow—though it has been in the throes of a decade-and-a-half-long building boom. Jingletown is the name Green Day chose as the place where their rock opera *American Idiot* takes place. It also is the home of the band's Jingletown Studios.

Originally built in 1998 as Studio 880, Jingletown Studios was, by 2001, where Green Day did much of their recording. In that time it had grown from one room to three. The facility also has offices and a conference room. The band bought the studio as they began recording *21st Century Breakdown* and renamed it Jingletown. They used it almost exclusively for their own projects until 2012 when they opened the doors to anyone wanting to pay for studio time.

People who have recorded there without a Green Day connection include VanLadyLove; metal super-group Meshiaak, featuring former members of Slayer, Anthrax, Tereamaze, and 4-Arm; Raphael Saadiq; Smash Mouth; and Samiam.

Run by longtime Green Day studio engineer Chris Dugan, it started out as "more of a home base, sort of a clubhouse for them," Dugan told the *Huffington Post*'s Melissa Webster. It was where *¡Uno!, ¡Dos!, and ¡Tré!* were recorded. As of this writing, the studio was being offered for sale with an asking price of $3.9 million.

Beyond all the other uses Green Day, Dugan, and the musicians that record there put it to, Jingletown also serves as parking for the members' collections of various vintage cars and motorcycles.

Otis Studios

As an *NME*-hosted walking tour of the band's new recording facility, Otis, displayed, the band likes to work in studios that are like clubhouses. The first floor is all business—a recording room a mixing console, analog and digital recording equipment, the bells and whistles of a modern studio. Then there is the room where the magic happens, a studio with many of their instruments (Tré has his cymbals literally stacked up behind his kit), amps and other tools for capturing music for later playback. Upstairs are sofas, surfboards, more guitars, a full-sized refrigerator, and a state of the art coffee maker. It gave them a private place to record *Revolution Radio*, as Jingletown had grown into a working studio and known location.

Broken Guitars

On April 3, 2016, Billie Joe cut the ribbon to announce the grand opening of Broken Guitars, a new music store in Oakland selling used instruments, not too far from 1-2-3-4 Go! Records. He had partnered with Bill Schneider, long time Pinhead Gunpowder guitarist, Green Day guitar tech, and frequent road coordinator for the band. The store focuses on used American-made instruments from companies like Fender, Gibson, and Gretsch, although not only vintage, collectable instruments. At the ribbon cutting, the store's inventory included around seventy-five guitars and Schneider's own proprietary, handmade amplifiers. The instruments tend to run between $400 and $800. The store also takes advantage of Schneider's guitar tech experience and offers professional repairs.

It was not Schneider's first venture into retail. Before becoming hooked into the Green Day whirlwind, he ran Univibe until his activities outside of retail forced him to close the shop and sell off his inventory. It is very hard to run a store when you are spending six months on the road.

The store also reflects Billie Joe's love of the instrument. He is alleged to have hundreds of Gibson Les Paul Juniors, some of which are likely to find their way into Broken Guitar's stock.

Extra-Musical Affairs—Clothing

In a Get Fuzzy comic from 2005, Rob wears (among other things) a Green Day T-shirt, which leads Bucky to accuse him of rocking "a 12-year-old skateboarder look." Green Day are a bit more fashion conscious than that, so much so that they have had excursions into the world of the schmatta business.

Adeline Street

In the immediate wake of *American Idiot,* Billie Joe and Adrienne partnered with Rock Steady Clothing to market a line of alternative/punk fashion, hoping to capture an "edgy look." They called the line Adeline Street, part of the record label of the same name. Billie Joe and Adrienne accepted "guidance" from Rock Steady, who made "their designs come to life." From the time Adeline Street launched in 2006, Billie Joe wore the clothing he and Adrienne designed in concert, on TV, and in magazine shoots to promote the line, making sure the items were available in stores before wearing them himself.

Adeline Street closed down three years later, announcing they had "decided not to move forward with future designs while Billie Joe and the guys are working hard on their follow up to *American Idiot*." The end of the clothing line had no effect on the record label.

Obedient Sons

Mike is a fashionable guy. Not only does he like to wear it, he likes to invest in it. In 2006, he took some *American Idiot* money and invested it in a designer sportswear company called Obedient Sons (eventually called Obedient Sons and Daughters).

OS owner and main designer Swaim Hutson told Sandra Nygaard of the *Daily News Record*: "Mike's a creative guy and he loves fashion. I always felt like he'd be the best partner, but I had trouble asking him for help. It got to the point where I just had to be persistent, so I flew out and met with him."

Mike discovered Obedient Sons at a store and sought Hutson out for more. Hutson had designed Mike's stage outfits and custom suits for award shows. Hutson and Mike even share the same birthday. "When I first saw their collections in whole," he said, "I was amazed with the strength, individuality and detail involved. Having worked with Swaim the last two years, I see a work ethic and passion that I can relate to. Seeing is believing, and I believe in Swaim and Obedient Sons."

When Hutson was going broke, Mike offered a limited amount of funding to be paid back on a firm schedule. This is clothing that demanded $250 for a shirt and $450 for a sweater at New York's Barney's Men's Shop. The clothing was confusing, even in intent, the collision of formal and casual, like a dress shirt and a tuxedo jacket with floral cutoffs. Indeed, a lot of their fashions called for short pants.

Eventually, the limited funding and strict repayments did not live up to the company's profits. The money Mike earmarked for the company was gone—or as *New York Magazine* put it, "The label's financial backer lacks the funds to continue to grow the brand." It would seem more a case of the willingness to allocate more funds. The Swains closed Obedient Sons and Daughters in the spring of 2009 but were still putting together a show for Fashion Week and taking the risk to find a new backer. They were hired by the casual fashion house Generra.

And More

The entire band was involved when they collaborated with surfboard maker and clothier Rusty on a line of hoodies with waterproof headphones built in to the drawstrings and a music player jack in one of the pockets. The Green Day line of hoodies featured "the original artwork from the band's classic albums."

The band, most of who are avid surfers when time permits, had been using Rusty boards for years. In a video tour of the band's new studio, Otis, on *NME*'s website, you can see a couple.

"When Rusty asked us to collaborate with them on their Wired Series, we jumped at the chance," Billie Joe said in a press release for the collaboration. "We identify with their creative spirit and desire to push the boundaries of fashion and technology."

Launched in conjunction with the Broadway musical version of *American Idiot,* the hoodies ranged in price from $59.50 to $79.50.

Mike also designed several pieces of footwear for Macbeth shoes. Mike's sneakers tended to be high tops. One design featured a "rugged military green upper, comprised of organic cotton, PET (recycled plastic fibers) and a recycled polyester woven material, while the black outsole consists of recycled rubber components from tires. Additionally, the adhesive is a water-based, synthetic, vegan glue." Mike donated his share of the proceeds to the National Military Family Association's Operation Purple, an organization to help the families of members of the US Armed Forces to stay connected despite current deployments.

Extra-Musical Affairs—Food

Having come a long way from the liquid dookie-inducing food of their pre-*Dookie* days, Green Day have become, if not gourmets, at least foodies. Mike is a longtime vegan. Billie Joe is a vegetarian. They all have an affinity for good coffee. They are also avid environmentalists, and this plays into their food-based businesses as well.

Oakland Coffee Works

If there was one thing that fueled Green Day, particularly in the studio, it was not bud. According to a lot of sources, Green Day albums tend to be fueled by coffee . . . an amazing amount of coffee. Coffee has become a major player in the Green Day oeuvre. They drink coffee between takes while recording.

Mike and Billie Joe had dabbled in making their own blends of coffee for years. The two of them took this passion for coffee and started their own brand of "designer coffee," Oakland Coffee Works, in 2013 (around the time Billie Joe ended his stint in rehab—twelve steppers tend to drink lots of coffee in lots of places).

The members of the band are also all about sustainability. They are all parents and worry about what they are going to leave behind for their children. They do work for ecological causes.

So as the company grew, they grew wary of the way coffee was packaged. The bags coffee comes in tend to not be biodegradable. There was a plastic lining in nearly all bags of coffee. This did not sit well with Billie Joe's and Mike's sustainability sensibility. "Experts told us that there was no sustainable way to package coffee without it going stale; it needs a one-way valve to breath," Mike told the *Daily Meal.* They wanted to do something about it, to keep their coffee fresh, but also to keep it environmentally sound—so did the neighboring San Francisco Coffee Company and its parent company, Rogers Family, of Lincoln, Nebraska.

"Come up to the lab . . . and I'll show you my favorite obsession." From the band's serious coffee jones comes Oakland Brand Coffee, their own blends.
Laurence Bordowitz

As bad as the coffee bag situation was, a new invention in the caffeinated beverage world was an even bigger environmental disaster. In 1997, the Green Mountain Coffee Roasters started packaging coffee in small plastic pods for the Keurig Single Cup Coffee System. It caught on in a big way because no one likes stale coffee. However, by late 2016, 18,000 spent plastic coffee pods were being thrown away every minute. The number of trashed K-Cups discarded each year, lined up next to each other, could circle the Earth more than ten times. It was enough to make the system's inventor, John Sylvan, wish that he had never conceived of the thing. Rogers Family had a different thought. They invented a biodegradable single-use cup that would make fresh coffee more sustainable but also keep it fresh. The proprietary packaging uses plant-based materials that include corn and sugar starches, and cellophane made from cellulose.

"We're a family-owned company, and we care a lot about our impact and the legacy we're leaving for our kids," Rogers Family president John Rogers said. "We wanted to be a company that solved the waste problem for the coffee industry, so we have invested more than five years of work and more than $2 million so far toward developing fully compostable pods and bags. Our goal is to influence the rest of the industry to adopt it, too. Mike and Billie Joe wanted to do the same thing, so we partnered so we could really make an impact."

Both the Oakland Coffee Company and the San Francisco Coffee Company use Rogers's new biodegradable packaging. The Oakland coffee became available at Whole Foods' stripped down offspring, 365, and also through Costco.com.

The goal, according to Mike, "is to provide exceptional coffee that is also sustainable."

To further this they started a charity called "Fueled by Love" that helps build infrastructure and supports the coffee growers at a grassroots level.

The day-to-day operations of the company are handled by Kate Kaplan, who took the position right out of UC Berkeley, where she spent a great deal of time working the student organic garden as student manager and became a UC Global Food Initiative Fellow. She told the University of California News that the company was allowing her to learn by doing: "Trying things out. That's what I do all day. We're learning from the ground up." Or, since it's a coffee company, the grounds up.

"We want consumers to have a choice that doesn't require a compromise," Mike said. "We want to make great coffee that supports [the coffee growers] and makes sustainable packaging accessible to everyone without pushing the added costs to our customers."

Rudy's Can't Fail

Once upon a time, Mike supported his music habit in the kitchen of a local restaurant in the East Bay, at a place called Nantucket in Crocker, California.

He has been described as a die-hard foodie. At the turn of the teens, his favorite restaurants included Pican, Le Cheval, and Dopo. As a musician in the Foxboro Hot Tubs, he has played at Rachel Ray's annual SXSW free beer, food, and music extravaganza, Forward. Mike hung out for the food. He and Tré demonstrated their comic ineptitude at making sushi with master sushi (and Iron) chef Masaharu Morimoto at an event that involved reducing an entire sixty-kilo (that's a bit over 140 pounds) bluefin tuna to sushi-sized pieces. Tré even played a drum solo on a kit made entirely out of pots and pans.

"I grew up hanging out in coffee shops at one and two in the morning," Mike told CBS News, "and I thought it'd be really cool to have a place open seven days a week where we could get a coffee or a beer and also bring a kid in and not have to wait an hour and a half for a waffle."

Mike wanted a diner that served vegan food and where "you could . . . bring a kid in and not have to wait an hour and a half for a waffle." *Laurence Bordowitz*

So Mike became one of four original founders of Rudy's Can't Fail, a high-end diner. The original Rudy's is in Emeryville, a town occupying a stretch on the shore of San Francisco Bay between Oakland and Berkeley. The restaurant has become a favorite of the animators at Pixar, which is across the street. In addition to usual diner fare, Rudy's serves vegan dishes (as befitting a place that is partially owned by a vegan) like mushroom burgers and tofu salads. It serves breakfast all day and stays open late.

The second Rudy's opened next to one of the band's favorite hometown venues, the Fox Theater.

"We didn't try to overthink it," Mike told Fender.com. "We just tried to put our own rock 'n' roll spin on it, give it good aesthetics and see what would happen. And serve good coffee."

45

Road to Acceptance (Speech)

Awards

In 1994, the video clip for "Longview" won the *Billboard* Maximum Vision award, given to a video clip that does the most to advance an artist's career. Green Day also won the Best New Artist award in the alternative/modern artist video category. They were the first awards the band ever won. They couldn't be there to accept the awards because they were doing one of their favorite things: playing a concert. Priorities.

Since then, Green Day has won a *lot* of awards. Now, on the face of it, that does not make them one of a kind, until you look at how many punk bands have won things like a Grammy or an American Music Award. Then the specialness of Green Day becomes a little clearer.

The Grammys

At the 1995 Grammy Awards, an upstart Green Day's major label debut, *Dookie*, won the Victrola statuette for Best Alternative Music Album. "Espionage," which was featured in the film *Austin Powers: The Spy Who Shagged Me*, was nominated for a Grammy Award for Best Rock Instrumental Performance.

American Idiot won Best Rock Album at the 2005 Grammys and was nominated for five others, including Album of the Year. The title track was nominated for Record of the Year, Best Rock Performance by a Duo or Group with Vocals, Best Rock Song, and Best Short Form Music Video. Rob Cavallo was also nominated for Best Producer of the Year, Non-Classical. The next year, "Boulevard of Broken Dreams" won Record of the Year honors.

Like its predecessor, *21st Century Breakdown* also won the Best Rock Album Grammy. Green Day were nominated for two others: the single "21 Guns" was up for Best Rock Song and Best Rock performance by a Duo or Group with Vocals (sound familiar?). A year later, *American Idiot: The Original Broadway Cast Recording* won the Grammy for Best Musical Show Album.

They Got Their MTV

MTV and Green Day have had a special relationship since the videos for *Dookie* kept the just home-from-junior-high-and-high-school crowd highly amused during the noon to 4:00 p.m. video slot. MTV has done specials about the band, including one of the Broadway show *American Idiot*, and Green Day has played their New Year's Eve events. They have also won a buttload of MTV Awards.

Green Day were given a Global Icon career achievement award at the 2016 MTV Europe Music Awards. They also played "American Idiot" and "Bang Bang" during the show. It reflected Billie Joe's mood on the red carpet, where he called politics in the United States "an American heart attack." They were edged out of the Best Live category by unabashed Green Day fans Twenty One Pilots.

In other MTV honors, Green Day was among the channel's 22 Greatest Bands. *Dookie* was No. 7 on VH1's 50 Greatest Album Covers, and Billie Joe was called one of the Alternative Rockers of 1995. That year, the video for "Basket Case" was nominated for nine MTV Music Awards: Video of the Year, Best Group Video, Best Metal/Hard Rock Video, Best Alternative Video, Breakthrough Video, Best Direction, Best Editing, Best Cinematography, and Viewer's Choice. However, they came home empty-handed.

American Idiot won seven of the eight MTV Video Music Awards it was nominated for in 2005. Six of those nominations were for "Boulevard of Broken Dreams," which won Video of the Year, Best Rock Video, Best Group Video, Best Editing, Best Cinematography, and Best Direction. They also won a viewer's choice award for the video to the title track.

In 2009, they took home three MTV Video Music Awards for "21 Guns": Best Rock Video, Best Cinematography, and Best Direction (again, sound familiar?). At the European Music Awards, they took home the Best Rock trophy and were also nominated for Best Group and Best Live Act.

The MTV Moonman, awarded at the Video Music Awards.

Deidre Woolard/Wikimedia Commons

Still More Awards

The Maximum Vision Award was not the only honor *Dookie* won. It made No. 3 (though perhaps No. 2 would have been more appropriate) on *Time* magazine's albums of the year and was its best rock album of the year. The readers of *Rolling Stone* called it the best album of 1994. In retrospect, *Rolling Stone* ranked it at No. 30 among the 100 Best Albums of the Nineties and called it the No. 1 record of the 40 Best Mainstream Albums in Alternative's Greatest Year, that being 1994.

In a similar list, *Loudwire* also placed it at No. 1. *Guitar World* ranked it at No. 13 in their albums that defined 1994. Of the 100 Greatest Albums from 1985–2005, *Spin* listed it at No. 44. The Rock and Roll Hall of Fame placed

Dookie at No. 50 on the organization's Definitive 200. *Dookie* was No. 33 on *Kerrang!*'s list of 100 Albums You Must Hear Before You Die and No. 2 among their 51 Greatest Pop Punk Albums Ever. It was among *Classic Rock*'s 200 Greatest Albums of the Nineties.

At the 2001 California Music Awards, Green Day won all eight of the awards that it was nominated for. The group won the awards for Outstanding Album (*Warning*), Outstanding Punk Rock/Ska Album (*Warning*), Outstanding Group, Outstanding Male Vocalist, Outstanding Bassist, Outstanding Drummer, Outstanding Songwriter, and Outstanding Artist. Outstanding!

Kerrang! named *American Idiot* the best album of the decade for 2000–2010. They also listed it at No. 13 in the greatest albums of all time. *Rolling Stone*'s readers named "Boulevard of Broken Dreams" the best song of the decade, *American Idiot* the best album of the decade, and the band best artist of the decade. *NME* listed *American Idiot* as the No. 60 album on their top 100 of that decade. NPR called it among the decade's 50 most important recordings. It fell in at No. 6 on *Entertainment Weekly*'s somewhat arbitrarily dated 100 Best Albums from 1983–2008. *Rolling Stone* called it the 22nd greatest album of its decade and the 225th greatest album of all time, and listed "Boulevard of Broken Dreams" at No. 65 on the list of best songs of the decade and *American Idiot*'s title track at No. 47.

American Idiot won Favorite Pop/Rock Album at the American Music Awards and was nominated for Album of the Year at the Billboard Music Awards. It was named Best Album at the MTV Europe Music Awards and was nominated for the title at the NME Awards. Both the Juno (Canada) and the BRIT Awards called it Best International Album. It appeared in several books about outstanding albums. The tour was nominated for a People's Choice Award in 2006. Green Day won that year's award for Favorite Musical Group or Band, and they won an American Music Award for Favorite Alternative Artist.

At the 2006 ASCAP Pop Music Awards—voted on by the songwriter, composer, lyricist, and music publisher members of the organization—Green Day was recognized twice. In a rare tie vote for Song of the Year, "Boulevard of Broken Dreams" finished in a dead heat with Mariah Carey's "We Belong Together." Green Day also took home the ASCAP Creative Voice Award, a career achievement kudos presented to artists whose work is "equally informed by their creative spirit and by their contributions to the role that a creator can play in their community." This all led to Billie Joe being named the Sexiest Person in Rock by *Kerrang!*.

21st Century Breakdown was nominated for a passel of awards that it did not win, including Best Album at the 2009 Kerrang! Awards and Album of the Year at the 2010 MTV Video Music Awards in Japan. At the 2010 NME Awards, *21st Century Breakdown* was nominated for both Best Album and Worst Album of the year. It won neither. It was nominated for Music Album Group at the 2009 Teen Choice Awards, as well.

The record hit No. 5 on *Rolling Stone's* Best Albums of 2009. Rhapsody placed it at No. 16 of the year's best albums. In 2010, the readers of *Kerrang!* voted the album No. 17 among the Best 50 Albums of the 21st Century, to that point. *21st Century Breakdown* won the Playboy Readers Poll for Best Rock Album. The band also won an American Music Award for Favorite Alternative Rock Music Artist. In the Spin 2009 Readers Poll, Green Day finished second in three categories to Pearl Jam: Best Live Artist, Album of the Year, and Song of the Year (for "21 Guns"). They also finished second to (gulp) Lady Gaga for Video of the Year. Billie Joe did win one: he followed his *Kerrang!* Sexiest Person in Rock honors the previous year with *Spin*'s Sex God of the Year, one of the poll's most coveted titles.

The Broadway production of *American Idiot* was nominated for three Tony Awards, including one for Best Musical. While it lost that one, it did win two technical awards for Best Scenic Design of a Musical and Best Lighting Design of a Musical.

Just before the musical opened in New York, Green Day got one of their more unusual accolades, winning a USA TV Network Character Approved Award. The kudos goes to innovators in their field who influence opinions, style, and people's worldview. That about sums up Green Day. They were also nominated for a People's Choice Award for Favorite Rock Band, which they lost to one of their opening acts, Paramore.

The Rock and Roll Hall of Fame

In 1995, Billie Joe told *Rolling Stone*'s Rich Cohen and Michael Rubiner, that if you believed everything that the media says about you, you "become, like, a parody of yourself," adding: "Look at people like Axl Rose. The guy's an idiot."

In 2012, Green Day found themselves inducting Guns N' Roses into the Rock and Roll Hall of Fame. Billie Joe started his speech by saying: "The first time I saw Guns N' Roses on MTV I thought, 'One of these guys could end up dead or in jail.' . . . The ride was not about parties, glamour, or power ballads. It was all about the seedy underworld of misfits, drug addicts, paranoia, sex, violence, love, anger, and the cracks of Hollywood." The good news for Billie Joe was that Axl Rose didn't show up for the induction.

It was not Billie Joe's first induction. Two years earlier, he had inducted the Stooges. At that induction, he described Iggy Pop as "the most confrontational singer we will ever see."

In 2015, the Hall of Fame committee rolled out the red carpet for Green Day. They were a first ballot lock. The band arrived in black tuxedos, all together. As they made their way inside, they signed autographs, posed for selfies, and shook hands with their fans.

During the ceremony, inductee Bill Withers made an observation that must have resonated with Billie Joe, as he called the event "the largest AA meeting in the Western Hemisphere."

Lawrence Livermore observed: "Green Day got the loudest reception of the night—including quite a few Beatlemania-style shrieks from the balconies—and played the loudest, too. They were the youngest of all inductees, and the only ones to have done some of their most important work in this century."

In his speech inducting Green Day into the Hall of Fame, Fall Out Boy's Patrick Stump said: "Without Green Day, there is no us. All of these bands that had really big success on the radio, they really kicked the door in for us."

Fall Out Boy's Pete Wentz said:

> [You] put out a scathingly political rock opera and somehow managed to make that career-redefining, that was insanely fucking punk rock . . . Everything you guys do is punk rock in the sense that you've never gone the easy route, the obvious route, the safe route. You've never repeated yourself . . . When a great band plays a set of their hits, there should be a lot of change . . . This is a band that's so in tune with their audience that they let a random kid onstage and play in the band . . . It is our great honor to induct Green Day into the Rock and Roll Hall of Fame.

In his acceptance speech, Tré said: "When we were on tour in our yellow Ford Econoline, we were playing punk clubs, squats, backyard parties, we were screen-printing T-shirts on Billie Joe's guitar case, sleeping on floors, couches, wherever we could. I didn't think back then that we'd be here now in the Rock and Roll Hall of Fame." He paused. "I thought it would take at least another year or two."

Mike also thanked "the hundreds of people whose floors you let us sleep on" adding: "Those were life-changing experiences and I wouldn't trade them for the world . . . I want to thank our friends and family at home for allowing us to be gone so much of our lives and still being there for us . . . Last but not least: to my two brothers behind me onstage here. Believe me, it's been way too many years to want to count. I love you guys and I'll see you at band practice."

Billie Joe went to the heart of matters: "My record collection is actually sitting in this room . . . I gotta thank my mom, Ollie Louise Armstrong . . . the one thing that I am so grateful for is all the music that was in our house . . . My house was like Rock and Roll High School . . . Mike is my musical soulmate and I love you so much and we've been through everything together, and I thank you for everything—your friendship, your family. I love you. . . . If there's one instrument I love to hear, and it's because my father was a jazz drummer, my brother is a drummer and my uncle is a drummer. I'm the oddball. But Tré is just phenomenal and just pushes and he's the most dangerous drummer on the planet."

Bibliography

"An Interview with Lawrence Livermore: An Inside Look at Green Day's Early Years." *Oocities.* Accessed July 28, 2015. http://www.oocities.org/greenday_timeofyourlife/Principal/Interviews/interview_with_lawrence_livermore.htm

"Billie Joe Gets Naked for Charity." *New York Post,* December 5, 1994.

"Didja Know—Useless Green Day Facts." *Green Day Authority.* Accessed August 6, 2015. http://www.greendayauthority.com/band/didjaknow.php?section=bands

"Exclusive: We Looked to Cartoon World for Comeback Inspiration, Reveals Green Day Frontman," *Daily Record,* May 3, 2009. http://www.dailyrecord.co.uk/entertainment/music/music-news/exclusive-we-looked-to-cartoon-world-for-comeback-1021040

"FMQB Exclusive: Inside Green Day: *21st Century Breakdown.*" *Friday Morning Quarterback,* April 27, 2009.

"Good Morning America Summer Concert Series, Central Park Rumsey Playfield in New York, NY." *Green Day Authority,* May 22, 2009. http://www.greendayauthority.com/tour/show/1411/

"Green Day: Album Left Green Day Singer Depressed." *Contact Music,* April 27, 2009.

"Green Day Chat." Green Day Community. November 11, 2016. http://www.greendaycommunity.org/forum/83-green-day-chat/

"Green Day's Death Pledge." *BANG Media,* May 5, 2009.

"Green Day: In the Studio." *Rolling Stone,* June 24, 2004.

"Green Day: Punk Icons, Broadway Tastemakers and . . . Video Game Stars?" *GQ,* April 28, 2010.

"Green Day: Rebel Yell." *Guitar World,* August, 2009.

"Green Day: Recognition at Last." *St. Louis Post-Dispatch,* July 14, 1994.

"Green Day Thank Vans, Fans, Rock & Roll at Hall of Fame: Read the Speech," *Rolling Stone,* April 18, 2015. http://www.rollingstone.com/music/news/green-day-thank-vans-fans-rock-roll-at-hall-of-fame-read-the-speech-20150418

"Green Day Webchat." *Guardian,* November 9, 2016. https://www.theguardian.com/music/live/2016/nov/10/green-day-webchat-revolution-radio

"Green Day—What Rock 'N' Roll Has Taught Us." *NME*, February 4, 2010. http://www.nme.com/blogs/nme-blogs/green -day-what-rocknroll-has -taught-us-1188465

"Green Day's *American Idiot* to Become a Movie." *Star*, April 13, 2011. https://www.thestar.com/entertainment/2011/04/13/green_days_american_idiot_to_become_movie.html

"In the Studio: Green Day." *Q*, June, 2010.

"In the Winner's Circle, Best Live Act: Green Day." *Q*, January 2011.

"Judy Greer Impressed by Green Day's Billie Joe Armstrong in First Movie Leading Role." *Associated Press*, October 16, 2016.

"Kevin Lemoine: FOH Engineer on Tour with Green Day." *Sound on Sound*, November, 2013.

"Konowitch & Cavallo Launch Classic Rock Vehicle." *Hits Daily Double*, October 4, 2016. http://hitsdailydouble.com/news&id=303228

"Q&A with Rock Photographer Bob Gruen." *Greenday.net*, November 23, 2011. http://www.greenday.net/news

"Rusty Announces Collaboration with Green Day." Press Release, February 3, 2010. http://www.grindtv.com/surf/rusty-teams-up-with-green-day/

Acosta, Dave. "Nirvana Producer Vig Tells Smart Studios Story." *El Paso Times*, October 18, 2016.

Alejandrino, Rosemarie. "Green Day Celebrates *Dookie* at Fox Theater." *Daily Californian*, February 25, 2016. http://www.dailycal.org/2016/02/25 /green-day-celebrates-dookie-fox-theater/

Ali, Lorraine. "Popular Music and the Loss of Anger." *Los Angeles Times*, July 15, 2016.

———. "Green Day's *American Idiot*." *Newsweek*, December 22, 2008.

Anthony, David. "Chris Carrabba and Adam Lazzara on Surviving the Emo Boom and Overcoming Fan Nostalgia." *A.V. Club*, June 1, 2016. http://music.avclub.com/chris-carrabba-and -adam-lazzara-on -surviving-the-emo-bo-1798247850

Ao, Bethany. "With 21st Century Grit, the Baltic Tackles the Music Industry." *Denver Post*, July 7, 2016.

Armstrong, Billie Joe. "Look For Love." 45 RPM Single, Fiat Records, #11, 1977.

———. "10 Questions for Billie Joe Armstrong." *Time*, June 26, 2010.

———. Acceptance speech at the Rock and Roll Hall of Fame Induction Ceremony, April 15, 2015.

———. Speech inducting Guns N' Roses into the Rock and Roll Hall of Fame, April 14, 2012.

———. Speech inducting the Stooges into the Rock and Roll Hall of Fame, March 15, 2010.

Atkinson, Ewan. "SWMRS: 'We Want to Give People a Different Way of Escaping.'" *DIY Magazine*, June 2, 2016.

Bergan, Tom. "Green Day: Still Touring and Still Terrific." *University News Syndicate*, November 3, 2016.

Bird, Ryan. "It's Time to Have Fun Again!" *Rock Songs*, September, 2012.

Bohn, Chris. "Desperation, I Recommend It." *Melody Maker*, December 29, 1979.

Borzillo, Carrie. "As Reprise Set Rises, It's Easy Being Green Day." *Billboard*, April 9, 1994.

Botica, Mike. "20 Eyes Looks to the Future." *Random Lengths News*, January 22, 2016.

Brackett, Nathan, and Andy Green. "Rolling Stone Music Now Podcast." *Rolling Stone*, August 25, 2016. http://www.rollingstone.com/music/news/music-now-podcast-billie-joe-armstrong-on-green-days-new-lp-w435701

Bradley, Bill. "Taking the Long View: Green Day Still Sneering After All These Years." *Daily Yomiuri*, March 8, 2001.

Bradman, E. E. "Holy Trinity! Mike Dirnt & Green Day Come Around with *¡Uno!, ¡Dos!, ¡Tré!*" *Bass Player*, January 2013.

Brown, Eric Renner. "Green Day, 'Revolution Radio.'" *Entertainment Weekly*, September 15, 2016.

Brown, Mark. "Green Isn't Blue Over Theft: After Songs Swiped, Band Started Over and Made *American Idiot*." *Denver Rock Mountain News*, November 17, 2004.

Browne, David. "Florence Welch on Covering Green Day, Quitting Drinking." *Rolling Stone*, May 11, 2016.

———. "The Green Day After." *Entertainment Weekly*, November 20, 1995.

———. "Q&A: Billie Joe Armstrong." *Rolling Stone*, September, 27, 2012.

Burgess, Aaron. "Billie Joe Is Interviewed About Upcoming Album." *Alternative Press*, November 28, 2008.

Bychawski, Adam. "Green Day's Billie Joe Armstrong Rushed to Hospital." *NME*, September 3, 2012. http://www.nme.com/news/music/green-day-112-1247791

Caramanica, Jon. "Pop-Punk Bands, Now Grown Up." *New York Times*, September 26, 2012.

Carter, Emily. "Green Day Confirm Heart Like a Hand Grenade Details." *Kerrang!*, October 9, 2005.

Carter, Nicole. "Grammys Give Sneak Preview of *American Idiot*, Green Day Musical Coming to Broadway." *New York Daily News*, February 1, 2010.

Case, Wesley. "Emily's Army, the Punk Offspring of Green Day, Makes Some Noise." *Baltimore Sun*, June 22, 2012.

Cashmere, Paul. "Green Day the Stage Show." *Undercover*, March 3, 2009. http://www.undercover.com.au

Chai, Yow Kai. "Demolicious." *Singapore Strait Times*, June 4, 2014.

Clarke, Paddy. "Play Time Is Over: Green Day Interviewed." *The Quietus*, November 14, 2016. http://thequietus.com/articles/21309-green-day-billie-joe-armstrong-interview

Clover. "Playing on Stage with Green Day!" *Green Day Authority*, November 29, 2009. http://www.greendayauthority.com/news/113/

Cohen, Rich, and Michael Rubiner. "Hot Band." *Rolling Stone*, May 19, 1994.

Cohen, Stephanie, and Hank Bordowitz. "MCY Interview with Pete Townshend." *MCY*, 2000. http://www.mcy.com

Colapinto, John. "Working Class Heroes." *Rolling Stone*, November 17, 2005.

Coleman, Mark. "Ode to Billie Joe." *Rolling Stone*, November 2, 1995.

Collins, Simon. "The Idiot Factor." *West Australian*, March 11, 2005.

Coulson, Nick. "Green Day Far from a (Stage) Dive." *Loyola Phoenix*, October 27, 2016. http://www.loyolaphoenix.com

Cridlin, Jay. "Now, How Punk Is That?" *St. Petersburg Times*, April 14, 2005.

Davidson, Vicky. "Hail to the Thief: Getting Their Album Master Tapes Stolen Was the Best Thing That Ever Happened to Green Day." *Glasgow Evening Times*, February 10, 2005.

Deitsch, Richard, Mark Bechtel, and Stephen Cannella. "Q+A Billie Joe Armstrong." *Sports Illustrated*, September 12, 2005.

Deusner, Stephen. "Green Day: Rock's Saddest Joke." *Salon*, July 16, 2012.

Di Perna, Alan. *Green Day: The Ultimate Unauthorized History*. Minneapolis: Voyageur Press, 2012.

Dirnt (Pritchard), Mike. Acceptance speech at the Rock and Roll Hall of Fame Induction Ceremony, April 15, 2015.

Dolan, Jon. "Zack Carper on Confronting Heroin Addiction, and Writing the Great, Grueling 'Too.'" *Rolling Stone*, October 15, 2015.

———. "Green Day, Angst on Fire." *Rolling Stone*, November 22, 2012.

Dziemianowicz, Joe. "Green Day's *Amerian Idiot* Doesn't Pack the Punch of a Broadway Musical." *New York Daily News*, April 20, 2010.

Earls, John. "Green Day Bassist Has Bass Lessons for the First Time." *NME*, July 18, 2016. http://www.nme.com/news/music/nme-36-1193227

Elder, Tanya. "Green Day Is a Gateway Drug to the History of Punk." *Green Day Mind*, March 20, 2010. https://greendaymind.com/2010/03/20/green-day-as-a-gateway-drug-to-the-history-of-punk/

Erickson, Anne. "Interview: Studio Talk with Mixer Chris Lord-Alge." *Gibson.com*, September 15, 2015. http://www.gibson.com/News-Lifestyle/Features/en-us/Interview-Studio-Talk-with-Mixer-Chris-Lord-Alge.aspx

Erlewine, Stephen Thomas. "AllMusic Review: *American Idiot* [The Original Broadway Cast Recording]." AllMusic. http://www.allmusic.com/album/american-idiot-the-original-broadway-cast-recording-mw0001987250

———. "AllMusic Review: *Awesome as F**k*." AllMusic. http://www.allmusic.com/album/awesome-as-fk-mw0002094541

———. "AllMusic Review: *Bullet in a Bible*." AllMusic. http://www.allmusic.com/album/american-idiot-the-original-broadway-cast-recording-mw0001987250

Fanelli, Damian. "Green Day Fan Wows Crowd with Perfect 'Dookie' Cover." *Guitar World*, October 26, 2016.

Ferrante Batista, Amanda. "An Interview with Green Day: One, Two, Three, Go!" *The Aquarian*, April 3, 2014.

Fitzgerald, Dan. "Green Day Hearkens back to *Dookie* Days, Remains Visually Pedestrian in 'Bang Bang' Music Video." *The Heights*, August 31, 2016.

Fletcher, Ethan. "Q&A: Mike Dirnt." *Diablo Magazine*, July 2011.

Foege, Alec. "Green Day." *Rolling Stone*, September 22, 1994.

———. "Green Day." *Rolling Stone*, December 28, 1995.

Fortnam, Ian. "The Biggest Punk Band in the World: Green Day." *Rock's Backpages*, 2002. https://www.rocksbackpages.com/Library/Article/the-biggest-punk-rock-band-in-the-world-green-day

Fantozzi, Joanna. "Wake Me Up When Caffeine Sets In: Green Day's Mike Dirnt Talks Up New Coffee Brand." *Daily Meal*, November 1, 2016. https://www.thedailymeal.com/news/entertain/wake-me-when-caffeine-sets-green-day-s-mike-dirnt-talks-new-coffee-brand/110116

Frankel, Ricky. "Demolicious." *PunkNews.org*, May 6, 2014. https://www.punknews.org/review/12589/green-day-demolicious

Fricke, David. "Billie Joe Armstrong (Cover Story)." *Rolling Stone*, November 15, 2007.

———. "Billie Joe, Norah's Dark Dream." *Rolling Stone*, November 21, 2013.

———. "Dookie at 20: Billie Joe Armstrong on Green Day's Punk Blockbuster." *Rolling Stone*, February 3, 2014.

———. "Green Day Ditch Rock Operas for Raw Punk LPs." *Rolling Stone*, July 5, 2012.

———. "Green Day Fights On." *Rolling Stone*, May 28, 2009.

———. "Green Day Go Bigger on *American Idiot* Follow-up." *Rolling Stone*, March 5, 2009.

———. "Green Day Strip Down, Turn it Up." *Rolling Stone*, September 13, 2012.

———. "Billie Joe Armstrong: The *Rolling Stone* Interview," *Rolling Stone*, March 14, 2013.

———. "The Dookie Chronicles." *Rolling Stone*, March 13, 2014.

———. "Tré Cool on Growing up Punk and Finding Green Day's Groove." *Rolling Stone*, May 15, 2009.

Friedman, David. "When Green Day Comes Around, Expect Fun." *News Times*, September 2, 2005.

Friedman, Roberto. "Short, Sweet & Somewhat Subversive." *Bay Area Reporter*, March 4, 2010.

Gaar, Gillian. "Green Day 2.0." *Goldmine*, April, 2011.

———. *Rebels with a Cause*. London: Omnibus Press, 2009.

Gabriella. "Billie Joe Armstrong—Green Day," *New York Rock*, April, 1998.

Gallo, Phil. "Green Day: The *Billboard* Cover Story." *Billboard*, July 16, 2012.

———. "Green Day Breaks on Top." *Billboard*, September 30, 2004.

———. "Green Day's Triple Play." *Billboard*, July 21, 2012.

Gamerman, Ellen. "'American Idiot's' Rebecca Naomi Jones on Green Day, Billie Joe Armstrong and Singing in Her Underwear." *Wall Street Journal*, April 2, 2010.

———. "Roll Over, Rogers and Hammerstein," *Wall Street Journal*, May 1, 2009.

Garcia, Leonardo Adrian. "How Do You Sleep?: 23 Highly Specific Rock and Roll Diss Tracks." *A.V. Club*, March 23, 2016.

Gardner, Elysa. "Green Day Goes Broadway for *American Idiot*." *USA Today*, April 18, 2010.

———. "Green Day's Take on Life in 2010." *USA Weekend*, July 16, 2010.

Garner, George. "The Best Green Day Album? Duh, It's *Nimrod*." *Kerrang!*, January 20, 2016.

Garondi, Pablo. "*Revolution Radio* Is Green Day Back on Straight and Narrow." *Associated Press*, October 7, 2016. http://www.lexisnexis.com/

Gilmore, Mikal. "The Curse of the Ramones." *Rolling Stone*, May 19, 2016.

Gokhman, Roman. "Bay Pays Tribute to Green Day's *Dookie* at 924 Gilman Benefit." *The Bay Bridged*, February 11, 2016. http://thebaybridged.com/2016/02/11/bay-pays-tribute-green-days-dookie-924-gilman-benefit/

Gold, Johnathan. "The Ballad of Billie the Kid." *Spin*, December, 1997.

———. "The Year Punk Broke." *Spin*, November, 1994.

Goodman, William. "Green Day: We Love the Who and Cheap Trick." *Spin*, May, 2009. https://www.spin.com/2009/05/green-day-we-love-who-and-cheap-trick/

Goodwyn, Tom. "Green Day Bring Reading Festival to a Standstill with Surprise Set." *NME*, August 25, 2012. http://www.nme.com/news/music/green-day-116-1251169

Gorman, J. P. "Green Day Sued by a Real American Idiot." *Cinema Blend*, November 2, 2006. http://www.cinemablend.com/music/Green-Day-Sued-By-Real-American-Idiot-1487.html

Graff, Gary. "¡Dos!" *Billboard*, December 1, 2012.

Green, Andy. "Billie Joe Armstrong on Green Day's Provocative New LP." *Rolling Stone*, August 11, 2016.

———. "Billie Joe Armstrong Talks 'Surreal' Hall of Fame Night, New Green Day LP." *Rolling Stone*, April 30, 2015.

———. "Twenty One Pilots: Inside the Biggest New Band of the Past Year." *Rolling Stone*, January 14, 2016.

Grimes, Courtney. "Green Day Frontman Billie Armstrong Talks Over His 'Floyd.'" *UltimateGuitar.com*, September 30, 2005. https://www.ultimate-guitar.com/news/interviews/green_day_frontman_billie_armstrong_talks_over_his_floyd.html

Gross, Terry. "Green Day's Billie Joe Armstrong Takes Broadway." *Fresh Air*, NPR, May 27, 2010. http://www.npr.org/2011/01/14/132908093/green-days-billie-joe-armstrong-takes-broadway

Gundersen, Edna. "Green Day Rising at the Dawn of a New Punk Rock Era." *USA Today*, January 20, 1995.

Hall, Russell. "The World According to . . . Green Day's Billie Joe Armstrong." *Gibson.com*, September 21, 2011. http://www.gibson.com/News-Lifestyle/Features/en-us/green-day-0921-2011.aspx

Harding, Courtney. "Green Day's *American Idiot* Hits Great White Way." *Billboard*, April 4, 2010.

Harrington, Jim. "It's Punk, It's Rock, It's Opera; On the Heels of *American Idiot*, Green Day Heads for S.F." *San Jose Mercury News*, November 29, 2004.

Harvilla, Rob. "Kerplunk: The Rise and Fall of the Lookout Records Empire." *East Bay Express*, September 14, 2005.

Hasty, Katie. "Interview: John Lydon on PIL, Sex Pistols, Green Day and the Olympics." *Hitfix.com*, May 22, 2012.

Hendrickson, Matt. "Green Day." *Rolling Stone*, February 24, 2005.

———. "Q&A." *Details*, May 2011.

Heisel, Scott. "Green Day Confirm They Are, in Fact, Foxboro Hot Tubs." *Alternative Press*, April 10, 2008.

Hiatt, Brian. "Green Day." *Rolling Stone*, September 22, 2016.

Hicks, Tony. "Green Day's *Idiot* Pure Genius." *Contra Costa Times*, September 22, 2004.

Hilson, Dave. "Green Day: Do You Have the Time to Listen to Them Whine?" *Daily Yomiuri*, March 28, 2002.

Howell, Peter. "Green Day: 3-Chord Fame in Just 3 Minutes Northern California Punks Get Big in the Blink of an Eye." *The Toronto Star*, November 24, 1994.

Ingham, Tim. "Green Day Album Trio 'Makes Perfect Sense': Warner Ramps Up Marketing for Ambitious Six-month Release Plan." *Music Week*, August 31, 2012.

Inskeep, Steve. "Billie Joe Armstrong, from Green Day to Broadway." *All Things Considered*, NPR, November 25, 2013.

Isherwood, Charles. "Stomping onto Broadway with a Punk Temper Tantrum." *New York Times*, April 21, 2010.

Jenkins, Mark. "It's Not Easy Being Green Day: The Sellout Band That Isn't Really Selling." *Washington Post*, December 24, 1995.

Johnson, Kevin C. "Punkers Blink-182, Green Day Tour Together." *St. Louis Post-Dispatch*, May 5, 2002.

Johnson, Neala. "A Fire Still Burns for Green Day." *Courier Mail*, May 14, 2009.

———. "Green & Gold." *Melbourne Herald Sun*, September 15, 2005.

———. "Punk Political Animals." *Courier Mail*, September 18, 2004.

Jones, Kenneth. "Brief Encounter with Michael Mayer." *Playbill.com*, May 22, 2010. http://www.playbill.com/article/playbillcoms-brief-encounter-with-michael-mayer-com-168672

Kandell, Steve. "Billie Joe Armstrong Meets Paul Westerberg." *Spin*, March 25, 2010.

Kemp, Bob. "English Rocker Claims Green Day Plagiarized His Song." *MTV News*, January 12, 2001. http://www.mtv.com/news/1437922/english-rocker-claims-green-day-plagiarized-his-song/

Keyes, J. Edward. "Green Day Moonlight as Foxboro Hot Tubs at Beer-Soaked Secret Show." *Rolling Stone*, April 26, 2010.

Kot, Greg. "*Awesome as F---*." *Entertainment Weekly*, March 17, 2011.

Kramer, Peter D. "Bringing 'Green Day' to Broadway." *LoHud.com*, April 20, 2010. http://listeningroom.lohudblogs.com/2010/04/23/bringing-green-day-to-broadway/

Krochmal, Shana Naomi. "Billie Joe Armstrong: Idiot Savant." *Out*, March 14, 2010.

Kuehnle, Alec. "Review: Green Day's 'Revolution Radio' Is an Angry, Reflective Story About the Passage of Time." *Daily Wildcat*, October 8, 2016. http://www.wildcat.arizona.edu/article/2016/10/review-green-days-revolution-radio-is-an-angry-reflective-story-about-the-passage-of-time

Kuzava, Luke. "Green Day Returns with the First Power-Popera." *Santa Fe New Mexican*, September 24, 2004.

LadyDragon. "Serena Williams Interview." *LadyDragon.com*, July 2, 2010. http://www.ladydragon.com/news2010/0307101.html

Lanham, Tom. "The Band You Love to Hate." *RIP*, April, 1996.

———. "Green Day: Older Louder, Snottier." *CMJ New Music Monthly*, 1997.

Leonard, Michael. "Billie Joe Armstrong's Gibson Guitars." *Gibson.com*, July 20, 2014. http://www.gibson.com/News-Lifestyle/Features/en-us/Billie-Joe-Armstrong-Gibson-Guitars.aspx

Lewis, Dylan. "Recovery TV." Directed by Janet Argall. Performed by Green Day. 1998. Sydney, Australia: Australian Broadcasting Company. Video.

Light, Alan. "The Idiot King." *Rolling Stone*, November 17, 2005.

Lipschutz, Jason. "Green Day's Album Trilogy: What Happened with '*¡Uno!*,' '*¡Dos!*' and '*¡Tré!*'?" *Billboard*, December 20, 2012.

Livermore, Lawrence. "I'm Larry Livermore. I Lived in the Mountains with No Electricity. . .," *Reddit*, December 2, 2015. https://www.reddit.com/r/IAmA/comments/3v6oqb/im_larry _livermore_i_lived_in_the_mountains_with/

———. "Green Day in the Hall of Fame." *LarryLivermore.com*, May 6, 2015. http://larrylivermore.com/?p=3065

Lloyd, Alice. "Backstage with [Spunge]." *Soglos.com*, February 23, 2016. http://www.soglos.com/music/40156/Backstage-with-Spunge

Lockett, Dee. "Billie Joe Armstrong and Lee Kirk on *Ordinary World*, Jamming with Fred Armisen, and Turning 40." *Vulture.com*, October 16, 2016. http://www.vulture.com/2016/10/billie-joe-armstrong-lee-kirk-on-ordinary-world.html

Longman, Will. "Five Minutes with Newton Faulkner: 'I Had a Huge Amount of Catching up to Do.'" *What's On Stage*, July 13, 2015.

Maher, Bill. "Episode 179." *Real Time with Bill Maher*. Performed by Billie Joe Armstrong, Bill Maher. April 9, 2010. New York: HBO. Video.

Maness, Carter. "Broadway Idiots." *New York Press,* April 7, 2010.

Mandell, Ryan. "SWMRS Hit the Funzone." *Independent.com,* January 22, 2016. http://www.independent.com/news/2016/jan/22/swmrs-hit-funzone/

Mapes, Jillian. "Butch Vig: Garbage Hiatus Clear Members' 'Baggage.'" *Billboard,* October 19, 2011.

Marks, Craig. "An American Family." *Spin,* December 1995.

Martins, Todd. "Snap Judgement: Green Day's *21st Century Breakdown.*" *Los Angeles Times,* March 2, 2009. http://latimesblogs.latimes.com/music_blog/2009/03/snap-judgment-g.html

Masterson, Andrew. "Green Day—Punk To Platinum." *The Age,* February 9, 1996.

Mathieson, Craig. "Time to Let Loose." *Sydney Morning Herald,* December 11, 2009.

McCabe, Kathy. "Day Lasts for a Decade." *Sunday Telegraph,* December 9, 2001.

McCarter, Jeremy. "*American Idiot,* Green Day's Show—Theater Review." *Newsweek,* April 19, 2010.

McCulley, Jeff. "Green Day Rule the Waves." *Daily Yomiuri,* January 18, 1996.

McCown-Levy, Alex. "Green Day Are Punks Afraid of Dying on the Uncertain *Revolution Radio.*" *A.V. Club,* October 7, 2016. http://music.avclub.com/green-day-are-punks-afraid-of-dying-on-the-uncertain-re-1798189020

McGonagle, Ryan. "Interview with Nick Ghanbarian of Bayside." *The Daily Slice,* May 11, 2014.

McNeil, Legs, and Gillian McCain. *Please Kill Me: The Uncensored Oral History of Punk.* New York: Grove Press, 2006.

Micallef, Ken. "A Simple Plan: Green Day and Butch Vig Devote Serious Time to Preproduction and Demos Before Recording *21st Century Breakdown.*" *EQ,* July 2009.

———. "Green Day." *Emusician.com,* September 11, 2012.

Michelson, Noah. "Billie Joe Armstrong Tells All." *Out,* March 19, 2010.

Milward, John. "Joy in Mudville." *Rolling Stone,* September 22, 1994.

Mitchell, Ben. "Cash for Questions: Green Day." *Q,* November 2012.

Mohan, Anne Marie. "Green Day Wants You to Start Your Day in a Green Way." *Packaging World,* November, 2016.

Mongredien, Phil. "Green Day: *Revolution Radio* Review—Punchy Punks Return to Form." *Guardian,* October 9, 2016.

Montgomery, James. "Green Day Exclusive: Yes, They Are Foxboro Hot Tubs, Just in Case There Was Any Doubt." *MTV News*, April 10, 2008. http://www.mtv.com/news/1585150/green-day-exclusive-yes-they-are-foxboro-hot-tubs-just-in-case-there-was-any-doubt/

———. "Green Day Moved 'To Tears' by *American Idiot* Musical." *MTV News*, April 20, 2010. http://www.mtv.com/news/1585150/green-day-exclusive-yes-they-are-foxboro-hot-tubs-just-in-case-there-was-any-doubt/

———. "Green Day Say Broadway *American Idiot* Isn't 'A Rated PG Affair,'" *MTV News*, March 25, 2010. http://www.mtv.com/news/1634702/green-day-say-broadway-american-idiot-isnt-a-rated-pg-affair/

———. "Green Day Talk Getting Their Own *Rock Band*." *MTV News*, June 7, 2010. http://www.mtv.com/news/1640821/green-day-talk-getting-their-own-rock-band/

———. "What's It Like to Sing with Green Day at Lollapalooza? Dan Michie Knows." *MTV News*, August 11, 2010. http://www.mtv.com/news/1645548/whats-it-like-to-sing-with-green-day-at-lollapalooza-dan-michie-knows/

Montgomery, James, and Kim Stolz. "Green Day Say Being a Punk Is 'Ground Zero for Us.'" *MTV News*, April 20, 2009. http://www.mtv.com/news/1610384/green-day-say-being-a-punk-band-is-ground-zero-for-us/

Morden, Darryl. "Green Day." *Hollywood Reporter*, September 20, 2004.

Morris, Jean. "Are We We Are," *Presbyterian Record*, September 2005.

MTV News Staff. "Black Day for Green Day." *MTV News*, July 27, 1995. http://www.mtv.com/news/506171/black-day-for-green-day/

———. "Former Green Day Managers Sue Band." *MTV News*, September 11, 1995. http://www.mtv.com/news/504635/former -green-day-managers-sue-band/

———. "New Found Glory, Taking Back Sunday, Turn out for Green Day DVD Premier." *MTV News*, November 16, 2005. http://www.mtv.com/news/1513869/new-found-glory-taking-back-sunday-turn-out-for-green-day-dvd-premiere/

Mueller, Andrew. *Rock and Hard Places*. Brooklyn: Soft Skull Press, 2010.

Mundy, Chris. "Green Daze." *Rolling Stone*, January 26, 1995.

News Desk. "Green Day: New Record Made Us Ill." *NME*, April 23, 2009.

———. "Kaiser Chiefs Surprised at Green Day's Good Behaviour." *Music-news.com*, May 26, 2009. http://www.music-news.com/news/UK/26852/Read

———. "The Killers 'Offended' by Green Day." *NME*, October 13, 2006. http://www.nme.com/news/music/the-killers-199-1317279

Newman, Melinda. "A Smart Start for Green Day: Trio Reclaims Punk Crown with *Idiot*." *Billboard*, October 9, 2004.

———. "After the Gold Rush." *Billboard*, January 7, 2008.

———. "Pat's Own Imprint: Green Day Manager Teams with Universal for Label." *Billboard*, July 17, 2004.

News Reporter. "Lady Gaga: 'I Used to Lick the Booklet of Green Day's *Dookie*.'" *NME*, September 8, 2009. http://www.nme.com/news/music/lady-gaga-522-1311823

Nygaard, Sandra. "Obedient Sons Secures New Investor; After Dark Days, Designer Swaim Hutson Inks Promising Partnership with Green Day's Mike Dirnt." *Daily News Record*, July 17, 2006.

O'Brien, Conan. "Green Day 'Welcome to Paradise' Late Night with Conan O'Brien, Episode 126." Performed by Green Day. Produced by Lorne Michaels and Jeff Ross. March 16, 1994. New York: NBC. Broadway Video.

O'Donnell, Kevin. "Green Day's *Revolution Radio*: EW Review." *Entertainment Weekly*, October 7, 2016.

O'Neil, Luke. "Blink-82 is Officially More Punk Than Crass, According to Spotify Study." *Noisey*, January 14, 2016.

Ortenzi, Rob. "From the Editor's Floor: Green Day, Part 2." *Alternative Press*, December 12, 2008.

Palmer, Jim. "No X Factor Regrets: Amelia Lily Talks to Us About Tours of Divas Show and Green Day Musical." *Richmond & Twickenham Times*, November 30, 2013.

Pareles, Jon. "Pop Review: Suburban Listlessness as Caught by Green Day." *New York Times*, December 5, 1994.

———. "Review: *Revolution Radio* Finds Green Day Still Unsatisfied." *New York Times*, October 5, 2016.

Pedersen, Erik. "Pop Disaster." *Hollywood Reporter*, April 23, 2002.

Perry, Claudia. "Seeing Green: Solid Sales, a Loyal Following—and a Lawsuit Are Rocking Green Day's World." *San Jose Mercury News*, October 9, 1995.

Perry, Neil. "Hero of the Bay." *Kerrang!*, January 24, 1998.

Peters, Mitchell. "21st Century Rock: Green Day Returns with a Rock Opera Thrashtastic Enough for its Old Fans—and New Ones." *Billboard*, May 9, 2009.

Porosky, Pamela. "Fear and Loathing in a Post 9/11 America: Green Day's Billie Joe Armstrong Rails Against Idiocy and Indifference." *Guitar Player*, February, 2005.

Reidel, David. "Melodramatic Fools? The Limit Brings Uncertainty to Disunity." *New Haven Advocate*, January 29, 2009.

Reighley, Kurt B. "Green Day Dawns Anew." *Advocate*, November 23, 2004.

Rix-Standing, Luke. "Classical Music for the Masses." *Nouse.co.uk*, May 17, 2016. http://www.nouse.co.uk/2016/05/17/classical-music-for-the-masses/

Roberts, Randall. "John Lydon's Latest Noise." *Los Angeles Times*, January 30, 2011.

Robinson, James. "Three Is the Magic Number." *Dominion Post*, September 20, 2012.

Rosen, Craig. "Green Day Grows Beyond Punk on *Nimrod*." *Billboard*, September 20, 1997.

———. "MCA Links with Green Day Mgrs. for (510) Label." *Billboard*, March 11 1995.

Rosenberg, Alec. "Learning from the Ground Up." *Berkeley News*, March 30, 2016.

Routhier, Ray. "Time for Punk: Two Bands Rock State Next Week; Green Day and Foo Fighters Will Stage Hard-Edged Shows in Lewiston and Portland." *Portland Press Herald*, May 7, 1998.

Ryan, Patrick. "Green Day's Billie Joe Armstrong: 'It Got Pretty Scary for a While.'" *USA Today*, October 6, 2016.

Saeed Saeed. "Green Day Rediscover Themselves on the Energising *Revolution Radio*." *The National*, October 3, 2016.

Schaffer, Athena. "Green Day Taking Extra Steps to Secure Most Pits, Fan Safety." *Amusement Business*, January 8, 1996.

Scheck, Frank. "Green Day's American Idiot a Tough Sell on Broadway." *Reuters*, April 22, 2010.

Schiewe, Jessie. "Hitsville High: The Unlikely Music Factory at Pinole Valley High School." *San Francisco Weekly*, April 6, 2016.

———. "The Electronic Duo Bob Moses Puts Canada on the Map." *San Francisco Weekly*, January 27, 2016.

Schonfeld, Zach. "Green Day: *Revolution Radio* Review." *Paste*, October 7, 2016. https://www.pastemagazine.com/articles/2016/10/green-day--revolution-radio--review.html

Sciacca, Annie. "What Does Green Day Coffee Taste Like?" *East Bay Times*, October 28, 2016.

Serpe, Gina. "50 Cent, Green Day top ASCAPs." *Billboard*, May 23, 2006.

Sharp, Tyler. "Review of Green Day's Impending Comeback Song Compares it to 'Early Punky Green Day' – News." *Alternative Press*, August 3, 2016.

Shutler, Ali. "SWMRS: 'We Wanted to be Our Own Band.'" *Upset Magazine*, February 12, 2016.

Smith, Dakota. "Green Day Trash NY Tower Records Store." *MTV News*, November 12, 1997. http://www.mtv.com/news/1849/green-day-trash-n-y-tower-records-store/

Smith, Nicky. "Green Day Crippled Punk Fascism." *Splice Today*, March 24, 2016.

Smith, Tracy. "Green Day Having the Time of Their Lives." *CBS News*, June 6, 2010. http://mobile-feeds.cbsnews.com/news/green-day-having-the-time-of-their-lives-06-06-2010/

Smith, Troy. "*Revolution Radio* Is Green Day's Most Heartfelt Work in Years." *Cleveland.com*, October 14, 2016. http://www.cleveland.com/entertainment/index.ssf/2016/10/revolution_radio_is_green_days.html

Snow, Mat. "Meet the Family: Ramones, Blondie, Talking Heads." *Q*, October, 1990.

Souter, Ericka. "Talking with . . . Billie Joe Armstrong." *People*, September 3, 2001.

Spanos, Brittany. "Billie Joe Armstrong's Son Jakob Danger Talks Debut EP, 'Musical Family.'" *Rolling Stone*, October 9, 2015.

Spin Staff. "Oregon Man Sues Green Day." *Spin*, October 20, 2006. https://www.spin.com/2006/10/oregon-man-sues-green-day/

Sprague, Debbie. "The Offspring *Smash* Review." Amazon.com, 1994. https://www.amazon.com/Smash-Offspring/dp/B000001IPL

Stamm, Chris. "Larry Livermore Made Lookout Records One of Punk's Most Iconic Labels – Then He Stepped Back and Watched it Die." *Williamette Week*, February 16, 2016.

Strauss, Neil. "Pop View: Has Success Spoiled Green Day?" *New York Times*, February 5, 1995.

Sullivan, James. "So You Wanna Be a Rock 'n' Roll Lawyer?" *San Francisco Weekly*, May 17, 1995.

Swift, Jacqui. "It's Our Most Ambitious Record. It Drove Us Crazier Than Any Other." *The Sun*, April 24, 2009.

Testa, Jim. "Green Day: Welcome to Paradise." *Jersey Beat*, March 1994.

Taylor, Charles. "A Wakeup Call for 'Idiot America.'" *Salon*, October 21, 2004. http://www.salon.com/2004/09/21/green_day/

Thomas, Andy. "Mikey Erg on the Preservation of Pop Punk." *Westword*, July 8, 2016.

Thomas, Fred. "AllMusic Review: *Demolicous*." AllMusic. http://www.allmusic.com/album/demolicious-mw0002627924

Thompson, Art. "Green Day's Jason White." *Guitar Player*, November 2009.

———. "Green Power: Billie Joe Armstrong Drives Green Day in New Directions on *21st Century Breakdown*." *Guitar Player*, November, 2009.

Trendell, Andrew. "Bruce Springsteen Opens Up About His Love for Green Day." *NME*, September, 29, 2016.

Trowbridge, Jacob. "Green Day: Ranking Their Albums from Worst to Best." *Whatculture.com*, January 22, 2016. http://whatculture.com/music/green-day-ranking-their-albums-from-worst-to-best

Tuttle, Nancye. "It's Green Day in Boston." *The Lowell Sun*, January 12, 2012.

Uhelszki, Jaan. "Pop Music – Green Day – Still a Bunch of Punks." *San Francisco Chronicle*, October 12, 1997.

———. "Pop Quiz – Q&A with Billy Joe Armstrong of Green Day." *San Francisco Chronicle*, November 19, 1995.

Usher, Shaun. "I Write for Myself and I'll Say Anything I Damn Well Please." *Lettersofnote.com*, May 9, 2011. http://www.lettersofnote.com/2011/05/i-write-for-myself-and-ill-say-anything.html

Vaughan, Andrew. "Unplugged: The Acoustic Side of Green Day's Billie Joe Armstrong." *Gibson.com*, April 13, 2011. http://www.gibson.com/News-Lifestyle/Features/en-us/green-day-0413-2011.aspx

Vaziri, Aidin. "Club That Launched Green Day in Danger of Closing." *Gibson.com*, May 4, 2010. http://www.lespaul.com/News-Lifestyle/News/en-us/Launched-Green-Day-504.aspx

Waddell, Ray. "Green Day, Blink-182, Others Team in the Name of Modern-Day Punk for Pop Disaster Tour." *Billboard*, March 2, 2002.

Walsh, Jim. "Olivia Kid Pumps Some Magic into Green Day Concert." *Saint Paul Pioneer Press*, July 16, 2000.

Webster, Melissa. "Chris Dugan at Jingletown Recording Studios." *The Huffington Post*, January 31, 2013. http://www.huffingtonpost.com/melissa-webster/chris-dugan-jingletown_b_2537407.html

Whyte, Danyel. "Green Day Trumpeter Brings His Journey to RCC." *River City College Viewpoints*, May 15, 2014.

Wilba, Rod, and Laura Riparbelli. "*American Idiot*." *Q*, December 2010.

Winick, T. J. "Billie Joe Armstrong Kicked Off Southwest Flight over Saggy Pants." *ABCNews.com*, September 4, 2011. http://abcnews.go.com/Entertainment/billie-joe-armstrong-kicked-off-southwest-flight-saggy/story?id=14445274

Winwood, Ian. "12 Steps to Revolution." *Kerrang!*, October 12, 2016.

———. "Get in the Van." *Kerrang!*, July 13, 2002.

———. "Nobody's Fools." *Kerrang!* Date unknown.

Wilks, Jon. "The Buzzcocks, Steve Diggle and the Story of 'Punk Soho.'" *Side Story*, February 10, 2016.

Young, Alex. "*Original Broadway Cast Recording – American Idiot.*" *Consequence of Sound*, April 29, 2010. https://consequenceofsound.net/2010/04/album-review-original-broadway-cast-recording-american-idiot/

Young, Clive. "Green Day Hits Broadway." *Pro Sound News*, July 2010.

Zuckerberg, Mark. "New Green Day Album Out This Weekend." Facebook, May 17, 2009.

Index

THE FAQ SERIES

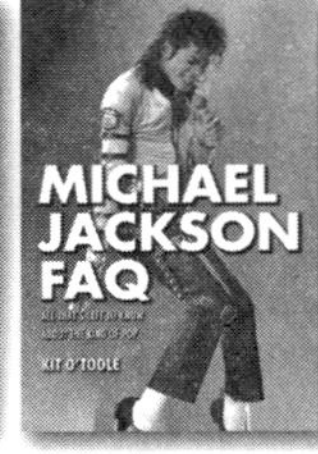

AC/DC FAQ
by Susan Masino
Backbeat Books
9781480394506 .... $24.99

Armageddon Films FAQ
by Dale Sherman
Applause Books
9781617131196 .... $24.99

The Band FAQ
by Peter Aaron
Backbeat Books
9781617136139 .... $19.99

Baseball FAQ
by Tom DeMichael
Backbeat Books
9781617136061 .... $24.99

The Beach Boys FAQ
by Jon Stebbins
Backbeat Books
9780879309879 .... $22.99

The Beat Generation FAQ
by Rich Weidman
Backbeat Books
9781617136016 .... $19.99

Beer FAQ
by Jeff Cioletti
Backbeat Books
9781617136115 .... $24.99

Black Sabbath FAQ
by Martin Popoff
Backbeat Books
9780879309572 .... $19.99

Bob Dylan FAQ
by Bruce Pollock
Backbeat Books
9781617136078 .... $19.99

Britcoms FAQ
by Dave Thompson
Applause Books
9781495018992 .... $19.99

Bruce Springsteen FAQ
by John D. Luerssen
Backbeat Books
9781617130939 .... $22.99

A Chorus Line FAQ
by Tom Rowan
Applause Books
9781480367548 .... $19.99

The Clash FAQ
by Gary J. Jucha
Backbeat Books
9781480364509 .... $19.99

Doctor Who FAQ
by Dave Thompson
Applause Books
9781557838544 .... $22.99

The Doors FAQ
by Rich Weidman
Backbeat Books
9781617130175 .... $24.99

Dracula FAQ
by Bruce Scivally
Backbeat Books
9781617136009 .... $19.99

The Eagles FAQ
by Andrew Vaughan
Backbeat Books
9781480385412 .... $24.99

Elvis Films FAQ
by Paul Simpson
Applause Books
9781557838582 .... $24.99

Elvis Music FAQ
by Mike Eder
Backbeat Books
9781617130496 .... $24.99

Eric Clapton FAQ
by David Bowling
Backbeat Books
9781617134548 .... $22.99

Fab Four FAQ
by Stuart Shea and Robert Rodriguez
Hal Leonard Books
9781423421382 .... $19.99

Prices, contents, and availability subject to change without notice.

Fab Four FAQ 2.0
by Robert Rodriguez
Backbeat Books
9780879309688 .... $19.99

Film Noir FAQ
by David J. Hogan
Applause Books
9781557838551 .... $22.99

Football FAQ
by Dave Thompson
Backbeat Books
9781495007484 .... $24.99

Frank Zappa FAQ
by John Corcelli
Backbeat Books
9781617136030 .... $19.99

Godzilla FAQ
by Brian Solomon
Applause Books
9781495045684 .... $19.99

The Grateful Dead FAQ
by Tony Sclafani
Backbeat Books
9781617130861 .... $24.99

Guns N' Roses FAQ
by Rich Weidman
Backbeat Books
9781495025884 .... $19.99

Haunted America FAQ
by Dave Thompson
Backbeat Books
9781480392625 .... $19.99

Horror Films FAQ
by John Kenneth Muir
Applause Books
9781557839503 .... $22.99

James Bond FAQ
by Tom DeMichael
Applause Books
9781557838568 .... $22.99

Jimi Hendrix FAQ
by Gary J. Jucha
Backbeat Books
9781617130953 .... $22.99